FOURTH
AND LONG

THE FIGHT FOR THE SOUL
OF COLLEGE FOOTBALL

JOHN U. BACON

SIMON & SCHUSTER PAPERBACKS

New York   London   Toronto   Sydney   New Delhi

Simon & Schuster Paperbacks
A Division of Simon & Schuster, Inc.
1230 Avenue of the Americas
New York, NY 10020

First Simon & Schuster trade paperback edition September 2014

SIMON & SCHUSTER PAPERBACKS and colophon are registered trademarks of
Simon & Schuster, Inc.

For information about special discounts for bulk purchases,
please contact Simon & Schuster Special Sales at 1-866-506-1949
or business@simonandschuster.com.

The Simon & Schuster Speakers Bureau can bring authors to your live event.
For more information or to book an event contact the Simon & Schuster Speakers Bureau
at 1-866-248-3049 or visit our website at www.simonspeakers.com.

Manufactured in the United States of America

1   3   5   7   9   10   8   6   4   2

The Library of Congress has cataloged the hardcover edition as follows:

Bacon, John U.
Fourth and long: the fight for the soul of college football / John U. Bacon.
        p.   cm
    1. Football—United States.   2. Football—Social aspects—United States.
3. College sports—United States.   4. Big Ten Conference (U.S.)   I. Title.
                    GV950.B33   2013
        796.332'63—dc23   2013016339
                ISBN 978-1-4767-0643-6
                ISBN 978-1-4767-6030-8 (pbk)
                ISBN 978-1-4767-0644-3(ebook)

To Terry McDonald, Maris Vinovskis,
David Rubin, Sharon Dilworth, and Nicholas Delbanco,
my mentors at the University of Michigan,
who taught me how to do this

CONTENTS

CHAPTER 1

"THE STAKES COULDN'T BE HIGHER"

PENN STATE

Mike Mauti grew up in Mandeville, Louisiana, just outside New Orleans. Mike Zordich grew up in Youngstown, Ohio, on the Pennsylvania border, equidistance from Pittsburgh and Cleveland.

Their fathers both played football for Penn State and went on to play in the NFL. Their dads revered Joe Paterno, as most of Paterno's players did. When Mike Mauti was born, in 1990, his dad, Rich, wrote a letter to Paterno, saying his only regret was that his son would never get the chance to play for the legendary coach.

Seventeen years later, in 2007, Mike Mauti made his official recruiting visit to the office of Penn State's head coach. But minutes before he did, he met another recruit outside the indoor practice facility: Mike Zordich, who'd already committed.

"I'll never forget it," Mauti said. "The first words out of his mouth are 'So are you coming or what?' I'm thinking, 'You know what? He's right.' But I didn't say anything to him or my dad. I wasn't planning to commit on that trip."

Of course, Mauti came to Penn State, and the two became inseparable.

That friendship would be tested—and not by each other, but by the extraordinary circumstances they would face during their years at Penn State. For these two, the moment of truth would arrive in late July 2012.

• • •

By 10:00 a.m. Monday morning, July 23, Penn State's football players had finished their workout, showered, and gathered in the players' lounge to watch NCAA president Mark Emmert's press conference, which was covered by virtually every news outlet in the country.

In a statement the players would long remember, Emmert said, "No price the NCAA can levy will repair the grievous damage inflicted by Jerry Sandusky on his victims. However, we can make clear that the culture, actions, and inactions that allowed them to be victimized will not be tolerated in collegiate athletics."

Emmert then laid out a series of penalties. One erased a wide swath of Penn State's rich history, vacating all victories from 1998 through 2011 — thereby dropping Coach Paterno from the perch of his profession, with 409 wins, down to fifth, with 298. The sanctions also threatened Penn State's future: a $60 million fine, a four-year postseason ban, and a drastic reduction in the number of scholarships the football coaches could offer recruits, from twenty-five down to fifteen a year, with a maximum of sixty-five — twenty fewer than Penn State's rivals could give out.

Emmert declared Penn State's penalties might be considered "greater than any other seen in NCAA history." Most experts believed they were second only to the infamous "death penalty" delivered to Southern Methodist University, from which the Mustangs had still not fully recovered twenty-six years later.

"Football," Emmert concluded, "will never again be placed ahead of educating, nurturing, and protecting young people."

Eight months earlier, on November 5, 2011, prosecutors had arrested Penn State's former defensive coordinator Jerry Sandusky on forty criminal counts, including the sexual assault of eight boys over a fifteen-year period, one of them in the showers of Penn State's football building. That put in motion a series of events that few could have imagined: it exposed the worst scandal in the history of modern sports; it led to the midseason firing of the iconic Joe Paterno; it prompted the hiring of little-known New England Patriots offensive coordinator Bill O'Brien; it resulted in Penn State's commissioning the Freeh Report, which concluded university leaders knew enough about what Sandusky had done, but cared more about protecting the university's image than his young victims; and it surely accelerated Paterno's decline and death — all within three months of Sandusky's arrest.

• • •

Those facts you probably know. What happened behind those headlines, you probably don't.

The players, coaches, and staffers in Penn State's players' lounge that Monday morning understood immediately that another provision of the NCAA's sanctions, which got far less attention outside that room at the time, threatened Penn State's season opener, just six weeks away: the one that allowed other schools to recruit Penn State's current players, who would be permitted to play for another team that fall without having to sit out a season for transferring. In practice, Emmert had declared open season for opposing coaches to cannibalize Penn State's roster, and all but encouraged Penn State's players to jump.

Just minutes after news of the sanctions broke, recalled Mauti, who had already defied the odds by reclaiming his starting position after missing the 2009 season when he tore the ACL in his right knee, and most of the 2011 season when he tore the ACL in his left knee, "Our phones were ringing—blowing up—with ten or twenty coaches calling right off. My high school coach had to turn his phone off because he got forty calls that day asking if I wanted to jump."

Just a couple hours later, while Mauti met with rookie head coach Bill O'Brien to address Mauti's fear that the program was on the verge of collapse, University of Southern California assistant coach Ed Orgeron called Mauti. "His kid went to my high school, so I picked up," Mauti recalled. "He asks me, 'What kind of guy is your tailback?' The coach didn't even know Silas Redd's *name*. Are you serious?"

Apparently serious enough to fly Redd—who ran for over a thousand yards in his sophomore year—out to LA, where USC had Snoop Dogg pick him up at the airport in a limousine. Everyone in Penn State's players' lounge assumed if the popular and talented Redd left State College, the floodgates would open.

That fear was well-founded. That same day, recalled starting senior defensive end Pete Massaro, an Academic All-American econ major, "One kid was telling me he was going and started listing a *ton* of guys in the freshmen and sophomore classes who were going to leave, too. I was *freaking out*. Next thing he said to me was 'Penn State football is dead.'

"I thought it was the end of Penn State football."

3

So did Mauti and Zordich. As was often the case, they had the same reaction at the same time: this will not happen on my watch.

After barely sleeping that night, they got up the next morning, Tuesday, July 24, at six. They immediately headed for strength coach Craig Fitzgerald's office to meet with him and Coach O'Brien, who didn't need to be persuaded about the gravity of their situation.

The seniors compiled a list of people they'd heard were planning to leave, and together they concocted a plan they hoped would stop the exodus before it started.

Before they split up that Tuesday morning, however, O'Brien moved to make a major decision.

"Coach was saying, 'We need to make a hard deadline,'" Zordich recalled. "'This can't go on forever. So I'm going to tell them, by August first, you're either with us or you're not.'"

It made perfect sense. Not knowing which players would still be on the team for the first game, just six weeks away, would make it almost impossible to conduct an effective practice and could be enough to make an already fragile team fall apart, piece by piece.

"I'm thinking, August first?" Zordich recalled. "That's one week. This dude's got balls." Zordich soon proved he had some, too. After initially agreeing, the more they talked about it, the more compelled he felt to speak up.

"I don't think that's a good idea," he finally said. "The players here don't know you well enough yet."

As soon as Zordich said it, Mauti decided he was right, and they explained why. Their reasons were both positive and negative: they believed the more the players got to know O'Brien and his program—which they viewed as a long-overdue step into the future, instead of relying endlessly on Penn State's glorious past—the more likely the players would be to stay; and second, if O'Brien threatened them with a deadline, it might create a panicked rush to the doors.

"You say, 'Now or never,'" Zordich said, "you're going to lose a lot of guys. They'll get scared."

"And make an irrational decision," Mauti added, finishing his best friend's sentence once again. "If we've got a deadline, word's going to get out to the coaches, and their phones are gonna blow up all over again the night before the deadline."

At that moment, Zordich and Mauti might have been the only college football players in the country with the temerity to question the decision of their head coach—a coach they already respected greatly—to his face.

At the next moment, O'Brien might have been the only college football coach in the country willing to listen.

O'Brien looked at Zordich, Mauti, and Fitzgerald, and then back to Zordich, thinking and weighing the options.

No one in that office had time to ponder the irony.

The NCAA sanctions were encouraging "student-athletes" to behave like athlete-students. They were putting the lie to the NCAA's own propaganda, which officially discouraged transfers because "student-athletes" are supposed to pick their schools for the education, not the athletic opportunities. But there Emmert was, inviting Penn State's student-athletes to jettison the university that graduated 91 percent of its student-athletes—a big reason many of them chose Penn State in the first place—to transfer penalty-free for bowl-eligible football programs.

Not only did it suddenly fall to O'Brien, Mauti, Zordich, and every Penn State player who stayed to protect their storied program from disintegrating, they could only do so by upholding the very values the NCAA itself could apparently no longer proclaim with a straight face.

OHIO STATE

In the early-morning hours of December 6, 2009, just a few hours after his undefeated Florida Gators lost the Southeastern Conference title game to eventual national champion Alabama, head coach Urban Meyer woke up, grabbed his chest, and collapsed.

His wife, Shelley, who'd been concerned about his health since he took the Florida job in 2005, didn't need to be convinced to call 911. An ambulance rushed to take Meyer to the hospital. Doctors determined it wasn't a heart attack he'd suffered, but they still couldn't pinpoint the problem.

The day after Christmas that year, Meyer announced he had "ignored my health for years" and would retire as Florida's coach after their Sugar Bowl game against his alma mater, Cincinnati.

The Ohio native ultimately decided to take a leave of absence for a few months, before returning to lead the Gators the next season to a disappointing 8-5 record. After Florida beat Penn State, 37–24, in the January 1, 2011, Outback Bowl, Meyer again announced his retirement, citing the same reasons he had the year before.

Thus, at the height of his powers, Urban Meyer did what few men in his profession would even consider: he left the game for the TV booth, where he spent the 2011 season critiquing other teams.

The same fall Meyer spent emerging from his living hell, the Ohio State Buckeyes spent entering theirs.

The Buckeyes' troubles paled next to Penn State's, but before the police arrested Sandusky, they were considered big news.

In December of 2010, a few weeks before Ohio State's Sugar Bowl game, five Ohio State players were forced to admit they'd sold some jerseys, mementos, and trophies to a tattoo-parlor owner. Predictably, he put them on eBay, and there's your scandal. Compared to the money USC boosters gave to Reggie Bush, and Mississippi State boosters gave to Cam Newton's father—all in the six figures—"Tat-gate" seemed pretty petty to most people, but to Mark Emmert and his staff, it was serious business.

In fairness to the NCAA, as Bo Schembechler himself once said, "Every single one of those rules came up because some coach was finding a way around them." This familiar cat-and-mouse game goes back to the inception of the NCAA itself—really, *why* it was founded—and even deeper, to one of the less appealing aspects of the American character.

"In his 1927 autobiography," sportswriter John Kryk writes, "[Amos Alonzo] Stagg perhaps wrote more than he realized when he contrasted the difference between the British and Americans in the matter of rules compliance. 'The British, in general, regard both the letter and the spirit,' Stagg wrote. 'We, in general, regard the letter only. Our prevailing viewpoint might be expressed something like this: Here are rules made and provided for. They affect each side alike. If we are smart enough to detect a joker or a loophole first, then we are entitled not only in law but in ethics to take advantage of it.'"

And that's why the NCAA was born: to close those loopholes.

Ohio State *had* told the players the rules—although the players initially claimed the university hadn't.

Yet, after Ohio State submitted its own report to the NCAA on December 19, 2010, the NCAA took all of four days to determine that five players would receive a five-game suspension—then allowed them to delay their punishment until the following fall, so they could play in the much-anticipated Sugar Bowl against eighth-ranked Arkansas on January 4, 2011.

The Buckeyes beat the Razorbacks, 31–26.

It soon surfaced, however, that star quarterback Terrelle Pryor had also traded a sportsmanship award from the 2008 Fiesta Bowl, a Big Ten title ring, and—most blasphemous to Buckeye backers—one of his gold pants charms, which Ohio State coaches and players have been given each time they beat the pants off Michigan, dating back to 1934. None of these discoveries increased the NCAA's penalties, but they did cause Buckeye fans to shake their heads in wonder at such disregard for their vaunted tradition.

Still, the whole thing seemed like a hill of beans until the spring of 2011, when head coach Jim Tressel got dragged into the investigation.

Ohio State's Jim Tressel era started on January 18, 2001, at a basketball game against Michigan. That night, when they introduced Tressel as Ohio State's new football coach at halftime, the Ohio native knew exactly what the fans wanted to hear.

He was hired on the heels of John Cooper, whose record at Ohio State was second only to that of Woody Hayes. But Cooper's teams lost to Michigan an inexcusable ten times in thirteen years—and in Columbus, you simply cannot do that. And you can't say the Michigan–Ohio State rivalry is "just another game," either—which might have been a bigger sin.

Knowing all this, Tressel wisely told the crowd, "I can assure you that you will be proud of your young people in the classroom, in the community, and most especially in 310 days in Ann Arbor, Michigan, on the football field."

The place exploded. At last, somebody *gets* it!

Tressel got it—and he proved it, beating Michigan nine out of ten times, including a record seven in a row. He also set Ohio State records for winning percentage in the modern era at .810, tied Woody Hayes's mark of six straight Big Ten titles, and won a national title in 2002—only the Big Ten's second since 1968.

Jim Tressel was clearly one heck of a coach. He was also pleasantly professorial—famed for his sweater vest, not his temper—and a great ambassador for the school.

But smoke always seemed to billow up behind him. His previous team, Youngstown State, won three Division I-AA national titles, but one of his stars got in trouble for taking money from a wealthy booster. The school got in trouble, but not Tressel.

When Maurice Clarett played on Ohio State's 2002 national title team, he later confessed, he took "golf, fishing, and softball as classes," which is not against the rules, but taking at least $20,000 in benefits is. "I was living the NFL life in college," he said. "I got paid more in college than I do now," in the United Football League. But Clarett got in trouble, not Tressel.

When Tressel was being investigated in 2011, a student reporter asked Ohio State president Gordon Gee—whom *Time* magazine ranked the best in the nation in 2009, the same year he became the highest-paid college president in the country—if he might fire Tressel. President Gee replied, "I'm just hopeful the coach doesn't dismiss me!"

Even after Pryor and company were caught selling trinkets, it was still chump change—until an e-mail from a former player-turned-attorney leaked to the press, indicating Tressel had lied to the NCAA about his ignorance of the violations—and not once, not twice, but three times. As usual, it was not the crime but the cover-up that did him in, giving even the supportive Gee little choice.

The Jim Tressel era ended on Monday, May 30, 2011, when he "resigned." But he would get to keep his national title and quickly landed a job at the University of Akron, where he had started his coaching career back in 1975 as a graduate assistant. He returned as their vice president for strategic engagement. It's hard to know what that corporate title entails, but we do know it doesn't include cleaning up the mess he left behind.

If the NCAA ran local law enforcement, whenever they pulled over a drunk driver, they would impound the car and let the driver hop in another one and drive off.

All this set up OSU's thirty-eight-year-old interim coach, Luke Fickell, and the Buckeyes for a historically horrible 2011 season. Ohio State struggled through a 6-7 campaign, including close losses to Michigan State, Penn State, and Michigan, Ohio State's first since 2003, and a final humiliation at the hands of the 6-6 Florida Gators in the TaxSlayer.com

Gator Bowl. The 2011 Buckeyes suffered the school's first losing season in twenty-three years, and only its second since 1966.

Near the end of the 2011 season, Ohio State had to make the most important hire most athletic departments have to make.

Ohio State's next head coach would be under immense pressure to win. To many Buckeye fans, Tressel's worst transgression was not getting the team put on probation, but getting blown out twice in national title games.

But could the Buckeyes' next coach also help the program's "image problem"?

Unlike NFL franchises, which simply hire the most talented coach available, schools like Michigan, Penn State, and Ohio State need to find a head coach who can not only win games, but also win over the lettermen, the loyal alums, and the fans. He needs to represent the entire school and even come to embody it.

Why Ohio State wanted Urban Meyer is obvious: after the prodigal son reached the apex of his profession, the Buckeye backers longed for him to return to his native land. But why would Meyer, a multimillionaire who had already won two national titles, want to leave a cushy job at ESPN to return to possibly the biggest pressure cooker in coaching?

During Meyer's happy hiatus, he made his first visit to his family doctor in years. The generalist determined in five minutes what the specialists couldn't diagnose after years of tests: Meyer's problem was not a heart condition, but merely esophageal spasms and acid reflux, which was resolved with a dose of Nexium, literally overnight. "The next morning," Meyer said, "I felt like a new man. And it got better."

But the catch was a familiar one to college coaches: both conditions were aggravated by stress, which the job provides by the bucket.

So why would he jeopardize his renewed health, his revitalized family life, and his rediscovered sanity to return to the sidelines—especially when it would include moving from Florida to Ohio, a trip most retirees make in the other direction?

No doubt additional money and fame have their appeal, but Meyer already had ample doses of both. More likely, having removed his biggest obstacle to coaching, he wanted to get back at it. For competitive personalities, there is naturally no substitute for actual competition. That it was the Ohio State Buckeyes coming after him tipped the scales.

No one understood the importance of "getting it" more than Meyer. He was born in Toledo and raised in Ashtabula, where he wore number 45 in honor of Ohio State's two-time Heisman Trophy winner Archie Griffin. He wasn't recruited by Ohio State, so he played at Cincinnati, then assisted Earle Bruce at Ohio State and Colorado State before becoming the head coach at Bowling Green, Utah, and Florida, while graduating 80 percent of his players. But Ohio State had been the team of his childhood dreams. Getting the opportunity to push them back up to their rightful station at the top echelon of the game was, for Meyer, more honor than duty.

When I spoke with Meyer between his first spring practice and summer training camp in Columbus, it didn't take long to understand why a man who had already won three division titles in six years in the SEC—a conference that was about to extend its streak of consecutive national titles to seven, including the two Meyer had won at Florida—wanted to return to the beleaguered Big Ten, which had won exactly two national titles in the previous forty-four years.

"Growing up in Ashtabula, Archie Griffin, Cornelius Green, Woody—man, that's all I knew," he told me. "I mean, that's *all* I knew. I'm not even kidding. I learned math by adding threes and sevens.

"But when you talk about Woody Hayes, and Bo Schembechler, and Earle Bruce, it's the same: you do it the right way, and you do it really hard. And there's always an academic component in there. That's what's special about those coaches: academic integrity, the big, old stadiums, the traditions that all these great schools have here. Growing up, the Big Ten was always the standard.

"To be a part of it again means a lot to a guy like me."

Meyer believed he would be a wiser coach, too, thanks to the year he had just spent analyzing games in ESPN TV's booth.

"I learned what all great programs have in common," he said. "It doesn't matter if they're running the spread, the wishbone, or a pro set, or if they run a three-four defense, or what league they're in. No, it's the alignment of the staff. If everyone's on the same page—if the CEO says this is how it's done, and nine coaches believe it—you have a shot. If you're not—if even one position group is off—you don't, and you're done.

"That means, when I ask [an assistant] for a quick answer, give me a

quick answer. Don't give me another question. And when I say something, I want it done.

"I need that responsiveness." Without being prompted, he added, "I
don't have that yet."

To get that, before 2012 spring practice even started, Meyer and his
new assistants were running through practices—without players. "We
practiced *practice*," he said, taking his already manic levels of prepara-
tion to new levels.

The tug-of-war between success and sanity had commenced.

One obstacle could not be avoided: Ohio State's probation, which meant
they would not be playing in the 2012 Big Ten championship or a bowl,
no matter how many games they won.

"It's the elephant in the room," Meyer acknowledged. "Completely
uncharted waters for myself, and for this program. How do you stay
focused without a championship game or a bowl game to play for? But
if we have a good year, we can still win the Leaders Division. So that's
number one on our bucket list.

"Number two," he said, then grinned, "well, you can probably guess,"
and it wasn't hard: beat "That Team Up North," a phrase borrowed from
Woody Hayes, who refused even to utter the "M-word." ("Show me a
good loser," he said, "and I'll show you a busboy.")

As if Meyer didn't have enough on his plate, he wanted to accomplish
something else, too: wipe clean the stain on Ohio State's reputation—
through more diplomas and fewer arrests. He had returned to Ohio State
to produce that familiar oxymoron, a professionally run program of amateur excellence.

"The stakes are extremely high," he concluded. "It's Ohio State. Do
you build up to next year? No, we simply try to win every game we play,
every year. It's Ohio State. There will *never* be a time at Ohio State that
we're worried about next year. We always want to win now. So, from
where I sit, the stakes couldn't be higher. And you can print that."

MICHIGAN

In 1989, on the twentieth anniversary of Bo Schembechler's first Michigan football team, he invited every Wolverine he'd ever coached back to Ann Arbor, for a long night of stories. The former players sat with their teammates, and each one stood up to give a brief introduction.

While Bo's first teams introduced themselves, Dave Brandon sat at the table with his 1973 teammates, wondering what he was going to say.

Brandon had grown up in South Lyon, just fifteen minutes north of Ann Arbor, where he became an all-state quarterback, good enough to attract the attention of Bo Schembechler.

Brandon had the good timing to join Bo's 1971–73 squads, which won 31 games, lost 2, and tied 1, with all three setbacks occurring in the last game of the season at the Rose Bowl or against Ohio State. But the excellence of those teams meant Brandon had to battle all-conference players at almost every position just to get on the field. Bo first tried Brandon at quarterback, behind Dennis Franklin, Larry Cipa, and Tom Slade, all of whom started at some point in their careers. Bo then moved Brandon to scout-team defensive end, where former all-American Reggie McKenzie used him daily as a tackling dummy, then to backup kicker, where he finished his career. Despite hundreds of practices, Brandon got in only one game.

Soon after Brandon graduated, Schembechler helped him get a job at Procter & Gamble's headquarters in Cincinnati—and that's when Brandon took off. He rose to chairman, president, and CEO of Valassis Communications, a former Fortune 500 company that sends advertising postcards to some 100 million homes every week.

So, after thinking through his career, when it was his turn to stand up at the football reunion, Brandon knew exactly what to say. His old coach Bo Schembechler liked his response so much, he could remember it verbatim years later: "Brandon gets up—and I've quoted this statement a hundred times—and he tells his old teammates, 'I didn't get in many games. I wasn't an all-American like a lot of you guys, or even an all–Big Ten player. Hell, some weeks I wasn't even on the All-Scout Team! But in the long run, I became an all-American in business.'

"They all cheered," Bo said. "People, believe me when I tell you, *that* is what we were trying to teach when I was head coach."

Brandon moved on from Valassis to work with Mitt Romney at Bain Capital. In 1998, the energetic Brandon won a statewide election to become one of the University of Michigan's eight regents. The next year Bain took over Domino's Pizza, which had been on the market for several years, and named Brandon its CEO.

So Brandon went to work simultaneously getting Domino's ready for an initial public offering (IPO) and courting the University of Iowa's president, Mary Sue Coleman, for interviews in Ann Arbor. Although almost everyone on campus seemed to believe the popular former business-school dean and interim president, Joe White, was a shoe-in—some journalists actually reported that he'd been named the next president—in 2002, the regents named Coleman Michigan's thirteenth president. Two years later, in 2004, Domino's IPO set the valuation record in the "Quick Service Restaurant" category.

After Brandon lost his 2006 reelection bid for regent, he lobbied Coleman and the regents to become Michigan's next athletic director. Michigan interviewed three current Division I athletic directors, all of whom had played or coached at Michigan, and Brandon, who had never coached or worked in college athletics before. That was also true of Michigan's previous four athletic directors, and might have worked in Brandon's favor.

"I'm more than just a pizza man," he said at the time. "Although I have not lived a career in athletics specifically as others have, I believe I bring a unique set of qualifications, interests, and experiences to the job."

The Associated Press added, "Brandon said his business background will help him manage an athletic department with a budget of more than $90 million, media and licensing agreements, and fundraising efforts under way in a sputtering economy. 'I view it as a selling organization for the entire university.'"

Universities have in recent years eschewed former coaches and university administrators in favor of corporate professionals to run their athletic departments—a list that includes Oregon, Rutgers, and Notre Dame. Fewer people wondered why Coleman would tap Brandon than why Brandon would want to take an 82 percent pay cut—not counting bonuses, stock options, and the like, which comprise the bulk of a CEO's compensation—for a job that promised more headaches, more scrutiny, and less privacy than running a Fortune 500 company.

"I can't think of many jobs in the world that I would pick up and leave that great company and great brand for," he explained, "but this is one. . . . I love the University of Michigan. I loved it when I was here as a student-athlete, [and] I've been connected to it ever since in one-way or another."

He started working well before his official start date of March 8, 2010, effectively assuming office after the announcement was made on January 5, 2010, and he's been on a mission ever since. If you send him an e-mail at 2:00 a.m., he often responds by 3:00 a.m. After he inherited the ongoing NCAA investigation of Michigan's football program's practice limits, he put on a veritable clinic of damage control through public policies and press conferences, causing his standing to soar among Michigan fans.

In former football coach Lloyd Carr's final years, Brandon had heard the masses grumbling about Michigan's slide into mediocrity. Then he heard that low roar rise to full-throated shouting when Carr's successor, Rich Rodriguez, finished his three seasons at Michigan with a 6-18 record in the Big Ten. Brandon was determined to do something about it.

If Michigan fans wanted more wins, he concluded, Michigan needed the best facilities and the best coaches. To get those things, he concluded, they needed to make more money to pay for them.

One of his first acts in office was to install gigantic, pro-style, four-sided scoreboards for the hockey, basketball, and football facilities—two four-thousand-square-foot versions for Michigan Stadium, the "Big House"—for an estimated $20 million. More recently, in late 2012, Brandon announced a master plan to renovate ten facilities and build seven new ones, including a field hockey renovation project for $10 million, new lacrosse facilities for $12 million, a pool expansion for $20 million, a new rowing/strength and conditioning center for $25 million, a new multipurpose gym for $30 million, and a new track facility for $90 million—plus "The Walk of Champions," which will create "one complete, contiguous athletic experience that will be as impressive in its scale as it is in its vision."

The department estimated the entire master plan would cost $250 million in 2012, but when he discussed it with the Regents in mid-2013, Brandon concluded the figure would be closer to $340 million.

Brandon's not afraid to make sweeping changes in personnel, either.

As he'd promised he would in speeches to alumni groups, he soon let over 85 of the department's 275 employees go, paying a couple million for buyouts, then increased the staff to 308. In those same speeches, he often mentioned his first hire would be a chief marketing officer, which reflected one of his principal missions, and changed the director of human resource's title to chief talent officer and had her report directly to him.

If Brandon isn't afraid to spend money, he has redoubled efforts to raise it, too, first by tripling the department's development staff, from nine to twenty-eight full-time fund-raisers to help cover the department's operating budget, which has grown from $100 million during the 2010–11 fiscal year to $137.5 million just three years later. (These figures do not include the capital expenditures above.)

Brandon also raised revenues by creating or increasing "seat licenses" for football, basketball, and hockey and closed off virtually all Michigan facilities to the public. The athletic department now charges for corporate events in the skyboxes ($9,000), for wedding receptions on the 50-yard line ($8,000, or $6,000 for one hour), and for school tours, which Michigan had provided free for decades.

Brandon's style might not please everyone he deals with, but he delivers what he promises. Under Brandon, the department increased its operating surplus to $15.3 million in fiscal year 2012, 72 percent higher than the previous fiscal year. In 2012, the Michigan football team alone generated $61.6 million in profits, second only to the University of Texas, which has the considerable advantage of its exclusive twenty-year, $300 million TV deal with ESPN.

Brandon has delivered more than dollars, too. After hiring Brady Hoke in 2011, the Michigan football team beat Notre Dame on the last play of the Big House's first night game, defeated Ohio State for the first time since 2003, and won a thrilling overtime game over eleventh-ranked Virginia Tech in the Sugar Bowl, Michigan's first BCS bowl victory since a young man named Tom Brady beat Alabama in the January 1, 2000, Orange Bowl.

In the 2011–12 school year, Brandon's first official full year on the job, the hockey team earned a #1 seed in the NCAA tournament; the men's basketball team won a share of its first Big Ten title since 1986; and the following fall, Michigan's other twenty-nine sports combined to run a close second behind Stanford, and ahead of such perennial all-sport powers as Texas and UCLA, in the Directors' Cup, which Michigan has never won.

If the Michigan athletic department had issued a 2012 annual report to its shareholders, it would have been the shiniest publication in college sports, packed with enough good news to make the competition envious. By those measures, its creator could be considered an all-American athletic director.

The Wolverines are not alone in spending millions, of course, engaged as they are in an arms race with the Buckeyes and the Southeastern Conference that shows no signs of slowing down. In Brandon's speeches to alumni clubs, service groups, and the press, he has been unabashed in laying out a simple equation: if you want titles, this is what it takes.

But it can come with some unexpected prices.

On Friday morning, April 20, 2012, while I watched workers set up the stage for the groundbreaking ceremony for Penn State's $104 million hockey arena the day before their football team's spring game, I took my weekly call from Ann Arbor's local sports-talk station, WTKA.

This being six days after Michigan's spring scrimmage, I assumed the morning hosts would ask me how Michigan's second-year coaches, who favored a pro-set offense, were meshing with soon-to-be senior Denard Robinson, the consummate spread-offense quarterback. So I was a little surprised when Ira Weintraub and Sam Webb asked me about the Michigan-Alabama game, scheduled more than four months away, on September 1 in Dallas.

It was already being hyped as a clash between two tradition-rich programs, both ranked in the preseason Top 10, and two tradition-rich conferences. But it was bigger than that, because the schools had struck a deal with the Dallas Cowboys' celebrity owner, Jerry Jones, to play the game in his shiny, new, $1.15 billion, state-of-the-art pleasure dome, nicknamed Jerry World.

They called the game the Cowboy Classic, a four-year-old version of the former Kickoff Classic, and it had come to represent the apotheosis—or nadir, depending on your view—of all that modern college football was becoming: the colossal, professional stadium; the seemingly endless corporate tie-ins; and the orgy of interest in a game between amateur athletes.

Although Michigan did not sell out its allotment of 17,500 tickets for the Sugar Bowl a couple months earlier, the athletic department had no trouble selling all 25,000 tickets for the Cowboy Classic, before they could even offer them to the general public. They were gobbled up entirely by Victors Club members: first to those with the most "priority points" (which they accumulate largely through donations), down to those with just one priority point. Thousands of fans with no priority points got shut out.

It was all the more impressive because the tickets for the Cowboy Classic weren't cheap: $125 for a seat in the rafters and $285 for one on the 50, plus $80 for parking across the street. Jerry World also offered standing-room-only tickets, which one website packaged with vouchers for a beverage, a hot dog, and a bag of chips for $89—and sold more than twenty-three hundred of them.

"Let's put it like this," the ever-quotable Jerry Jones said the week of the game. "I'm going to compare it even to the Super Bowl. They're two different events—but this is the hottest ticket . . . of any game or any event that we've had at that stadium."

Michigan would net $4.7 million for the Cowboy Classic matchup with Alabama, the highest payout ever for a Kickoff Classic/Cowboy Classic season opener. After the department publicized that fact, fans were surprised to hear Brandon announce he would not be sending the Michigan Marching Band to the game because the athletic department couldn't afford the $400,000 travel expense. That decision lit up sports-talk shows across the state.

If one symbol separates college football from the NFL, it's the marching bands. When the band plays, all the alums in the stadium travel back in time to their college days. Some fans angered over the decision included big donors, who ultimately stepped up to cover half the cost of the band's trip. Leaving the band behind for a big game proved not to be an option—at least in 2012.

As the arms race escalates, Brandon does not seem terribly interested in slowing down to ponder it all. He is too busy pressing full steam ahead. "I don't talk the past," he said several times in his first year as Michigan's athletic director. "I create the future."

He might just be right.

If the future of Penn State was in the hands of its players, and Ohio State in the hands of its new head coach, Michigan's was in the hands of its new athletic director.

NORTHWESTERN

In the early eighties, while Penn State was winning national titles, and Ohio State and Michigan were winning Big Ten titles, the Northwestern Wildcats were setting a record of their own: the longest losing streak in NCAA history.

After the Wildcats finished second in the Big Ten in 1970 and 1971, behind only Ohio State and Michigan respectively, they couldn't manage even one five-win season for almost a quarter century. Northwestern's stadium seats 47,130 people, less than half as many as Michigan's, Ohio State's, and Penn State's, but they hadn't sold it out for a single game since 1963. In 1978 and 1980, Northwestern's attendance for the entire *season* was less than what Michigan attracted for a single game.

The football program came by its incompetence honestly: from the top. In 1981, after the team had lost its twenty-ninth straight game, Northwestern's then-president, Robert Strotz, told the student paper, "I think having a bad football team can help academic standards." Apparently, President Strotz believed a losing squad could convince the high-browed that you must be serious about school, or else your football team would surely be better.

Spend any time in Evanston and you'll be struck by how every single alum—no matter when he or she graduated—can recite the president's quote verbatim, more than three decades later. His words are carved that deeply into their collective psyche.

"He actually came out and said that publicly!" said Eric Chown, '85, equally amused and appalled—a typical reaction.

Not surprisingly, given such support, the week President Strotz said this the Wildcats lost that Saturday's game to Michigan State, 61–14, and the next one to Ohio State, 70–6, to extend its record losing streak to 31—and fuel rumors they would soon be dropping out of the Big Ten. When the team hit 34 straight losses to secure the record, the students tore down the goalposts and, in the spirit of a Bronx cheer, started chanting, "Lake the posts!"—then rushed the white pipes down Central Street and into Lake Michigan.

Since the "Mildcats" went 35-128-1 during Strotz's fifteen-year reign, you have to assume he, at least, was thrilled.

18

Apathy was in their DNA. The few fans who showed up to see loss after loss after loss had a favorite cheer: "That's all right, that's okay. You're going to work for us someday."

It wasn't always that way.

Unlike Ohio State and Penn State, who were the tenth and twelfth teams to join the Big Ten, respectively, Northwestern is a charter member, forming the world's first academically based athletic conference in 1895 with Michigan, Purdue, the University of Chicago, the University of Illinois, Wisconsin, and Minnesota.

The Chicago Maroons, led by Amos Alonzo Stagg, took seven of the Big Ten's first twenty-nine football titles. But by the midtwenties, the boys from Northwestern got the upper hand on their Southside cousins, which accelerated the demise of the Maroons. When they finally dropped out of the Big Ten after the 1939 season, Northwestern assumed the mantle of "Chicago's team," until the NFL's Bears captured the public's attention for good in the 1950s.

Along the way, the Northwestern "Purple" became the "Wildcats," so named by a sportswriter for their tenacity in a 1924 game against the Maroons. They took five Big Ten titles by 1936, won the 1949 Rose Bowl, and usually beat Michigan and Ohio State a few times each decade.

Until, that is, 1972, when the Dark Ages descended upon Evanston.

The seeds of the Wildcats' awakening were planted in 1991, when they hired Gary Barnett from Colorado's 1990 national-title staff. One of his first recruits was a young man from Carl Sandburg High School on Chicago's South Side named Pat Fitzgerald. Few would have guessed it then, but together those two would change Northwestern's fortunes.

When Northwestern introduced Barnett at a basketball game, he told the crowd, "We're taking the Purple to Pasadena!" Since the Wildcats had made only one appearance in the Rose Bowl, in 1949, it sounded crazy—but he believed it. Even crazier, his players did, too.

"Losing so much was sort of a badge of courage," former athletic director Rick Taylor (1994–2003) told me. "I never bought into that. The university would never allow such failure to continue in any other field, so why ours?"

The Wildcats finally emerged from their twenty-three-year slumber in 1995, the same year Henry S. Bienen became Northwestern's fifteenth president. While Bienen certainly didn't seek to transform Northwestern into an Ohio State wannabe, he didn't confuse failure on the football field for academic excellence, either.

Although Barnett's first three teams finished sixth, tenth, and tenth in the Big Ten, the 1995 Wildcats stunned Notre Dame in South Bend for the first time since 1961, then beat the Wolverines in Ann Arbor for the first time since 1959, followed by victories over Wisconsin, Penn State, and Illinois to finish the Big Ten season undefeated for the first time since 1936.

The impossible had happened: the Purple was going to Pasadena. The entire nation cheered on the 'Cats, who were celebrated on the Wheaties box.

The next year, rather amazingly, the Wildcats beat Michigan again and won a share of another Big Ten title.

The school raised $20 million for long-overdue stadium renovations and started planning for a new indoor practice field, too. "Given our facilities," President Bienen said, "Gary's been recruiting with one hand tied behind his back."

The arms race, it seemed, had been joined.

The stadium was renovated, and an indoor practice facility, Trienens Hall, was completed in 2001, but that didn't stop the Wildcats from a vertiginous fall back to earth, finishing eighth in the eleven-team Big Ten in 1997, and dead last in 1998, with an 0-8 conference record.

If any of the Big Ten's "big three" had gone 0-8—in any year, for any reason—the local papers would have plastered the unbearable disaster across the front page and put the actual Apocalypse on the second.

But at Northwestern, a funny thing happened: not much.

No one freaked out. They didn't search their souls to determine where they had lost their way. They didn't wonder what deep-seated flaw in their collective character the winless year had revealed.

When the Wildcats win, it wakes up the whole campus. But it's a bit of a lark. Nice, but not necessary. The day after the Wildcats finish a winless Big Ten season, the faculty and the students wake up and walk across the street to one of the greatest universities in the world.

After Barnett left Evanston in 1999 to return to Colorado as the head coach, Northwestern hired Miami University's Randy Walker. His arc mirrored Barnett's, peaking with a Big Ten title in 2000, followed shortly by a return to tenth place two years in a row.

When the fifty-two-year-old Walker died in 2006 of a heart attack, Northwestern hired his understudy, thirty-one-year-old Pat Fitzgerald. The promotion made Fitzgerald, Northwestern's only nonkicking all-American between 1982 and 2000, the youngest Division I head coach in the country, by a full five years.

If Northwestern has a golden boy, the flat-topped, square-jawed Fitzgerald is surely it. No one could understand Northwestern, and how it works when it works best, better than Pat Fitzgerald.

If Meyer's marriage to Ohio State makes perfect sense, the same is no less true for Fitzgerald and Northwestern.

Consider this: the coaches at the big-time programs would never take a job like Northwestern's. The Wildcats have all the obstacles those coaches have worked so hard to get beyond, including a small stadium, fewer fans cheering for your team than your opponents, rare coverage by the national media, second-class facilities, and none of the academic back doors many teams have traditionally used to get their stars through school. Yet the team still graduates 97 percent of its players—a higher rate than that of the student body at large—and it would be higher still if the formula counted the team's fifth-year engineering students.

Most coaches believe Northwestern is the toughest place to win in the Big Ten—and Northwestern's record up to that magical 1995 season stands as solid proof.

Yet, all those reasons are exactly why Fitzgerald loves coaching the Wildcats, even declining overtures from Michigan's Dave Brandon after he fired Rich Rodriguez in 2011. Fitzgerald is competitive, but he agrees with the priorities of his alma mater, which proudly places academics ahead of athletics in funding, facilities, and favoritism. He even claims the university's higher standards make it *easier* for him to produce winning teams—something no one who had not played at Northwestern would ever claim.

If it is, in fact, harder to win the Wildcat way, it's surely more fun when they do, as just about every Hollywood script about the underdog will attest.

Not only does Fitzgerald know Bienen's successor, President Morton

Schapiro, would never say, "I hope Fitzgerald doesn't fire *me!*"—he knows athletic director Jim Phillips wouldn't say it either. Fitzgerald makes roughly $1.3 million a year—significantly less than the $2 million Division I head coaches average at public universities, and about the same as President Schapiro. There's a message in that. At Northwestern it's clear the football coach works for the athletic director, the athletic director works for the president—and the relative power accrues accordingly.

The question is, Can that chain of command produce a football team that can beat Michigan or Ohio State?

When Fitzgerald became Northwestern's head coach in 2006, it took him two seasons to lift the Wildcats from 4-8 to 9-4. But, just like Barnett and Walker, he found success hard to maintain in Evanston, where his teams steadily slid down to eight, seven, and six wins, capped by four straight losses in progressively weaker bowls. The last point was a touchy one for the Wildcats, who had won just one bowl game—in 1949.

"You look on my shelf over there," Fitzgerald told me, sitting at a table in his office, "and we have two stuffed monkeys."

"The first one goes back to 1995. We hadn't beaten Iowa in something like twenty straight years. [Twenty-one, actually.] One of our teammates, Chris Hamdorf, went to Iowa City High, so his parents bought us all stuffed monkeys before that game. We beat 'em [31–20]—and our guys destroyed those monkeys!

"My first time back to Iowa City as the head coach, seven years ago, I brought that monkey out. We beat 'em again [21–7, in an otherwise disappointing 4-8 season]—and our guys destroyed that monkey in the locker room after that game. So, that monkey was two for two.

"The new monkey, the big one, is for our bowl game. We've brought that along for the last four bowl games."

The problem was, the new monkey was undefeated—and therefore unharmed—and had been around long enough to start feeling more like a gorilla on their backs.

But in the summer of 2012—with their head coach secured through 2020, a $220 million budget set aside for a new facility on the Lake Michigan shoreline (one designed for *all* students, not just varsity football players), $24.6 million coming in from the Big Ten alone, more than Notre Dame's $15 million from NBC, and a four-year president in place who understood what athletics could do for Northwestern—hopes were once again high in Evanston.

"We have everything we need to be a champion now," Fitzgerald said in late July. "And we have some things that no one else in the country can say they have."

Like Barnett, Fitzgerald actually believes this. And he leverages Northwestern's advantages through clever recruiting, usually bypassing the four- and five-star players Ohio State, Michigan, and the SEC scoop up, to secure recruits who are strong students, captains of their team, and from winning programs. They also have to commit to Northwestern early and expect to stay for five years to develop as players and graduate. If Fitzgerald can find all that, he believed the Wildcats could compete with anyone in the league.

If the football gods could give him something extra—such as a senior class not just willing but eager to meet on their own time to ensure they're getting the most out of their team—Fitzgerald believed they could beat anyone and perhaps claim their fourth Big Ten banner since his junior year.

Fitzgerald's confidence in his alma mater was admirable—but was it misplaced? Did Northwestern truly have enough to compete with the best in the Big Ten? And even if they could battle the big boys, could they do so without losing their values—or their sanity?

Having dropped one win a year for three straight years—with the next stop being the dreaded "bowl ineligible" five-win season—2012 was sure to provide some answers.

Other teams would fight for the 2012 Big Ten title, of course, including Michigan State, which had leveraged its football prowess after World War II to join the Big Ten and become a world-class research university, and Nebraska, which had sacrificed over a century of success in the Big 12 conference to escape Texas and its stability-shattering TV deal, to join a conference it barely knew. Was it a mistake? The 2012 season would offer plenty of answers there, too.

If all these players, coaches, athletic directors, and presidents would be under tremendous pressure in 2012, it was nothing compared to the scrutiny college football itself would receive.

The sport was under attack for myriad sins, including academic fraud, the exploitation of amateur athletes by millionaire coaches and athletic directors, a profoundly corrupt bowl system, and the rank hypocrisy of the NCAA. By 2012, college football had attracted more critics than the IRS—and not just the usual skeptics such as Murray Sperber and Rick Telander, but writers like Taylor Branch and Joe Nocera, who usually focus their lasers on Capitol Hill and Wall Street.

"I swear," Charles P. Pierce wrote in April 2012, "the NCAA uses a dictionary from beyond the stars. It's taken longer than it did for golf and tennis, and even longer than it took for the Olympics, but the amateur burlesque in American college sports is on its way to crashing and the only remaining question is how hard it will fall. The farce is becoming unsupportable."

It was no longer just college sports' critics who were saying this, either, but former players—who were pushing class-action lawsuits to redress financial and physical exploitation—and the fans, whose seemingly boundless passion for college football appeared to be approaching some boundaries, after all. The exponential increases in ticket prices, seat licenses, and TV time-outs were testing the loyalty of even the most rabid fans, who were starting to foster an embryonic protest that showed signs of growing into a full-scale revolt.

The lines were beginning to form. On one side, the players and the fans—the true believers—wanted to keep what they had, while on the other, the suits—athletic directors, league commissioners, the NCAA, and TV—were trying to extract more and more from the very people who comprised the heart of the enterprise.

In the eye of this storm sits the Big Ten.

The Big Ten might be the nation's oldest, biggest, and richest conference, but could it catch up to the Southeastern Conference on the field, where the Big Ten had fallen woefully behind? Or had the locus of football power, like the Midwest's economy and population, moved to the South and West, where academic research and NCAA rules didn't seem to be such high priorities?

Given the Big Ten's unique place in the pantheon of college football—the exemplar that has combined academic power, athletic prowess, and commercial popularity, with a minimum of miscues before 2010—the conference, its twelve-hundred-plus football players, and 17.5 million fans aren't merely canaries in the coal mine. They're the coal miners.

The Big Ten has four distinct models to face the future: the pure passion of Penn State's players; the no-nonsense professionalism of Ohio State's coaching staff; the corporate-style control of Michigan's money-focused athletic department; and the old-school, presidential-driven approach of the Big Ten's only private school, Northwestern.

If the Big Ten can't compete while keeping its programs clean and complementing the academic mission of its schools, then no conference can. The entire enterprise will have to be deemed a failure.

The world's first academically based athletic conference now stands as the last, best hope for nationally competitive, reasonably clean college football to make its stand.

When Urban Meyer declared that "the stakes couldn't be higher," he was discussing the Ohio State Buckeyes season ahead, but he could have just as easily been discussing the entire sport.

CHAPTER 2

PATERNO'S LEGACY

Mark Emmert, in his press conference announcing Penn State's sanctions, promised that football would never again come ahead of education. While critics questioned his sincerity, few questioned his logic.

They should have. In yet another cruel twist of irony, Joe Paterno's career makes the point.

A few weeks after Paterno led the Lions to victory in the January 1, 1983, Sugar Bowl, earning the program's first national title, Penn State's thirty-two-member Board of Trustees invited him to speak. If they expected him to give a friendly recap of the team's historic achievement and thank them for their support, they were in for a surprise.

"We have never been more united, more proud," he told them, "and maybe it's unfortunate it takes a number one football team to do that."

Then he abruptly shifted his focus from the football team to the faculty: "It bothers me to see Penn State football number one, then, a few weeks later, to pick up a newspaper and find a report that many of our academic departments do not rate up there with the leading institutions in the country."

He didn't stop there, laying out a direct approach to elevating the entire school: recruit better teachers. "We have some. We don't have enough of them." Next, he said, Penn State had to recruit "the star students that star professors get excited about." The way to do all that, he said, was to raise more money to pay for endowed chairs, scholarships, better labs and libraries. "Without a great library, we can't be a great university."

According to Joe Posnanski's book *Paterno*, the coach told the trustees they needed to raise $7 million to $10 million over the next few months—a staggering sum at the time—while Penn Staters were still flush with their feelings over the football team's triumph, and the iron was hot.

"I think we can be more than we are," Paterno said, "and make students better than they think they are."

His challenge was simple: to make the university as good as the football team, a strategy employed to great effect at the University of Chicago, Notre Dame, and Michigan State, among others.

And they needed to start doing it now.

Without Penn State's elevated academic ambitions, it is less likely that seven years later the school would have reached out to join the Big Ten, or vice versa. Yes, the Big Ten offered geographical proximity and athletic excellence, but also a better academic reputation than other athletically competitive conferences. The Big Ten gives all members access to the Committee on Institutional Cooperation, which fosters collaboration among researchers and graduate students of the Big Ten, a conference that generates $8 billion in research annually and produces 16 percent of the nation's PhD graduates. Until Nebraska lost its accreditation just before joining the league in 2011, the Big Ten was also the nation's only athletic conference whose every school was a member of the prestigious Association of American Universities, which requires world-class levels of broad-based research—something not even the Ivy League can claim.

Joining the Big Ten also forced Penn State to raise its game by expanding the airport and highways needed to make Happy Valley—which Bob Knight famously called a "camping trip" when Penn State started Big Ten play in 1993—more accessible, and by building the 15,261-seat Bryce Jordan Center for basketball and concerts.

Paterno's team, however, showed it belonged in the Big Ten from the start. In just its second year, 1994, the Lions notched Paterno's fifth undefeated season, took the Big Ten title outright, then beat Oregon in the Rose Bowl—but once again finished second in the polls, this time behind Tom Osborne's Nebraska team.

In the Big Ten, Penn State's graduation rate has consistently ranked second only to Northwestern's and ahead of the average for all Penn State students. Paterno's African-American players—a demographic too often neglected in big-time college athletic programs, if not higher education itself—usually graduated at or above the team's average, placing them far ahead of both the university's and the nation's average.

By January 1, 1995—twenty-nine years after Paterno became Penn State's head coach, and twelve years after his speech to the trustees—by any measure you wanted to pick, Paterno's guidance of his football program, and the university itself, had to be considered an unqualified success.

Which is why some of even Paterno's staunchest supporters thought 1995 marked the perfect time for the sixty-eight-year-old coach to make the perfect exit. "Step down then? After 1994? Are you kidding me?" he told Posnanski. "Why? I never even thought about it."

In the spring of 2012, I accompanied new coach Bill O'Brien and a few other coaches on a bus tour of Penn State's alumni clubs. At Pittsburgh's classically opulent Omni William Penn Hotel, built in 1916, I talked with an older attorney, who told me about the last conversation he'd had with Paterno a few years earlier.

When this lawyer told Paterno he was contemplating retiring, the coach grabbed his lapels, shook him, and shouted, *"Do you wanna die?!"*

For Joe Paterno, the choices were that simple.

The following fall of 1995, Penn State introduced its next president, Nebraska's Graham Spanier. Moving from Lincoln to State College might not have looked like a promotion in 1965, the year before Paterno became head coach, but it certainly did by 1995. Adding a little intrigue, the Cornhuskers were the very team that had just received a few more votes to nudge the undefeated Lions out of the way for the national championship—something Spanier had the presence of mind to make sport of at his first press conference, in addition to Nebraska's contract with Coke, and Penn State's with Pepsi.

"What a difference a day makes!" he said with a grin, trading his red hat for a blue one, "because yesterday I thought Nebraska deserved the national championship. I used to drink Coke. But today it's Pepsi, and maybe Penn State should have won it."

Everyone laughed, the Lions loved it, and the president and Penn State embarked on an unusually harmonious honeymoon. But Spanier, like Paterno, wasn't bashful about his ambitions. Early in his tenure, Spanier told a gathering of faculty: We're a Big Ten university. Let's act like it!

He wasn't talking football, but research.

"This is a standard phrase around here," said Michael Bérubé, an English professor. He was awarded the Paterno Family Professorship in 2001, which he felt compelled to abdicate in the fall of 2012, the same year he was named the president of the prestigious Modern Language Association, the first in Penn State's history. "We could have competed with Notre Dame for T-shirt sales for the rest of our lives—until we joined the Big Ten. Once you do that, now your benchmark isn't Notre Dame football, it's Michigan's and Indiana's and Illinois's graduate schools—and all of a sudden your libraries start to look pretty puny and your grants rather minuscule.

"It's really one of the main reasons I came here [from Illinois]. The graduate programs here were better funded. And not just in the sciences, but in the humanities as well."

They were soon better staffed. According to former assistant dean Ray Lombra, in the past ten years Penn State's liberal arts faculty grew by 50 percent, from 240 to 360.

Since Penn State joined the Big Ten, federal research grants have tripled, to $780 million.

When the Academic Ranking of World Universities released its list of the top one hundred research universities in 2012, Penn State ranked forty-ninth—one of five Big Ten schools in the top fifty—the kind of recognition Penn Staters could only have dreamed of when Paterno provoked the trustees back in 1983. The university had met his challenge, and had become the equal of the football team.

"When I think of Penn State," men's volleyball coach Mark Pavlik said to alumni groups on the bus tour with Bill O'Brien in the spring of 2012, "I think of ordinary people, doing *extraordinary* things."

It is not a crime to coach too long or to succumb to pride. But at Penn State, when the two biggest leaders' blind spots overlapped, it led to tragedy.

Sometime after Penn State's sterling 1994 season, Paterno's passion for the position began to wane. This is not surprising for a man in his seventies and then eighties who had spent his life pursuing a punishing profession. But the players noticed, and the effects were corrosive.

I first met the players on the 2012 Penn State team on April 20, 2012, the day before their spring game, and started a dialogue that lasted past their season-ending banquet, seven months later. The notes from those conversations alone filled over eight hundred single-spaced, typed pages—enough to fill three books this size without a word from the author. They spoke with admirable candor on just about every topic that came up in our long, wide-ranging discussions.

Except one.

Almost every member of the 2012 Penn State football team had been recruited by Joe Paterno. Many had fathers or older brothers who had played for Paterno at the height of his powers. The players from Pennsylvania were raised on stories of the iconic coach and grew up believing in Paterno and the Penn State mystique.

So whenever the conversation turned to their time playing for Paterno, they spoke slowly, and carefully. They knew the legend, and the power it still possessed with their classmates, the lettermen, the six hundred thousand Penn State alums, and over 2.5 million fans nationwide. They knew the avalanche of calls and e-mails they would receive if they ran afoul of the faithful, something many of them had already gotten a hint of during the Sandusky saga—and that was enough.

But they also knew Paterno's image, hammered out of steel long before they had arrived, did not match what they had experienced, and they had too much integrity to deny it.

Naturally, most of the players liked being recruited by Penn State. If they hadn't, they would have gone somewhere else, where they would probably have had a much easier time of it, on and off the field, and perhaps even gotten illicit payment for their labors. But that's not what they signed up for.

"I was offered money," Mike Mauti told me matter-of-factly, of his recruitment by other programs. "The schools that do it don't come out and say they're going to give you this or that, but their players tell you how it works.

"I had all these coaches calling me, offering all this stuff, guys telling me to hold out until signing day. 'You wait long enough, they'll rate you five-stars.' Do the hats on the table and all that. Never been my style. Never been about the flash."

Just about every elite prospect sooner or later gets offered some forbidden fruit. Unlike many, if not most of them, Mauti was unimpressed. He credits his father for keeping him "supergrounded."

And his father, Rich, gives all the credit to Paterno, who, in the mid-seventies, turned the all-American lacrosse player from Long Island into an NFL special-teams starter. It was Rich's dream for his son to play for Paterno, but since Mike was born in 1990, that seemed impossible. But after Mike Zordich asked Mike if he was coming "or what?," Mike Mauti found himself in Paterno's spacious office, where he noticed the conversation was fundamentally different from the ones he'd had at other schools.

"The other coaches were always telling me how good I was and showing me the flash, the rings and all that," he recalled. "With Joe, we didn't talk about me. He never once said anything about how good I was."

Paterno was transparent, offering the young phenom nothing more than a chance. "You have a great opportunity here" was all he promised. "After that, it's up to you what you make of it." That was it, Paterno's entire pitch. "All right, kid, what are you thinking?"

Before Mike answered, he thought back to Zordich asking if he was coming. "So I just kind of blurted it out: 'Coach, I want to come here!'"

Rich Mauti's head whipped around. "What a minute, Mike, are you sure about that?"

Paterno walked around his desk and put his hand on Rich's shoulder. "Aw, shut up, Mauti! You heard the kid's coming!"

"And that was it for me," Mike recalled.

This was the Paterno approach in a nutshell: no bells, no whistles, no bull. His offers—to everyone, always, whether they were five-stars or nobodies—were as straightforward as a firm handshake: the chance to get a good education at a good school and play football in a tradition-rich program. If you accepted, there would be no dancing in the end zone, just a lot of hard work, sacrifice—and success.

For every player I talked to on the 2012 team, however—over three dozen—it went downhill from there.

In his last years, Paterno was hardly coaching at all, particularly after 2006, when a Wisconsin player ran into him on the sidelines and injured his leg just below the knee. He started watching the games from the press box, and never wore a headset. After he recovered, he returned to the sidelines, where he still didn't wear a headset, carry a clipboard, or seem to talk to anyone who was calling plays. The game seemed to pass him by.

He no longer ran the team meetings, the offensive meetings, or the positions meetings, rarely even attending those staples of a college football program. The staff joked privately that the less Paterno got involved, the better things usually went.

Paterno, freed from almost all coaching duties in his final years as the titular head of the program, would often leave for lunch, then return to the football building to shoot the breeze with some staffers. When practice rolled around, every position group was already doing its own thing—discussed at length in various meetings earlier that day—when Paterno felt the urge to weigh in. When he did, he often confused the situation, got the players' names wrong or just yelled at them by their numbers.

After Paterno delegated so much of the coaching duties to his assistants, they tended to cling to the symbols of the Paterno Way, while missing their meanings.

"Shave your face, cut your hair," Mauti said, recalling the mantra. "If we weren't shaved for a practice, we would have to work out on Saturdays in the off-season, or guys wouldn't start during the season. Just stuff like that. It got almost to the point where that's all that mattered, and you start to wonder, 'Why are we doing these things?'"

"I was in the middle of a pregame stretch on the field," Zordich recalled. "I'm getting focused, and [one of the assistants] walked up to me and asked, 'Why didn't you shave?' Dude, I'm trying to get ready for this game. And this is what he's worried about?"

Penn State was not the first storied football program to rely too much on its past at the expense of its future, and Paterno was surely not the first coach to linger longer than he should have. In big-time college football, these are the rules, not the exceptions. By 2011, few programs could claim to have accrued a richer tradition or a better reputation than Penn State had. From the outside, it looked like Camelot. But that view did not match the reality the players faced on the inside every day.

No, the program did not channel money to the players, write their papers, or pump them with steroids. They were clean, they went to class, and they graduated. But over time, the pristine image of the Penn State program, which had drawn them to State College in the first place, had become as reliant on reputation as reality, and Paterno's persona had become as much burden as blessing.

This is why I heard almost every Penn State senior I talked to say some version of this line: "We felt like we were protecting an image. And only we knew it."

Six days before Sandusky was arrested, the Nittany Lions' record stood at an impressive 7–1, with their only loss coming to eventual national champion Alabama. They were riding a six-game winning streak, and life looked pretty good in Happy Valley. But even before the Sandusky bomb hit ground zero, the Penn State locker room was anything but tranquil.

On October 29, 2011, Penn State hosted 6–2 Illinois, which had just lost two close games. Neither team could score in the first half, thanks partly to Penn State quarterback Rob Bolden's ineffective play.

"Bolden was having a tough day," Mauti recalled, "and our defense is going ape-shit on the sidelines because they won't put in [Matt] McGloin."

Joe Paterno's son, Jay, coached the quarterbacks and had always favored Bolden, a four-star prospect from a suburban Detroit prep school. When Bolden arrived in 2010, Jay immediately installed him as the starter, ahead of sophomore walk-on Matt McGloin.

About Joe Paterno, the Penn State players had decidedly mixed feelings. But about Jay, I found no such division of opinion. It all came to a head that afternoon.

In the midst of Bolden's breakdown, defensive captain Drew Astorino had seen enough. He picked up the headset to yell at Jay in the press box, "Get that motherfucker out of this game right now!"

At halftime, the players made a full sprint for the locker room. "Lot of guys were looking for a fight," Zordich recalled. "They'd been waiting for this."

Jay Paterno played right into their hands, storming into the defensive meeting room, yelling, "You motherfuckers! You think you can get on this headset and talk to me like that?!"

In a room full of angry defensive players waiting to explode, Jay Paterno provided the match. The players jumped up and charged him, throwing chairs out of the way to get to him. Were it not for a respected assistant coach pulling Jay out, then holding his hands on the doorjambs to block the players from getting to him, many players believe Jay wouldn't have gotten out of the locker room unharmed.

"That dude," Mauti concluded, "was an example of everything a coach should not be."

In the game's final three minutes, McGloin directed an 80-play drive, capped by Silas Redd's three-yard touchdown to give the Lions a 10–7 win—Joe Paterno's 409th career victory, thereby surpassing Eddie Robinson as Division I's winningest football coach.

Six days later, the Penn State players' private unhappiness would be eclipsed by one of the most public tragedies in the history of college sports.

The weekend of November 5, 2011, the Lions had a bye week, so the players, coaches, and staffers enjoyed that rarest of things: a fall weekend free of football. Most of them left town, including longtime equipment manager Brad "Spider" Caldwell, who headed up to his camp on a beautiful lake in Vermont to enjoy a few days of peace and quiet and to mow the lawn for the last time that year.

"No phone, no TV," he said, smiling. "Love it."

As a result, however, he didn't hear anything of Sandusky's arrest that Friday. Finally, at four-thirty Saturday afternoon, Spider was sitting on his riding mower when his neighbor walked over with his iPad.

"Hey, Brad," he said tentatively, "I don't know if you've seen this."

When he showed Spider the article—Sandusky arrested, athletic director Tim Curley and Vice President Gary Schultz stepping down—Caldwell couldn't believe it. Months later, recounting the day in the equipment room, he began shaking his head, and his eyes reddened.

"Your first reaction," he said, "is to look around and realize you have to put it all on hold. Our world is going to change. This is going to get ugly.

"Then you think of the kids. You just can't believe it. I just felt so bad. Just devastating news." No Penn Staters I talked to ever forgot, however they were affected by the NCAA's sanctions, who the real victims were.

Caldwell spent the rest of the November weekend reading what he could, and crying.

Most of the players didn't even know who Sandusky was until they saw his picture on TV. Only then did some of them recognize him as the "old guy who worked out here once in a while."

Their reactions were pretty swift. "They used to hang people at the Centre County Courthouse in Bellefonte," Mauti said, "and frankly, I would have been okay with that. Hell, give us the rope, and we'll do it for you."

This would prove to be the reaction of Sandusky's jury, eight of twelve of whom went to Penn State or worked there and spared him little.

Many of the Penn State people I talked to were sad to see Athletic Director Tim Curley put on administrative leave while he awaited his trial. They understood why: he was technically Paterno's boss, and Sandusky was on Curley's payroll during the first part of Curley's eighteen-year run as athletic director. Far more damning, Curley had been accused of perjury, which didn't give the university much wiggle room to retain him.

But as a State College native who'd worked his way up from the equipment room to become athletic director, he'd made many friends along the way, and no enemies I discovered. Most believed he got caught up in the decisions made by others and didn't have the strength to speak up. In this, he was far from alone.

His likability might have been his downfall. He worked to avoid confrontations and tough decisions. As one colleague said, "Tim was so indecisive, if he was offered steak and potatoes on one plate, and chicken and rice on the other, he'd starve."

Unlike most Big Ten universities, whose presidents pick their athletic directors, at Penn State replacing the AD fell to the trustees. That was yet another unique problem Penn State faced.

At Michigan, state voters elect two regents to the eight-person board every two years, for eight-year terms. At Ohio State, the governor appoints nineteen members to the board for nine-year terms, except the two student members and three charter trustees. At Northwestern, the twenty-person executive committee appoints fifty more members to a board, but because it's private, they are immune to the Open Meetings Act and Freedom of Information Act (FOIA). More important, the Northwestern board divides the duties up into smaller committees, and those appointed have no conflicting agendas, so the university runs as smoothly as any in the country.

Penn State, however, is governed by a board of thirty-two trustees, composed of the university's president; the governor; the state secretaries of education, agriculture, conservation and natural resources; six appointees by the governor, nine elected by alumni, and six elected by Pennsylvania agricultural societies—harkening back to the school's founding as a land-grant college. Six additional trustees are elected by a board representing business and industry enterprises. It's safe to conclude that Penn State's board is the most unwieldy in the Big Ten.

After Curley stepped down, the board named one of its own, David Joyner, to replace him. Joyner had been an all-American defensive lineman who was also an NCAA finalist wrestler at Penn State in 1971. He graduated from Penn State's medical school and became an orthopedic surgeon, focusing on sports medicine. He worked with both the World Football League and the USOC, and was elected to Penn State's Board of Trustees in 2003, 2006, and 2009, taking one of the nine seats reserved for alums, voted on by alums.

Nonetheless, Joyner was an odd choice for athletic director.

That Joyner had no experience working in an athletic department was an obvious weakness, but one university presidents had overlooked elsewhere, including at Michigan, in favor of business experience. But what business experience Joyner had wasn't exactly a ringing endorsement for his candidacy. In 2002, he founded a company which operated a chain of gyms called C-5 Fitness. In 2006, the company filed for bankruptcy. Joyner and his wife, Carolyn, were out of money themselves and lost their home.

When the board, on which Joyner still served, put Curley on administrative leave, Joyner lobbied to become the acting athletic director—which paid $396,000 a year—and thanks to his colleagues on the board, he got it. Billionaire trustee Ira Lubert arranged for the Joyners to stay in one of his homes in State College, and another in Hershey.

This attracted the attention of the Pennsylvania auditor general, who released a report a year later, in November of 2012, stating, "This movement gives rise to reasonable public perceptions of insider influence and conflicting interests, particularly when the movement involves persons at executive levels."

Penn State ignored the warning.

If Joyner passed muster with his colleagues on the board, he didn't fare as well with the players.

After losing their second game of the 2011 season to third-ranked Alabama, the Lions went on a roll, rattling off seven straight victories to earn a tie for first in the Big Ten, and a No. 12 ranking nationally, with just three games left. They seemed poised to take another Big Ten title and send Paterno off a winner.

Then the scandal broke.

They lost the next weekend to Nebraska, 17–14, and got shellacked the final weekend by Wisconsin, 45–7. In just three weeks, they dropped all the way from a possible berth in the Rose Bowl to the lowly TicketCity Bowl in Dallas. What would normally be a disappointment became, in the leaderless program the players suddenly found themselves inhabiting, a dilemma: Should they decline the bowl invitation?

To answer the question, captains Devon Still and Drew Astorino called a players-only meeting in December of 2011 with just one item on the agenda: to stay or to go.

"It was a very diplomatic meeting," offensive lineman Mike Farrell recalled. "We were leaning toward going, but there was a solid faction against. But the arguments on both sides were great. The guys who didn't want to go were saying, 'Hey, we go down there, and our coaches will be freaking out. They don't know if they have a job when they come back, or where they'll be next year. How will they be able to coach?'"

While this discussion rolled on, former all-American linebacker Shane Conlan—captain of the 1986 national title team, and former teammate of Mike Zordich's father (also Mike)—was on campus and caught wind of the meeting. He asked one of the players going in to bring out Mike Mauti.

"What the fuck are you all doing?" Conlan asked Mauti. "You better get these guys to go. You'd all be seen as spoiled brats."

Mauti returned to the room and asked to speak. "I just talked to Shane outside," he told them, "and he was telling me what it would look like to these former players if we didn't play. If we stand for the values that Penn State stands for, we have to eat it. We have to go. There's no choice.

"So here it is, majority rules," Mauti said. "Who wants to go? Raise your hand, right now."

"Boom," Mike Farrell said. "It was eighty or ninety percent. Obvious."

"Okay," Devon Still said. "We're going."

Facing a nation that had turned on them, at a university that suddenly had no leaders—with the interim president, Rod Erickson, and the acting athletic director, Dave Joyner, not daring to say a public word on their behalf—the players managed to conduct a civil town-hall meeting and come to a mature decision. All seem settled.

Until, that is, Mauti walked outside the room to retrieve Dr. Joyner, who had been cooling his heels outside while the players were deliberating.

"'We're ready for you,'" Mauti recalled saying. "He didn't ask me how it went, or anything. He was just all pissed off because he'd been waiting outside for twenty minutes."

Joyner marched to the front of the room, visibly agitated, and said, "I thought I was coming here to talk to a group of men, but I didn't realize there was a bunch of children in here, whining about not going to a good bowl game and getting screwed!"

"Before he could finish that sentence," Farrell recalled, "Devon made a sound, and stood up to stay something. But Gerald [Hodges] stood up first and said, 'Hold up, hold up, hold up! We're in here talking like men, to make this decision, and you come in here disrespecting us!'"

This set Joyner off on another tour of his biography, which they had already heard a few times in his first few weeks on the job. "Everyone was selling him to us," Mauti said. "All-American wrestler, football player, doctor. Look, honestly, we didn't care. We're getting blasted by the media, and Erickson and Joyner were nowhere to be found. Joyner was a former member of the board. The suit was already on him. What we needed was someone to stand up."

Instead, Joyner made an ill-advised argument that, because the school had to pay the NCAA $60 million, the bowl payout was a good way to get some of that back. This elicited more sounds and comments from the players, and the meeting devolved from there. Players complained that Joyner had gone AWOL while the program was getting ripped by the national media, and Joyner repeated his list of accomplishments before becoming the acting athletic director.

"You better show me some respect!" he demanded.

By this time, Gerald Hodges was standing up and pointing back at Joyner. "No, no, no. My father said, 'I'm only going to respect someone who respects me.'"

The two started walking toward each other, creating a commotion loud enough for Coach Larry Johnson Sr., waiting outside, to come into the room, hold Hodges, and literally escort him out.

Finally, Devon Still had his chance to speak. "We already decided," he told Joyner. "We're gonna go."

"Oh," Joyner responded.

"From that point," Mauti recalled, "Joyner was apologizing to us. 'We're sticking up for you guys, and we're fighting for you guys out there.'"

"And no one said anything," Zordich said, "because we knew nothing needed to be said. They weren't doing anything to stick up for us. Not on TV. Not on campus. Anywhere."

After O'Brien was named the head coach, the entire senior class told him they did not want to see Joyner or Erickson on the field before the games. Joyner must have felt some contrition—or embarrassment, take your pick—because he respected their wishes, not setting foot in front of the team again until the 2012 banquet.

After the Lions dragged themselves to the TicketCity Bowl in Dallas, where they lost to the Houston Cougars, 30–14—their third loss in their last four games—the media chorus declared Penn State's collapse would continue into the next season, if not longer. But Spider Caldwell's right-hand man in the equipment room, Kirk Diehl, saw the seeds of their renaissance after the team's last bowl practice, on December 31, 2011.

While Diehl was cleaning up the locker room, Massaro and Mauti were finishing their rehab. They asked him, "What's going to happen in January?"

"You always try to have an answer for them, but I didn't," Diehl recalled. "I said, 'We don't have the slightest idea. But I know it's going to take you guys, as fifth-year seniors, to hold this team together. When a new coach comes in, it'll come down to how you guys respond to it.'

"And they said, 'Okay, when do we get started?'"

The players were in. They just needed a coach.

With Graham Spanier, Gary Schultz, and Tim Curley out of office, and Joe Paterno dying, the lettermen naturally sought stability. They wanted Joyner to stay inside the family by hiring defensive coordinator Tom Bradley, who had assisted Paterno since he'd finished playing for Penn State in 1978. But if Joyner felt compelled to clean house, the lettermen hoped he would go after Penn Staters Al Golden, head coach of the Miami Hurricanes; Mike Munchek, the NFL Titans' head coach; or Greg Schiano, the head coach for the Tampa Bay Buccaneers, whom many had thought would succeed Paterno years earlier.

But one of the trustees suggested Joyner reach out to the offensive coordinator for the New England Patriots. How unknown was he? When *Sports Illustrated*'s veteran NFL writer Peter King was asked what he knew about Bill O'Brien, he said, "I wouldn't know him if he walked into this room right now."

For his part, O'Brien knew more than a little about Penn State. He had followed his father and brothers to play football at Brown, Paterno's alma mater. After he became a graduate assistant, in 1992, he wrote to Paterno directly, on Brown University stationery: "Dear Coach—congratulations on a tremendous season. . . . I am at Brown coaching the inside linebackers. I have enclosed a résumé. I would be extremely interested in any grad assistant positions. Regards, Bill O'Brien."

Paterno replied with a handwritten note in the margin: "Hi Bill— thanks for this. I'll keep you in mind if we have something that would be appropriate for you. All the best, Joe Pa."

When the O'Briens were packing up to move to State College, Bill's wife, Colleen, shouted, "You won't believe what I found!" The letter is now framed, and hangs on O'Brien's office wall.

When O'Brien first told New England Patriots head coach Bill Belichick about Penn State, Belichick encouraged O'Brien to apply. "It's still Penn State," Belichick said.

Joyner asked for O'Brien's résumé and a cover letter, which O'Brien sent via FedEx, per Joyner's request. After hearing nothing back for eight days, O'Brien called Joyner, who said they had never received the envelope, although FedEx had recorded it as signed for. O'Brien gave Joyner the tracking number, and a staffer eventually found the envelope in a mailroom. For a program that was about to see one of its most revered assistant coaches get what amounted to a life sentence for raping boys, the lack of due diligence was stunning.

Penn State liked O'Brien enough to pick him up in the school's private plane and start the interview on the flight back to State College. O'Brien had gotten on the plane equipped with a thick binder, full of his plans for Penn State. At Belichick's insistence, O'Brien had also practiced interviewing with him for hours, even as the playoffs approached.

"I could *never* repay him for that," O'Brien said. "And let's face it, if I don't work for Bill Belichick and I don't coach Tom Brady, I don't get this interview. I work hard—but a lot of guys work hard. If I don't have those two guys, I don't have this opportunity."

After Joyner and company finished their questions, O'Brien had a few of his own, including the elephant in the room: How would the ramifications from the Sandusky scandal affect the program moving forward?

While they admitted they were probably going to face expensive lawsuits and settlements, they assured him these were all criminal matters, and beyond the jurisdiction of the NCAA.

In their defense, precedent seemed to be on their side. Whenever a college athletic program got itself in trouble with the law—big trouble—the NCAA usually steered clear, sticking to how many minutes a week student-athletes are allowed to stretch, the distance they can travel in a car with an alumnus, and whether they are allowed to put cream cheese or jam on their free breakfast bagel. (They are not.)

In the summer of 2003, Baylor basketball player Patrick Dennehy disappeared. During the investigation, head coach Dave Bliss portrayed Dennehy as a drug dealer to explain how the player might have paid his tuition without a scholarship. But authorities soon discovered teammate Carlton Dotson had shot and killed Dennehy. The NCAA got involved only in those aspects of the case that triggered its rules on paying players and the like, but left the legal matters for law enforcement. Likewise, the NCAA stayed out of two infamous lacrosse cases: the Duke incident, when three members of the team were falsely charged with raping a stripper; and the University of Virginia tragedy, in which George Huguely V murdered his girlfriend, fellow lacrosse player Yeardley Love. In both situations, the NCAA left the criminal investigations to the legal authorities—and wisely so. It would have been tantamount to assigning a serial-murder case to meter readers.

Several Penn State insiders, however—both inside and outside the football building—warned Joyner and others that the NCAA might make an exception in the Sandusky case. To be safe, they urged Joyner, Penn State should hire attorneys with experience negotiating with the NCAA, and start building bridges before the reports emerged.

Joyner replied that Penn State had never had a major infraction before and was not likely to get one now—ignoring that Penn State's entire compliance department consisted of one man, who was not likely to find much over the years, if there was anything to find.

The insiders' advice was ignored.

Not knowing any of this, Bill O'Brien signed on the dotted line.

CHAPTER 3

URBAN'S STORY

If Bill O'Brien was walking into the Happy Valley swamp largely blind, Urban Meyer had a much better map of the landscape he'd be navigating in Columbus.

After all, the man had been born in Toledo in 1964 and raised in Ashtabula, a town of about twenty thousand people, known mainly as a throwaway line in Bob Dylan's classic "You're Gonna Make Me Lonesome When You Go."

Kids grow up tough in Ashtabula, a shrinking coal port in the northeast corner of the state, but Meyer probably grew up tougher than most. His grandfather had been killed in a German concentration camp, and after the war, his mother, Gisele, ended up on the wrong side of the East-West divide. Not content to die in East Germany, she crawled underneath a barbed-wire fence to escape, lived in a West German basement for three months, then took a ship to New York.

"Germans at the time thought the US was all palm trees and sunshine and smiles," Urban told me. "But when her ship arrived, the New York City sanitation workers were on strike. Her first three weeks in America she spent walking past mountains of garbage and avoiding rats the size of Volkswagens."

Although most Europeans find American football mystifying, Gisele Meyer loved it. Being Catholic, she naturally cheered for Notre Dame and dreamed her son would one day become the Fighting Irish's head coach. Her son loved the game even more, but Notre Dame less. In Ashtabula, if you wanted to fit in, there was one thing you had to do, but only one thing: back the Buckeyes.

Meyer didn't need to be told. When he was just five or six, he recalled, his mom dragged him out of the house to run an errand during the Michigan–Ohio State game—at the outset of the Ten Year War between Woody Hayes and Bo Schembechler.

"I couldn't believe we were leaving the house. We had to go to some outside mall, and when I heard the PA system playing the game, I just stopped, cold." Meyer was mesmerized, and even his tough, Teutonic mom had a hell of a time getting her son to move.

He played almost every play at Saint John High School, but after he failed to get Earle Bruce's attention at Ohio State, he played two seasons of professional baseball before accepting the University of Cincinnati's offer to play defensive back. When his college career was over, he knew he didn't want to leave the game, but he also knew he couldn't stay as a player.

Coach Bruce came to the rescue, hiring Meyer as a graduate assistant at Ohio State.

"What I admire most about Coach Bruce is what the fans of That School Up North love about Bo: he's always honest and direct. Those two were very much alike.

"This kind of world is hard. And the whole idea of following all these rules—not everyone does it. But there was never a time when Coach Bruce said, 'Let's find a way around something.'

"There's nothing like having a conversation with someone who has the guts to say things people don't like. 'This is the way it is.' It's rare, and Earle has it. The honesty, the toughness—that's the only way you can operate. And sometimes you get criticized for it. At the end of the day, you can't please everyone."

When Bruce was fired by Ohio State, then later hired by Colorado State, Meyer eagerly followed. Bruce taught him more than plays. "He always said the two groups most overlooked were the former players and the students." Bruce worked hard to keep both groups appreciated and involved.

After five years there, and five more at Notre Dame—which thrilled his mother—in 2001 Bowling Green offered Urban Meyer his first head-coaching job. Sadly, it was after his mom had passed away. Meyer took a team that hadn't had a winning season in seven years, including a 2-9 season before he arrived, and pushed them to 8-3 and 9-2.

Next stop, Utah, where Meyer took the Utes to records of 10-2 and

12-0 in 2004, capped by swamping Pittsburgh, 35–7, in the Fiesta Bowl, for a Top 5 ranking. He won just about every Coach of the Year trophy, including the Woody Hayes Award.

Notre Dame, which had just fired Tyrone Willingham, came calling. But Meyer, whose mother had named him for a pope, surprised almost everyone when he swerved south to Florida. His connection with Coach Bruce, however, only grew stronger. He continued to call his mentor almost every week, about everything from discipline issues, to hiring questions, to scheduling.

"I like to get his opinion on how we're doing things," he said. "He knows me as well as I know me. If I'm overreacting, or struggling with the balancing act that's so hard to achieve, he'll say something."

The depth of trust between them was manifest in 2006, Meyer's second season in Gainesville. He had led the fourth-ranked Gators to the SEC title game against Arkansas. If USC somehow lost against a weak UCLA team—which was a long shot—Florida could steal the Trojans' invitation to the national title game against top-ranked Ohio State. But that didn't seem very likely.

At the team breakfast before the SEC title game, "I'm not doing well," Meyer recalled. "I'm loaded up pretty tight. I've got such tunnel vision, I don't even know Coach Bruce is sitting right next to me at my table. I feel a nudge. I look. It's Coach Bruce."

Bruce all but shouted, "Hey! How you doing!?"

"Honestly? I'm not doing too good," Meyer admitted. "I'm too tight. I need to lighten up, loosen up."

"What the hell is wrong with you?!" Bruce asked.

The waitstaff, cleaning up around them, must have thought it was crazy, this seventy-eight-year-old man screaming at Meyer.

"Let it go! Relax!" Bruce said, but seeing that he wasn't getting through to his protégé, he grabbed Meyer's shirt with both hands and said, "Let the m#*%@# go!"

"Now he has my attention!" Meyer recalled.

"How did you get here?" Bruce asked him. *"How did you get here?!"* He punched Meyer's chest. "Relax! Let your kids play. *That's* how you got there!"

On Meyer's game sheet, he wrote down, "Let the m#*%@# go!"

Meyer knew his 2006 Florida team had great defense—led by Coach

Greg Mattison, who would join Brady Hoke's staff in 2011, with amazing results—but not a great offense. "We ran a lot of trick plays and reverses and fake punts," Meyer said. But it worked well enough in the first half, when the Gators jumped out to a 17–0 lead and held a 17–7 advantage at halftime.

When they returned to the locker room, "everyone's cell phone was buzzing—almost like music," Meyer told me. "Our SID was pasty white. He said, 'You won't believe this. USC just lost.'

"Now, I know the players know. They're all grabbing their phones. I almost panicked."

Instead, Meyer turned to his players and said, "Hey! You guys want to play for it all?"

"Yeah!"

"Then let's play for it all!"

Of course, the Gators naturally responded by throwing two interceptions, which the Razorbacks converted to go ahead, 21–17, just two minutes into the third quarter.

"It's loud," Meyer recalled. "We have no momentum. They've got Darren McFadden and Felix Jones. I thought, this could get ugly fast."

When Florida got the ball back, they couldn't get anything going. Facing fourth and 10, from their own 12, Meyer looked down at the words on his game sheet and, for the first time that night, really read them. "Let the m#*%@# go!"

All right, he thought, here we go. He called "Blitz at Nine"—a fake punt. Even his players couldn't believe it.

"I remember thinking, 'If this doesn't work, you lose your job.'" That might not have been an exaggeration.

"I don't even watch it," Meyer said. "My mouth was sandpaper. I turned to talk to Chris Leak. I wasn't really talking to him. I was just trying to look like I wasn't calling a fake punt! I had to look somewhere else. I grabbed him—and it went silent. And then I heard the crowd—and I knew he'd made it. Hell, he got the damn first down, and three times more—maybe twenty-five yards.

"The players will tell you that, after the fake punt worked, they *knew* we were going to win the game." And Florida did, 38–28.

"If the fake had failed, I think that would have been tough to rebound from. College football is all about momentum. Momentum is everything."

Meyer's mom was gone, but his dad was still with him. After the Gators beat the Buckeyes for the national title, 41–14, *Sports Illustrated* reported, Meyer walked back to the sideline to see his father.

"Well," Bud Meyer said, "it's about time you did that."

After Ohio State hired Meyer on November 28, 2011, between their loss to Michigan and their loss to Florida in the Gator Bowl, he didn't waste any time putting his stamp on the program. When Meyer walked into his first team meeting that day, he did not start with the usual pleasantries— hello, thanks, great to be here. He told them all to sit up straight in their seats, then pointed out those who weren't sitting straight enough.

"He grabs your attention right away," 2012 captain Zach Boren told me. "That first meeting was intense. *Intense.* But that's something we needed. We'd gotten complacent around here. He was all serious, all business."

Of the four coaches featured here, if you wanted to go get a beer, Meyer might be the fourth one you'd pick. They all have deeply competitive personalities, but Meyer is wired just a little tighter than the rest. But he did not come to Columbus to have a beer with you. He came to run the table—and his yearlong campaign started that day.

Buckeye fans bristle when Michigan head coach Brady Hoke refers to Ohio State as Ohio—which is the name of the state, or an entirely different state university, located in Athens. Likewise, Michigan fans roll their eyes at the Buckeyes' recent custom of referring to their school as *The* Ohio State University. This would suggest the university was the state's first, though Miami University in Oxford was founded in 1809, sixty-one years before Ohio Agricultural and Mechanical College was born in 1870 and later became Ohio State. It would suggest Ohio State was the best school in the state, but for years Miami was harder to get into, while great liberal arts colleges such as Oberlin, Wooster, Kenyon, and Denison have been highly rated for a century—not to mention Case Western.

The Ohio State University? More like *an* Ohio State University.

Just a generation ago, if you had earned a diploma from any high school in the state of Ohio, you were automatically, by law, granted admission to Ohio State—hardly the foundation for competitive excellence.

"Over the past two decades," former Michigan president James

Duderstadt told me, "Ohio State has invested heavily in its academic programs and today ranks as one of the nation's leading research universities. They have become very competitive in attracting outstanding faculty and students."

"Ten or fifteen years ago," said Michigan professor John Hagen, who has served on many national panels in his forty-five-year career, "you wouldn't even list Ohio State in the top three or four in the Big Ten academically, but they did a big fund-raising campaign a few years ago, and I hear they're doing another one, so they can offer higher salaries and get some more of our star faculty. They're not just competing with us in athletics anymore."

If you grew up in Ann Arbor in the seventies, as I did, the most hated man in your universe was not Leonid Brezhnev, but Woody Hayes. A close second, however, was one Archie Griffin, who not only was the only two-time Heisman Trophy winner, he was a certified Wolverine killer. He faced four of Schembechler's best teams, all ranked third or fourth in the country, three of them undefeated, and walked away with three wins and a tie—which were the first four Michigan–Ohio State games I watched.

If you want to really ruin your day, talk to Mr. Griffin for an hour and discover he is the epitome of all that is right about college football.

It is enough to make a Michigan man want to throw up.

Archie Griffin grew up, as they like to say, in the shadow of the Horseshoe, the fourth of eight kids, seven of them sons—all of whom played serious football. In the Buckeye State, that means everything. On Friday nights, the entire town empties into the local stadium. That included Archie's father, James Griffin.

"He would always be there," Archie recalled. "That might not sound like anything to you, but he worked three jobs: at Ohio Malleable, a steel casting company; another for the City of Columbus; and a janitorial service. He worked days, and he worked nights. That had to be awfully hard."

To see his kids play Friday nights, James Griffin would take his vacation time. "That *was* his vacation," Griffin said. "To watch his kids play football Friday nights. He loved doing that. When I think of him, that's what I think of first. And every time I say that, it gets me choked up."

This time was no exception. To maintain his composure, the impossibly energetic Griffin had to pause and look out the window on the Olentangy River rolling outside his office.

It will come as a shock to most football fans that Griffin visited Michigan and seriously considered going there. But he went to Ohio State, partly for his father, but also for the man in the baseball hat, the short-sleeve shirt, and the black tie.

"I loved the man. I think about him every day—and I mean that. Not a day goes by that I don't think about Woody Hayes. Something he would have said, in the course of the day, comes back into my mind.

"The biggest thing he talked about in meetings, year after year after year, was paying it forward. Paying it forward. You've been blessed, so you need to give back and give the next generation a chance."

Naturally, that list includes number 45 himself. Griffin and his wife, Bonita, founded the Archie Griffin Fund and have endowed six scholarships at Ohio State, and not in football or basketball, but in the Olympic sports.

But Griffin's greatest gift for his alma mater is his career itself—the one *after* football. In the state of Ohio, his name probably runs second only to his old coach's. Griffin could have made himself a wealthy man quite easily through sales, public relations work, even TV and radio, to name just a few pursuits. Instead, he returned to his alma mater in March 1984 to work in the athletic department, but left his comfort zone in 2004 to lead the alumni association, which now has a half million dues-paying members, thanks to his leadership.

"Now that I'm fifty-eight, I love my football, I love my Buckeyes, but I love this university as well, and what it can do for the people of the state of Ohio. For me, it's vastly more important. But I know without football, we wouldn't be this big, or this powerful. It's the drawing point.

"The president of the university can't draw that. The president of the *United States* can't draw that! It's like Bear Bryant said: 'You can't rally around a math class.'

"When you think about it, it's true—but getting people on campus actually *helps* the math class. And football *does* that! When people get drawn in, they can see what this place is all about.

"You get less support from the state now, so you need donors—and that's where football helps, too. That's why so many people know who we are, and what we do here.

"I'm not going to say all five hundred thousand alums are huge football fans, but I've gotta tell you, it's a big point of interest! We have alumni who are very proud of Ohio State, and we hear about it—especially when things are not going well! The tattoo issue. When something like that happens, you see how passionate they are. And they want it fixed! But it really shows you that they care."

When I visited Griffin in 2012, some 211,000 alums had already shown they cared by raising $1.5 billion of a $2.5 billion campaign, "But for Ohio State," to benefit the university's fourteen colleges, which have rapidly been climbing the national and even world rankings the past decade.

"They're still not Michigan," Professor Hagen said, "but now they're certainly right up there."

And that's true top to bottom. A friend of mine had little trouble getting in some two decades ago, but was surprised to learn from the admissions department in 2013 that her out-of-state daughter would need a 3.6 GPA and a 28 ACT just to be considered.

In its most recent ranking, *U.S. News & World Report* named Ohio State the eighteenth-best public university in the country. Thirteen of Ohio State's graduate programs ranked in the top ten, and the university itself earned the title of best public university in the state.

Given all this, you just might have to concede that, by 2012, the state school in Columbus had, in fact, become *The* Ohio State University.

Curse that Archie Griffin, anyhow.

Such academic ambitions, naturally, did nothing to lower the temperature of the seat Urban Meyer found himself sitting on. If anything, the university's growing stature and confidence—and the football program's central role in sparking it—only put more pressure on Meyer's new position.

The legions of Ohio natives who have bolted north to Ann Arbor includes Heisman Trophy winners Desmond Howard and Charles Woodson, plus dozens of All-Americans. But Craig Krenzel is one of the few native Michiganders who chose to play for Ohio State, and he did so in memorable style, quarterbacking the Buckeyes to their first win in Ann Arbor in fourteen years, breaking a streak that dated back to Earle Bruce's last game in 1987. Then he led Ohio State to the 2002 national title, its first since Woody Hayes's 1968 team. Along the way, Krenzel earned a 3.75 GPA in molecular genetics.

He decided to leave the premed path for business and now provides commentary for 97.1 The Fan in Columbus, alongside Mike Ricordati.

"Is coaching Ohio State the biggest pressure cooker in the country?" Krenzel asked. "It's up there. But that all depends on how you perceive pressure, and where it comes from.

"When you play at Ohio State, the fans don't expect more from you than you do. Those are the kinds of players this place attracts, and if you don't have that mentality, you don't last very long here. If you have that mentality, it's a pressure-packed situation, no doubt, but it's pressure packed because you're a perfectionist.

"What I just described is exactly how Urban Meyer is wired. He is as intense as it gets. I look at how he coaches, his expectations, his transparency, and I think it's a breath of fresh air in this age. Recruits are usually sugarcoated and schmoozed, but he just says, 'You'll earn everything you get. I'll make you a better football player—but you're gonna earn it.'

"Nobody expects more out of him than he does. The man is a perfectionist."

At Ohio State, in the wake of NCAA sanctions and a 6-7 season, Meyer only ratcheted up his perfectionist tendencies, seeking not only to run the table, but to do so with high graduation rates and little drama. To do what Tressel did, in other words, minus the headlines and headaches.

Meyer already knew the price he could pay for his perfectionism: his family and his health. But instead of backing off, he just added two more goals to the list: more time with his family, and more sanity at season's end.

"I've always had a great fear of being that old guy who says, 'I missed out,'" he told me. He was not talking about failing to win a Big Ten banner at the school he grew up cheering for, or suffering a near miss for his third national title. He was talking about his family.

The previous generation of coaches—Woody, Bo, and Bear's—made no apologies for being utterly consumed by the endless duties of their jobs, which they expressed regret over only after they retired. But this generation—squarely including Fitzgerald, Hoke, and O'Brien, who are all committed husbands and fathers—is determined to do it differently. Yes, the job is still consuming, but they stubbornly insist on protecting time with their wives and kids.

At midcareer and midlife, Meyer was attempting to join his peers in being a full-fledged father. He credits Bob Stoops, the Oklahoma coach, for being the first to say, "'I'm going to take my kids to school.' In this business, you usually get chastised for that. Legendary coaches never did things like that." Because of Stoops, and those who followed in his footsteps, Meyer said, "It's starting to change."

It is now common for these coaches to invite their families to practices, team dinners, and other functions that were strictly off-limits in the old days, and Meyer planned to take advantage of the new norms to avoid sacrificing his family life during the madness of a Big Ten season.

Meyer knew none of those goals would be easily achieved, especially given his starting point on each front.

To the Buckeye faithful, however, it all looked like a no-brainer: plug in a high-powered coach to a high-powered program, and national titles will surely follow. Meyer knew it wasn't that simple—witness the quick divorce between Michigan and Rich Rodriguez just eleven months earlier.

And Meyer knew something the fans didn't: when summer practice began, unlike Fitzgerald, Hoke, and even O'Brien, Urban Meyer still didn't have his team.

"The kids wouldn't let us coach them," he told me. "There was pushback."

Hardworking senior cocaptain Zach Boren "was actually one of the biggest offenders. He was always asking, 'Why are we doing this? We didn't do it this way before! We won games and went to the Rose Bowl!'

"Whenever you take over a new program," Meyer said, "there's going to be pushback. But this was getting old."

Going into the 2012 season, Meyer had plenty on his plate, by any standard: expectations of a perfect season, a cleaned-up program, a high graduation rate, and a historic, university-wide fund-raising campaign, plus his own hopes of maintaining a healthy, happy family life.

But he would be unlikely to achieve any of those goals if he didn't win the hearts and minds of the men wearing the gray helmets.

When fall camp started, he still hadn't.

CHAPTER 4

THE OUTSIDER

When Bill O'Brien signed his name on that dotted line, he might not have had any more idea what the NCAA had in store for Penn State than Penn State's new leaders apparently did. But he had no illusions that their troubles were behind them—the court cases alone could drag on for years—and he already knew how tricky coaching could be even under normal circumstances. And these were far from normal circumstances.

For their part, Penn State's leaders might have been whistling past the NCAA graveyard, but to their credit, they got a few things right. Even they knew enough trouble lay ahead to conclude they had no choice but to hire someone outside the family for their next football coach, and to give him a free hand in hiring an almost completely new staff. O'Brien wisely kept stalwarts such as coaches Larry Johnson Sr. and Ron Vanderlinden, and equipment managers Spider Caldwell and Kirk Diehl. But as for the rest of Paterno's staff, most of whom had served with Sandusky, Penn State avoided the problem of having a dozen coaches still on payroll who might have to answer more questions about what they knew, when they knew it, and what they did or didn't do about it—which could keep even the best coaches hopelessly distracted from doing their jobs.

But Penn State's leaders did not fully recognize why this would be the mother of all transitions: no football program was so haunted by both its past *and* its future. If this coaching transplant was going to take, O'Brien and his players would have to outrun both.

At major college football programs, smooth transitions are still the exception, not the rule, especially when the new guy is following not just a legend, but a suddenly tainted one.

Unlike their NFL counterparts, the best college coaches are not interchangeable parts. You don't simply install one here or there, flick a switch, and watch them light up the college football world. Too often, schools embark on a blind date, with neither party knowing enough about the other before heading to the altar. Las Vegas weddings tend to end in Las Vegas divorces—just ask the people at Michigan. Both sides had better know what they're getting into and be ready, willing, and able to bridge the gap between them.

Tradition can be a great help here. No matter what sordid stories would emerge—and as Penn State's lawsuits roll out, those could only get worse—the uniforms, the mascot, and the band were blameless and could be leaned on by the faithful to remind them of the values they hold dear.

When they introduced Bill O'Brien on January 6, 2012, as the school's fifteenth coach—and only its third since 1950—famed lettermen such as Franco Harris, Todd Blackledge, and LaVar Arrington publicly complained the university had just picked a man with no ties to Penn State's celebrated tradition, and no experience as a head coach. Of course, both charges were true and resonated with many alums and lettermen.

But the current players—many of whom had secretly grown unhappy with the program they had joined—immediately took to the unassuming, energetic O'Brien, his cutting-edge football formulas, his pedigreed staff, and his benignly insane strength coach, Craig Fitzpatrick, who led them on predawn conditioning runs in the dead of winter wearing a T-shirt and shorts. By the time of the annual Blue-White game on April 21, marking the end of spring practice, O'Brien felt close enough to his players to end his halftime locker room speech by telling them, "Now let's give the fans something to look forward to this fall. Keep it moving, keep it sharp—and, hey, don't cheap-shot your teammates . . . assholes!"

He turned to the door with perfect comedic timing. The players cracked up, snapped their straps, and jogged out the tunnel behind their new coach. He had them.

But having them under those conditions—tough as they surely seemed at the time—looked positively simple compared to having them in the rough seas ahead.

● ● ●

On Sunday, July 22, 2012, O'Brien got word that the NCAA would be issuing its punishment sometime the next day. The coaches debated canceling the Monday-morning training session, but the players urged them not to. Their summer work had built up to their "max out" day to set their personal records before taking a week off, then returning to start a month of full-blown practice and three months of games.

Monday morning, Coach O'Brien walked through the weight room while the players were lifting to let them know he had just learned the sanctions were going to be announced at ten, right after their training session ended. He told them they would meet as a team in the players' lounge to watch the press conference.

"But that only jacked us up, like we needed to get ready for the news, to prepare ourselves," recalled starting offensive lineman John Urschel, a redshirt junior who was already pursuing his master's degree in mathematics, with a 4.0. "We just had a ton of great, positive energy—one of the best lifts we've ever had."

After they set a pile of personal bests, when they sat down in the players' lounge to watch Mark Emmert announce Penn State's punishment, their energy was quickly redirected.

"Guys were getting pissed, yelling at the TV," Urschel told me. "It was pretty severe—a lot more than we thought it would be."

Just two years earlier, Emmert himself had held up Penn State as a pillar of all that was right about collegiate athletics. Just one year earlier, you'd be hard-pressed to find a university or a state with greater pride in its football program, which stressed "Success with Honor"—and seemed to live up to it.

Now it was the football program that threatened to bring down the very university it had helped build.

For the people watching in that players' lounge the question, stripped down to its essentials, was this: Could Penn State's program, and the traditions that went with it, survive the season intact? Did they have a future worth fighting for?

O'Brien immediately led everyone into the team room, where he draped his left arm over the podium and spoke directly to his shell-shocked squad.

"I just remember how matter-of-fact and truthful he was," longtime equipment manager Kirk Diehl recalled. "He was probably as surprised as anyone, but he didn't sugarcoat it. He said—and I'll never forget this—'We're not here to understand the rules. We're here to follow them. It's my obligation to tell you that you are free to go anywhere you want, with no penalties. However, if you stay, I promise you, you will never forget it.'"

"He really felt for us," Urschel said. "He didn't say anything that wasn't true. He didn't try to minimize what the NCAA had just done. He didn't beg us to stay. But he stressed the positive: 'You still get to play football in front of 108,000 rabid fans. You still get to be on TV. And most important, you will still get a great education.'"

The bond between the new coach and his players had grown stronger, but if O'Brien was going to keep his team together, he still had lots of work to do—and not a moment to spare.

"Were we in danger of a complete collapse?" seventeen-year defensive-line coach Larry Johnson Sr. wondered aloud. "No question. The threat was as real as it could be."

It quickly became obvious that Penn State's interim president, Rod Erickson—a nice guy who had been an effective provost, but was clearly in over his head in his new role—its acting athletic director, Dave Joyner, and its deeply dysfunctional board of thirty-two trustees, who did not even know each other's names, were too busy working damage control for their university and themselves to spend any time defending the current players. It is not a stretch to say the survival of Penn State football would be left almost entirely to the coaches and the players.

That Monday night, O'Brien set up a conference call with the parents of his 120 players. From this town-hall phone meeting an idea came to him—a simple one by the standards of every other college football program, but not Penn State's. The next day, O'Brien walked down to see Spider Caldwell in his equipment room to follow up on this idea. "How difficult would it be," O'Brien asked, "to put these guys' names on the backs of their jerseys?"

At Penn State, this was tantamount to asking if it would be a big deal if the pope replaced his ceremonial miter with a backward baseball cap.

Caldwell, who started working in the equipment room as a student in 1983, recoiled. "My first reaction was 'Oh, no, the lettermen are going to go bonkers.' And I knew Bill had promised, originally, never to change the jerseys. That nameless jersey is so sacred to our former players.

"But when I heard the reasoning behind it—that he wanted to honor the guys who stayed, and it will mark a break—I thought it was a great idea. But I wasn't at all sure the lettermen would agree."

O'Brien's relationship with the old guard, which could create a chain reaction of problems if it went sour, was a real concern. But that first frenetic week, it was easily eclipsed by the fear of an exodus of players, with no time to replace them before Penn State's first game, against Ohio University on September 1.

The lettermen and the current players might have had different perspectives on Paterno and O'Brien, but they had far more in common than not, including being the first groups to grasp the full threat Penn State football faced.

Tuesday, July 24, 2012: The morning after Emmert's announcement, Mike Zordich woke up at six to work out at seven. "First thing I do, I look at my phone, and I already had a bunch of calls from [opposing] coaches. Fuck. That meant everyone else was getting them, too."

When he first saw Mauti in their living room, "Dude" was all he had to say. "I looked at him, looking at his phone, and he's got the same thing happening. And I said, right then and there, 'Look. I'm staying.' And once I'm staying, he's staying, so now the question is, who else is gonna stay?"

Convinced of the program's impending doom, the two went straight to their favorite sanctuary: strength coach Craig Fitzgerald's office. It was attached to the weight room, which looked out onto the emerald practice field of real grass, surrounded by pine trees and the Nittany Mountains beyond—one of the most beautiful settings in the Big Ten, and the league's only campus with mountains. But they knew scenery was not going to save their team.

"What are you guys hearing?" Fitzgerald asked.

The two seniors cut to the chase, rattling off all the teammates they'd heard were leaving. "We just started writing names on legal pads," Zordich said, "listing who was in and who was out, trying to figure out if this guy leaves, is this guy gonna follow, so will it trickle down? We practically made a playbook of who's getting calls, from where, and who's gonna stay."

Fitz looked at the list. If even half the players they had listed on the "Gone" side of the ledger actually left, Penn State might not have enough players to run a decent practice, let alone compete on Saturdays.

Fitzgerald muttered, *"Holy shit,"* then grabbed his phone to call O'Brien in his upstairs office. Not long after he started relaying what the seniors had told him, O'Brien interrupted Fitzgerald: "Hold it. I'll be right down."

Bill O'Brien left his spacious, carpeted office, dashed down the stairs, and joined Fitz and the two seniors in the smaller, rubber-floored room. O'Brien knew this was no time to stand on ceremony.

He saw Mauti and Zordich, normally as upbeat as any players he'd coached, slumped in the couch against the window.

"When Coach showed up, our body language, sitting around, was basically 'We're screwed,'" Mauti recalled. "We weren't hiding anything. It was too late for that."

While O'Brien and Fitzgerald sat and listened, the two seniors started reading the names of dozens of teammates they had learned were about to bolt to other campuses. O'Brien had coached these players for only six months, but he had no reason to doubt them. He'd been hearing most of the same things they had, and some they hadn't.

He looked at them, then at Fitzgerald, then exhaled. He knew he had to make some big decisions—decisions that could determine the very fate of Penn State's football program—and he had to make them fast.

"The four of us sat there," Mauti recalled, "and started making a new list, going over everyone we knew about. Then we started strategizing on what to do—who would call who, all that. And then we just started calling everyone—players, parents, roommates, everyone we could think of—basically re-recruiting our own team to stay."

The four men agreed on virtually everything, except one seemingly minor point: O'Brien thought he should set a deadline for players to declare whether they were in or out. How could they run an effective fall camp without knowing who would still be on the team for their first game?

At first, the two seniors agreed, but after letting it sink in, Zordich said he thought it might backfire; opposing coaches would hear about the deadline and start pounding the players' phones all over again. The younger players might panic and make a bad decision. Then Mauti chimed in, arguing that the more the players got to know O'Brien, his staff, and their cutting-edge program, the more likely they would be to stay.

O'Brien looked at Zordich, Mauti, and Fitzgerald. He knew he had to make a decision, one that could make or break the historically stable program he had just inherited. And he had to make it that instant.

"You've got to understand," O'Brien told me, "all four of us, nobody knew what to do. Nobody ever had to know! The entire staff was on vacation—it was our last summer break—so nobody was around. The setting was important.

"The key is you're talking about two very mature guys, *smart* guys, Penn State guys, whose dads were heroes here, who've already been through a lot. I love these kids and I wanted them to stay, so we were just trying to figure out the best thing to do."

After scanning their faces one more time, O'Brien started nodding and finally said, "Okay. Then that's what we'll do."

At another team meeting that afternoon, O'Brien soft-pedaled the idea of a deadline, telling the players assembled, "Just be respectful of me and the coaching staff and your teammates."

"And that was the cool part," Zordich said. "Coach listens to us. He's open to what we're saying, and he has enough trust in us to try it our way. And that's what he did."

Since top-down, CEO-style management seemed to be all the rage at other athletic departments around the country, O'Brien's approach to vital decision-making looked unorthodox, if not downright crazy. But, as he said, unprecedented events had also made it necessary. Nobody had ever sailed these waters before, forcing him to rely more heavily on his seniors—and they on him—and a North Star they couldn't always see behind the clouds. It was undeniably scary—but when it worked, it was undeniably thrilling, too.

"Looking back on it," Mauti concluded, shaking his head in both disbelief and pride, "that was a serious meeting."

• • •

The four men split up and started working their phones, contacting every member of the team, some of them several times. "We had a whole operation going," Zordich said. "This was nuts."

"I have never used my phone that much in my life," Mauti recalled. "We started at seven Tuesday morning and went to ten thirty that night. Then we said, 'Let's get back to Fitz's office at six thirty tomorrow morning and start all over.' So Z and I would get up, go to the building, and do it all again. We only slept a couple hours a night that week."

For all the calls they made to their teammates, the players received almost as many from coaches across the country. The long list included a call from a longtime assistant Mauti knew well, who resigned after Penn State picked O'Brien.

Therefore, when Mauti saw the name of his former assistant coach pop up on his cell phone that day, the senior linebacker assumed he was calling simply to offer his support. So, Mauti took the call. But after a few pleasantries, the coach made it clear the purpose of his call was to see if any Penn State players might want to transfer to a school where a friend of his was the head coach.

Mauti told him flatly that, no, no one at Penn State was interested in transferring anywhere, least of all Mauti. That call surprised Mauti, but not as much as a long text he received that same day from University of Georgia quarterback Aaron Murray. Although the two had never met, Murray was texting on behalf of their new strength coach, John Thomas, who had been Penn State's strength coach for twenty years, until he left in the same wave that had swept the others out.

To hear that these two former Nittany Lions coaches, who had just months earlier spoken of Penn State as a devoted family, were now trying to tear that family apart was more than Mauti could bear. So Mauti decided to put an end to it. "Look, we appreciate your interest," he replied to Murray, "but no one is looking to go anywhere.

"And please do me another favor. On behalf of the entire Penn State team, please tell JT to go fuck himself."

We don't know if Murray passed on Mauti's message to John Thomas. But we do know Mauti received no more text messages from anyone at the University of Georgia.

• • •

Mauti's message to Thomas aside, the seniors followed O'Brien's example on this point, and every other: do not worry about predators, whom
O'Brien knew they couldn't stop anyway. The NCAA had set the new
rules, and the new rules said competing programs could poach Penn
State's program without penalty.

Within twenty-four hours, coaches from around the country weren't
just calling and texting Penn State players. They were setting up shop
in the parking lot of Penn State's football building, waiting for players to
come out to sell them on transferring to their school. Many of the players
stayed inside the sanctuary of the football building as long as they could,
in the hopes of waiting the coaches out.

On Wednesday, Adrian Amos and Stephon Morris, roommates and
fellow cornerbacks, both tweeted, "We have chosen to stay at Penn State
and opposing coaches are outside our apartment, was that the intention
of the NCAA?"

Actually, that was precisely the intention of the NCAA. Instead of giving Penn State the death penalty—for which the NCAA leaders might
themselves be castigated—they would let the vultures finish the job for
them. Of course, given the setup, Penn State's fate ultimately wasn't up
to the NCAA or the scavengers on the phone or in the parking lot. It was
up to Penn State's players, who would vote with their feet.

"Silas [Redd] was basically our first domino," Mauti said, referring to
the Lions' soon-to-be junior running back, who had finished third in the
Big Ten as a sophomore with 1,241 rushing yards. "There were a lot of
guys who were waiting for him to make his decision. We almost drove to
his home in Connecticut—"

"—because we knew USC was going to visit his home," Zordich
cut in.

"We figured," Mauti said, "whether Silas stayed or left, the longer he
drew out that process, the more he isolated himself from the rest of the
team."

"And the longer he waited," Zordich said, "the more we could talk to
the other guys, who might influence other decisions."

"If he'd gone right away—"

"—it would've instantly cost us five or six guys, good players," Zordich
said. "At least."

• • •

Given the endless rumors of departures, Mauti and Zordich knew if they were going to keep their team together, they had to do more than just make phone calls and visit their teammates.

"At first, Coach is telling all of us, 'Don't talk to the media,'" Zordich recalled. "Which makes sense. He didn't want us stirring it all up. But when we met again, I said, 'All these people are hearing about how many players are supposed to be leaving and how it's all falling apart. And that's not what's happening here. We're *sticking*. We're working our asses off. We're *together*. We need to go out there and tell *them* that.'"

"The media was making a story where there wasn't one," Mauti said. "Really, no one had left yet. And the guys who *had* left were already injured or walk-ons or whatever—reasons that had nothing to do with the sanctions."

Once again, after O'Brien listened to his seniors and weighed the new data, he was not afraid to alter his original strategy. He gave them permission to contact ESPN and offer a statement. ESPN jumped at the chance, inviting the seniors to broadcast their announcement from the practice field Wednesday morning. Live.

At O'Brien's request, the duo shared their plans with the Penn State athletic department's PR staff, which asked to see their proposed speech. Mauti and Zordich walked over to Spider's office, typed their speech out on his computer, and e-mailed it to Assistant Athletic Director for Communications Jeff Nelson, who sent back a revised version, highlighting the things the office wanted them to say.

"We read it, and we looked at each other," Mauti remembered, "and we said, 'Nah, this ain't us.' Then we balled it up and threw it in the trash."

They went back over their original notes and divided up the lines. "You'll say this, and I'll say that." And that was it. But right before they went on camera, they asked a few teammates in the weight room if they wanted to come out to show support. Everyone there said, "Sure," and walked outside.

Well, almost everyone. When math major John Urschel saw them, he asked, "Do you guys have notes?"

"No. Why?"

"Do you know what you're going to say? Because this is going live. It's going to go everywhere. It's going to be big."

"Jeez, John," Zordich said. "I was doing fine until I talked to you! Now I want to shit my pants! Thanks!"

Armed with Urschel's unconditional support—he walked out with them—the two seniors bravely stepped outside anyway to face the ESPN cameras, surrounded by thirty-some teammates who had interrupted their workouts to join them.

"We want to let the nation know that we're proud of who we are," Zordich said into the camera. "We're the real Penn Staters. We have an obligation to Penn State, and we have the ability to fight for not just a team, not just a program, but an entire university and every man that wore blue and white on the gridiron before us."

"No sanction, no politician, is ever going to take away what we have here," Mauti said. "This is what Penn State's about—fighting through adversity—and we're going to show up every Saturday and raise hell. This program was not built by one man, and this program sure as hell is not going to get torn down by one man."

Three minutes after they started, they were done.

"Good thing they taped from the chest up," Zordich told me, "because my right leg was shaking the whole time!"

ESPN ran the piece in its entirety many times, which generated dozens of comments on air, hundreds of e-mails, and a wide range of reactions. Some expressed nominal support for the players, who had nothing to do with the Sandusky tragedy. Others called them everything from "Paterno apologists" to "child rapists." And still others pointed out that only thirty teammates stood behind them, unaware they had come out spontaneously and the rest were in class, where they were supposed to be.

But all these reactions missed the point. The public and the press are so accustomed to consuming packaged hype pumped out by PR people that when we finally witnessed something rare—unscripted authenticity—we missed it. For all the official promotional spots constantly telling us how committed student-athletes are to the ideals of college sports, and how those ideals prepare them for life, when we saw the real thing, we didn't see it for what it was: a group of young men defending the fundamental values of intercollegiate athletics.

If the public missed it, Penn State's coaches caught it.

Defensive line coach Larry Johnson Sr. was sitting in his office when he saw the players walk out onto the grass field below. An hour later, he heard that they had made a statement. When he watched it, "I was impressed. I was emotionally charged that these young men knew it was about a lot more than football."

By inviting players to admit that playing football was more important than remaining at their university, the NCAA sanctions, quite unintentionally, had given Penn State's players an opportunity to prove the opposite.

"I think, at that moment, our team got solidified," Coach Johnson said. "I think guys who might have *thought* they were in were *really* in after that.

"I think it was critical. I really do."

The next day, Thursday, July 26, O'Brien would fly out for the annual Big Ten Media Days in Chicago. But before he did, he was trying to think of something else, *anything*, that might help ensure he'd still have a team when he returned Friday afternoon.

"Man, we were doing all we could—meeting with the players every day—to keep them on the team," O'Brien said. "We decided to have each of the coaches give a speech that night on some adversity they'd overcome, and how they'd handled it."

All the coaches knew how to connect with the players—a skill that usually comes with the territory—but the most memorable speech, by all accounts, was Larry Johnson Sr.'s. Johnson played and later coached at the high school made famous in *Remember the Titans* and led his teams to three Maryland state titles before coming to Penn State in 1996. He quickly proved to be an excellent recruiter and a topflight coach.

A few years earlier, Illinois had called to see if he would be interested in becoming the Illini's defensive coordinator—a promotion from D-line coach. When his players heard about it, they said, "If he leaves, we're going with him."

"I try very hard to build relationships with young men outside of football," he told me, "and I've turned down things because, I tell them, 'You guys are important.'"

"The D-linemen, they love that guy—for all the right reasons," Zordich said.

Johnson is an unusually calm, self-possessed man, a former deacon with a deep baritone. When he speaks, he has a way of looking deep into your eyes that makes you give him your undivided attention.

That night, when he took the floor of the team room, he told them, "My message is simple. Everybody has a role. We are given a road, and we choose how we travel that road. We've been chosen to do something extraordinary, something that's never been done before.

"This is bigger than just football. To be able to look back on your lives when you have kids who are fifteen, sixteen years old, and they ask you, 'Hey, Dad, have you ever faced adversity?'—you will say, 'Yes, this is what I was given, and this is what I've done.'

"So you see, we're here for a reason, and we have a job to do."

"Near the end, you could see him tearing up," Zordich said. "His voice was cracking. It was pin-drop stuff. He had us. Coach Johnson—he should get a whole lot of credit for keeping this team together."

"Our D-line has some of our best athletes," Mauti added, players such as Jordan Hill and Pete Massaro. Once Coach Johnson secured the D-line to stay, "we built it out from there. Make no mistake: Coach O'Brien got us through this. But Coach Johnson's leadership during this time cannot be overstated."

Seeing how well the coaches' speeches were received, O'Brien had another inspiration: "Penn State has the largest letterman club in the country, over a thousand guys. I thought, 'Let's invite them in to talk to the team, about what it means to play here.'"

Good idea, but no small feat. O'Brien's secretary, Christine Laur, sent out over a thousand old-fashioned letters that day, which arrived at most of the lettermen's homes Friday. O'Brien had invited them for a meeting that coming Tuesday, a workday, with just five days' notice.

"And let's be honest," O'Brien said, "State College is still not exactly the easiest place to get to."

O'Brien had no idea what the response would be—not only to his invitation, but to his decisions that week, including putting names on the jerseys—but he didn't have any time to worry about it. The morning after the letters went out, Thursday, July 26, O'Brien woke at 4:00 a.m. to get to work, then hop on Penn State's private jet to fly to Chicago for the annual Big Ten media circus.

Naturally, Penn State would be center stage.

CHAPTER 5

FOUR TEAMS, FOUR GOALS

Thursday–Friday, July 26–27, 2012: "Hello! And welcome to the forty-first annual Big Ten Media Days."

The Big Ten's always affable assistant commissioner for communications, Scott Chipman, stood at the podium to welcome the five hundred journalists at Chicago's McCormick Place.

The league started hosting this media event in 1971, when the Big Ten actually had ten teams and no TV network and allowed each member only two televised games per season. Woody Hayes coached Ohio State, Bo Schembechler coached Michigan, and Joe Paterno coached Penn State, which was still twenty-two years from playing in the Big Ten. No one in the Big Ten sold out every game.

Forty-one years later, the Big Ten had twelve teams, the nation's biggest stadiums, the most living alumni (4.4 million), and the most fans attending games—over 6 million in 2011. Four of those stadiums drew 100 percent or more of capacity, eight of them 90 percent of capacity or more, and all twelve drew 70 percent or more. Of the nation's twenty-one schools with the highest attendance, seven of them were in the Big Ten, fully a third.

Big Ten teams played ninety-six regular-season games in 2011, and every single one of them was on TV, many on the league's own Big Ten Network. Just five years old, the BTN was by far the most successful conference TV network, going out to 53 million homes and paying out $24.6 million to each team in 2012 alone.

This kind of growth generates a tremendous amount of money, and with it, power. But you could argue such unprecedented growth *requires* this very concentration of power just to manage it. If contemporary athletic directors sounded increasingly like corporate CEOs, with endless talk of branding and business models, market value, and return on investment, they had cause: the Big Ten had become a stunningly successful business.

Big Ten Commissioner Jim Delany had played on two of Dean Smith's Final Four teams at North Carolina and captained the 1970 squad, then graduated from UNC's law school. He was entering his twenty-fourth season as Big Ten commissioner and deserved the lion's share of the credit for the league's unprecedented success. After listing the Big Ten's impressive highlights, he said, "I couldn't stand up here without addressing the Penn State case."

And he did, in comments that ran a full page, before opening the floor to questions. Over the next thirty minutes, with admirable candor, he fielded eight questions—seven of them pertaining to Penn State in some form. A reporter pointed out that all four of the Big Ten's marquee football programs—Nebraska, Michigan, Ohio State, and Penn State—were currently on NCAA probation. He asked the commissioner what that did to the league's reputation.

After describing it as a "fair question, and one I've thought about," Delany separated the four schools' situations. It was a big leap from Nebraska's minor infractions over textbook-purchasing policies, he said, to the Ohio State coach "who lost his job for not being honest about answering questions about tattoos," to the tragedy at Penn State. "I think it's intellectually and morally difficult to even discuss those things in the same sentence."

But Delany pointed out that no one, least of all him, had ever claimed the Big Ten had a spotless record. "In fact," he said, "if you look at history . . . we've had, I think, thirty-two [NCAA probation] cases in thirty years. We've had thirteen basketball cases; fifteen football cases. We've had a few cases of academic fraud. But some are much worse than others."

In other words, the present wasn't as bad as it seemed, partly because the past wasn't as great as believed. It was a refreshingly honest assessment.

Since the Sandusky case, he said, the Big Ten office had been intent on getting to the core issue: "institutional control, concentration, and power." For comparison, he cited the NFL and the NBA, where there was no question who the owners were. But it was not nearly as clear who was in charge of a university's football program "because power is diffuse [among] trust-ees, presidents, faculty, athletic directors, compliance directors."

It's worth noting, however, that the athletes and the fans did not make Delany's list of power brokers. The leverage each possesses—to play or not to play; to pay or not to pay—are considered givens, when they're considered at all. For all the perceived cracks in the edifice of college football, and all the suggested patches, few of the would-be repairmen are even entertaining the possibility that either players or fans might ever call it quits.

These hypotheticals would be largely academic if millions of fans did not prefer college football to the pros. Why do they?

College teams were organically and spontaneously created more than a century ago by the students, just for fun.

The NFL and all its teams since were created by league executives, lawyers, and chief marketing officers, just for profit.

Almost every Division I college football team predates the oldest NFL teams by three or four decades. Most schools built their current stadi-ums before most NFL teams built their first—or second, or third. Col-lege football is one of those few passions we have in common with our great-grandparents.

College teams play on college campuses, where students actually go to school. The students feel as connected to these campuses as they do to their homes—and this connection typically lasts for life. That also goes for the jocks, who live in the same dorms as the geeks; they take classes in the same buildings; and they eat at the same pizza and burger joints everyone else does. Just about anyone who went to college has a story about running into the big man on campus.

NFL players make millions and live in gated communities. You're not likely to meet them, no matter how many years you pay to watch them play. Their teams play in big cities, and they don't have homecoming games.

College teams never threaten to change their colors or move to Okla-homa City if you don't build them a new stadium—at taxpayer expense. No, they play in the nation's oldest, grandest stadiums, surrounded by lush green lawns, old trees, and two-story homes where students live. They have marching bands and fight songs and quirky customs that go back a century.

NFL teams play in sanitized, soulless domes—usually subsidized by the taxpayers—with loud scoreboards that tell you exactly what to yell and exactly when to yell it, all surrounded by vast oceans of asphalt.

The NFL's rules are constantly tweaked to create as much parity as possible—which is why every team seems to finish 9-7 or 7-9. The margins are so close as to render the competitive differences almost meaningless. The Pittsburgh Steelers' Larry Foote told me most games boil down to three or four mistakes. Pro football functions like a giant gumball machine, jumbling players around the league, then spitting out winning teams virtually by dumb luck.

When you hear the score of an NFL game, you have to stop and think, Was that expected, or an upset? But when Utah beats Alabama, or Navy beats Notre Dame, or Appalachian State beats Michigan, you don't need to check the latest polls to know something historic just happened.

Pro teams choose their players, but college players choose their teams—which leads to another major difference: universities, because they started long before their football teams, represent a particular set of values, priorities, and strengths that stamp the teams that wear their name. It was for this very reason the Big Ten presidents formed their conference. If these players were going to represent their schools, they reasoned, they should do so honorably.

In 1941, Michigan's legendary Fielding Yost said at his retirement banquet, "My heart is so full at this moment and I am so overcome by the rush of memories that I fear I could say little more. But do let me reiterate . . . the Spirit of Michigan. It is based upon a deathless loyalty to Michigan and all her ways; an enthusiasm that makes it second nature for Michigan men to spread the gospel of their university to the world's distant outposts; a conviction that nowhere is there a better university, in any way, than this Michigan of ours."

But the beauty is this: the fans, alums, and players at Ohio State, Penn State, and Northwestern—and dozens of other schools—all feel the same way. When college teams compete, it isn't just a game between two teams. We see it as a battle between two ways of life. Is there a single professional team that can claim anything like this?

This is why, when schools are caught violating NCAA rules, it bruises the identity of their fans. But when the New England Patriots were caught filming opponents' hand signals, did their fans hang their heads in shame? No, it was just a passing nuisance.

Professional teams don't stand for anything more than a can of pop. The players go on strike, the owners lock them out, and they repeat the cycle every five or ten years, as needed, for more money. Their fans respond in kind, often caring less about the actual teams in their state than the fantasy teams on their computers—or the point spreads in their paper, and the wallets in their back pockets.

About 17 million people attended NFL games in 2011, but almost twice that many, 33 million, participated in fantasy football leagues—as pure an expression of the players-as-gumballs model you could conceive. The sites that host those fantasy leagues don't even bother posting versions for college football because virtually no one plays fantasy college football. College football fans actually care about college football, not just its parts.

If the NFL has benefited greatly from fantasy football fans, it's nothing compared to the viewers it attracts through gambling. (Several NFL franchises were actually founded and owned by gamblers.) The NFL is a $9-billion-a-year business (helped considerably by the $17 billion it extracted from taxpayers for its stadiums). But that doesn't include the piles of money gamblers bet on the NFL, which, by most estimates, is approaching a billion dollars a year. Of course, plenty of college football fans bet on their games, too, but I've found it as rare to hear them talk about the point spread at a sports bar as it is to *not* hear NFL fans discussing the same subject during their games. The two fan bases are not motivated by the same things.

In other words, many of the NFL's "fans" are simply fellow travelers, along for the ride for ulterior motives. That simply isn't the case with college football fans, whose devotion is based on a passionate attachment to their team.

The same fellow travelers label could be applied to NFL players. As Jerry Seinfeld said, professional players are traded so often, you're really just cheering for your team's jerseys. Those *teams* don't even represent their cities—six of the NFL's thirty-two teams have moved a total of eight times since the Super Bowl started in 1967. If the Rams play in Los Angeles or St. Louis, what difference does it make?

Of the 124 FBS Division I teams, not one has ever moved, gone on strike, or been locked out. Ever.

College athletes are more passionate playing for a scholarship than pro athletes are playing for millions. And we admire them more for this very reason. It's the difference between citizen soldiers volunteering for the army and hired Hessians. Give us the doughboys, the G.I. Joes, and the grunts fighting for a cause.

And this is why we watch: not for perfection, but passion — the same reason over a million fans watch the Little League World Series every summer. This point is easily proven: the worst team in the NFL would crush the best team in college football, every year. Yet college football is the only sport in the world that draws more fans to its games than the big league teams it feeds. The attendance at Michigan, Ohio State, and Penn State home games typically averages 50 percent more than that of the NFL teams in those states — and often doubles it. No minor league baseball or hockey team comes close to matching the attendance of their parent clubs.

This basic truth escapes both the proponents of paying players and the NCAA executives who try to squelch minor leagues from starting: college football is selling romance, not prowess. If ability were the only appeal, we'd move NFL games to Saturday and watch those games instead. But if you lose the romance of college football, you will lose the fans of college football.

Joining a hundred thousand like-minded strangers solves a modern problem, too. The Dalai Lama and Mother Teresa have both noted that the great disease of Western civilization is loneliness. Yes, it's possible to be lonely in a crowd — but not this one.

Studies show our endorphins spike when we're marching in formation, singing in unison, or cheering together in a stadium. Where else can you be certain a hundred thousand other people are feeling exactly what you're feeling, exactly when you're feeling it? This is why such places are more important now than ever.

Think about it. The Big Ten's twelve teams do not play one game this season that's not televised. You can sit back in your easy chair right at home and watch every game for free. Likewise, every song in the world can be purchased for a few bucks, and every movie is on DVD. Yet we still go to concerts, movies, and games, just as our ancestors did almost century ago. If Beethoven, Humphrey Bogart, or Fielding H. Yost visited those places today, they would think almost nothing had changed.

We need to be together. We need to share something we care about with strangers. And to fill that need, you could do worse than Big Ten football.

"We have too much *pluribus*," filmmaker Ken Burns said twenty years ago, "and not enough *unum*." If that was true then, before the flourishing of designer news stations, gated communities, and the Internet, it is surely more true now. College football stadiums are now one of the few remaining places where we connect across race, religion, and politics. And we do it with vigor.

Dr. Ed Zeiders, the pastor of St. Paul's United Methodist Church right in downtown State College, has seen what the football team can do for the faithful in ways others might not.

"We are desperately needy," he told me. "We need something to cheer about and rally around. Our culture is devoid of these things.

"We need a place to stand, and a people to stand with, and a cause to stand for. That is not original with me. That came out of World Methodism. And those three propositions hold the key to healthy and value-oriented living.

"I've taught and preached that for a lot of years.

"I have this belief that academics should be that unifying principle, but the evidence points to something else.

"Sports has the capacity to make that happen. That can get skewed and twisted, especially in the marketing side of the equation, but my interest in sports is more in the community that forms around them.

"Obviously, football's an important consideration for us—they've been very good here for many, many years—but part of what my wife and I enjoy is the friendships we create in the stands. There is an *ease* with which sports fans connect with each other. The sport has a tendency to create an environment, and a way for people to live vicariously through their teams. And in the case of Penn State it has the potential to hold up something that is admirable and unifying."

I've spent four of the past five years following Big Ten football players at close range, and I can tell you that, with few exceptions, they are hard-working, honest guys who care deeply for their school and their team-mates. For many fans, when their favorite running back breaks through the line into the end zone, then simply hands the ball to the ref and celebrates with his teammates, he represents our cherished Midwestern values at their best.

One Wolverine fan who lost his dad at a young age wrote to Michigan's athletic director that "Michigan football is my father."

A foreign concept, perhaps. But not to us.

Our love for college football is irrational—and that's where they've got us.

Back at McCormick Place, after each coach gave a fifteen-minute speech in the main room, they joined three of their players to meet with smaller media groups in the room next door.

I have no idea what kind of players each coach left back on campus, but the ones they brought to Chicago were not just smart, sincere, and well-spoken—the kind of guys you'd want to hire for your company— they demonstrated the kind of message control that political campaigns could only dream of.

Urban Meyer, as the first head coach to migrate from the SEC to the Big Ten in . . . as long as anyone can remember, had to field the usual questions about the Big Ten—repeatedly.

Characteristically, he didn't sugarcoat his answers.

The SEC had "won a bunch of national championships," he said, and were clearly "the kingpin in the BCS bowls." For Ohio State to catch up to the best of the SEC—and by proxy, the rest of the Big Ten to do so, as well—he believed it needed faster, more athletic players. "But the defensive front seven is the difference in the SEC right now," he said, which entailed everything, from recruiting to coaching.

He pointed out, however, that eight of the twelve Big Ten teams had started running some version of the spread offense. "That's obviously a drastic change historically."

When yet another reporter asked Meyer what the Big Ten had to do to catch up with the SEC, he said simply, "We have to win, and win some bowl games. The bottom line in all this is the same: to win."

When Meyer first laid out his expectations to his new team, Zach Boren recalled, "We knew we were in store for a long, hard ride—and that's why we came to Ohio State. That's what we signed up for."

"I was off-the-charts excited," senior linebacker Etienne Sabino said. "His passion, his enthusiasm for the game, his sense of urgency for us as players—that's what we needed."

When the inevitable bowl-ban question came up, fellow senior John Simon provided the team's stock answer: "We're going to treat every game like a bowl game."

Of course, some "pretend bowl games" are bigger than others. When someone asked Meyer if he needed to do anything extra to motivate his team for the Michigan game, he looked surprised. "I hope not. I hope we're really good by then. If we're not, maybe I'll have to make up some secret slogan and put them on T-shirts. But if you have to do that, you're already in trouble.

"So, no, I don't think so. It's the greatest rivalry in college football, a game I've known all my life. Buckeye Nation is very clear on what it expects from that game."

His expression suggested that he intended to give it to them.

Michigan head coach Brady Hoke arrived with co-captains Denard Robinson and Jordan Kovacs and junior offensive tackle Taylor Lewan, who had flirted with the NFL after his sophomore year and was expected to jump after the 2012 season, possibly as a first-rounder.

Robinson's and Kovac's prospects looked a little different. Robinson capped his first year as Michigan's starting quarterback in 2010 by winning the Big Ten MVP award. Then he watched the staff that recruited him get broomed, and his numbers slip as a junior under new offensive coordinator Al Borges, who favored the NFL passing attack to the system Robinson was born to run, the spread offense. While Michigan's defense jumped, leaped, and pole-vaulted its way from 110th to 17th in the nation, a stunning achievement, the offense seemed to be going the opposite direction, though surely not as fast.

When Rodriguez's staff was fired, many assumed Robinson would transfer to a spread-option program, perhaps one closer to his home in Deerfield Beach, Florida. But he had promised his parents he would get his Michigan degree and told his teammates that he would not leave them. His word proved good on both fronts.

For Kovacs, whom Rodriguez plucked from a campus tryout, every day wearing the winged helmet was gravy. His dad had walked on for

Bo Schembechler, but only got in a few plays. Jordan found himself starting in his third game, a thrilling win against Notre Dame, and finished his junior year as the team's leading tackler. So, here he was, an unrecruited walk-on turned cocaptain of the sport's winningest program—with no desire even to try out for the NFL draft. As a movement-science major with a 3.1 GPA, he didn't need the NFL to consider his college career a success.

As for Hoke, he was fresh off his 11-2 "rookie season." If any coach had a happier honeymoon than Hoke's, on and off the field, it was hard to remember. From the fans to the guys on the front line, the affection for the second-year coach seemed universal. "I love him," said David Molk, who won the Rimington Trophy in 2011 as the nation's best center. Molk is not given to gushing, but of Hoke he said, "He's a great coach, he's a great mentor, he's a great friend. He's every single thing you want a college coach to be, and he does it flawlessly."

But it also marked Michigan's fourth year without Paul Bunyan, the big, ugly trophy that goes to the winner of the Michigan–Michigan State game, and Michigan's seventh year without a Big Ten title. And that, everyone on the small stage said repeatedly, is what they wanted.

After Michigan's return to glory in 2011, one reporter asked, were expectations in Ann Arbor the highest ever?

"I think it's funny that everyone says that," Hoke replied in his permanently hoarse voice. "This is Michigan," he added, using the phrase Dave Brandon had since trademarked. "Those expectations are to win Big Ten championships every year. For people to say expectations are higher—they've always been high. That's why you're at Michigan—that's why these guys come to Michigan. They haven't changed. They've never changed."

Just minutes into Hoke's introductory press conference, it was not hard to see why Michigan fans had taken to him so completely. The man knew the maize-and-blue gospel, chapter and verse, and he sang it from the heart.

"Having lost the Paul Bunyan Trophy four years in a row," a reporter asked, "has the Michigan State rivalry become more important?"

"We've got three tremendous rivalry games," Hoke said. "One on a national level [Notre Dame], one on a state level [Michigan State]—an

74

hour apart—and the Ohio rivalry . . . is important," he said, getting a laugh.

The players, however, were more willing to admit the Michigan State game had loomed larger with each loss to the Spartans—particularly the previous year's defeat up in East Lansing. Michigan fell behind early and couldn't catch up, losing 28–14, with fans giving the offense the most withering criticism of the season.

"We didn't come out ready," Robinson said, "and we didn't play Michigan football."

After saying almost the exact same thing, Lewan added, "Hopefully we can change that this year."

"We had a bitter taste after last year's game," Kovacs confessed, "and I can still taste it."

They were all wise enough to leave out one reason they did not come out ready: when they returned to the locker room after warm-ups, they were surprised to find the athletic department had put gaudy uniforms in their stalls, which required them to change in the ten minutes they usually spent going over their assignments and getting mentally ready. Changing uniforms is a more cumbersome process than you might think, since simply getting a jersey on or off requires the help of the guy next to you to get your shoulder pads off, too. The linemen usually have their knee braces taped, and those have to come off, too—which resulted in equipment managers frantically slicing the original pants just to get them off fast enough.

Alternative uniforms are Brandon's idea, not Hoke's, but the head coach was also smart enough not to mention it. Nor did he mention Brandon's habit of coming in Sunday mornings to watch the coaches break down film from Saturday's game, or chest-bumping Hoke's players on the sidelines after big plays. If President Mary Sue Coleman owed a debt to Brandon for his early and unexpected advocacy, so did Hoke. Neither was likely to speak a discouraging word.

When another reporter mentioned how close the Wolverines had come to winning their division in 2011 and asked what that showed, Denard Robinson cut him off:

"It shows us we didn't accomplish our goals. We want to be the Big Ten champions."

How hungry are you?

"We're not the Big Ten champs, are we? So we're still hungry."

Another reporter followed up with Hoke: "Why did you say last season wasn't a success?"

"Because we didn't win the Big Ten title."

"How do you get over that?"

"You win it," Hoke said. He was not smiling.

In the breakout room, Northwestern's representatives let the press know that these were not your father's Wildcats.

Head coach Pat Fitzgerald opened with two points. One, they'd been to four straight bowl games, a first, and the previous year's senior class had won more games than any other in school history.

The bad news came next. "Two, because we know how to win, we're disappointed we haven't won enough," Fitzgerald said. He entered the 2012 season with a 40-36 career record, which put him second all-time at Northwestern behind only the 49-45 mark of Lynn "Pappy" Waldorf, who coached the Wildcats from 1935 to 1946.

"I can't tell you I put one win ahead of the others," Fitzgerald said, "but I can tell you I'm ticked off about the thirty-six losses.

"To get to this point is easy. The next steps are the hard part."

When a reporter asked Fitzgerald why it had been so tough for Northwestern to win in the past, he replied, "We don't have time for that conversation. But I can tell you why we're having success now: great young men, who are unified and willing to work for our goals. Since 1995, Ohio State, Michigan, and Wisconsin are the only schools to win more Big Ten titles. Gary Barnett told us, 'Expect victory.' Now, we expect championships."

The players picked up the tune from there. Senior offensive lineman Brian Mulroe said, "We haven't [won a bowl game], and it hurts the seniors." Junior quarterback sensation Kain Colter, a premed student from Colorado, said, "We all want to be part of something special here, and that means winning a bowl game."

Senior linebacker David Nwabuisi was the most direct: "We've been to four straight bowl games, but the wins, the records—none of this will matter if we don't get that bowl win."

They were hanging it out there pretty far, setting up an all-or-nothing proposition, and they were every bit as serious as the Buckeyes and

Wolverines were about their goals. If you swapped their ties and lapel pins and tweaked the quotes, you'd have a hard time discerning which player went to which school.

Rivalries and reputations aside, these guys had a lot more in common than not.

No team at the Big Ten Media Days gets ignored. Every Big Ten team is either near a major city or is the biggest deal in its state, so they all get pretty good coverage. But in 2012, Penn State easily got more reporters and more questions than Ohio State, Michigan, and Northwestern combined.

That expectation initially led O'Brien to decide not to send any players. He didn't want to bring anyone who might still be on the fence—like Silas Redd, their biggest star—nor subject others to relentless questions about everything from Jerry Sandusky to the NCAA sanctions to Silas Redd's future.

But after the players showed up on the practice field for a seven-on-seven scrimmage at six thirty Thursday morning, O'Brien once again trusted his instincts, which had not betrayed him that summer. He found Mauti and told him, "On second thought, if we don't send any players, we'll look like we're hiding out, and that becomes the headline. So, you want to do this?"

"Helllll, yeah! Let's do it!"

"Can you be at the airport in an hour? You got a suit?"

Mauti was game. Because his suit hadn't been dry-cleaned recently, he borrowed fellow linebacker Glenn Carson's, headed to the airport, and joined O'Brien, standout defensive lineman Jordan Hill, a quietly intense leader, and John Urschel, the team brainiac.

That meant Zordich was staying behind. "At first I was pissed," he told me, with typical candor. "I should be going! But once Coach explained it to me—'Z, I need you back in State College, holding it down with Fitz'—it made sense."

When I asked Zordich if he was certain O'Brien wasn't just blowing smoke to appease him, he responded with one of the few dead-serious expressions of our many hours of conversation.

"Nothing he says is smoke," Zordich said. "At this point, we have a ridiculous amount of trust in each other."

• • •

O'Brien's faith was vindicated by the poise his three players demonstrated, starting with the obvious questions about the NCAA sanctions, just three days old. O'Brien gamely pointed out the trustees had already come out with a statement about those. "Now it's time to move forward and turn the page."

Fat chance.

The reporters then focused on the four-year bowl ban. "Nothing against the bowls," O'Brien said, but "I think about the stadiums in which we play—including ours, with 108,000 people—what bowl game can say that? I'm probably going to get in trouble for this, but coming from the NFL, there's only one game that matters, and that's the Super Bowl. Unless you're in the championship game, how much difference does a bowl game make compared to playing in front of 108,000 people?

"I understand bowls are an important part of college football, but there are other things to play for."

There were also other things to worry about. O'Brien was far more concerned about the NCAA's cutting Penn State's scholarships down from twenty-five a year to fifteen, and from a total of eighty-five to sixty-five. Worse, Penn State was not allowed to replace any of the players who quit or transferred.

The vacated victories affected the past. The bowl ban affected the present, but to O'Brien, was largely cosmetic. The scholarship sanctions, however, endangered the future of the program. But no one asked about that.

"Can you give us any update on the Silas Redd situation?"

"No," O'Brien said—and nothing more, which got some chuckles.

But he would tell me that night he was hoping like hell to keep Redd in the fold. Yes, Redd was the most talented player on the team, but O'Brien knew they were relatively deep in the offensive backfield, with Zordich, former receiver Bill Belton, and others ready to step up. O'Brien was most eager to hear Redd say he was staying because that would ensure almost everyone else would, too. While O'Brien sat there taking questions in Chicago, he had no idea what Redd was thinking back at his home in Connecticut—but O'Brien was checking his phone every chance he could, waiting for an update.

● ● ●

O'Brien, arms folded, answered every question with a flat expression until someone asked him why he'd changed his mind about bringing his players with him.

"I want these guys to hear this answer," he said. "This has not been the easiest week. A lot of people were asking to go home this weekend. But I asked them to come here because this is a representation of what Penn State is all about.

"They have a lot of pride in Penn State, in the university, and most important they have a tremendous commitment to each other. What else can you say? You talk about three stand-up guys—*tough* guys—and fantastic representatives of Penn State, guys who go to class." He then pointed a thumb to Urschel and finally grinned. "The guy to my left has a 4.0 in math.

"I've obviously been around some pretty good leaders. I told these guys the other day, these are some of the best leaders I've ever been around."

When it came to goals, the Lions did not talk about winning them all, like Ohio State; they did not talk about taking a Big Ten title, like Michigan; and they certainly did not talk about winning a bowl game, like Northwestern. For Penn State, it was much simpler.

"The key," O'Brien said, "is to keep this 2012 team together, and right now . . . we've got a bunch of kids back at State College sticking together."

As mission statements go, it paled in comparison to the others. But of the four goals, it was surely going to be the toughest to achieve.

After a full day of press conferences on Thursday, and another half day of nonstop interviews on Friday, the event finished with a lunch for over a thousand players, coaches, and fans. While the tables were being cleared, everybody was ready to go home—but no one more so than the people from Penn State.

On the bus ride to the airport, a spent O'Brien sat next to his wife, Colleen, reading his texts to see if there was any word from State College on players staying or going. Nothing.

Mauti couldn't even manage that much activity. "I was completely drained," he told me. "I was in and out of sleep on the bus until we got to the plane."

When they got off the bus, Mauti remembered vividly, O'Brien and he looked like the walking dead. But Athletic Director Dr. Joyner suddenly appeared, joking around with his wife, Carolyn.

"I honestly didn't know they were even [in Chicago] until we got off the bus," Mauti told me. "I hadn't seen him the entire two days."

When the group walked onto the tarmac to retrieve their bags from the cart to put on the plane, Mauti said, "I kind of pulled O-B aside, and I remember saying this specifically, 'Coach, [Joyner] thinks this is a game. This is all a big joke to him.'"

They climbed wearily onto the small private plane. After Mauti collapsed in the back, he noticed a cooler next to his seat, so he opened it and discovered a couple of cold Budweisers. Mauti is not a big drinker—his father doesn't drink at all—"but you know what?" he remembered thinking, "This is exactly what I need right now. So I just cracked it open and started drinking it. And O-B looked back and kind of gave me a smile. There was only one person on that plane who deserved a beer more than me, and that was him. But Joyner looked back at me, let's just say, 'disapprovingly.'

"I looked right back. I'm thinking, 'We've been out here fighting for our program all week. We didn't get *one* question about football. Not *one*, the whole time. We were answering nonstop questions about Penn State, about the NCAA, about Sandusky, you name it. And it's not like *he* was facing the media—or on his phone all week trying to keep the team together back home.'

"So my look back was, 'You don't like this? Do something about it.'"

Mauti stared right back at Joyner and slurped his beer. After a while, the staring contest ended when Joyner turned around.

Before the plane touched down back in State College, Michael Mauti, for one, had concluded that whatever they would need to make it through that season, it was not going to come from their interim athletic director.

CHAPTER 8

NIGHT OF THE LETTERMEN

O'Brien's letter to the eleven hundred lettermen started hitting their mailboxes on Friday, July 27, when he was still at the Big Ten Media Days in Chicago. He had no idea what to expect, but by Monday, July 30, the lettermen made it clear they were with him. Almost every one of them sent some word of encouragement, and fully half confirmed they would find a way to get to State College to support the team Tuesday night.

"Man, five hundred guys showed up!" O'Brien said. "The airport was packed with private jets. Some of these guys have done pretty well. It was a scene, man. Amazing."

He met the lettermen in the Holuba indoor practice facility, where they sat in rows of seats on the artificial field, before the players arrived. He had a speech prepared, but once he saw all the lettermen together, he threw it out. He thanked them for coming—underscoring how impressive their dedication was—then he got to the point. "These guys don't care about the Freeh Report. They don't care about the NCAA sanctions. They don't care about who you think should have been named the head coach, either. I'm the head coach, and you're just going to have to accept that."

If any of the lettermen thought the little-known head coach lacked backbone, that notion was quickly dismissed that night.

"We all have to realize why we're in the position we're in," O'Brien told them, hitting one of his most repeated points. "We've got to stop arguing about that, and keep moving forward."

With that in mind, O'Brien laid out why he'd asked them all there: to reach the players by speaking to the traditions of the program that had defined it for decades.

What the players *did* need to hear, O'Brien told them, "is what only *you* know: what it's like to play in the great games, in this great stadium, against the Buckeyes and the Badgers and the Wolverines. About what it's like to graduate from Penn State. About what you learned here, and what it means to you now, when you look back.

"That is what they need to hear."

"It's funny," recalled Spider Caldwell, one of the few people left who knew almost everyone in the building that night, "he talked to them like they were *his* football players—guys like Jack Ham and Todd Blackledge and Franco Harris, guys who are older than him—and you could see them glued to him. 'Yes, sir! This is the Penn State coach talking!' Their 'player mode' kicked into high gear."

The unheralded O'Brien seemed to have them. But that wasn't the point of the evening. The question remained, would the lettermen reach the players and vindicate all the effort executing this night required?

O'Brien asked Lydell Mitchell, Franco Harris, Matt Millen, Todd Blackledge, Jack Ham, and some lesser-known players who had become great successes in business to speak to the team. All the talks were fast and fiery, delivered by strong speakers who spoke from the heart.

Most agreed the most powerful speaker was the last one, Matt Millen— who is as hated by Detroit Lions fans as he is beloved by the Penn State faithful. "Forget about what you lost," he told them. "This is what you *have.* I can only promise you, you will have a brotherhood. You may not realize it now, but that's worth more than anything."

"All those lettermen, they had the benefit of hindsight," Zordich said. "That's why they wanted to talk to the kids thinking about leaving. Look, those guys who were thinking about leaving had good reason: they wanted to win games and play in bowls, not deal with all this crap. But they're so young they don't realize the impact they can have on this place and the history here. The lettermen were there to tell them about that, how it looks when you're fifty."

There were a number of ovations that night, but when Millen finished the last speech, the players jumped to their feet and cheered for a solid minute.

"After *that,*" Craig Fitzgerald said, "we all told the lettermen, if someone doesn't want to stay after this, they weren't Penn State guys in the first place."

By just about any measure, the night was a remarkable success—for O'Brien with the lettermen, and for the lettermen with the current players. O'Brien's gamble had paid off handsomely.

But for Spider Caldwell and Kirk Diehl, one big question still hadn't been answered: Would the lettermen accept O'Brien's one-week-old plan to put the players' names on the jerseys, or would they mutiny?

"I was grimacing and grinding my teeth all day," Spider confessed. Whenever former players come to town, their first stop is Spider's equipment room, to say hello and find out what's going on. "To hear them complaining about [the names] every time," Spider said, "and for me to have to explain the coach's reasoning every time, would be very draining.

"They had all heard about the names, and after the speeches, they came up to me and were all so supportive of it, saying, 'What a great idea.'

"They all realized, too, that we're in uncharted waters."

O'Brien and company had pulled a few rabbits out of their hats that week, but everyone knew they could still lose their team at almost any moment.

A few players did leave, of course, including kicker Anthony Fera, who transferred to Texas to be closer to his mom, who suffers from multiple sclerosis; and Justin Brown, a wide receiver and kick returner who transferred to Oklahoma. While they did not constitute a critical mass, it could quickly become one.

The key, everyone agreed, was Silas Redd. A week after the sanctions, he still hadn't left—but he hadn't committed to staying, either.

During the first weekend after the sanctions, between the Big Ten Media Days and the Lettermen Night, USC's Lane Kiffin flew Redd out to LA—presumably after learning his name—where Snoop Dogg's picking him up at the airport in a limousine apparently made an impression.

The suspense finally ended the day after the lettermen spoke, when Redd called Zordich: "Z-man, don't tell anyone, but I'm going to USC tomorrow."

"I was his fullback," Zordich told me. "He's lived with us. He's been our roommate. It was a special relationship. So when he tells you to keep it private, you got to be a man about it and keep your word. I didn't tell anyone."

Losing their best offensive player was undeniably bad news, but they could accept it if Redd's departure did not start the dominoes dropping. If, in other words, Zordich and Mauti's theory that the longer the players stuck around, the more likely they were to stay, proved true—and O'Brien was right to take their advice.

Eight days after the sanctions hit, Silas Redd proved to be a domino of one. No one followed that day, or the next.

Days later, a few players did leave, but no one of great importance to the team's prospects. Pete Massaro, the senior defensive end who "freaked out" when he heard how many teammates planned to transfer just hours after the NCAA sanctions were announced, did some final accounting: "The freshman I talked to listed a ton of people in those two classes who were going to leave—and only two of them left. Those meetings helped. A lot."

But just to be sure, O'Brien had one more card to play: Rick Slater, who had walked on to the Penn State football team a decade earlier when he was already in his late twenties. He went on to join Navy SEAL Team Six. Yes, the very same unit that killed Osama bin Laden.

Slater walked to the front of the team room, wearing cargo shorts, a brown T-shirt, and a brown flannel shirt. Then he very deliberately emptied his pockets of his cell phone, his keys, and his wallet, leaving them all on the table, then grabbed the podium.

"Gentlemen," he said, "it is an honor to be here."

He told them why: as great as it had been playing an important role on Navy SEAL Team Six, walking on at Penn State was a greater honor.

He then pulled his belt from his cargo shorts to show them the proof: a navy-blue belt, the exact same kind the Penn State players use to hold up their practice and game pants.

"This belt," he said, "I pulled from my pants after my last game at Penn State. And this is what I wore when we went on our mission against Osama bin Laden."

Needless to say, Lieutenant Slater had their undivided attention.

He then told them of SEAL Team Six's mission to Pakistan, and how things had not gone according to plan. A vital chopper had crashed, just as two had in President Carter's failed mission to free the hostages in Iran in 1980. When that happened, the SEALs knew from their training, they were required to ask, "Can we finish the job, or do we pull out now?" They called base camp and quickly got this reply:

"Charlie Mike."

"That's the military alphabet," Slater explained, "for 'CM.' For us, that means 'Continue Mission.'

"So we did."

The room erupted. They got the message.

The Penn State players' cause was not taking out an evil terrorist, just winning a few college football games—but they believed in it.

"Everyone who's still here," Urschel told me, "has made a choice."

A clear one. As Leo Tolstoy said, "Happy families are all alike; every unhappy family is unhappy in its own way."

The players who were unhappy departed for a wide variety of reasons: family or opportunity or freedom from sanctions or just better weather. But the ones who stayed all stayed for the same reasons. They knew what they were up against, but they also knew why they wanted to stay: for Penn State, for the football program—past and present—and for the coaches, but mainly for each other. A little over a week after the sanctions hit, the players who remained shared an uncommonly uniform set of beliefs.

"People think we're gonna lose games, that we'll be lucky to go six and six," Zordich told me at the time. "People think we forgot how to play football. They don't know us! This team is stronger than it's ever been.

"Our whole thing is—all this crap—we've been the ones suffering the consequences. When we talk in public these days, we walk a fine line. We can't say much. But somebody has to pay the price for what we've been through. We can't do it through the media. We can't do it in the courts. So we will do it on the football field.

"We've done all this, we've got to make it worthwhile. We can't do all this, then say, 'Seven and five is good enough.'

"It's not."

CHAPTER 7

WE KNOW WHO WE ARE

The people running the Big Ten, of course, had other things to worry about.

Surrounded by a sea of tsunamis, in which everything you thought just yesterday was going to be there forever was blown away a day later, the nation's oldest college conference increasingly looked like an island of sanity and stability.

Nationwide, the long-static conferences started shifting about two decades ago, when college football's Division I independents began looking for conferences to call home, and most found them. That included Penn State, after Paterno failed to convince other regional independents like Boston College, Rutgers, Syracuse, West Virginia, and Pitt to create their own conference, only to see them join the Big East. The Big Ten eagerly accepted the Lions for a few reasons, one of which was "Northwestern insurance." Concerned that the Wildcats—still deep in their Dark Ages, and flirting with the Ivy League as a possible out—might fail to emerge from the depths, the Big Ten thought adding an unwieldy eleventh team was a small price to pay to ensure it wouldn't be stuck with an even more awkward nine teams.

When these independents joined conferences, it made college football more stable, not less so. But the next round of moves would not have such a calming effect on the sport.

All seemed relatively secure in the college football world until 2010, when the conservative Big Ten—which had added exactly one school in the previous half century, Michigan State, and lost none—reached out to Nebraska.

• • •

Neither party entered the dialogue lightly. The Cornhuskers were one of the charter members of the conference that became the Big Eight. The conference dominated the Great Plains for almost a century and featured some of the greatest rivalries in college sports: Missouri-Kansas, rooted in the Civil War, and of course Oklahoma-Nebraska, one of the sport's best running duels. From 1912 to 2010, those two teams played eighty-six times, including every year from 1928 through 1997.

The string stopped not because of any lack of fan interest—which was still sky-high—but a lack of opportunity. In 1996, the Big Eight accepted four schools, Texas, Texas A&M, Texas Tech, and Baylor, from the Southwest Conference, which had disbanded under the weight of its own corruption. The Big 12 put Oklahoma and Nebraska in different divisions, which caused them to skip their series five of the next thirteen years.

Other problems quickly arose, particularly with Texas, which demanded and received a larger slice of the revenue pie than the schools that had been in the conference from the beginning. Things went from bad to worse when Texas split off entirely from the conference TV contract to sign a separate deal with ESPN, worth an unheard-of $300 million over twenty years.

For the Cornhuskers, the writing was on the wall.

When Big Ten commissioner Jim Delany met with Tom Osborne, Nebraska's legendary coach-turned-athletic director, Osborne explained the Big Eight thought it was expanding, while the Texas schools thought they were merging. "So, who's in charge? There was no congealing."

"Tom said it was an eye-opener," Delany told me. "You always have your disagreements and your aggressive coaches [in any conference], but there was always a sense of a common purpose among people in the Big Eight, and they had generally gotten along remarkably well."

The Longhorns' money grab poisoned the waters, prompting a number of Big 12 schools to consider new homes. For Nebraska, the Big Ten looked especially appealing.

"Relatively speaking, we've always had more sharing than other conferences," Delany said. "We've never had any special deals. Everyone gets the same slice of the pie, always has, and no one has seriously questioned that."

To the people at Nebraska, that meant they would be treated more equitably in their first year in the Big Ten than they had been in their hundredth season in the conference Nebraska helped found. Their welcome included a check from the Big Ten Network for $22 million—almost twice as much as the Big Eight would pay.

For the Big Ten's part, they were not looking, but they were curious.

"Eleven is not the best number in the world," Delany said. "It's a prime number, is about all you can say about it. But it was just going to be that way for a while because we weren't looking to add a school just to make a nice round number. We were not going to add a school that didn't have strong research elements, that didn't aspire to be good in a lot of areas, and didn't have a broad-based athletic program. Sports like baseball, women's volleyball, and wrestling don't always have big popularity, but they do have an incredibly loyal fan base."

Nebraska had all of those elements, and something more: a compatible personality.

"I knew," Delany recalled, "after meeting with the Nebraska people after just a couple hours that there was a fit there, partly because we were talking the same language. There was an immediate congruency.

"Neither side needed the other—neither side was desperate—but we felt we could both benefit. And they understood, we were offering an expansion, not a merger."

Tom Osborne and company concluded Delany's offer sounded pretty good—and certainly better than what they were getting from the Big 12.

The courtship couldn't have gone better. Big Ten fans almost universally applauded the addition of Nebraska, and Nebraska fans were relieved to jump from the Big Eight to the Big Ten. But the marriage's first year presented some bumps in the road.

If you're the Big Ten, and you suddenly have twelve teams, what do you do—change the name to the Big 12? No, because that name was already taken by Nebraska's former conference—which, naturally, now had ten teams. So the Big Ten decided to keep its name—and change everything else, starting with the logo.

Now, to handle all this, they could have asked regional artists to draw on the Big Ten's unparalleled 115-year history and come up with something simple, honest, and authentic, or paid one of the league's thousands of art students a hundred bucks to make a new logo, the way Nike did years ago to create the swoosh. Or it could simply have opened up a contest to the league's 17.5 million fans, who would have jumped at the chance for nothing.

Instead, the Big Ten gave the assignment to high-priced international image consultants—"branding experts"—and then let them tell Big Ten fans what they were supposed to like. The conference hired Pentagram Design—a "multi-disciplinary design firm with offices worldwide," in London, New York, Austin, and Berlin, whose "culture of interchange . . . adds tremendous value to all creative thinking," and whose "core competencies" include "futurizing."

For about the salary of a Big Ten athletic director (at the time, anyway), Pentagram Design put their best people on this assignment—and after months of experimenting, their seven-person Project Team emerged from their undisclosed location to give us the solution: put the word BIG over the word TEN. It was sobering to realize we helped subsidize this expensive effort through tax breaks for the nonprofit Big Ten and its member institutions.

The logo Pentagram came up with turns the *I* in BIG into a 1, and makes the G look like a zero, like this: B1G. Right below the number 10, they put the word TEN, which is how many teams were in the Big Ten from 1953 to 1992. The color they picked for this avant-garde logo is a strange shade of light blue—the kind your printer makes when it's running out of ink—which might explain why not one of the twelve Big Ten teams has ever put that color anywhere near their uniforms.

The response was immediate—and negative. *Time* magazine said the logo "looks as if it needed an elementary-school stencil and an oven timer to complete." One sports website, in a piece titled "New Big Ten Logo Looks Like It Took 25 Seconds to Make," wrote, "The Big Ten unveiled a new logo on Monday, and it looks, well, it looks like someone was assigned the redesign, completely forgot about it and then scraped something together on Microsoft Paint a few minutes before it was due."

The fans were less forgiving.

The league's most beloved traditions—from trophies like the Little Brown Jug and Floyd of Rosedale, to Wisconsin's "Jump Around" and Ohio State's "Hang on Sloopy," to Michigan's banner and Penn State's whiteouts—were created spontaneously and organically. The process to create the logo was the opposite—and fans responded accordingly.

Having come up with an expensive, wildly unpopular logo, the Big Ten turned its attention to naming its two new divisions. They threw out suggestions such as East and West—they had swapped a couple teams out of alignment—and others such as Lakes and Plains, and Hayes and Schembechler (in honor of two of the league's greatest coaches), and settled on Legends and Leaders, which stand for nothing and nobody.

The normally stoic Big Ten fans once again went ballistic—and this time, the Big Ten's actual leaders heard them.

"We've had enough experience with names and expansion and development of divisions that we know that you rarely get a ninety percent approval rating," Delany told WGN 720 AM in Chicago. "But to get a ninety percent nonapproval rating was really surprising. It showed that we didn't connect with our fans in a way that we wanted to. It's humbling, to say the least, because we're trying to build fan bases, not push them away.

"We're still listening and trying to figure things out. We'll try to do a little education, let it breathe a bit, and then probably revisit it after the first of the year."

But they didn't, and the names stuck.

The league had much more success actually creating the divisions, which was no small trick. Delany and his staff had to solve a logic game with a dozen conditions, including geography, rivalries, and competitive balance. After Delaney gave his team the ground rules, he left for the Big Ten Media Days luncheon kickoff and was amazed to discover they had managed to get the whole thing sorted out before he returned.

"Of our seventeen main rivalries," he told me, "we were able to keep twelve, and the five we didn't keep annually, they'll get them about half the time due to crossover play."

Even geographically it worked out better than expected, with only Michigan and Michigan State moved to the "western" division, and Wisconsin and Minnesota to the "eastern" side. The rest stayed on their side of the dividing line.

Of course, no such divisions can be perfect. "Geographically, Wisconsin was hurt the most," Delany told me, "and they lose their rivalry with Iowa and potentially Nebraska—but there was just no way we could draw a line, East and West. Barry [Alvarez, Wisconsin's AD] has provided great leadership."

Alvarez had also been a good sport, understanding that not everyone could get what he wanted and that each had to put the greater good first—the very spirit that was lacking in the Big Twelve and threatening to break it apart.

But the divisions presented another potential pitfall, and a big one: they threatened the Michigan–Ohio State rivalry.

Ten years ago, ESPN viewers voted the Michigan–Ohio State football game the best rivalry in the nation. Not just in college football, or football in general, but in all sports. Since 1935, it's held a privileged spot as the last game of the Big Ten season. More college football fans have seen this rivalry, in person or on TV, than any other.

But when the Big Ten added Nebraska, the rivalry's future was in jeopardy.

So that raised a few possibilities—not to mention plenty of rumors and fears. If they kept Michigan and Ohio State in the same division, the teams could never meet in the title game. But if they put them in different divisions, they might have to play again in the title game just one week later. One rumor had the league moving the game from its traditional date at the end of the season to October—or even interrupting the rivalry, without any guarantee of playing every year.

The fans, former players, and reporters responded with their "usual level of cool maturity," as Dave Barry would say, "similar to the way Moe reacts when he is poked in the eyeballs by Larry and Curly." One Ohio politician introduced a resolution demanding the game never be moved.

So what'd the Big Ten leaders finally decide? They surprised the many critics of their logo and division names and came up with a format that's intelligent, even elegant. They listened to their constituents and established the Michigan–Ohio State game as a "protected divisional crossover" at the end of the season, right where it belongs.

The conclusions were clear enough: when the people who run college football listen to the fans—by adding Nebraska, and maintaining traditional rivalries—things work well. When they don't—think logo and divisional names—they don't.

It's a simple lesson, but would the Big Ten—not to mention other conferences and the NCAA itself—heed it?

• • •

If the Big Ten's decision to add Nebraska created some unintended by-products inside the league, it was nothing compared to the chain reaction the small spark started outside the Midwest, throwing the nation's biggest conferences into major upheaval—perhaps the biggest in the history of college sports.

After Nebraska bolted to the Big Ten, former Big 12 brothers Missouri and Texas A&M bolted to the SEC, and Colorado went to the Pac-10, along with Utah, making it the new Pac-12. Shortly thereafter, Syracuse and Pittsburgh announced they would be leaving the Big East to join the Atlantic Coast Conference.

Those changes aren't as geographically twisted as seeing Marquette and DePaul—and even, for a little while, Texas Christian, Boise State, and San Diego State—join the Big East. Which raised the question: Just how *big* is the East, anyway? Big enough to swallow half the Midwest and chunks of Idaho, Texas, and California?

By the time the dust settled, all eleven major conferences had gained or lost at least one member.

In the aftermath, I was struck by how many people who don't care too much about sports seemed to care a lot about this. For nonsports fans, college conferences are kind of like your parents as you get older. You might not check in with them every day, but it's good to know they're there, something you can count on in an uncertain world.

Nothing defined our nation's regions better than our conferences used to.

What is the Midwest? Depending on who's talking, it could span from western Pennsylvania to Montana, from North Dakota to Oklahoma. But when someone said "Big Ten Country," you knew they meant the Great Lakes states. The Big Eight connected the Great Plains states—nearby, maybe, but night and day to those of us who live here. The Southeast Conference connected the Deep South and was fundamentally different from the Atlantic Coast Conference—which was exactly what it said it was. The Ivy League—well, that's a label unto itself, while the Big East linked the biggest schools in the biggest cities in, yes, the East. It all made perfect sense. It fit.

These bonds were part of our very identity. Of course, each school's students, alums, and fans think their conference is the best and can even give you specific reasons why it's better than the one next door, but fans from all conferences felt a connection to the center, and it held. What these conference schools all had in common was sometimes hard to pinpoint, but—to paraphrase Supreme Court justice Potter Stewart's famous line about pornography—we knew it when we saw it. When the university presidents founded these conferences, they sought kindred spirits—and they were amazingly successful at finding them.

Somehow Iowa has more in common with Wisconsin than it does with Iowa State—and all parties seem to understand this intuitively, just as we all knew where to sit in the high school cafeteria. No one told us, but we knew where we belonged.

These conferences were so stable for so long, it was easy to identify with them. Schools bragged not just about their teams, but about their conferences, painting their league logos on their fields and their courts. If you wandered into a sports bar in any of those college towns, hanging overhead you would see the banners of every member of their league—and that meant the banners of their *rivals*, too. And no other sport has rivalries like college football has rivalries.

I have never attended Indiana or Wisconsin or Michigan State, but I've visited them many times. I can get around their beautiful campuses and talk knowledgeably to their alums in Chicago bars, where everyone seems to end up.

But suddenly, by the fall of 2012, the whole jigsaw puzzle had been tossed up in the air, and all for two reasons: greed, and fear—the fear that some other football team would make more money on its TV deal than you did on yours.

The frantic, thoughtless redrawing that followed was akin to the way the British carelessly carved up the Middle East in the 1920s, without knowing the difference between Sunnis, Shiites, and Kurds, with disastrous results we're still living with to this day. This mindless game of musical chairs threatened many of the biggest reasons why millions of us prefer college sports to the pros: geography, affinity, stability, and identity. And it tore apart rivalries that go back to the birth of modern sport.

When the *Wall Street Journal* asked Bill Martin, Michigan's former athletic director, about the state of the game, he said, "We're chipping away at what makes college football unique."

When I followed up with him, Martin added, "The *last* thing you want college to do is become a professional environment. The *last* thing. Don't let the NFL be your model.

"Take the band. That's one of the most unique appeals of college sports. There's not a professional team in the country that wouldn't love to have the quality of a college band playing—and for free! Let 'em play!"

Martin couldn't answer one question, however: How many more chips can college football take before we can no longer distinguish it from the pro game?

The tornado that rearranged the college football landscape seemed to soften it for the NCAA to build a playoff system right in the middle of it all—something it had longed to do for years, for a simple reason: money. Unlike March Madness, which would generate a record $1 billion in advertising revenue alone in 2013 that went straight to the NCAA to distribute, the NCAA didn't make a dime off the bowl system. The bowls did.

When NCAA president Mark Emmert announced Penn State's sanctions on July 23, 2012, he bolstered the NCAA's new "get tough" image—just in time to return to the podium a week later to announce the long-awaited creation of a four-team playoff, whose TV rights alone would be worth $5.64 billion over twelve years, or about $470 million a year, all for three games.

So, after decades of debate, it was finally upon us—a bona fide Division I college football playoff. But in fairness to the NCAA, it was a committee of twelve university presidents—not coaches or even athletic directors, but presidents—that approved the plan to create a four-team playoff for college football, the last major sport to have one.

So what if college football had somehow survived without a playoff since students from Rutgers and Princeton played the first intercollegiate game in 1869? That was twenty-two years before James B. Naismith invented the game of basketball, thirty-four years before the first World Series, and fifty-one years before the National Football League was even formed, let alone mattered.

In the past forty years the game's leaders have tacked on enough bowl games for virtually every team still standing to play in one, from twenty-two teams to seventy—which is more than half the Division I schools currently fielding football teams.

But that wasn't enough, so they added a twelfth game, which schools have used to play tomato cans like Arkansas–Pine Bluff, Prairie View A&M, and Gardner-Webb (not to be confused with the furniture chain), solely to grab another payday on the backs of unpaid players. Then they piled on conference title games, too—increasing the total games a division winner could play from eleven to fourteen, just two shy of the NFL's regular season.

But we need a playoff now, they told us, to take the competition out of the hands of computers and pollsters and to settle it *on the field*.

How are they going to fix that? Instead of picking *two* teams based on polls, strength of schedule, and computerized rankings, they are going to have a selection committee pick *four* teams—based on polls, strength of schedule, and computerized rankings. Problem solved.

So, instead of the third-ranked team complaining that it got screwed out of a title shot, the *fifth-place* team will now do all the whining. Another problem solved.

A four-team playoff will not end arguments, just expand them. It won't heighten the regular season—something unique to college football, where every game actually matters—it will diminish it. It's not going to shrink the schedule, but extend it. It won't reduce injuries—especially concussions—but increase them.

Here are a few other sure bets: the playoffs will result in more insane incentives in coaches' already insane contracts. In the 2012 national title game, LSU head coach Les Miles would get a $5 million bonus if his Tigers beat Alabama—which would have doubled his salary for coaching sixty minutes of football.

But LSU lost, and maybe that's not a bad thing. How many coaches, faced with a star receiver who got caught plagiarizing a paper, or a quarterback with a concussion, would have had the integrity to do the right thing and bench those players—and forfeit a $5 million payday?

However many currently exist, it's a safe bet that, with these temptations, there will be fewer in the future.

In the Big Ten, at least, stability still seemed more the rule than the exception. Nebraska finished its first season in the league in 2011, to great acclaim. The Cornhuskers didn't win the division, but their team and their fans won over the Big Ten faithful wherever they went.

For Delany's part, when I talked with him in August of 2012, he seemed content with the twelve-team league. For a man who played basketball at the highest level in the ACC, his grasp of Big Ten football culture seemed secure.

"What makes us unique? I would say, first, our history—117 years—would be one big differentiating factor.

"Second, our location and our culture. There is something essentially Midwestern about our character. I realize there's loyalty every place—every school, every conference—but the Midwest is a very stable place culturally, and I think given to greater loyalty than most places.

"Adding Penn State and Nebraska didn't change that. The schools we added are in contiguous states. That was important to us.

"We're not going to add teams to add teams. We like what we have. That doesn't mean we couldn't expand, or we won't. But it's like I said about Nebraska, it has to be a good fit.

"When you sit down and talk with their people, you know it when you see it."

CHAPTER 8

"IT ALL STARTS SATURDAY"

Saturday, August 11, 2012, 5:30 a.m.

Bill O'Brien is preparing to dash out the door to go to the office.

That's all the more impressive because he'd had two or three beers with his brother Tom in his kitchen the night before—the only time he'd had to catch up with him in months. They talked about their parents, their kids, Bill's team, and Bill's half-joking final assessment: "Given the sanctions, if we end up no better than .500, they'll probably fire me in two or three years."

He hadn't considered the worst-case scenario: they wouldn't.

Five hours later, he was up—an average night of sleep, for him. He wolfed down a nutrition bar—ninety calories—and a cup of yogurt, leaving the spoon in the sink. He muttered about the fifteen or so pounds he couldn't seem to get rid of—on his way to Dunkin' Donuts. You can take the man out of Boston—the chain's spiritual center—but you can't take Boston out of the man.

"Love this place," he said, pulling into the parking lot in the darkness. He bought a $2 coffee and headed back out to his van.

I asked the guy at the counter if he knew who that was. He looked up, stared for a moment, then said, "Nope."

He was saved by his coworker. "Oh, that's Mr. O'Brien," she said. In a month, just about everyone in the state would know who Mr. O'Brien was.

So, who is Mr. O'Brien?

William James O'Brien was born in 1969 in Dorchester, Massachusetts, the third of three boys. His father, John, a big, amiable guy partial to khaki pants and plaid, button-down shirts, played football at Brown just a few years after Joe Paterno himself, and his sons followed in his footsteps.

But Bill O'Brien probably got his fighting spirit not from his former football-playing dad, but his polite, petite mom. Anne O'Brien dresses like Miss Manners but, if provoked, she could probably take the etiquette queen.

While sitting on a couch in Bill's office next to her husband, she was cajoled into telling a familiar story. Because Bill attended St. John's Preparatory School in Danvers, about thirty minutes from their home in Merrimack, he carpooled home after practice every day at five thirty with two other kids. The mother of one of them, Russell, never picked them up, and one day on the drive back, Ms. O'Brien casually asked him why.

"My mom works," Russell said. "She's a teacher."

That's all Anne needed to hear. "And here I am, *a librarian*, working till five every day, when the teachers get out at three." At the next stoplight, two miles from Russell's home, she turned to him, sitting in the backseat, and said, "Get out! Get out, Russell, and walk home!"

And that's exactly what the stunned Russell did, while Bill and his classmate cracked up.

"You ask any of my buddies that story," Bill said, "they all know it. My friends love my mom."

When St. John's played rival Malden Catholic, fans from both schools had to sit on the same side—never a good idea, of course. The entire game the Malden parents chanted, "St. John's sucks! St. John's sucks!"

The diminutive Anne O'Brien stayed silent, until St. John's won the game on the last play. She stood up, pointed her finger at the Malden parents, and said, "We'll see who sucks now!"

"We had a reunion [last year]," Anne said, "and the parents just *love* telling that story."

"They don't have to," Bill said. "Everyone already knows it."

At Brown, O'Brien played defensive end and linebacker on unremarkable teams. He had no illusions about playing pro football, but that didn't matter because he always knew what he wanted to do: coach.

"He wasn't all that big or fast," recalled Jim Bernhardt, who served as Brown's defensive coordinator and now works as O'Brien's special assistant—a fancy term for "trusted right-hand man." "But he was tough and smart, and very hardworking." Bernhardt did not bother adding the obvious: those are qualities that make great coaches.

After O'Brien graduated in 1993, he stayed at Brown as a graduate assistant football coach, until a similar position opened up at Georgia Tech. Head coach George O'Leary called Bernhardt and said, "I need someone smart enough to get into grad school here, and dumb enough to coach football for nothing while doing it."

Bernhardt didn't miss a beat. "I got the perfect guy for you."

And that's how Bill O'Brien started his coaching career.

Monday, August 27: "All right, we *have* to get this right," O'Brien said.

It was seven o'clock on a Monday morning, and O'Brien's assistants had already been up for a couple of hours themselves, yet were every bit as alert as he was. O'Brien wasn't directing this message to them, though, but to video coordinator Jevin Stone, who has a staff of three and an office second in size only to O'Brien's—which tells you something about how a modern program functions.

"You have to break tape down differently," O'Brien said flatly. "I look at this stuff by personnel and situation, not by possessions or game time. All those cut-ups—if you guys want them, fine, but they're useless to me."

Stone took notes.

"First thing I do is take out the two-minute plays. I want those separated and labeled. In mine they're not labeled.

"I do it backwards as the week goes on. I start on Monday by looking at the two-minute defense, then their red zone, then third downs. So then all I have is first and second downs left by the end of the week. And that's how I want them broken down and labeled. Got it?"

"Got it."

"Good."

How coaches work with film today mirrors how investment banks started handling loans in the 1980s. As Michael Lewis described it in *Liar's Poker*, bankers three decades ago discovered they could cut up loans into their components, bundle those parts in big chunks, and create a new commodity.

Likewise, a head coach might watch an entire game, start to finish, once. But after that, it's all situational: offense, defense, running plays, passing plays, red zone, and the like. When coaches are scouting their opponents or breaking down practice film, they care even less about the game itself and more about the individual components. When they're looking at film, they're far more scientists than fans.

They didn't notice, for example, that in this game between Ohio University and Bowling Green University—two ancient MAC rivals—the stands were virtually empty. If it happens outside the lines or doesn't involve the team they're scouting, coaches simply don't care. If the bleachers collapsed or the other team's quarterback was on fire, they probably wouldn't notice—unless the defensive end on the team they're scouting failed to tackle him.

"This is a five-game breakdown," O'Brien said to his staff while watching Ohio's defense on the screen. "Out of fifty plays, they only called three plays of diamond," a common defensive setup.

"These guys don't tackle very well," he added as an aside. "These could've been big plays if Bowling Green could run better."

Like blackjack, which rewards only those players who know how to double-down and split pairs at the right time, football only rewards those teams that know how to break the big play—on offense or defense. And that's what they were looking for: the opportunities Ohio might give them to go big, be it exploiting a slow cornerback, taking advantage of a linebacker's failure to read a play-action pass, or a coordinator's weakness for blitzing too often. They knew they weren't going to beat many teams that season by grinding out endless 4-yard gains.

O'Brien saw plenty to admire, however: "You look at this, and you know: they're gonna try to strip the ball, every play. They're good at that.

"We'd better be ready."

Monday, August 27: A few hours later, O'Brien was working the overhead in the team room, which looks like a movie theater with a blue-and-gray carpet, folding seats with blue cushions, plus retractable desktops. Many players took notes, some just sat and listened, but everyone paid attention. They knew they would be graded in a few days, on national TV.

"This is the best Ohio team in the Frank Solich era—or probably ever," O'Brien said. He read his players some confident quotes from Ohio's players, then said, "They will be very aggressive. They will try to strip the ball every time. And Matt [McGloin], if you think you can just lob it up the middle to [tight end Matt] Lehman all day, you got another think coming.

"But they have trouble with tempo—which is surprising, since they practice against a fast offense every day. They can't get lined up fast enough. They'll have trouble with NASCAR," which was Penn State's code name for their hurry-up, no-huddle offense. "So let's get that going from the start and run 'em down."

When they were on defense, O'Brien explained, they had to stop quarterback Tyler Tettleton, the son of major league All-Star catcher Mickey. "He can run, he's athletic, he can throw. We've got to contain him. If we don't, it's gonna be a long day."

O'Brien turned off the overhead, the lights went up, and he stood up to look directly at his players. Knute Rockne, it's said, never dressed himself. Clothes fell on him. When O'Brien's coaching, he could be the great-grandson of the Notre Dame legend: baggy, blue sweatpants and a gray sweatshirt, with his trademark towel draped over his shoulder.

But also like Rockne, when O'Brien spoke to his players, he knew how to reach them. He paced around slowly, hands on hips, then stopped, looked right at them, and raised his right hand to punctuate his points.

"I was thinking about this earlier today, watching tape in my office. You have done everything we've asked you to do, to this point. You've worked hard in the weight room. You've stuck together.

"Everybody is involved. Everyone's dressing Saturday. One team.

"But this whole thing boils down to twelve weeks. Twelve weeks! That's it! I'm just telling you the truth.

"Follow your seniors. And, seniors, you've got to lead.

"It all starts Saturday. And it will come faster than you think."

Thursday night, August 30: On any football team, the importance of the quarterback is obvious. On Penn State's 2012 team—with a new staff, a new system, and the NCAA propping the door open for their players to leave—the pressure on the position might have been the greatest on any team that season.

O'Brien had decided that position would be filled by "the fiery red-headed Irishman from Scranton," as strength coach Craig Fitzgerald described the walk-on-turned-starter, thereby putting Matt McGloin ahead of Robert Bolden, Jay Paterno's favored signal caller.

"McGloin got all the receivers together this summer," Fitzgerald said. He got them all to run routes and seven-on-seven drills, then walked down to the football building to watch film on his own every day.

"And he never shuts up! You *can't* shut him up. He's not intimidated by anything, and he's gonna speak his mind.

"I love 'im."

At the team's dining hall, on another beautiful late-summer night, you could watch the sun start its descent over Mt. Nittany, while enjoying a first-rate meal of—well, just about everything you could think of: steaks, lasagna, chicken, stir-fry. And those were just the entrées.

McGloin sat down with his center, Matt "Stank" Stankiewitch, offensive guard Eric Shrive, and equally massive defensive end Pete Massaro, to plow down a few thousand calories each. All four were raised in eastern Pennsylvania's rich football culture, the Keystone State's answer to *Friday Night Lights*: small, blue-collar towns, whose steelworkers and coal miners still fill the stands every Friday night, whether they have kids in school or not.

Sit down at any college football team's dinner, and you are quickly reminded just how local a game college football really is. Almost everyone on the team played with or against at least one teammate, and usually half of them. And they never forgot.

McGloin started on the West Scranton High School's varsity basketball team as a freshman and went on to set the school record with over 1,300 career points. He thought basketball might be his ticket, but, he says, "I never focused on one sport."

"He never passed the ball, either," added Shrive, a high school teammate, stealing the stage from Stank, who usually handled comebacks.

When Louisiana native Mike Mauti moved to State College, he had never met anyone from Pennsylvania. But as soon as he met Matt Stankiewitch, Mauti said, "I knew immediately: that is what someone from Pennsylvania looks like." Tall, beefy, and strong, with his bright red hair cut in a perfect flattop, Stank played the stereotype of the offensive lineman to a tee: a free-speaking smart-ass, safe in the knowledge that, like all linemen, he would rarely be quoted. He grew up in tiny Orwigsburg, Pennsylvania, about ninety minutes south of Scranton, and he still

remembered the first time he met McGloin, at midfield for the pregame coin toss.

"He wasn't anything like I thought he was when I met him in high school," Stank said. "The dude didn't say anything. I figure, shy guy."

"I let my performance speak for itself," McGloin said.

"That is not true," Massaro corrected.

"Now, I know: this guy can't shut up!" Stank said. "I remember when I tried to sack him—"

"Key word: *tried*," Shrive underscored, since he had faced Stank that night.

"I think he threw for four miles that game," Stankiewitch said. "You know why they passed so often? Because they knew if they ran, they had to go through *me!*"

Stank's teammates busted on him for that, then turned the conversation to the Big 33, an annual all-star game that had pitted the best thirty-three players in Pennsylvania against their counterparts in Ohio for over fifty years. A stunning stat: of the forty-seven Super Bowls, every single one of them has featured at least one player from the Big 33. From Pennsylvania alone, the list includes Joe Namath, Joe Montana, Dan Marino, Brian Kelly, and Kerry Collins, and from Ohio, Orlando Pace, Ben Roethlisberger, and Archie Griffin.

"The Big 33—we were all picked for that," Stankiewitch said, waving his glass of Gatorade over the dining hall, before pointing to McGloin. "But not him."

"They picked John Laub instead," Massaro said.

"Sunseri got picked, too," McGloin recalled. "He took my scholarship to Pitt. Where's Laub now?" McGloin asked, feigning ignorance with a cocksure grin.

"I have no idea what he's doing now," Stank said.

"I think he went to Richmond," Massaro answered.

"And I'm starting at Penn State?" McGloin asked, then drank his Gatorade. "Hm. Interesting."

After enjoying his little joke, McGloin said, "I got looks from some schools. I went to camps. I talked to a couple Lehighs and Colgates, but I really wasn't interested in playing D-II. Then Penn State called and wanted me to be a preferred walk-on. After seeing the campus and the facilities, that was it."

In doing so, McGloin became the first member of his family to attend college—which most of the guys at the table could also claim.

When I told McGloin I had seen him light up Michigan's defense for 250 yards and 41 points in 2010—in the first start ever for a walk-on quarterback under Paterno—Stankiewitch cut me off:

"Don't feed his ego."

"He doesn't need it," Massaro agreed.

"He can't even fit his head through the doorway as it is," Stank added.

McGloin turned to me. "I gotta deal with this shit every day."

"You notice McGloin's not on the 'watch list' for any awards this year?" Stank added.

"I'm not!" McGloin said. "Nothing new there."

Everyone in that dining room knew, however, that all the rest of them combined would not receive half the scrutiny the unheralded quarterback would face, and from all directions: generations of fans, alums, lettermen, and classmates, not to mention the media, which would be watching Penn State more closely than virtually any other team in the country that season.

One way or the other, the redheaded walk-on from Scranton would be remembered.

Before dinner ended, I asked them who was keeping the team together.

"O-B," Massaro said without hesitation, "and Mauti and Zordich. The Bash Brothers."

"Me and McGloin and [Miles] Dieffenbach," Stankiewitch countered, "we're the Blood Brothers. When there's blood on the ball or McGloin's hands or his pants, he's always asking, 'Who's bleeding?' Usually, it's me."

Shrive rolled his eyes, then turned to me. "What Massaro said."

I met with the Bash Brothers an hour later in a study room at the Academic Center.

"The world's crazy right now," Mauti said. "Everything we thought was so stable—our program, our school, our reputation—all of a sudden, you don't know what's going on outside the building."

"It's all crazy outside these walls," Zordich clarified, "but in our own little world, in our little bubble here, nothing's even a *little* wrong, to be honest. In all seriousness, we're happier now than we've ever been here."

"That's across the board," Mauti said. "Every guy will tell you that."

The irony was not lost on them. Between them, they had turned down LSU, Ohio State, and a host of other top programs to come to Penn State, in the hopes of having the same experience their fathers had: values over victories, unequaled camaraderie, and the pursuit of noble goals. But they didn't truly start having that experience until the staff that coached their fathers had left.

But they also knew the very values Paterno had instilled in their fathers—dedication, integrity, sacrifice—their fathers had instilled in them. Now they were relying on those same values to lead the team in Paterno's absence. In a sense, they were the grandsons of Joe Paterno.

How far those values could take them also depended on the new staff.

"One of the biggest things they did for us was give us our confidence," Zordich said about O'Brien and his assistants. "The relationships we have with our coaches—it's only been six months—are nothing like we ever had before. I've never been closer to any team in my life than this one, this season. Once we're playing, and playing well, a lot of this will be in the past."

Zordich was naturally focusing on his final season.

O'Brien did not have that luxury. He had to take a longer view. Even if they survived this season, he knew harder ones would follow. But failing his first season would all but guarantee worse to come.

For Penn State to outlast the NCAA's four-year sanctions, succeeding in 2012 was utterly necessary, but not sufficient.

Saturday, September 1, 2012: The two-mile journey to Beaver Stadium from the Toftrees Resort, where the Lions spend Friday nights before the game, runs along two-lane roads, complete with a police escort with sirens blaring. This forces cars to pull over for the team's famed blue buses to pass—but instead of being upset, the drivers were thrilled to see the blue caravan, honking their horns and giving fist pumps out their windows.

The buses passed a handful of barns, dozens of hay wheels, and hundreds of cows—all of them owned by Penn State. Were it not for the people who rode these buses—who usually wore their headsets and bobbed their heads silently to music to get psyched up—that's what Penn State would be today: a glorified cow college.

A half mile from the stadium, the buses started passing tailgaters, who cheered and flashed handmade signs:

WE ARE ONE.

PRIDE.

And a string of people holding up one letter each to spell W-E A-R-E P-E-N-N S-T-A-T-E.

The energy built block by block. When the blue buses pulled up to the stadium tunnel, the band blasted the fight song, and several hundred fans packed the walkway and covered the grass embankments. At least a hundred of them waved navy-blue signs with white lettering that said YOU STAYED WITH US, while an equal number waved white signs with navy-blue lettering that said WE STAND WITH YOU.

One player whispered, "Goose bumps."

McGloin got off first, per O'Brien's wishes.

The cheering the players received was not just loud, but had a warmth to it, expressing as much appreciation as excitement. A few players put on their sunglasses to hide their shiny eyes as they walked through the crowd, then took them off when they entered the dark tunnel.

They went directly to their stalls, where every single one of them stopped to stare at something no Penn State player had ever seen before: their jerseys hanging from the hooks with their names on the back. They gawked and ran their fingers over the letters, then took photos with their cell phones and sent them to family and friends.

"Never thought I'd *ever* see this!" Mauti said.

Mike Fuhrman put it another way: "Sweet as fuck!"

This went on for a solid ten minutes. Whatever the lettermen, alumni, and fans thought about this break with tradition, the response among the players was unanimous. They loved it.

They eventually returned to their normal routine of light stretching, shooting the breeze, and reading the game programs left in each stall. Flipping through his, Matt Lehman, who had made the team the previous spring during an all-campus tryout, said, "We're, like, 0 and 130."

"What?"

"Well, according to the NCAA, we haven't won a game in twelve years."

In the parking lot outside, and in the stands above, the fans were enjoying arguably their favorite hour of the week, tailgating and getting pumped up before a big game. But for the coaches in the locker room underneath them, it was the most agonizing hour of the week—and in this case, probably the year: waiting for the first game to begin. They alternated between forced small talk and silence.

Mac McWhorter—one of three coaches on O'Brien's staff who'd won a national title—looked calm. But, he admitted, "The jitters are on the inside."

O'Brien was the most visibly impatient, rapidly tapping his foot and doing nothing to hide it. Of course, if they lost, he'd be the one who would have to answer for it.

Coach Stan Hixon, who had won a national title at LSU, was the calmest of the bunch, putting on his reading glasses to peruse the morning paper.

"Did you have the French toast?" O'Brien asked his lieutenants, his foot still tapping away. "It was pretty good. The whole training table is pretty good."

A few nods, then more silence.

"Steve, what time is it?" defensive coordinator Ted Roof asked.

"Ten twenty."

"Sheesh," Roof said. "The hands of time are standing still."

They stood up, sat down, put their baseball caps on, took them off, got some gum, chewed it for a minute, then spat it out. They went to the bathroom, washed their hands, drank some water, and repeated as needed. They told stories, but they were only half listening—even to their own—with long silences between each one. Prisoners on death row, waiting for the governor's call, are only slightly less anxious.

"Been a long time since I played a noon game," O'Brien said.

"When you're winning," Roof said, "you play later."

"Even in the NFL," O'Brien said. At New England "we were always on Sunday night, or Monday, or Thursdays. Never at noon."

"Same with the SEC," Roof said, then added, with more than a little sarcasm, "That's another place where the NCAA is so good about inter-vening on behalf of the welfare of the student-athletes. You play a night game on the road, you get home at five in the morning—then get up in a few hours and start the whole thing all over again. Why? Hey, wait a second! We can make a buck here!"

The choir agreed, but more silence followed. There was nothing to add.

"I think we need to get 'em to turn the AC down," O'Brien said. "We could hang meat in here!"

McWhorter looked up. "Sixty-five minutes? Shit—time's *creepin'* in here!"

O'Brien loudly clasped his hands. Then he unclasped them. Then he clasped them again—and repeated the cycle. He finally lay down on the carpet to stretch his legs. "I just need to get ready to run for the introduc-tions," he said. "See how long that damn tunnel is?"

For the first time, everyone laughed out loud.

"With the lettermen lining the ropes and all, it's a hundred yards! I'll probably pull every hamstring in my legs. I just don't want to trip—or have someone run over me, like fucking Hodges!"

More nervous laughter, but the relief didn't last. Silence returned.

"You rush, rush, rush all week," Roof said, "then it's *errrr*," imitating squealing brakes. "Tick. Tock. Tick. Tock."

"First time I've coached in real pants in forever," O'Brien said, refer-ring to the khakis he was wearing instead of his usual sweatpants. "I think it's pretty interesting Joe [Paterno] wore a tie. Woody, Bear, Landry, they all wore ties. I find the history of college football fascinating."

More silence.

"Getting off the buses—how great was that?" O'Brien asked. A few coaches had already run to the field to work with their position groups. The remaining coaches nodded. "That's one thing you don't get with pro football. I love the band! Got that from my mom. Four-hundred-piece band? Can't beat that!"

A minute later, O'Brien looked up at the digital clock with the big red numbers again.

He had made it. It was time.

He put on his hat and headed out for the first warm-ups of his head-coaching career.

• • •

Beaver Stadium is the only venue in the Big Ten where the fans see the players between the locker room and the tunnel. Lions fans take full advantage, waiting for an hour under the stands, forty deep on both sides of the walkway, to scream and yell their support, which echoes under the concrete stands. The players act cool, just as they do walking off the buses, but it clearly gives them a jolt.

On O'Brien's way back to the locker room after warm-ups, a few dozen lettermen stopped him to give him handshakes and man-hugs. Jay Paterno stood among them, near the locker room, wearing a light-blue shirt and a tie, just like his father had for so many Saturdays. He gave O'Brien a friendly handshake, but then yelled for McGloin, who turned around and smiled, but their hug seemed to mean less to McGloin than to Paterno, who turned away, choked up.

Back in the locker room, O'Brien had switched to his normal coaching mode. His time in purgatory had finally ended.

Just a minute before it was time to take the field, O'Brien told his team, "The last eight months you have put in the time and the effort like no other team I've ever been around. You *deserve* to win today.

"We're not going to be perfect, and that's okay. Play the next play! Play the next play! Play hard. Play fast.

"Encourage your teammates — and let's fucking go!"

"*Yeah!*" the players yelled, snapping their helmets and walking behind their leader.

This was no spring game.

The fans under the stands were loud during warm-ups, and louder still right before kickoff — as loud and crazy as any I've seen.

From the dark reaches under the stadium, the players walked toward sunlight. At the end of the tunnel, the ushers slowly swung open the huge stainless steel gates to the field. The players rushed past the cameramen, the band, and the cheerleaders, through a path lined by young varsity athletes and aging football lettermen.

O'Brien was right: the entire run was close to a hundred yards. But he didn't pull a hamstring or trip, and Gerald Hodges didn't fall over him.

The cheering was not just loud, but sustained. The fans had been waiting for this moment for ten months. They longed for it every time their school absorbed another blow, which seemed to arrive daily. They needed this.

This was football. This was their team. There would be no investigations or news reports today, or any need to criticize or defend their alma mater. Just a bunch of college kids running out onto the grass in their famed midnight-blue jerseys, with the stark white numbers—and, for the first time, their names on the back.

Ohio won the coin toss and elected to defer—which, actually, was just what Penn State wanted. The idea was simple: Don't waste any time. Drive the ball down there, get some points, and get the crowd going.

On this day, that wouldn't take much.

The Lions could only return the opening kickoff to their own 12—and even that was enough to solicit a hearty cheer.

From there, Bill Belton ran for 8 yards, and McGloin hit Allen Robinson for 6 more—and the first first-down of the brand-new season. They kept rolling right up to Ohio's 49-yard line, where they faced fourth and 2. For sixty-two years, Rip Engle and Joe Paterno would never have given a thought to doing anything other than punting.

O'Brien never gave a thought to doing anything other than going for it—which brought another cheer from the crowd. Penn State's defense stood ready to go, helmets on, in case the offense came up short.

McGloin took the shotgun snap—even more surprising on fourth and 2—then hit his man, who gained 9 yards.

The defensive players nodded vigorously. "All right! All right!"

If that's what the new era of Penn State football was going to look like, that was okay with the defense, and the fans.

The sun was out, the place was packed, and the Lions were driving, just like old times. The offense was headed to the end zone—and the first morsel of good news in almost a year. A touchdown would hardly solve their problems—past, present, and future, with the tragedy still hanging overhead, the sanctions setting in, and the endless court cases to follow—but it would provide a scrap of salvation.

McGloin handed off to Belton—Silas Redd's replacement, converted from receiver—who cut through the Ohio line for a decent gain, until the Bobcats stripped the ball, just as O'Brien had warned they would.

The Bobcats recovered the ball on their 21-yard line. Penn State's first drive was over.

But everyone knew Penn State's strength was defense. Mauti stopped their first play for 4 yards, then, on third and 1 at Ohio's 30-yard line, he fought past his blocker to stuff the runner, short of the first down. He jumped up and punched the air, screaming—which sent the crowd into a frenzy.

Late in the first quarter, McGloin took the snap on first and goal from Ohio's 6-yard line. He dropped back, looked around, and started scrambling. One of the lettermen standing on the sideline couldn't help himself: "Throw it away! *Throw it away!*"

McGloin probably should have, but instead he found Belton, who finished the easy trip to the end zone.

Touchdown! Penn State, 7–0.

O'Brien, who'd been working hundred-hour weeks for several months, did not resemble his famously stolid mentor Bill Belichick. O'Brien's reaction was that of a first-year Pennsylvania high school coach, jumping up and down, patting his players' helmets and backs and yelling at everyone coming back to the sideline. He was holding nothing back. He loved them, and they loved him back.

In the stands, fans who were wearing T-shirts proclaiming STILL LOUD, STILL PROUD were just that, giving a full-throated defense of their university for the first time in ten months.

They launched into their trademark cheer: "*We are* . . . *Penn State!*"— repeating it at least twenty times, as if they needed the opening touchdown as an excuse to reassert that simple declaration.

Neither team could get much traction the rest of the half. After the Bobcats suffered another three-and-out, they set up to punt from their own 25. But the Lions rushed in, blocked it, and three plays later, McGloin found walk-on Matt Lehman with a pass in the right flat. Lehman clutched the ball as he turned upfield, rumbling as only a tight end can through a handful of Bobcat defenders, all the way to the end zone. It was Penn State's second touchdown of the O'Brien Era—and the first of Lehman's career.

When the half ended, 14–3, the players trotted back up the tunnel, which was lined with so many students in T-shirts hanging over the rail it looked as if the players were running into a white cloud.

• • •

The stadium was rocking, but the locker room was all business.

"How much time?" O'Brien asked his coaches, to start his first half-time as Penn State's head coach.

"Twenty minutes."

"Let's decide what to run on the first play of the second half," he said. "They haven't stopped NASCAR yet," the code name for their no-huddle offense.

"They're sucking air out there," Mac said of the Bobcat defenders. "If we can get farther ahead, I wouldn't mind running the two-minute drill on them, to put the nail in the coffin."

O'Brien nodded. "I think we need to throw one up on them, Stan."

"I agree," Hixon said.

They separated the offense and the defense into two classrooms, which looked a little silly with three-hundred-pound men in full uniform sitting in rows of school chairs. In the defense's room, Ted Roof drew a huge 0 above the word TAKEAWAYS. They had not created a turnover yet, which obviously did not please Coach Roof.

O'Brien started with the offense. "We need to get rid of this mentality: I don't want you to be cocky, but you gotta realize, *we're good!* We're *better* than they are! In my opinion we should have put twenty-eight points on these guys that half. We're just stopping *ourselves* with third downs and turnovers!

"Play with confidence!

"Remember this word: *finish!* I don't give a damn what happened in the past. We're here now! *You're* here now!"

The Bobcats took the kickoff to start the second half and worked their way to Penn State's 43-yard line. From there, on third and 7, Tettleton dropped back, saw his receiver over the middle, and fired.

Tettleton apparently didn't see safety Stephen Obeng-Agyapong, gliding right into position to make the interception, nor Penn State's Malcolm Willis, right behind Obeng, already camped out to make a virtual "fair catch" on the same pass. If Obeng could make the catch—for Penn State's first takeaway of the season—he had plenty of grass in front of him, and few Bobcats, presenting him a good chance to complete the "pick six" that would give his team a 21–3 lead, and enough momentum to finish the game the way O'Brien had instructed.

But the ball bounced through Obeng's hands, high enough to float over Willis and right into the hands of Ohio's Landon Smith, who jogged to the end zone.

Instead of 21–3, the scoreboard read 14–10, and the game was on.

Penn State's players were as resilient as any in the country. They'd already proven that. But self-reliance and self-assurance are not the same things. Their confidence was fragile—and that's what the Bobcats attacked in the second half.

First games can set the tone for a successful season—or a disappointing one. That kind of pressure exposes cracks that enthusiasm, camaraderie, and determination cannot cover.

From that point forward, Penn State's offense exhibited a surprising inability to convert third downs—with McGloin missing simple passes, and the receivers dropping too many of the accurate ones—and Penn State's defense displayed an equally surprising inability to stop the Bobcats on third downs. Penn State's coverage was generally quite good, but Tettleton revealed himself to be the quarterback they thought he was, eluding near sacks time and again, then putting the ball exactly where it needed to be for his receivers—who never seemed to drop the ball.

That's how the Bobcats scored again—and again—giving them three unanswered second-half touchdowns to take a 24–14 lead with 2:55 left in the game.

"C'mon, guys!" a fan pleaded, leaning over the rail. "Let's gooooo!"

A few thousand had left, but most had stayed, reduced to begging for something good to happen. Another McGloin interception sent a few thousand more to the exits, but with the seconds ticking down, the student section revived, bursting into another round of *We Are! Penn State!* After the game ended, they repeated it endlessly, while the players and coaches trundled up the tunnel, heads down.

The fans, at least, were not giving up.

The players took off their uniforms and pads, some almost violently. There followed one of the saddest sounds in sports: the hiss of the showers. In a losing locker room, that is what you hear.

The assistants and players had completed their duties for the day. But for O'Brien, the second-worst part of the week, right behind the hour before the game, had arrived: facing the press. He was calm throughout, hunched over, giving straight, clipped answers. He probably said, "I have to coach better, and that starts tomorrow," a half dozen times. He was blaming no one but himself.

An hour after the game ended, O'Brien finally returned to the largely empty locker room, where Spider and Kirk Diehl were still working. O'Brien walked past the few assistants still getting dressed, straight into his rarely used head coach's room. With the door open, he slumped in the big chair, then threw a few things around.

Boom! Crash! Bang!

The sound of losing was the same in every locker room in America.

He grabbed a stat packet, revealing the source of his discontent. Seventy plays for Penn State's offense, for 352 yards. Well, he expected that. Not bad, but they had a long way to go. But 88 plays for Ohio, for 499 yards? Penn State's defense hadn't been able to stop the unranked Bobcats. O'Brien muttered a few curses, then whipped the pages against the wall.

He had good reason. On their home turf, against a team from the middling Mid-American Conference, on a perfectly dry, calm day, Penn State had been beaten, fair and square.

That was bad enough. But looking ahead, he had to wonder: if they couldn't beat these guys—under ideal conditions, in front of a hungry home crowd—who *could* they beat?

How many losses could these players—who had already put the whole school on their shoulders—withstand, before they finally cracked?

CHAPTER 9

PAIN AT THE PLEASURE DOME

September 1, 2012: While Penn State's misery deepened, the rest of the Big Ten managed to win their opening games that afternoon. Most of them were warm-up wins over tackling dummies like Indiana State and Southern Mississippi, but even at that, Iowa had to come back from a 17–9 deficit to squeak by Northern Illinois, 18–17, and Wisconsin had to hang on for dear life against Northern Iowa, 26–21.

True, it looked like Urban Meyer was bringing the Buckeyes back to form quite quickly in his debut, a 56–10 smackdown of Miami of Ohio. Michigan State played the Big Ten's only ranked opponent, No. 24 Boise State, and won, 17–13. And the Wildcats gave early notice that they warranted the league's attention by pulling off a win against Syracuse, the only BCS team on the Big Ten slate that afternoon, in a 42–41 overtime victory.

But when it came to the central question—did the Big Ten still belong among the big boys?—opening day didn't offer much evidence either way until the contest everyone wanted to see started at 7:12 central daylight time: second-ranked Alabama, the returning national champions, against eighth-ranked Michigan, the Big Ten's Great White Hope.

Whatever national reporters weren't in State College that day were in Dallas, and with good reason.

Throughout the summer of 2012, I constantly heard one question: "Are you going down to Dallas?"

Behind the repeated query were a few unstated assumptions: hardcore Michigan fans expect to go to all the big games, and they expect all fellow followers of the Wolverines to do so, too; their optimism for the

Wolverines—and by proxy, the Big Ten—had overcome their doubts; and, hey, it promised to be a hell of a show, and who doesn't like to see a good show?

Most of the Alabama fans drove nine hours across I-20 from Tuscaloosa to Dallas that day, though Tide fans in one row of Section 101 had come from North Carolina, St. Louis, and Alberta, Canada.

Most Michigan backers flew down, but those who drove split their twenty-hour drive by stopping over in Memphis or St. Louis. Many arrived a day early to take a tour of the shiny new Cowboys Stadium, one of the rare stages impressive enough to become part of the show.

Because it was just 1971 when the Cowboys moved into their last home—the famed Texas Stadium, with the rectangular hole cut in the roof so "God can watch his team play," as the fans claimed—you might think the Cowboys wouldn't need another one anytime soon. But you'd be wrong.

According to Rutgers University's Judith Grant Long, the United States is home to ninety-nine major league baseball, football, basketball, and hockey rinks, arenas, parks, and stadiums. The teams that play in those places have received taxpayer subsidies totaling $21.3 billion. That's *billion*, with a *b*—and only two of those stadiums even made a profit.

The taxpayers' willingness to pay those subsidies—or vote for their representatives who do—helps explain why eighty-nine of those ninety-nine stadiums have been built since 1970, including Philadelphia's Veterans Stadium, Pittsburgh's Three Rivers Stadium, and Cincinnati's Riverfront Stadium. All three have already been demolished and replaced, this time with two stadiums each, one for football and one for baseball. That marks nine new stadiums for those three cities alone in the past four decades—and well over one hundred major league stadiums nationwide. And we're not done.

Americans—and only Americans—have entered the era of the disposable stadium.

It doesn't have to be this way. And in Canada, it isn't. Canada is home to six NHL teams, one NBA team, and one Major League Baseball team. But Canadians don't pay for their stadiums. The teams do, which makes sense. Canadian taxpayers instead pay for their schools, which also makes sense. Guess whose students rank third, fifth, and fifth in reading, math, and science, respectively, and whose rank fourteenth, twenty-fifth, and seventeenth?

Taking candy from a baby may be immoral, but taking money from students and giving it to millionaire athletes and billionaire franchise owners should be illegal. The critics of big-time college sports have plenty of easy targets, but those who think college sports should function more like the pros are severely overestimating the sanity of the latter.

The phenomenon of disposable, taxpayer-funded stadiums is not only foreign to foreigners, but also to American college football fans. Beyond the considerable benefit of being a tax-exempt educational entity, the University of Michigan—like all universities—does not ask taxpayers to pay for its stadiums. You never hear about any college team holding the local taxpayers hostage by threatening to leave for Nashville or Jacksonville if they don't build the school a new stadium. Which is just one more thing that separates college football from the pros—for now.

The firewall that previous generations of athletic directors have built and maintained to protect college sports from being overrun by the professional leagues—by, for example, prohibiting the Chicago Bears from renting Northwestern's stadium, which the Big Ten feared would blur the lines between pro and college football—seems to be eroding, and fast, based on the display in Dallas that day.

Jerry Jones captained Arkansas's 1964 national championship team, then made a fortune through Jones Oil and Land Lease. Soon after he bought the Cowboys in 1989, he fired the franchise's only head coach to that point, Tom Landry, and its longtime general manager, "Tex" Schramm, whose duties Jones himself assumed. For these reasons, and his George Steinbrenner–esque ego, an online poll of *Sports Illustrated* readers in 2003 determined Jones was the most hated sports personality—in Texas.

Just five years after Jones bought the team, he asked the taxpayers to renovate the twenty-three-year-old Texas Stadium, including construction of executive suites, to allow him to make more money. When they didn't promise everything Jones wanted, he started a bidding war among the Dallas suburbs of Grapevine, Coppell, and Arlington, to see who would give him the most.

Arlington "won," by pledging $325 million of the estimated $650 million needed to build a state-of-the-art stadium. When Cowboys Stadium was finished in 2009, at One Legends Way, the estimate proved to be a little off. The final price tag was $1.3 billion, or twice the projection.

What do you get for $1.3 billion? Everything you want, plus a few things you never knew you wanted, starting with the world's largest dome, the world's largest column-free interior, and the world's two largest high-definition TV screens, which span from 20-yard line to 20-yard line, weigh six hundred tons, and cost $40 million—$5 million more than the entire Texas Stadium cost to build in 1971. The TV screens are bigger than the basketball court that appeared under them during the 2010 NBA All-Star game.

The stadium boasts eighty-five thousand seats, the third most in the NFL—although it would rank fourth in the Big Ten, and barely ahead of Nebraska and Wisconsin. But it's so big it can fit another twenty thousand standing fans without alarming fire marshals, partly due to the Party Pass areas behind each end zone. If you have to leave your seat to head to the concourse, or one of the 10 gift shops (the biggest covering eighteen thousand square feet), or one of the 824 concession stands that serve everything from sausage to sushi, or one of the 342 executive suites—which cost between $100,000 and $500,000 per season—you can still watch the game on one of five thousnd Sony LCDs installed throughout the stadium. Or you can admire one of the eighteen original works of art commissioned for the stadium.

The locals have given the stadium a number of nicknames, from the regal Cowboys' Cathedral to Jerry World to the less sophisticated Boss Hog Bowl to Jones Town and, yes, the Death Star. Before too long, however, all those monikers will be replaced by whatever corporation pays $100 million or more for the naming rights.

At 8:00 a.m. on September 1, about the same time the Penn State players started boarding the blue buses, ESPNU began broadcasting outside Cowboys Stadium, followed by ESPN's *College GameDay* from 9:00 a.m. to 11:00 a.m. Although it was eight hours before game time, the parking lot was already packed.

The fans lined up behind the set, hooting and hollering. One Alabama fan waved a sign that said NO, THAT WASN'T A UM PUNT. THAT WAS

A DENARD ROBINSON THROW! A Michigan fan countered with a placard that declared CIVIL WAR CHAMPS.

After the broadcast finished, some fans killed the eight hours to kick-off at the U-M alumni club's official tailgate on Collins Street, which offered drinks, a large barbecue spread, and some shade to give people refuge from the hundred-degree temperatures, all for a cover charge of $40. But far more did what came naturally in the stadium's huge parking lot: tailgate as if they were pros. Which, of course, they were.

Eric Miller and I go back to the fourth grade. He grew up in Ann Arbor, met his wife at the University of Michigan, and has watched two children graduate from U-M, too. He now lives near Cleveland, where he's contended with Buckeye fans for almost two decades. He's a friendly and funny guy, but with enough fight in him to defend his alma mater—repeatedly—in his adopted state. But none of that feistiness was needed on that opening weekend in Dallas.

"Our pregame tailgate consisted of buying a canopy, a cheap table, coolers, ice, cups, and beer from the Walmart across the street from the stadium, then drinking for four hours," he told me. "But our crimson-clad tailgating neighbors could not stand seeing us tailgate in such a 'Northern manner.'"

So, without warning, their new friends in red heaped a metal bin of meat on Miller's table "about twice the size of the one that tipped the Flintstone mobile on its side. I don't know the origin of the meat, or how they got it to taste so good, but it just fell off of the enormous bone, and the small parts that didn't were gnawed off caveman style. It was that good."

Another friend of mine, Steve Chronis, flew down with four comrades, but he didn't have quite as much fun. He was looking forward to tailgating because he suspected that might be the highlight of the day for Michigan fans. But the hundred-degree heat made the prospect of grilling bratwurst less appealing. They stuck to the beer, downing it fast before it got warm, and put ice on their heads to cool down. "Everybody was fighting to get under the three square feet of shade the only tree in the parking lot provided," he said.

Chronis was also impressed by the Alabama fans' hospitality, but he couldn't help but notice their idea of tailgating was closer to our idea of a cocktail party or a wedding reception. Of course, it could be that Tide fans talk about the same things at their cocktail parties and wedding receptions that they do at their tailgates—namely, how good their football team is, and why it's so much better than everyone else's. On opening day, they covered all the usual reasons, but they could have added one more: the Midwest's population has drained into the South, following the jobs.

At about 5:00 p.m., two hours before kickoff, the tailgaters escaped to the comfort of Jerry World, cooled by an eleven-thousand-ton air conditioner—the main reason the stadium's utility bill can exceed $20,000 on a single hot day, like this one.

In April of 2012, Michigan athletic director Dave Brandon sent band director Scott Boerma an RFP, or a "request for proposal," which is how CEOs ask for a sales pitch. Brandon told Boerma to put together a page of bullet points explaining why Boerma thought it would be better for the band to fly to Dallas for the season opener against Alabama, on September 1.

"We did so," Boerma told me, "and we turned it in. We never expected Brandon to fly us down, but we hoped. At that point, it was my assumption that we would have a conversation about those bullet points, most likely making compromises on both sides. But a few days later, we heard that the answer was simply no. And that was it."

Boerma and his band were stunned, but not as much as their loyal following, who blasted the decision through just about every medium available. For a week in late April, the band's fate dominated Ann Arbor sports-talk radio—a first, to be sure. Invective aside, the callers' main complaint was that if Brandon eliminated a home game or the possibility of an attractive home-and-home against Alabama for the chance to play in Jerry World primarily for the record paycheck, as he stated, then why couldn't Michigan afford the $400,000 it would cost to take the marching band? After all, the band had to be one of the main attractions of college football Jerry Jones surely expected when he invited two college teams to play in his pleasure dome.

There seem to be a few reasons behind Brandon's initial decision. A $4.7 million payday sounds like a lot, but according to MGoBlog's Brian Cook, it was actually about $300,000 less than Michigan would have made if Brandon had scheduled Alabama for a home-and-home series, on the same terms Michigan had with Notre Dame. The deal looks even worse when you take into account the team's travel costs to Dallas, and the substantial revenue from parking and concessions Michigan would have kept for a home game—not to mention the excitement such a game would generate among season-ticket holders from the day it was announced. Cook concludes, "This supposed financial windfall simply does not exist."

But if you looked at Brandon's initial decision to leave the band behind purely from a short-term business perspective, it made sense. The band trip would cost real money, coming right off the bottom line, but would not necessarily influence the outcome or ticket sales or TV ratings. Fans would not wait in long lines to buy Michigan Marching Band uniforms—be they classic or "alternative"—and EA Sports was not champing at the bit to put Michigan's drum major on the cover of its next marching-band video game.

If you bring it back to the simple question of keeping your fans happy, however, Brandon's decision was as foolhardy as the CEO of Cracker Jack eliminating the prizes at the bottom of the boxes because, hey, you can't eat them, and those things cost money. If there is one component of college football that distinguishes the irrational, romantic notions fans feel for their favorite sport from the streamlined sensibilities of the pro game, the marching band might be the best place to start. It is the prize at the bottom of the box.

Shortly after Bill Martin became athletic director in 2000, he commissioned a survey titled "Fans Speak Out on Game Day Experience," by his good friend, Republican pollster Bob Teeter. The response rate alone told them how passionate Michigan fans were about their team. While most consumer surveys attract a 6 to 8 percent rate of return, fully 64 percent of the three thousand Michigan fans randomly selected responded—or about *ten times* the average.

When these season-ticket holders were asked to rank the importance of twenty-three aspects of the game-day experience, the survey readers weren't too shocked to find seat location atop the list, with 88 percent of respondents ranking it "important." But the marching band finished a close fourth, with 83 percent, two places ahead of the final score, and four ahead of the quality of the opponent. Thus, whether the Wolverines won or lost, or which team they were playing—in other words, the *football game*—was less important to the fans than seeing the marching band. After all, the band remained undefeated.

Brandon took some hits for his decision from fans, who flooded his e-mail account, but donors soon stepped up to cover half the $400,000 tab, leading some to believe the whole incident was a ruse to get someone else to pay the bill. But band director Scott Boerma wasn't buying it. "I do not think he planned on the backlash," Boerma told me, "nor do I think it was some clever way to get donors to pony up for it. Dave was genuinely surprised."

After Brandon finally capitulated, he told the Detroit Economic Club in August that it was all a "misunderstanding," akin to a "family squabble." He said he had agreed from the outset to fund the $100,000 necessary for the band to take buses down to Dallas, allowing them to play concerts along the way.

"The band changed their mind," Brandon said. "They decided they didn't want to be in buses and they didn't want to play their way to Dallas, and they came and said, 'We're planning on coming to Dallas, everybody's planning on coming to Dallas, but we're not going to ride in buses—we're going to fly in a jumbo jet and here's what it's going to cost.'"

But band director Scott Boerma recalls the dialogue differently. "I think it's important for people to know that we never 'changed our mind.' We never agreed to busing down and playing gigs along the way. We offered to look into that possibility, but when we did, we determined that it really wouldn't be best for all concerned, especially because it would be the weekend before classes started, and we would lose several days of our pre-season rehearsals, when we prepare for the entire fall ahead. We never refused to bus down, as Brandon said. We were never given the opportunity to refuse anything, because there was no follow-up conversation.

"When it all hit the fan, I made sure that it wasn't the band students and staff causing a commotion. We just laid low and waited for it all to work out. If the decision to not take the band down remained intact, we would have been fine with that. It was Brandon's decision; he was paying the bills, and that's his business."

Of course, after the fans expressed their outrage over that decision, and the donors ponied up, the trip was on.

• • •

My friends back in Ann Arbor watched the game on TV, something seven of us have been doing together for almost two decades when the Wolverines are away. While our gang wouldn't pass for a scientifically selected "focus group," we're probably pretty typical not only of Michigan fans, but of Big Ten fans in general. An anthropologist watching us would have little difficulty identifying our tribe and our shared rituals.

In our "gang of seven" (to which we've added spouses and kids), nine of our fourteen parents earned at least one degree from U-M, and five of them work there. Only one of us didn't earn at least one degree from Michigan, and three of us have worked for U-M ourselves. We've also earned degrees from Kenyon College, Williams College, and the Universities of Georgia, Wisconsin, and Ohio State, so we have a few points of comparison. But for all of us, when it comes to sports, Michigan is where our loyalties lie.

It started before we were even aware of it. For me, it was the 1972 Rose Bowl, when the third-ranked Wolverines appeared to have a 12–10 victory locked up to secure an undefeated season, and a shot at a national title, only to see sixteenth-ranked Stanford connect on five straight passes, then kick a field goal to win 13–12. I was seven, in a house filled with adults and kids, and I remember everyone being very happy, then suddenly very unhappy. I didn't know what was going on, but I knew whatever it was, it must have been important.

The others in our gang were similarly indoctrinated, even those who went to grade school in Minnesota, Illinois, or Connecticut, because their parents had gone to Michigan or were from there, and they raised them that way.

Paul Barnett, aka Barney, was a high school hockey teammate of mine who is now a county prosecutor. He is the son of two U-M alums who both played in the marching band, and his dad still plays in the alumni band during homecoming weekends.

During Ohio State week, Barney and his fifth-grade buddies would go around their neighborhood with their cornets and trombones, ringing doorbells and playing "The Victors" and "Let's Go Blue!"—Christmas carols for Wolverine fans.

"If we lost," he recalled, "it would ruin my month. I still have bitter memories of certain games, like the loss to Purdue at Purdue in 1976, and the sixteen-to-nothing loss at Minnesota in 1977." Because we're all part of the same tribe, he didn't need to add that Michigan had gone into both games ranked number one.

"I was connected to it. Michigan was *us*, and we were *Michigan*. All the kids in school felt the same way. There were no—*no*—Michigan State fans."

Before we had given any thought to where we wanted to go to college, we already knew Michigan's players, records, rivals, and traditions. We were hooked—and it didn't have anything to do with what we knew about the school itself, which wasn't much.

A few of our classmates would go on to play for Michigan, which is what happens when you grow up in Ann Arbor—or Columbus or State College or just about anywhere in Big Ten country. Unlike the NFL, in college football, the best players near you tend to go to the best program near you.

For us, that included Andy Moeller—whose dad, Michigan assistant coach Gary, would replace Schembechler in 1990—and Jim Harbaugh, whose dad, Jack, was also an assistant coach. Harbaugh, like Bob Seger, went to Tappan Junior High, named after U-M's first president. In ninth grade, two members of our gang, Tim Petersen and Brian Weisman, comprised Harbaugh's starting backfield.

Of course, Harbaugh went on to become Michigan's Big Ten MVP quarterback, a star in the NFL, and then the head coach of Stanford and the San Francisco 49ers. Petersen and Weisman switched to tennis and soccer, respectively, which probably better fit their five-eight frames. If you stretched it, you could say they were eventually replaced by Walter Payton and Marshall Faulk. Well, sort of.

All of this comes up with remarkable regularity in our e-mails, ostensibly intended to plan a simple Saturday get-together. These e-mails should have nothing to do with anything that happened thirty years ago—but they always seem to have everything to do with it. We had become Michigan fans long before we went to college. We have remained Michigan fans long after we graduated.

Rest assured, the same immersion method applies to kids who were raised on Penn State and Ohio State football, Indiana and Purdue basketball, and Wisconsin and Minnesota hockey. And that's what makes the whole league work: whether we admit it or not, we *want* the other schools' fans to be as passionate about their teams as we are about ours;

otherwise, what's the point? Where's the fun in beating someone who doesn't care about the game in the first place?

But this doesn't mean we can't be critical of our alma mater. In fact, probably no one is *more* critical of these schools than the alums. This became obvious over lunch the week after the Alabama game, when the gang recounted their "talking points" from the watch party that Saturday.

"The Cowboy Classic?" asked Brian Weisman, one of Harbaugh's former junior high tailbacks. "It was a poor idea, poorly explained."

"There's no good reason for it," Barney said. "And no good reason for leaving the band behind, either."

"I don't think it's *all* about the bottom line with Brandon," Weisman said, "but that's always the first foot he puts forward, and it often doesn't look or feel right with a public institution established for education first. It has a corporate feel to it. Tacky. With all the commercialism of the Cowboy Classic—the JumboTrons and the expensive tickets and the TV coverage—was it a college game or a pro game?"

"It was a pro game," said Keith Severence, who had gone with a friend whose company was being entertained by Tyson's Chicken and therefore got to sit in one of those fancy suites drinking gin and tonics and eating sushi. "It was a lot of fun, but it wasn't college. And afterward, you had nowhere to go." After all, Jerry World is surrounded by a massive parking lot—and little else.

"The Cowboy Classic was made for TV and nothing else," Weisman concluded. "It's a serious compromise from what could have been a great home-and-home series," one where Michigan fans could have walked Alabama's campus and eaten at mom-and-pop shops like Houndstooth and visited the Paul W. Bryant Museum, and Tide fans could have walked Michigan's "Diag" and visited Pizza Bob's, Blimpy Burger, and Mister Spots—no chains in the mix.

Nonetheless, none of us even considered not watching the game, in person or on TV. And either way, we gave Jerry Jones and the two schools' athletic directors exactly what they wanted: a chance to make money off us.

Just inside the stadium's east entrance, the Ann Arbor–based souvenir chain M Den set up a tent to hawk Michigan apparel and jerseys designed for this game, attracting a line of customers longer than the field they would soon be watching. It took Scott Bell, a former student of mine at Michigan who's now a *Dallas Morning News* sports reporter, about thirty minutes just to get inside the tent—and once he did, still two hours before kickoff, the ravenous fans had already emptied a number of cubbyholes and racks.

The money makers didn't stop there. Both schools posted ads inside the stadium, something Michigan has made a point never to do in the Big House, and ran more ads on the jumbo TVs for—well, for just about everything. Even alcohol was for sale—another Big House no-no. If you were willing to wait in line for ten minutes or so, you could get a good ol' twelve-ounce Miller Lite for a mere $8.50, which buys twelve of them at the Walmart across the parking lot, with a buck-fifty change.

Even at those prices, those drinks came in handy for Michigan fans.

Michigan entered the game a 14-point underdog. A point or two might have been attributed to Brady Hoke's decision, announced the day before the game, to leave starting running back Fitzgerald Toussaint at home due to his DUI conviction a month earlier.

"The decision was not easy, but I feel it is in the best interest of this program and for these kids, and those always will be my priorities," Hoke said in a press release. "It's about teaching life lessons, and if this helps these kids or someone else make a right decision later, then we've won. That is ultimately what we are here for, to help them grow and mature to become better sons, fathers, husbands, and members of society."

Hoke's decision was roundly heralded by Michigan fans as proof that their program was not run by a win-at-all-costs coach, a virtue they value deeply—and one pro fans wouldn't even consider.

But even without Toussaint, a genial young man who had led the 2011 team with 1,041 yards, Michigan fans were almost uniform in their belief that, if Denard Robinson could just get rolling, Michigan could pull the upset.

"Hey, Appalachian State beat *us*, right?" State Street Barber Shop's Bill "Red" Stolberg said, back in Ann Arbor. "If they can do it to us, we can do it to 'Bama!"

As votes of confidence go, I've heard stronger. But two things became clear early, then often: First, though the crowd was evenly split between the two schools, the folks in crimson were twice as loud—*before* anyone had scored. Second, Touissant's presence would have made little difference.

Thanks to Alabama's "containment" defense, Michigan's coaches felt compelled to keep Denard Robinson in the pocket—where he is at his most uncomfortable and ineffective. He proved it when the Wolverines' first six possessions ended with four punts and two interceptions.

Michigan's defense, however, looked as if it might be up to the challenge when it sent the Tide's potent offense to the sidelines after its first three downs. Unfortunately for the Wolverines, that proved to be the rare exception. Alabama quarterback A. J. McCarron and company scored three straight touchdowns in the first quarter alone to take a 21–0 lead, which they expanded to 31–0 with 4:31 still left in the half.

It was all over but the shouting, which Tide fans happily provided by the decibel. Wolverine fans had little to cheer for until halftime, when the Michigan Marching Band took the field. I'm told the Michigan fans in Dallas did, in fact, enjoy every note.

When they'd signed the deal months earlier, Jerry Jones compared this game to the Super Bowl. He didn't realize just how right he'd be: the event provided weeks of hype and unbridled commercialism, followed by a fizzle. This game would have fit in just fine among the many forgettable Super Bowl blowouts of the seventies and eighties.

The final scoreboard read 41–14, Michigan's two touchdowns coming off two Robinson bombs, but the fans knew the real score: if the best of the Big Ten was going to compete with the cream of the SEC, it still had a ways to go.

"The 'Bama fans were treating us like Michigan fans treat Michigan State fans," Steve Chronis said. "Now I know what it feels like to be a Sparty."

Michigan's football truck, festooned with the winged helmet, rode through the night to get to Schembechler Hall the next morning. While the equipment managers unloaded the gear, and the coaches graded the players, the Wolverines refocused on their original mission: get good enough, fast enough, to win their forty-third Big Ten title.

On the season's first day, they discovered national acclaim was out of reach for at least another year.

CHAPTER 10

THE BRAINIAC BOWL

If you want to see what a Big Ten school that doesn't care about football looks like, all you have to do is revisit Northwestern between 1972 and 1991. Within those twenty years you have two eras: the Bad Years, from 1981 to 1991, when two coaches led the 'Cats to a record of 20-79; and the Really, Really Bad Years of 1976 to 1981, when they posted a record of 3-62.

That's no typo. Three victories against 62 defeats. If the team had flipped those numbers around, the Wildcats would be considered the greatest dynasty of the modern era. Only the Washington Generals, who get paid to lose to the Harlem Globetrotters, had a worse record.

"We won three games in six years," said Northwestern's current president, Morton Schapiro. A celebrated professor, he has written five books and over a hundred academic articles on the economics of higher education, and he possesses a savantlike ability to conjure scores, records, and even the dates of big games for all of Northwestern's nineteen varsity teams. He follows them assiduously through GameTracker, which provides every pitch, shot, and play. "We were three and sixty-two—and one! We tied one in there." And he was correct.

"But it wasn't just six seasons of losing. It was two decades."

Again, he was right. And it wasn't just embarrassing. It was costly.

"Northwestern was losing a lot of money for the conference," recalled Jim Duderstadt, who served as Michigan's president from 1988 to 1996.

"Back then they had shared gates, and Northwestern wasn't really interested in making the investments necessary to help out," he told me. "They were losing about ten million dollars a year in the early nineties, and with about ten thousand students, that's about a thousand dollars per student to stay in the Big Ten.

"They're much more Ivy League–like than Big Ten. If they could have conveniently moved into the Ivy Leagues, they would have done it."

In fact, Duderstadt recalled, before he became president in 1988, "They actually explored it in the eighties, with a serious proposal to the Ivy League, but both sides ultimately backed away."

And what if Northwestern had followed through on its proposal to drop out of the Big Ten?

A decent model of that alternative universe can be found just fourteen miles down Lake Shore Drive in Hyde Park—home of the University of Chicago.

In the late 1800s, it had become fashionable for America's richest men—Cornell, Vanderbilt, Stanford, Rice, and Duke, to name a few—to create colleges in their names. But the richest of them all, John D. Rockefeller, named his school after its home: the University of Chicago.

In 1891, a year before they opened the doors, the university hired a Yale professor, William Rainey Harper, to become its first president.

Harper's first hire was not a vice president, a provost, or a dean, but his former Hebrew student Amos Alonzo Stagg, a coach trained by Yale's Walter Camp himself, the father of football. Both Rockefeller and Harper knew the fastest way to put their new school on the map was to make a splash in the sensation sweeping the nation—and therefore became the first school to leverage football success for academic prestige, a model later followed by Notre Dame, Michigan State, Penn State, and now Ohio State.

According to John Boyer, dean of the University of Chicago since 1992—and the most knowledgeable historian on campus—Harper focused more on the graduate schools than the undergraduate program. "But counterbalancing this was Harper's incredible love of student life," Boyer told me. "He recognized the school needed a vibrant culture, loyal alums, and successful—underscore *successful*—Big Ten athletics."

President Harper hired the right guy. Stagg made the Maroons strong enough fast enough to join the brand-new Big Ten in 1895, winning five of the league's first eighteen titles, and two more in 1922 and 1924. Chicago's seven Big Ten football titles were not exceeded by Iowa until 1990, by Wisconsin until 1993, and by Purdue or Northwestern until 2000. Eighty-eight years later, Indiana, Michigan State, Penn State, and, of course, Nebraska have yet to pass Chicago's mark.

Stagg invented the Statue of Liberty play, the man-in-motion, and the end-around. Knute Rockne himself once said, "All football begins with Stagg." That might be a bit hyperbolic, but there is no discounting what Stagg did for the game, the Big Ten, and the University of Chicago. In fact, Stagg might have done his job too well, gaining such notoriety for his school that he and his team were no longer needed.

"We were already the third-wealthiest university in the country by 1910, behind only Harvard and Yale," Boyer explained. "By the 1920s, many of our schools and colleges were in the number one or two spot nationwide."

Chicago's fifth president, Robert Maynard Hutchins, served from 1929 to 1951. According to Robin Lester's authoritative book, *Stagg's University: The Rise, Decline and Fall of Big-Time Football at Chicago*, Hutchins decided the university's undergraduate program had grown so strong through a new Great Books curriculum that, by 1939, it wouldn't matter much if he killed the football program.

Of course, Hutchins's contempt for athletics in almost all forms didn't help. "Whenever I get the urge to exercise," he famously said, "I lie down until it goes away."

His disregard for organized collegiate athletics was even greater, as captured in this classic: "Football is to education what bullfighting is to agriculture."

It's a safe bet, however, that if Chicago's teams hadn't tanked in their last fifteen seasons, Hutchins would not have been so predisposed to cut the squad.

After Stagg won Chicago's seventh and last Big Ten title in 1924, he managed only one winning season in his next eight and was fired. Stagg's successor, Clark Shaughnessy, never achieved a single winning season in his seven-year stint, despite coaching Jay Berwanger to the first Heisman Trophy in 1935.

"Even in the twenties," Dean Boyer told me, "we had a difficult time fielding successful teams, and then the market for our team collapsed. The Bears were at Wrigley Field, and Northwestern was on the rise, so attendance and wins began to decline. This continued into the thirties."

In 1939, the Maroons managed to beat Oberlin and Wabash (now Division III schools), but suffered four straight midseason losses to

Harvard, Michigan, Virginia, and Ohio State, by a combined score of 254–0—an average of 63.5 to, well, 0, of course.

"Looking at scores like that, what can Hutchins do?" Boyer asked, "He wasn't going to keep putting a team like that on the field to represent this university. Really, Hutchins was killing off a program that had already died."

But Hutchins's revamped undergraduate offerings atrophied, too. By the 1980s, the University of Chicago had become a serious success, but a joyless campus. A popular T-shirt on campus featured THE UNIVERSITY OF CHICAGO on the front, and on the back, WHERE FUN GOES TO DIE.

When the late, great Notre Dame coach Frank Leahy once said, "A school without football is in danger of deteriorating into a medieval study hall," this is what he was talking about.

As a result, Boyer recalled, applicants stayed away in droves. When he started at the university twenty-one years ago, the school had a 71 percent admit rate. In other words, just about everyone who could do the work and bothered to apply to one of the world's most prestigious universities was all but guaranteed admission.

"The education has always been first-rate," he said. "But you can't sell that just by itself anymore."

So, what to do about it? Liven up the atmosphere by bringing back big-time sports—as Connecticut and Buffalo have done—or come up with another plan?

Characteristically, Chicago opted for Plan B—and executed it cleverly.

"We were not investing enough in residential life—in dorms, and dining halls, the theater, sports," Boyer admitted. "We were not paying attention to the world beyond the life of the mind. We may not need tailgating, but you need nice dorms, good dining halls. And the university made significant improvements in all those areas, investing massively."

Chicago also put good money into a new arts center on campus, first-rate pools and gyms—Hutchins's hatred of exercise notwithstanding—and even Division III athletic teams.

"Sports are important to us," Boyer said, "but it's not the tail wagging the dog. We require calculus for all freshmen—admissions are very tough—but we have very good teams in cross-country, tennis, and soccer, among others. They're all competitive, they have a good time, they make lifelong friends, and the alums think it's great. But the most popular campus activity is theater."

Chicago's formula is working. The 71 percent admit rate the school had twenty years ago has dropped to just 9 percent, making Chicago more selective than any university outside of Harvard, Yale, and Princeton—a truly dramatic turnaround.

"What we do isn't for everyone," Boyer acknowledged. "But it's working very well for us."

By the early nineties, Northwestern's football team had been almost as bad, on and off the field, as Chicago's had been during the Maroons' death rattle. It probably wasn't too hard for Northwestern's leaders at the time to understand President Hutchins's decision to pull the Maroons out of the Big Ten in 1939. But seeing a great university such as Chicago struggle to get high school seniors simply to apply probably gave Northwestern's executives pause.

During the football team's two lost decades, Northwestern was still a great university, populated by world-class professors and ambitious students from around the country and the globe, who loved their school. But, like Chicago, the place lacked something just about every other Big Ten student body could take for granted: fun.

According to the authoritative *Insider's Guide to the Colleges'* 1995 edition, Northwestern students' primary social outlet was "going to the library. . . . The social scene is very uptight for a large university."

Evanston itself often struck outsiders as a tight little town, and for good reason. In 1851, local Methodist lay ministers founded Northwestern, and their leadership helps explain why there are still eighty churches in a college town of about seventy thousand people. In its twentieth year, the school absorbed the Evanston College for Ladies and named its president, alumna Frances Willard, the first dean of women. She stepped down in 1874 to become the leader of the Woman's Christian Temperance Union, the driving force behind Prohibition—which is also the reason Evanston does not have a single bowling alley to this day. It's not too surprising, then, that as late as 1995 Evanston had just one liquor store in the entire city and not a single bona fide bar.

Evanston, in short, could have used a little levity—but the football team was only equipped to provide comic relief through horrible seasons.

Northwestern's president and athletic director could have left well enough alone or attempted an experiment like Chicago's. Neither option seemed too appealing, however, especially since Chicago's plan hadn't yet borne fruit, and even if it did, two such universities in the same county might flood the market for that niche of students who prefer theater to football.

Instead, Northwestern's leaders wondered, what would happen if Northwestern's football team actually—gasp!—started winning games.

Enter Gary Barnett, who had just led Colorado's offense, under head coach Bill McCartney, to that school's only national title in 1990. Barnett's mere arrival signaled things were changing in Evanston. "Northwestern used to be a place to hang your hat while you made calls for your next job," former athletic director Rick Taylor told me. But when Northwestern started paying competitive salaries, they started attracting competitive coaches.

Two new NCAA rules also helped the Wildcats: the eighty-five scholarship limit, which kept teams like Michigan and Ohio State from hoarding all the good players; and Proposition 48, which mandated certain academic minimums for incoming freshmen—and prompted parents to start asking recruiters about graduation rates. Suddenly, Northwestern's high academic standards were transformed from a liability to an asset. To make sure the more talented recruits weren't overwhelmed by Northwestern's classrooms, Barnett instituted mandatory tutoring for all freshman players, which all programs do now.

The players also developed a confidence beyond their record. When Northwestern was recruiting Pat Fitzgerald—a self-described "Irish-Catholic kid from the South Side who heard Notre Dame scores announced at mass every Sunday"—he recalled going to a campus party with two Wildcat linebackers. When they asked him where else he was looking, and he said Georgia Tech and Notre Dame, "I'll never forget what they said: 'Would you rather *play* for Notre Dame or *beat* Notre Dame?'" he told me. "That took me back, made me think."

As it should have, since Northwestern had not won in South Bend since 1961. Their faith was that deep-seated.

These were all essential steps, but that still left the actual winning of games. In Barnett's third season, 1994, the Wildcats split their first seven games, 3-3-1, before losing their final four contests. They finished the season last in the Big Ten in offense, last in defense, and last in turnovers—but first in punting.

Barnett told them, "Keep priming the pump. The water is about to come up." The players believed it long before their fans did. That summer, fifty players decided to stay in town to work out through the sweltering heat wave, more than double the usual number.

The Wildcats opened 1995 against ninth-ranked Notre Dame. Before the game, Barnett told his team that when they won—not if, but *when*—they were not to carry him off the field because they had bigger games ahead.

It worked. Northwestern pulled off the upset, 17–15—just as Fitzgerald's recruiters told him they would—then went on to sweep the Big Ten en route to the Wildcats' first Rose Bowl appearance since 1949.

Everyone loved the 'Cats because they were the embodiment of the little engine that could, besting the traditional football machines at their own game.

Almost two decades later, the Wildcats' revival remains one of the most popular stories in the history of college football. The team's turnaround was unforgettable—but the effect that team had off the field might have been more dramatic.

The Monday after the Wildcats clinched the 1995 Big Ten title, I camped out in Evanston for the week to write a story for the *Detroit News* on the impact this meteor of a team had had on the campus and the town. It didn't take long to recognize how a successful football team could energize even the normally dour Northwestern students, the restrained town of Evanston, and even the stodgy faculty, who started discarding their stoic silence for adolescent yelps of joy not heard in these parts since . . . well, ever.

"It's finals week and people are more concerned with Rose Bowl tickets than finals," one sophomore told me, "and that's *never* happened around here."

Case in point: On the Friday before the season finale against Illinois, in a highly competitive chemistry course with over two hundred students, an acclaimed professor produced a beaker full of a bright, orange solution. While explaining the chemical principles that governed his experiment, he stirred up a second, blue solution in a flask. When he finished, he poured the blue solution into the beaker of orange solution, which just happened to be Illinois's color, and—shazam!—the two solutions suddenly burst into Northwestern purple. The lecture hall erupted in cheers.

The football team's success even had a salubrious effect on the school's relations with Evanston and Chicago. Town-gown relations here have always been a bit rockier than in other Big Ten towns, partly because Northwestern is the league's only private school, and the hardest for the locals to get into. Its campus sits on a large chunk of Lake Michigan shoreline, which can make the relatively small town envious, particularly of the school's tax-free status.

But, during the 1995 team's unprecedented roll, every storefront in downtown Evanston, from hair salons to antique stores, put purple in their windows. As longtime resident Donna Streibich Curtis observed, that one glorious season "has *done something* to this town."

It had also done something to Chicago, which had been searching for a college team to call its own for decades. Chicago is twice as close to Evanston as Detroit is to Ann Arbor or East Lansing, yet for years both Michigan and Michigan State had a stronger gravitational pull on their state's biggest city than Northwestern did on Chicago. In the midst of Northwestern's great 1995 season, however, the same papers that used to give more print to a Notre Dame loss than a Wildcat win were devoting half the front page to headlines like "Cats Win Big Ten."

"Our identity's done a one-eighty, and we're just sitting here in the middle watching it spin around," said Jennifer Brown, a first-year student in 1995 from San Diego. "The ripple effect is amazing. It's affecting everything."

The evidence was everywhere at once. The Northwestern Sailing Club found it could solicit more corporate support because of the football team's success. "They know who we are now," said Beth Holland, a sophomore who called on those sponsors. "I had to learn [star tailback] Darnell Autry's football stats just to talk with these guys."

Rebecca Dixon, who was in charge of admissions and financial aid, told me applications for "early decision" were up 23 percent from the previous year. And every Monday after football games "our phones are ringing off the hooks," she said.

It was surely ironic that the bigger the senior football players, the higher the freshmen applicants' SAT scores. One junior admitted, "I wouldn't want to be in next year's applicant pool."

The 1995 Wildcats accomplished all this without making any deals with the devil. The academic standing of incoming Northwestern football players was second only to Stanford's in Division I-A. True, of the seventy-one players from the 1995 Northwestern team who'd declared majors, twenty-two were enrolled in something called "organizational studies," and a few others listed majors such as "psychological services" and "communication studies," which will not be confused with computer science. But they won't be confused with the traditional jock loopholes, either, because Northwestern doesn't offer them.

"It's been just a miracle kind of season," said Ken Kraft, the associate athletic director who'd seen enough Wildcat campaigns to know. "Even if you make two holes in one, the second one's not as much fun."

And that's the catch: everyone knows it's simply impossible to re-create the magic of 1995. The perennial loser overcoming all odds is not a story line you can repeat, and Hollywood has yet to make a film about an admirably average team. So the question becomes, How much of the magic from that unforgettable season can Northwestern keep alive—and at what price?

Sixteen years after Pat Fitzgerald won his second Big Ten title as a player in 1996, he would embark on his quest for his first as a coach, with fifty-five returning lettermen, thirteen returning starters, and all his specialists coming back.

The 2011 seniors had won more games than any other Northwestern class and had gone to four straight bowl games, a first. And there was this surprising statistic: since 1995, only Ohio State, Michigan, and Wisconsin had won more Big Ten titles than Northwestern's three—and Wisconsin had passed the 'Cats only the year before. You could win a lot of bar bets with that one, even in Chicago.

To win their fourth title since 1994, the Wildcats would have to battle division rivals Michigan, Michigan State, and Nebraska, but they would not have to face Ohio State in the regular season, nor in the title game, since the Buckeyes were ineligible for postseason play. They had to travel to Penn State, but most experts were predicting the Lions would throw in the towel before the Wildcats got there in October. If there was a year the stars were aligned for the 'Cats to grab another banner, 2012 was it.

But even if the Wildcats fell short of exploiting this rare opportunity, Northwestern would still be Northwestern. "Academically," Fitzgerald said, "2011 was an unprecedented year for us." The team had a 3.04 GPA, a 94 percent graduation rate—higher than the student body's—and thirty-two players on the Academic All–Big Ten team, a record even for Northwestern.

"But most importantly," Fitzgerald said, "we take great pride in being the number one school academically in the Football Bowl Subdivision [for APR]. So we believe we're the number one [football] school academically in the country."

Northwestern's 107 football players on the 2012 roster were pursuing twenty different majors, including seventeen in economics and eleven in engineering. Offensive lineman Patrick Ward runs six feet seven and 320 pounds, "but his most impressive stat is his 3.94 in mechanical engineering," President Morton Schapiro told me. "I'm hoping he goes to the NFL, but if not, he'll be the world's largest engineer."

Patrick Ward aside, most Wildcats can't simply bowl over the corn-fed boys at Wisconsin and Iowa, so they have to outwit and outwork them. But Northwestern is a good place to attract the kind of players who can do just that.

"I think everything about us is unique," Fitzgerald told me. "So why stop on campus? The way we recruit is unique, too.

"We approach it as a challenge to find the right fit. How do we define that fit? It starts off the field. I want leaders. I want guys who want to be a little unique. When they're the captains of their high school teams, that usually requires them to step out of the box a bit and be a little bit more mature, which typically leads to a better academic kid—and that fits in here.

"And we like finding winners. An overwhelming majority of our players played on league-champion, sectional-champion, even state-champion teams. And they *led* those teams."

Fitzgerald was recruiting a mind-set first, a body second.

"So we don't get a dozen five-star kids. Whose opinion is that? *What do I care?*

"There's a young man out there right now with offers from every school in the Big Ten. But when we watched him play, he was injured early in the game, so he went back to the bench, put a towel over his head, and sat there the rest of the game. Didn't cheer for his teammates or talk to anyone. I don't know if he even watched the game. So, right now, every school in the Big Ten wants him—but not us."

It's not hard to see what Fitzgerald saw in the quarterback he actually recruited, junior Kain Colter, a three-star player out of Colorado. His father, Spencer, played safety for Colorado's 1990 national championship team and went on to become a high school football coach. Kain's mother, Stacy, is a legal analyst for Chipotle.

"My parents definitely preached to me, 'Get your education,'" he told me, wearing a white, button-down shirt, a navy-blue tie, and a gray sport coat. "You want to make your degree count."

Football, then, was sold to him as a means to an end. He received offers from Air Force, Arizona State, Nebraska, Texas Christian, and Colorado, among others. But, he said, "I really didn't want to go to a program with a whole lot of tradition. I wanted to go somewhere where they were going to build something. I liked Stanford for that reason. I was committed to Stanford my whole junior year, but I ended up getting hurt, and they brought in another quarterback."

That's how Colter became the Wildcats' quarterback—and how he got his nose bent out of shape, which is virtually a prerequisite to play at Northwestern.

"I wasn't a four- or five-star guy coming out of high school," Colter told me. "None of us were. But the guys we get for our team haven't been told how great they were, how amazing they were, their whole lives. They come to college with a chip on their shoulder. They want to prove they can compete at this level, and they want to work for everything. They're going to do anything for the team—so many guys on this team change positions, without complaint—and those are the guys we look for."

That included Colter himself. When Northwestern's 2011 quarterback, Dan Persa—who had been considered a preseason Heisman Trophy candidate—was healthy, Colter played tailback and receiver. But when Persa went down with a freak ankle injury, Colter filled in at quarterback. He did all three jobs so well—running for 654 yards and 9 touchdowns, catching 43 passes for 466 yards and 3 more touchdowns, and hitting 55 of his 82 passes for 673 yards and 6 more touchdowns, against only one interception—that in 2012 Colter was Northwestern's leading returner in passing, receiving, and rushing, surely the only player in the country who could claim that.

Because the other ten players on Northwestern's offense usually aren't bigger or faster than the guys across the line, it's especially important that Northwestern get a quarterback who fits their system: a smart, quick, coachable leader who can run the spread offense, a system designed to help smaller teams compete. When the Wildcats find their man, they are surprisingly dangerous. The 2012 Wildcats knew Colter would be the key.

If that was Colter's principal mission in Evanston, it would be enough, but Colter was determined to make the most of his opportunity, majoring in psychology with an eye toward medical school. That meant time-consuming labs—so many, he had to miss off-season workouts and seven-on-seven drills his first two years to attend them.

"It's tough. It's *really* tough," he told me. "Labs are usually later in the day, and those take three hours, so it's really tough to get that in. Sometimes I just want to give it up and focus on football, but you have to look at the long run: all of us in this room will have our football careers end sooner or later. You definitely have to have a backup plan, and that's something that Northwestern really helps you with.

"But if you want to be a great football player," he added, still turning it over in his mind, "you have to do a lot of extra work—lifting, watching film, doing drills. If you want to go to the NFL, there's only one time to do that, and it's now."

He's also received a bit of fame—but only a bit. Once you've "made it" as a college football player, you can look forward to being depicted in EA Sports' college football video game. (You can also look forward to EA Sports, the NCAA, and member schools keeping all the profits.) Having started most of 2011, Colter figured he had to be in the video game this year—and he was, on their national third team.

"I was excited!" he said with a laugh. "I bought the game, ran home, opened it up, and put it in—and I ended up being a white guy with red hair."

Only at Northwestern.

• • •

Every head coach I talked to cited his team's academic standing, underscoring how seriously his program took the student side of the student-athlete equation, and they were utterly sincere, with the numbers to back it up. But Northwestern was alone in arguing the team's academic success was central to their success on the field. It was not simply a matter of declaring, "We take school seriously, too," but "*Because* we excel academically, it helps us compete on the field."

When I asked Fitzgerald about this, he straightened his back and set his jaw like he was warming to a familiar fight—one he'd already waged as a Northwestern recruit and player, and now as the head coach. "So I want to know, why do these people think we *can't* win with bright guys? We win *because* they're bright guys! We think we've got the best leaders and the brightest guys in the Big Ten. That's *how* we win! And this school *helps us* recruit them."

If the NCAA wanted a spokesperson to explain how its core values actually translated to victories, Fitzgerald would make a fine selection. You could argue, however, that more than other coaches, he could afford to put values before victories.

"We can do that here," he told me, "because our president, our AD, our trustees, and our fans have the right kind of compass. They understand who we are, and they embrace it, with no excuses."

Everyone in Evanston still credits President Bienen for his pioneering support of Northwestern football, and his successor, Morton Schapiro, has cranked it up another notch. A former dean at USC, and president of Williams College, Schapiro immediately impresses visitors with his uncommonly engaging manner, his incredible memory and voracious curiosity, and the breadth and depth of his interests. One of those interests is varsity athletics.

"Morty," as he introduces himself, made this manifest immediately after being named Northwestern's next president in December of 2008, nine months before he would assume the office. President Bienen was nice enough to invite him to the December 29, 2008, Alamo Bowl, against Missouri. Schapiro eagerly accepted and stayed in San Antonio for the entire week, meeting everyone and addressing the team two days before the game, starting a tradition that continues to this day.

"Morty gives us great talks when he visits practice," defensive end

Quentin Williams told me. "He's very impressive, very charismatic, and a great speaker. It goes over very well."

"What Morty's meant to this program," Athletic Director Jim Phillips told me, "you can't measure. He's been unbelievable."

"The whole [athletic] ramp-up started with President Bienen," Vice President of University Relations Alan Cubbage said, "but when Morty shows up at the games, for all our teams, it's a clear demonstration of institutional commitment."

Schapiro is an unapologetically avid sports fan—especially of the Wildcats, of course—but not as an end in itself.

"I was in New York talking to our alumni last week," Schapiro told me on a rainy April day in his office. "Northwestern—it's not the kind of place where the first question you get from the alums is about football. But it comes up, every time. They wanted to know about the bowl game, and about our new basketball coach. They take a great interest in our teams and can keep in touch with the school this way," something that's harder to do through an econ class.

Athletics also keeps the school in front of future students, especially since the Big Ten Network started broadcasting games coast to coast. "When a Northwestern tennis match is being shown in San Antonio," Cubbage said, "it helps our coaches recruit, but it also gets our name out there for everyone. BTN has broadened the reach of the schools."

But at its roots, Schapiro stressed, if athletics aren't for the people on campus, something's amiss. "The faculty and staff take a lot of pride in our teams," he said, "and it's a great part of the college experience."

That is something Schapiro takes seriously. He still teaches an economics class twice a week, he accepts dozens of invitations from students to dine at their dorms or fraternities or apartments, and he attends every varsity competition he can—usually a few each week. It's all part of building a sense of community on a campus where more students come from both coasts than from the state of Illinois.

"USC has sixteen thousand undergraduates," Schapiro told me, "and most Big Ten schools have more than that. You're not going to know them. Eight thousand students is all we have, which makes it a little different and gives us a smaller, more intimate campus.

"People are always saying, 'I'm going to this game or that game.' You ask them why, and they say, 'I don't know much about the sport, but my suitemate is on the field hockey team, my fraternity brother is on the soccer team, or my church buddy is on the women's lacrosse team.' They're going to support their friends. I think that's more common here. The teams bring us together and give us something to cheer for."

This helps Northwestern establish a few tenets necessary to every vibrant learning community: a common identity, lifelong loyalty, and a happy campus.

"Once in a while," Fitzgerald told me, "I have to remind people around here: the current students, down the road, are your alums. And if they had a good time here and have good feelings about the place, that's when they give back. If they didn't, I don't think they're opening their wallets for you. President Schapiro has done a magical job bringing it all together."

However, Northwestern has already learned—just as Chicago did— that simply *having* a Big Ten football team doesn't do much for your school. If it's the laughingstock of the league, you might be better off without it.

"We've made a commitment that athletics would be important," AD Jim Phillips said. "Does that mean the tail's wagging the dog? That won't ever happen around here. I never lose any sleep wondering what my head coach is up to, and we'll never be confused about why the athletic department is here. It's to support the school's educational mission.

"It isn't winning at all costs, but either you're going to get into the game or you're not. We keep score! We keep score of *U.S. News* rankings and Nobel Prize winners, too! Why would we accept any less than the standards of excellence the institution was founded on?"

Northwestern's renewed commitment to athletic success has convinced everyone the school belongs in the Big Ten, and can play with the big boys.

"I don't think anyone wants us to go D-III anymore," Schapiro said. "We're very happy in the Big Ten. When you look at our nineteen sports, we're really pretty good. In the last nine seasons, our women's lacrosse team has won seven national titles. We've won"—he pauses to do the math in his head—"one hundred and eighty-two games and lost just ten."

But even at Northwestern, football is the focal point.

• • •

142

That brings us back to Pat Fitzgerald. The support he enjoys is essential, but winning games is still largely up to him. That starts with finding the special class of players who can win in Evanston and value what Northwestern offers.

"I don't know what being Ohio State means," he told me. "I never played there. I've never coached there. But I do know what being Northwestern means. And we know how to find the kind of people who will appreciate it."

Case in point: defensive end Quentin Williams. He was a tenth grader at Central Catholic in Pittsburgh when his mom died. His father, an urban planner, his brother, Nate, and he had to start making their own meals. One load was lifted when Nate, a linebacker, got scholarship offers from Duke, Virginia, and North Carolina, but he was captivated by Fitzgerald, the same way Fitzgerald had been captivated by Barnett.

Two years later, Fitzgerald came after Quentin, who was not particularly big or fast but, he told me, "I was always taught that football is a team game. I was a captain in high school, and we won state our senior year," all but defining Fitzgerald's ideal recruit.

Quentin was leaning toward Stanford until he asked his brother about Fitzgerald. "He couldn't think of anything negative to say: 'I love that man.'"

Still, Quentin was the last Northwestern recruit to fax in his letter of intent. But by 2012, all his doubts had been erased. "This was the best decision I've ever made."

Going into his fifth year—which is strongly encouraged in the Northwestern program—Williams and his classmates wanted more. After Fitzgerald's "welcome back" team meeting in January of 2012, receiver Demetrius Fields gathered team leaders Kain Colter, David Nwabuisi, and Quentin Williams together in the team room. "It was the first time in my career," Williams recalled, "the seniors got together *after* Fitz left the leadership meeting. We were sick and tired of losing. We were sick of watching senior classes fall short. You could see it in our eyes that day. We didn't care how long the meeting took. We were determined."

"In 2011," Colter added, "we had tons of talent. But for some reason, we just threw away too many games we should have won. We noticed we weren't close enough as a team. You play harder for guys you know and respect. So in that meeting, we decided that was the main problem, so we were going to start working as a team, eating as a team, doing everything together to get closer."

The idea was to make their attitudes contagious. "Take the team by the hand," Fitzgerald told them. "It's your team. Show them how to do it."

Being contagious didn't necessarily mean being polite—or even liked. "We had to call some people out sometimes," Williams said. "It wasn't fun, but it was necessary."

We journalists often write about coaches who "have" their teams—when their players are following not just their rules and playbook, but buying their philosophy.

Michigan's Brady Hoke had his team from his first team meeting in 2011. O'Brien had fought to keep his team through the off-season, and despite the NCAA's best efforts, he had succeeded. Meyer still didn't feel that he had his team, but he was working on it.

But at Northwestern, not only did Fitzgerald have his team, but, in a real sense, the university did, too. Most of the players had declined schools like Stanford, Georgia Tech, and Virginia to wear the purple. They knew what Northwestern offered—and they had decided that's what they wanted.

The question remained: Would that translate to another 6-6 season, capped by another bowl loss—or worse? Or would that create something better, even historic?

Just like the university it hosts, Evanston doesn't have that much in common with the rest of the Big Ten college towns. This might seem irrelevant, but, unlike pro teams, who up and leave one city for another whenever they get a better offer, college teams are forever married to their schools and their towns. How this love triangle interacts, and what accommodations each party makes for the others, tells you a lot about all three.

Because the Wildcats wouldn't kick off until 7:00 p.m., central time, I went searching on another perfect fall Saturday for the best of Evanston's five bars (yes, five) to watch the early Big Ten games.

Matt Albers, an Ann Arbor native, former Michigan State hockey player, and Evanston transplant, suggested we meet at the Bluestone bar and restaurant on Central Street, just a few blocks from Northwestern's Ryan Field. It's a nice spot, with dark wooden walls, tables, and chairs, brightened by a big picture window, with a park just down the street, but because it lacked the grit of Ann Arbor's Brown Jug, or State College's Rathskeller, or Columbus's Plank's Café, the Bluestone felt more like a chain bar. They don't blast college fight songs or even rock and roll, but pipe in Norah Jones's mellifluous voice.

They have the complete collection of Big Ten helmets on a shelf over the bar, but the walls were plastered not with Northwestern frames or even Big Ten pennants, but banners taken from golf flagsticks around the country and the world, more than a hundred.

I had stumbled upon something I'd never before seen: a golf bar, unattached to a golf course. It turns out the owner is a friend and occasional caddy of Luke Donald's, a Northwestern alum who became the world's top-ranked golfer in 2011. It says something that the only bar close to Northwestern's stadium is based less on the football team than an English golfer. But Donald married a classmate and still lives here, which says something, too. The place grows on you.

Albers loves Evanston and the Wildcats, as do his wife and kids, who are big fans of the teams and Coach Fitzgerald. "I have such respect for him, and what he does," Albers said, expressing a universal sentiment. But part of the Northwestern experience is undeniably foreign to a man who grew up in Ann Arbor and graduated from Michigan State.

"Last season," Albers reported, "Northwestern's basketball team could have gone to the NCAA tournament for the first time ever if they'd won their last game. So my friends went early to Buffalo Wild Wings, thinking it was going to be packed. Before a big game at State, every bar within five miles of campus is packed. But we were damn near alone! Maybe three or four tables of people, max."

Then things turned stranger. "Ten minutes into the game, a bunch of people show up, and a girl takes the microphone, and she says, 'It's time for Harry Potter Trivia!'"

I cannot do justice to the expression on Albers's face.

"Harry fucking Potter? Are you *shitting* me?

"If there was a home opener at Michigan or Michigan State and there was no school, it'd still be sold out. At Northwestern, if a big game fell on the same week as final exams, they would be studying. Okay, that's what they *should* be doing—but it's still strange!"

We were soon joined by Roger Williams, forty-one, a former all–Big Ten wrestler at 177, and Jack Griffin, a Northwestern teammate who won the NCAA title at the considerably lighter 118. They both now work in Northwestern's development office.

"How bad was it?" Williams asked rhetorically, of Northwestern football's Dark Ages. "Before my senior year, 1994, they never charged students to go to the games, and we could come and go as we pleased, all game." Even at that, most students rarely bothered to leave the parking lot.

For years, when Northwestern was losing, Griffin recalled, "The students would start that stupid chant, 'It's all right! It's okay! You're gonna work for us someday!' I hated that chant, but we're past that now."

Williams nodded vigorously. "Any question about Northwestern leaving the Big Ten—or getting kicked out—all that ended in 1995. We expect to win every game now, and that's what we're thinking when we take the field."

Their confidence was well deserved and hard earned. What President Schapiro, Jim Phillips, and Pat Fitzgerald had accomplished was nothing short of heroic, but their stated goal wasn't a Big Ten title or perfect season, but something far more modest: their first bowl victory since 1949. But, if that trio of leaders was replaced by less committed or talented people, or if Michigan and Ohio State made it impossible to keep up in the arms race, individual heroics could be rendered irrelevant. Northwestern would either have to quit being Northwestern, or quit being in the race.

What would Northwestern be like today if it had left the Big Ten during the dark decades?

"Without Big Ten football?" Griffin asked. "We'd be a top-notch research institution."

Nothing wrong with that, of course. But the belief that you don't need big-time football—which Chicago proved—should not be confused with the belief that you don't need something special to attract freshmen and unify the campus—which Chicago also proved.

The question is, could the 'Cats keep their cake and eat it, too? Northwestern is the Big Ten's smallest school, with only about eight thousand full-time undergraduates, plus some eight thousand graduate students, who are far less likely to attend the games. The next smallest, newly joined Nebraska, has nineteen thousand undergrads, and the rest have somewhere between thirty-two and fifty-seven thousand total students, dwarfing the little engine that could.

This creates a particular challenge for Northwestern, even in Chicago. "Of the twelve current conference schools, ten have more alumni *in Chicago* than we do," Athletic Director Jim Phillips told me. "We're eleventh right now, ahead of only Penn State, whose alums are mostly in the East. And that gap between us and the others will only grow in the years to come."

Leave it to a Northwestern athletic director to spin that as a positive. "We try to embrace this," Phillips said, "and stay connected with all the Big Ten fans in the city. It's not that we want you to dismiss the school that you went to—but you can have your second-favorite team. And we want that to be us!"

It seems to be working. By almost any measure—season-ticket sales, corporate sponsorship, revenue, website hits, and hours of community service—it's all going in the right direction. Since Phillips took over in 2008, Northwestern's attendance has grown 60 percent. In 2011, they set their attendance record against Michigan with 47,330 fans, two hundred more than capacity. Even the students go to the games now, usually leaving their tailgates to head to the stadium in the middle of the first quarter.

"They want to win," Albers chipped in, "but if they don't, the pride is still in the school, not the team. If Michigan loses, my dad [a distinguished neurologist at U-M Hospital] is still grumpy on Monday. It ruins his week—and he spends it talking about how they should have gone for it on fourth down."

Wildcat fans don't want to be the University of Chicago, but they don't want to be Michigan, either. Like Goldilocks, they think they've got it juuust right. But their contentment should not be confused with complacency.

"Losing used to be okay," Griffin said. "Not with the coaches or the players, but the students and alums became numb to it. The losing streak had almost become a badge of courage. But they expect more now, and they care about winning. We're ready to take the next step. Since Fitz's class, we've shown we can do it here. In basketball, we're ready to go from the NIT to the NCAA tournament. In football, we're ready to win bowl games."

And therein lies the rub: Once you start caring, you've put one foot on the treadmill. When you get a taste of winning, you want another, and before you know it, you've got both feet on it, and you're running.

● ● ●

We settled in for the noon game, Penn State at Virginia, which had problems of its own.

UVA's new president, Teresa Sullivan—who had been a popular provost at Michigan—had been the target of a coup attempt by board member Helen Dragas, a real estate developer. She felt Sullivan had been dragging her feet on changes Dragas wanted, changes that would run the very university Thomas Jefferson had founded more like a corporation, Dragas's stated goal. Dragas's changes included cutting the budgets of unprofitable programs like classics and German, and pursuing something she called "strategic dynamism."

Dragas had broad support among the other board members, who included executives and lawyers from Wall Street, General Electric, a coal company, a nursing home, a beer distributor, and the son of conservative televangelist Pat Robertson. Many were UVA alumni, but few had any professional experience in higher education.

The *Huffington Post*'s analysis of the board's e-mails concluded, "Members of the board, steeped in a culture of corporate jargon and buzzy management theories, wanted the school to institute austerity measures and re-engineer its academic offerings around inexpensive, online education, the e-mails reveal. Led by Rector Helen Dragas . . . the board shared a guiding vision that the university could, and indeed should, be run like a Fortune 500 company."

Dragas and her biggest ally in the pursuit of "strategic dynamism," a former Goldman Sachs partner and hedge fund manager named Peter Kiernan, based their vision of the University of Virginia not on deep research, respected studies, or conversations with academics, but by gleaning from several recent columns in popular publications.

"Reading a few op-eds and articles in the *Times*, the *Wall Street Journal*, and the *Chronicle of Higher Ed* does not qualify you to make definitive judgments about hugely complex issues such as the promise and perils of online learning," said John Arras, director of the UVA Bioethics Program. "We are dealing here for the most part with a bunch of amateurs who think they know everything, but really know very little about the academic culture and what makes us tick.

"A successful real estate empire is not at all like a university. These people are talking about cutting classics—Greeks and Romans, the foundations of Western thought—because it's not profitable enough."

Tal Brewer, the chair of UVA's philosophy department, took a longer view. "There is this sort of shift in the zeitgeist," he said, characterized by "adoration of the business mind as capable of bringing clarity, organization, and efficiency to any kind of institution. . . . I just think that's a deep mistake. . . . What's happening at other kinds of institutions around the country is now coming home to roost in higher education."

The shift is not only happening in other institutions, but other universities.

"I don't think necessarily the boards of visitors in the Virginia public institutions are the worst example," said Robert Kreiser, of the American Association of University Professors. "Texas is the place where this has gone to the extreme, where first [George] Bush and now [Rick] Perry have been filling the boards with political appointees who are favorably disposed to a view of higher education which is very corporatist and not understanding of what the academic mission should be about."

Texas governor Rick Perry has since taken it further, letting the billionaire-oilman-turned-University-of-Texas-business-school-teacher, Jeff Sandefer, gather data on Texas A&M's professors to determine who's making money for A&M, and who's losing it. Sandefer then listed their results in black or red ink and divided the faculty members into five categories: coasters, dodgers, sherpas, pioneers, and stars. According to the *Austin Statesmen*, he has also concocted a list of recommendations to reform the school: "Award bonus pay to teachers based strictly on student evaluations, put more emphasis on teaching productivity and less on research, split budgets into separate amounts for research and teaching, and treat students like customers."

When Sandefer tried to do the same thing at the University of Texas, however, the alumni association stood up to protest in support of the faculty, and the two sides seem headed for a historic battle.

At Virginia, the students and faculty rebelled in force, too, defending President Sullivan from Dragas and company, and forcing them to reinstate her within days.

Would a similar takeover of the nation's biggest athletic departments prompt a similar rebellion by players and fans? And if the battle between economic and academic interests is not fought there, where will the front line be drawn?

• • •

Penn State's players had simpler things to worry about: winning their first game in almost a year. They started out with a determined seventeen-play drive, converting three third downs and two fourth downs—the last a quick, confident read by Matt McGloin to a wide-open Kyle Carter, right over the middle, for an early 7–0 lead.

But they lost their early momentum when Anthony Fera's replacement, Sam Ficken, missed three straight field goal attempts—from 40 to 20 yards, the latter snapped from the 3-yard line—and an extra point, too.

Penn State's defense was as good as Ficken's kicking was bad. Mauti forced a fumble, Jordan Hill grabbed an interception, then Mauti forced another fumble. Late in the game, Mauti recovered a third fumble, after which he ran off the field with the ball held high, jumping and hollering, as if the ball had everything he'd ever wanted inside it.

The Lions held a shaky 16–10 lead with eight minutes left in the game when they had to punt again. On the Cavaliers' final possession, they converted a third-and-16 on their way to the end zone to take a 17–16 lead with just 1:27 left.

The camera focused on a Penn State fan, mouth open, hands on face, head tilted back—a perfect symbol of the accrued agony of ten months of bad news, big and small, without relief. ABC then flashed a graphic: the last time Penn State had started the season 0-2 was 2001, when they finished 5-6.

The 2012 Lions remained poised, calmly moving the ball from their own 27 to Virginia's 25-yard line in just eight plays. This set up Sam Ficken for another chance, a 42-yard field goal attempt with one second left on the clock.

As Ficken set up, they flashed his career stat line: 2 for 6, 43 long, 2 for 3 PATs. Today: missed left, missed right, missed right, and made the last one, from 31 yards out. The stage was set perfectly for the shaky sophomore to be the hero, for the team to run off with a thrilling victory, and for everyone to fly home to a grateful campus.

The Virginia coach kept his head down, unable to watch.

The ground was dry, the wind was light, the angle was dead straight, and the snap was good. So was the hold.

Ficken stepped into it, but as he approached, his form was clearly off. His left shoulder opened, driving his leg and twisting his body to the left, which is exactly where the ball went: far left.

The Lions had to fly home heavy with the knowledge that they had not won a game since November 19, 2011.

ABC cut immediately to the Big House, which was a sea of maize for Michigan's home opener against Air Force.

The Falcons might have been undersized, but they were tough, they ran the tricky triple option, and just like every other team visiting the Big House since the Appalachian State Horror of 2007, they played without fear.

With the Wolverines hanging on to a 31–25 lead with just 2:45 left, Air Force got the ball back on their own 20-yard line, giving Michigan fans reason to dread another 0-2 start themselves. Greg Mattison's defense held, however, and one more Big Ten team escaped a nonconference disaster.

Ohio State broke free from Central Florida in the second half to win 31–16. But Nebraska, Purdue, Wisconsin, and Iowa were not so lucky, falling to UCLA, Notre Dame, Oregon State, and Iowa State, respectively.

A couple hours before Northwestern's kickoff, the Big Ten was already a disheartening 5-5 on the day. Illinois would get crushed later that night by Arizona State, 45–14. So the league was looking to the former "Mildcats" for some redemption against the only other SEC school the conference would play in the regular season.

It wasn't just Northwestern fans or Big Ten backers who should have been pulling for the Wildcats, however, but every person who cares about college football. Because if Northwestern could not compete with this squad, this coach, this athletic director, this president, and this approach, then the entire enterprise of college football would be taking another big step toward becoming a glorified minor league.

By 5:00 p.m., the Bluestone had finally filled up, with the bar about evenly divided between Northwestern purple and white, and Vanderbilt black and gold, often at the same table. As one Northwestern fan said, "This is the Friendly Bowl."

While not as dramatic as Northwestern's unforgettable 1995 season, in 2008 the Commodores had executed a similar rags-to-almost-riches story. They have not won a conference title since 1923, and between

1986 and 2001 they averaged just over one league win a year. But in 2008 they went to their first bowl game in fifty-three years—and actually won it, earning the envy of everyone in Evanston. Then they went to another bowl game in 2011, setting expectations higher in 2012.

A Vanderbilt fan proudly quoted their coach, James Franklin, saying Vanderbilt should lose players only to Cal, Stanford, Notre Dame, and Northwestern. It was a point of pride for both schools—right up to President Schapiro.

The Association of American Universities (AAU) has only sixty-two members, Schapiro explained, and only twenty-six are private schools. When you take out the seven Ivy League schools in that group, and such universities as Emory, Brandeis, and Washington University in St. Louis—all of which play in a Division III league with Chicago—you're left with exactly seven private members of the AAU that play Division I football: Duke, Tulane, Rice, USC, Stanford, Vanderbilt, and Northwestern.

"When people ask me why don't we play our peer institutions in football," Schapiro told me, "it's because there are only six! There just aren't a lot out there.

"But I believe you are who you play, so it's nice to play other schools that are different from the mainstream.

"We like playing Vanderbilt."

An hour before kickoff, the crowd started walking a few blocks down Central Street, which could double as a movie set for small-town, 1950s America. If you didn't know better, you might think the throng was headed to Mustard's Last Stand, an inspired hot-dog joint with a line going out the door. Their actual destination was Ryan Field, which only presents itself when you reach Mustard's Last Stand. Ryan Field is just another building on the block, the antithesis of a Jerry World plopped down in an ocean-sized parking lot. Ryan Field might be the smallest stadium in the Big Ten, with a capacity of 47,130, but it's also the only one that reminds you of a neighborhood ballpark.

A parking lot can speak volumes about a stadium. The one framing Ryan Field wraps around the stadium in a U and holds only about 1,500 cars, not tens of thousands. The asphalt is faded, rolling, and cracked, the kind you might find in front of abandoned shopping malls.

But the tailgaters didn't seem to care. Roger Williams, the former

Northwestern wrestler, set up shop with his classmates, all former Wildcat athletes themselves, who had become successful professionals. Back in the day, they said, the students dominated the parking lot, but when they barred the fraternities from tailgating, that changed everything.

From the local law enforcement's point of view, however, that wasn't all bad. "Oh, yeah, I remember the frat-party days," the oldest officer in a circle of three told me. "I remember when they managed to set the asphalt on fire, and that pretty much marked the end of that."

"Now you have to pay to get in the game!" one of Williams's friends exclaimed, a complaint which would not get much sympathy from Michigan, Ohio State, or Penn State fans, who fork over a few hundred bucks for the same honor each football weekend.

Another difference from their college days: they were actually talking about the game beforehand and had clearly given it some thought during the week.

"We're three-and-a-half-point underdogs tonight," one reported without surprise. "We're rarely favored—even at home."

None of which dampened their optimism. When they made their predictions, every one of them picked the 'Cats.

Of all the elements of Northwestern and its football team that had changed since they were students in the early nineties, the fans' newfound confidence might have been the most striking.

"Go 'Cats!" they said, put down their beers, and walked to the stadium—before the game had even started.

Game time fell right at dusk, on a cloudless, sixty-one-degree evening, with the setting sun glowing off the prettier campus buildings. Beyond the shoreline, Lake Michigan spread the entire width and breadth of the horizon, flat as glass. You can see nothing else from the press box. The scene rivals the view at Penn State, looking out on Mt. Nittany.

From just beyond the north end zone, where the Northwestern players got dressed in the football building, they ran out under an awning, charging down the sloped, perfectly manicured grass, through two columns of the marching band. The official attendance was just 31,644 that night, but the cozy confines made it feel like twice that.

Because the students weren't due back for another three weeks, Northwestern officials were pleasantly surprised to host their largest season opener since the game following 9/11, when the need to be together was unusually high, and a solid Michigan State team was in town.

The crowd cheered a little louder when they saw the team's new uniforms, which brought back the classic "Northwestern stripe," a thick horizontal band, sandwiched between two thin ones, first popularized in the 1920s. The crowd cheered again when the players ran over the end zone, newly painted with the same Northwestern stripe.

But new uniforms and fresh paint cannot protect you from a good opponent, and Vanderbilt's first drive clearly showed they were a serious, well-coached team. Led by Aaron Rodgers's little brother, Jordan, they ground out 77 yards in 13 plays to take the early 7–0 lead. The teams traded field goals to end the half at 10–3, but the scoreboard hardly did the first two quarters justice.

Neither school could boast the kind of "big uglies" you see playing for their conference opponents, but both teams played smart, sharp, and fast football. Not three yards and a cloud of dust, but rollouts and end arounds and reverses, with the occasional Statue of Liberty thrown in for fun—the kind of clever football fans like to watch.

During halftime, I left the press box to take a tour of the eighty-seven-year-old building. Entering the stadium under its Romanesque columns, you first notice an actual grill, bigger than a Chevy Volt, blazing away under the stands, filling the concourse with the sweet smell of a dozen backyard barbecues.

Just past the south end zone, opposite the locker room and the football building, the grounds crew has built an arced ramp of grass that runs up right to the stands, which form a parallel arc. The first row of seats sits about five feet above the field, close enough to feel the speed of the game, but high enough to see what's going on—with nothing in between but a three-foot-high chain rope. The space between player and fan shrinks after a touchdown, when the lucky Wildcat often runs up the grass incline toward the crowd.

In those seats, I came across a young couple enjoying a night out. Justin Mangin, a 2006 Michigan State graduate, brought his girlfriend, Courtney Chambrell, a University of Georgia alumna—both of whom work in Chicago—for what can only be called a cheap date. "We got our tickets on StubHub for four bucks each," Mangin told me. "Four bucks!

Hell, the face value is eighteen. We paid about that for tickets to the Michigan game here last year, and that was the most expensive one so far.

"I love college football," he added, explaining why they weren't out painting Chicago red. "After living in Florida for five years, it feels nice to be back in Big Ten country."

"It's a nice family atmosphere," Chambrell said, an interesting comment from two single people with no kids. She even preferred the experience to the celebrated Georgia football weekends, when women wear fancy, black-sequined outfits and high heels. "Oh, I'm enjoying this a lot more. High heels are not fun walking up the bleachers. I want to wear a sweatshirt!" She wore a purple scarf and a Northwestern-style N decal on her cheek, to match Mangin's "eye-black" sticker.

"We like to root for the home team," he said.

"Hey, we want to fit in and make friends," she added.

It wasn't hard to do at Ryan Field. If the Big House is impressive, the Horseshoe intimidating, and Penn State's Erector Set just plain loud, Ryan Field might be the Big Ten's most lovable home. At times, it felt less like a Big Ten Saturday than a high school Friday night, the kind that takes place in small towns all across America, where everyone comes out to support the team and see old friends.

Midway around the arc, a dozen kids from the Evanston Township High School football team sat together, with a few parents behind them. They wore their team jerseys because they were proud to be 3-0. They went to four or five Northwestern games a year, they said, because they liked the town, the team, and the university.

"At first, they were a doormat," their junior quarterback, Ryan James, told me. "But now they've turned it around. The stadium gets louder every year. Now everyone knows them around town."

I had to test this theory. Did he have a favorite player?

"Yeah!" he said. "The quarterback. What's his name?"

Kain Colter?

"Yeah, him!"

When I asked them where they wanted to go to school, I heard Auburn, Chapel Hill, Illinois, and Michigan—but not Northwestern, perhaps due to the high admissions standards, or the cost, or because they knew only one person who had gone there, their line coach, Keegan Grant, who had risen from walk-on to Wildcat starter by 2010.

But none of that mattered when Northwestern tailback Venric Mark dashed up the right sideline, past the Vanderbilt bench, right toward the Evanston high schoolers, then made a quick cut, straight to the end zone. The refs called him out of bounds along the way, but the end-zone crowd was on full alert.

Just a little bit farther down the arc, at the far end, I found a gang of eight-year-olds standing at the chain rope, whipping their jackets over their heads.

"Our uncle has season tickets," said Nicholas Alvey, who was "almost nine. I like it here because I can run around with people."

"I like seeing really cool plays and stuff, and getting signatures from the players," Leo Dlatt told me.

His favorite?

"The quarterback!"

His name?

"I'm not sure."

The people I'd met, from the twentysomething couple to the high school players to these eight-year-old kids, were fans not so much of individual players, but of the team—and really, the experience.

Just a few plays later, Mark broke through again, cut to the middle, and ran right to the end zone—touchdown!—then continued running up the grass ramp to the fans, where he stopped to point at them. They were standing on their feet across the arc, at eye level—the Big Ten's version of the Lambeau Leap.

The kids went crazy.

I've been to every conference stadium, and I've liked them all except the Minneapolis Metrodome, which the Gophers leased from 1982 to 2008—marking the only time a Big Ten school had to rent its "home field" or play indoors. All but two of the Big Ten stadiums were built before the Great Depression, and at the risk of sounding older than I am, they don't build 'em like they used to. Even today's technology can't give a building character—or memories.

But of all the league's great stadiums, the south end zone at Ryan Field might just be the best place in the Big Ten to watch a game.

Mark's touchdown gave the Wildcats a 13–10 lead, their first of the game, with 9:28 left. For two teams with flashy offensive systems, led by two capable, exciting quarterbacks, the game was surprisingly low scoring.

The Commodores tied the game with a field goal, but the 'Cats came right back with a field goal of their own to regain the lead, 16–13, with 2:01 left. On Vanderbilt's next play, the 'Cats sacked Rodgers, forced a fumble, and smothered it.

When Colter was simply trying to run out the clock, he found a seam and took off for the south end zone, electrifying Ryan Field and the end-zone-arc inhabitants once again to seal the 23–13 victory.

The temperature had dropped to the fifties, clouds covered the moon, and rain had started coming down softly, then hard—but no one seemed to care.

On the other side of the stadium, the students—thousands of whom had showed up three weeks before classes began, though most lived far from Evanston—weren't going anywhere. A few wore gigantic purple sombreros, more than a few wore purple leggings—men *and* women—and at least two groups had painted their chests purple and white.

President Schapiro ran from the team's bench to the corner of the end zone, right past the student section. Recognizing their president, whom many of them had met along the way, they started chanting, *"Mor-ty! Mor-ty!"*

President Schapiro acknowledged the students with some fist pumps, then ran up to the ever-anxious athletic director, Jim Phillips, who had been pacing in the rain around the north goalpost, arms folded, wearing his shirt and tie, with no coat or umbrella.

"When it's close, Jim won't talk to anyone," one staffer said. "He has to worry by himself."

President Schapiro gave Phillips a big hug, then threw his arm around him, and pivoted him to the student section while raising Phillips's arm like a ref introducing the winner of a championship bout. The students went crazy again and Phillips's worried face finally broke into a great grin.

When the game ended, the coaches and the players ran to midfield to shake the hands of their cerebral peers from the SEC, then charged over to the student section at full speed. They stood just a few feet from the five-foot-high wall and—with the band's help—started singing their fight song, "Go U Northwestern," one of the league's best, punching their purple helmets into the air on the beat.

This has become a happily common custom in the Big Ten, but never is it more personal and intimate than it is in Evanston, where the players are singing to the students, and the students are singing to the players, and it's small enough that everyone can see each other's face. Players often pointed to a particular student and smiled, and vice versa, during their serenade.

They actually knew each other, and not as player and fan, but as classmates. If the Chicago Bears had ever actually played here, it would never be the same.

It was raining hard. It was getting cold. It was becoming miserable. And everybody was thrilled.

Northwestern is the only Big Ten school I've visited that holds its postgame press conference not in a separate press area, but in its team room—perhaps because they're the only school that never moved its football building from the stadium end zone, where most programs built them a century ago. The arms race has since separated the two buildings at just about every other school.

The Big Ten's team rooms are all pretty similar, resembling small movie theaters, with the chairs and carpet in some permutation of school colors, and motivational slogans and goals painted on the walls. Still, they all reveal something about each school.

On the right wall of Northwestern's, for example, they picture not their Big Ten titles, their colossal stadium, or their most famous players, but a black-and-white photo of their students, clearly ecstatic after a big victory, with chests painted to spell out WILDCATS.

In the back, they've painted THE WILDCAT WAY and AS HARD AS YOU CAN, FOR AS LONG AS YOU CAN.

On the left side of the room, they've listed the goals of a Northwestern football player:

BE A CHAMPION

PREPARE FOR LIFE

GET A NORTHWESTERN DEGREE

Against this backdrop, Coach Pat Fitzgerald took the stage and sat down at a table.

He delivered the requisite praise for Vanderbilt and his defense, and predictable concerns over his offense. When a reporter asked about the

Big Ten's troubles that day—final tally, 6 and 6—Fitzgerald answered honestly, "Sorry to hear that from our brothers in the league. But we're not a good enough football team to put the league on our shoulders."

I asked if the relationship between the students and the team had grown since his freshmen year. "I don't think it has anything to do with me," he said with a grin, "but I think it's because we're very active on campus. We've got an unbelievably tight-knit family, and as a university I think we're very close. Everyone's involved in everyone's lives.

"We've had great student support for a number of years. But when you see those kinds of numbers, for a home opener when it's raining and the students aren't even in school yet, it was awesome! It's a privilege for us to play for them."

Clearly, the contagion the seniors had hoped to spread was catching, and their coach knew it.

He closed by saying, with another grin, "I look forward to not reading whatever you guys write." It got a good laugh from the most collegial beat in the Big Ten.

Then he added something you don't often hear from big-time football coaches: "Our game next week [against Boston College] is at two thirty. I cordially invite each and every one of you. Thanks for coming down. Be safe going home in the rain—and go 'Cats!'"

The players followed their coach, delivering more of the usual answers, but in a manner you'd expect from twenty-five-year-olds. The only quote that stood out came from Venric Mark, the small tailback who crashed through to the end zone and then celebrated with the fans. "Our destination isn't done yet," he said. "We're only two games in."

But they were one-third of the way to another bowl bid, and a chance to do something no Northwestern team had done in sixty-four years.

CHAPTER 11

"IF WE COULD JUST WIN ONE"

The most beloved living figure of Penn State football is not John Cappelletti or Todd Blackledge or Ki-Jana Carter, or any of the eighty-eight all-Americans who have worn the navy and white. This guy has never even thrown a pass, scored a touchdown, or made a big tackle—because he can't.

Brad Caldwell was born with a severe case of scoliosis. The condition cost him part of his left shoulder blade and a few ribs and gave him a bit of a hump, leaving him slightly bent over. He grew up in Curwensville, a former brick-manufacturing town in west-central Pennsylvania. When Caldwell was in eighth grade, his science teacher, Mike Keely, convinced him to become the junior high football team's equipment manager. Caldwell reluctantly agreed, but before long, the varsity coach called him up—and changed his life forever.

Adding to the self-consciousness every high schooler feels, the five-foot-two Caldwell had to wear a back brace. Working with the football team gave him an identity, a sense of belonging, and forced him out of his shell. He was hooked and followed his new passion to Penn State when he enrolled in 1983.

Caldwell got his nickname one day when he was joking around, crawling across the locker room floor on all fours to pick something up. Defensive lineman Joe Hines said, "You look like a spider!" It stuck with everyone. Well, almost everyone. Although even his best friends call him Spider, with his blessings, Paterno never did because his wife wouldn't let him. "That was Joe," Caldwell said with obvious affection.

Caldwell, his top lieutenant, Kirk Diehl, and a few interns are responsible for outfitting 120 football players, organizing some two thousand jerseys and two thousand pairs of cleats, and replacing any piece of equipment at a moment's notice, right on the sidelines. (Caldwell's wife, Karen, is a skilled seamstress and repairs the jerseys.) During the season, Caldwell and Diehl work eighty-hour weeks, minimum.

When you're in the Penn State locker room before a game and you hear a huge cheer suddenly go up in the concourse, that's because Spider tried to sneak out the door to get something from the sidelines, but the fans and the lettermen saw him and gave him a spontaneous ovation. When the lettermen return, their first stop is the BRAD "SPIDER" CALDWELL equipment room, according to the plaque outside the door. When the coach's son, seven-year-old Michael O'Brien, was riding in the van with his mom one day, he said, "Everyone in the football building is nice. But Spider is the nicest."

I have yet to meet anyone who disagrees with Master O'Brien's assessment. But in the spring of 2012, when the Sandusky scandal was consuming everything, for the first time in his twenty-nine years at Penn State, Caldwell started asking himself, "Do I really want to keep doing this? This isn't the Penn State I knew."

After O'Brien told him and Diehl how important they were to Penn State, and Caldwell watched the seniors that off-season not only stay but step it up, Caldwell knew he wanted to stick it out at least one more year to see this team through.

But his resolve, like everyone else's, had to be tested after the Lions' painful 17–16 loss to Virginia, their worst start in a decade. When I arrived in State College the day after, I fully expected to see cracks running through their foundation. That was the national pundits' prediction, convinced Penn State football was on the verge of crumbling, right on schedule—and arguably by the NCAA's design.

But, contrary to the forecasts, the Penn Staters were not giving up. At Wednesday's Quarterback Club, they planned for 290 people, but 350 showed up. In a normal season, 0-2 would have sent fans jumping off the bandwagon. In 2012, it caused more to jump on. Likewise, the coaches, staffers, and players weren't running for the exits, or even eyeing them, after a particularly tough loss.

I found Spider, "Captain Kirk," and their interns folding the first of eight hundred towels that week—just a small sample of the forty thousand towels Caldwell has folded in his career. Caldwell admitted that when Ficken missed the final kick against Virginia, "It was just a kick in the gut.

"But it's coming," he said. "We'll get there. The attitude has been good. Really, it's been amazing. None of the usual rumblings after a loss like that: 'I'm sick of this!' 'This is crap!' And you always get some whispering after losses, people pointing fingers—it's human nature—but not this time. We've been through so much together that no one's pointing fingers. I've heard *not one word of that*, and after a game like that, that's a first in all my years here.

"We're hungry. They're dying for it, but we can handle this and move on. Something positive is gonna happen.

"We know it's gotta happen."

"We have a very big game," O'Brien said, standing in the center of the team-room stage, hands on his hips. "We need this to get back on track. Once we get *one*—this one!—we'll be rolling. But we have to get that first one.

"We have to."

At the team dinner that night, quarterback Matt McGloin said, "I think we're playing well at times. But something always happens, and we get screwed up. We just have to string it together."

He adjusted the ice pack on his elbow—something you see a lot of at training tables once the season starts. Probably a dozen players were sporting similar packs, wrapped to their shoulders and hips and knees.

"I took one hit right here, on my funny bone," McGloin said, pointing. "Some three-hundred-pound guy."

"He wasn't three hundred pounds, because that would be my guy," Stankiewitch said, sticking a cube of steak, dripping with A.1. sauce, into his mouth, then pointing his fork at McGloin. "*My* guy didn't get to you."

"Okay, okay," McGloin said, wincing a bit while readjusting the pack. "A six-six D-end did. Hurt just as much. Then another guy hit it again, same place. Not sure if the bone's chipped or it's just a ligament. I came back in—and at that point you don't pay too much attention to it—and threw for two touchdowns, 197 yards, and no interceptions. But we came up short."

No matter what players or coaches tell you, they almost always know their stats, down to the penny. But in Penn State's case, it was not a cliché to say the players felt their many good individual performances in the Virginia game—including a great fake punt and four takeaways—were wiped out by the big stat: 0 and 2.

"The plane ride home—it's kind of to the point where you're so frustrated, you can't say anything," McGloin said. "What did we do wrong? Am *I* doing something wrong? You have to question yourself. Then you pull everything together, you talk it over, and you keep fighting. And that's why this senior class stuck it out.

"We've dealt with so much adversity in the past ten months, being 0 and 2 shouldn't faze us."

"We don't *like* it," Stank clarified.

"Exactly—we don't *like* it," McGloin said, "but it will make us work harder, stick together, and do our jobs."

In the meantime, out in LA, Silas Redd ran for almost 200 yards for USC that weekend, and Justin Brown was starting a promising career year as a wide receiver at Oklahoma, while kicker Anthony Fera missed the first four Texas games with a groin injury. But all three were winning games and enjoying life without the stigma, the judgments, and the endless e-mails the Penn State players had to face every day.

Back in Happy Valley, wide receiver Shawney Kersey and kicker Matt Marcincin dropped off the team, though—thanks to the NCAA's sanctions—they could keep their scholarships, and if they screwed up in school, it would count against the team's average, which could cost the Lions still more scholarships.

If the folks who ran the NCAA had set out to design an experiment to prove the student-athletes' commitment to their school and their studies was greater than their need for glory on the gridiron, it's hard to imagine they could have done a better job than what they'd created for Penn State's players that fall.

During a practice two weeks earlier, offensive line coach Mac McWhorter told his players, "We're looking at film for Ohio for their twist percentage." That is, how often they employed a certain defensive strategy. "On third down and seven-to-eleven yards, they twisted 49 times out of 361."

Offensive guard Miles Dieffenbach turned to John Urschel and asked, "Ursch—what percentage is that?"

Urschel looked down for just a moment, came up, and said, "About . . . 13.6 percent. But you should check my math."

With whom, exactly?

Every team has its academic stars, but only Penn State has John Urschel. As a redshirt junior, Urschel was in his fourth year at Penn State. He had already earned his bachelor's degree in mathematics, so three of his four math classes were PhD-level courses, including Math 551: Numerical Solutions to Ordinary Differential Equations, and Math 597-B: Discrete Differential Geometry and Applications.

You get the idea.

"Tuesdays and Thursdays are the easy days," he told me, giving me false hope. It was ten thirty on a Thursday morning. While we waited for Math 597-B to open its doors, he told me how he got there.

Urschel's mother is an attorney, and his dad played football at the University of Alberta while attending medical school. He turned down the Canadian Football League to become a surgeon. After he retired, he went on to earn a master's in economics, then another in mathematics, then another in industrial engineering, "just for fun," John said.

When John was in kindergarten, the principal called his mother for a conference. "My mom loves to tell people this story—*loves* to," John said.

"We need to talk to you about John," the principal said. Urschel's mother, Venita Parker, was naturally a little nervous, but it only got worse when they explained why.

"They thought I was mentally challenged—retarded," John said. "They said, 'He's not interacting in class, he's not playing with others, he's not even looking at us or paying attention.'"

"No," Ms. Parker insisted, "my son is not mentally challenged."

They were equally insistent that he was. They planned to hold him back a year and put him in a class for slow learners.

His mother wouldn't budge, finally demanding that they give her son an IQ test. They did—and young John got every single math question right. The principal issued no apology. Ms. Parker moved her son to a different school, where he excelled.

Football, however, didn't come as easily. "I don't really have any doubts about my math talents," he said. "But I *work* at football."

The big schools weren't biting for a two-star defensive lineman out of Buffalo. By late December of Urschel's senior year, he thought he was headed to Princeton, and he was okay with that. But a month later, Penn State called, offering him the next-to-last scholarship available. He visited, he liked it, and he committed on the spot.

But the Monday after Urschel's weekend at State College, Stanford head coach Jim Harbaugh called him directly, inviting him to fly out to Palo Alto. Urschel thought about it—but not long. "I had committed to Penn State during my weekend here. I know a lot of guys would break it, but when you make a commitment, you make a commitment. You don't have much more than your word, you know?"

Besides, he realized, "They have good academics here, and it's paid for. I wanted to take that burden off my parents."

But Urschel's dilemma, strangely enough, wasn't over. After earning his bachelor's in the spring of 2012 as a redshirt sophomore, he faced a rare predicament. If he wanted to keep playing football, he had to go to grad school. No problem, for him. But the byzantine NCAA rules allow all graduate-school students to go anywhere they like and play immediately, without sitting out a year like normal transfer students.

So, Urschel's options opened up once more. He applied to Penn State, Stanford, and Northwestern. He then faced another twist: the programs he applied for—a master's in applied mathematics at Northwestern, and a master's in computational mathematics in engineering at Stanford—Penn State doesn't offer.

The temptation grew greater in the spring of 2012, when Stanford's math department offered Urschel an academic scholarship, something they rarely do for master's students, which was worth a cool $96,000 a year. "I could put thirty thousand dollars in my pocket, after tuition. I had a chance to be a math student, put away a little money, and play football for a good program."

He could also have avoided dealing with whatever sanctions the NCAA would give Penn State, and the grief that would surely go with it.

"It's funny how things work," he said. "When I got my second chance to go to Stanford, I wanted to stay. It feels different when you *decide* to stay."

This is the double-down Urschel and his Penn State teammates had to make. Like all Penn State football players before them, they enrolled knowing what would be expected of them, on and off the field. But after the sanctions hit, and the NCAA threw Penn State's door open for them to leave, they had a choice. They could bail out, avoid the hassles, and maybe get some of the extra stuff everyone was always talking about. Or they could stay, knowing that not only they would be expected to be clean, go to class, and graduate—just as before—but it would be *all* they would get out of the program. No title games, no bowl games, and lots of scrutiny from people they'd never met. Those who stayed would carry the team on their backs—including its rich history—and with it, a large chunk of the university itself.

In other words, Christmas would come only after the NCAA's Grinch had cleaned them out. Would it still feel like Christmas?

Urschel embraced his decision, and Penn State—public opinion be damned—just like his teammates had.

The NCAA, however, has not impressed Urschel as much. That spring, he had been asked by Penn State's world-renowned Professor Jinchao Xu to join him and his graduate assistant Xiaozhe Hu to compose a grant proposal, and Urschel eagerly accepted. "If the grant goes through," he said, "and in all likelihood it should, I would get paid in the high twenty thousands, or the low thirty thousands. But the NCAA is probably going to say no, I can't take the money. If and when the grant money actually comes in, I'm going to formally petition and see what they say."

But he was far too smart to assume logic would carry the day with the NCAA.

At ten thirty we walked into a small classroom that probably hadn't changed since the building was constructed in 1938, right down to the black chalkboards at the front of the class. The room barely fit fifteen people, thirteen of whom were Asian or Asian-American, all of whom wore glasses. The remaining two were John Urschel and yours truly. Once class started, I quickly discovered that fourteen of the fifteen people understood what the hell was going on.

You can guess who the fifteenth person was.

My life has given me the opportunity to feel stupid many, many times—but I can say, without equivocation, that I have never felt dumber than I did that day. Walking the streets of Taipei, Tokyo, or Thailand, staring at signs I couldn't possibly read, I felt more literate than I did in that class, staring at Professor Xu's incomprehensible squiggles, running endlessly across those boards.

Near the end of class, Professor Xu said something that must have been a whopper of a joke, because it made the entire class chuckle.

After class, Urschel explained it to me, more or less. "It was a 'determinant joke,'" he said—and really, who isn't a sucker for a good ol' determinant joke? "It usually includes complex sums involving cofactors, but when put in context in differential forms, it came out to a very simple equation. And that was the joke."

Get it?

I didn't, either.

Walking out together, on a beautiful day, Urschel said to Professor Xu, "The last few classes were very abstract, so it was good to see some concrete, real-world examples."

For the first time all day, I could not stifle my laughter—even if it was at my own expense.

Urschel bid Professor Xu good afternoon and continued across the quad. "Penn State has been really good to me," Urschel said, clearly satisfied with his decision. Given everything the university had already gone through in 2012—from Paterno's passing to Sandusky's trial to the NCAA sanctions and now an 0-2 start—that was saying a lot.

If the NCAA was, in fact, setting up an obstacle course to test the faith of the Penn State players like Job himself, Urschel's conclusion might constitute the gold standard for student-athlete testimonials.

He still believed in the student-athlete ideal—and not because of the NCAA, but in spite of it.

Probably no critique of the NCAA was more withering and garnered more attention than the cover story Pulitzer Prize winner Taylor Branch wrote for the *Atlantic* monthly in the fall of 2011.

In his piece, titled "The Shame of College Sports," Branch laid out the case against NCAA control of college athletics. He started with an anecdote from a 2001 gathering of the Knight Commission on Intercollegiate Athletics, which had been formed in 1991 to save college sports from being swallowed by the money it was generating.

Sonny Vaccaro, a sports-marketing executive who had made a name for himself setting up lucrative sponsorships between Nike, Adidas, and Reebok and the top college athletic programs, addressed an august body of former college presidents and NCAA and USOC directors.

"I'm not hiding," he told them. "We want to put our materials on the bodies of your athletes, and the best way to do that is to buy your school. Or buy your coach."

"Why," Penn State president-emeritus Bryce Jordan asked, with thinly veiled contempt, "should a university be an advertising medium for your industry?"

"They shouldn't, sir," Vaccaro said, with a smile. "You sold your souls, and you're going to continue selling them. You can be very moral and righteous in asking me that question, sir, but there's not one of you in this room that's going to turn down any of our money. You're going to take it. I can only offer it."

"Boy, the silence that fell in that room," former UNC system president William Friday told Branch. "I never will forget it."

Of course, it's not just the sneaker companies pouring millions into college athletic departments. Just about every major television network does, too, not to mention countless donors, sponsors, and bowl backers. Most of them get their money back, many times over, or they wouldn't write the checks in the first place. They make so much—the TV contract for March Madness alone has grown from $16.6 million a year to $770 million in just thirty years—they could still leave enough crumbs on the table for the SEC to gross more than a billion dollars a year in 2010, and the Big Ten to do so two years later.

Head football coaches at Division I public universities now average more than $2 million a year, an increase of 750 percent (adjusted for inflation) since 1984, which is about twenty times more than professors' salaries increased over the same period. In 2012, the highest-paid state employee in twenty-seven states was a football coach, and in thirteen it was a basketball coach. The number of states whose highest-paid public employee was a university president? Four. The explosion in CEO pay, and the rationales that go with it, would be a fair comparison.

As Branch writes, "When you combine so much money with such high, almost tribal, stakes—football boosters are famously rabid in their zeal to have their alma mater win—corruption is likely to follow."

The twist is that temptation has subsumed the enforcers, too, transforming the NCAA from mere sheriffs to saloonkeepers, too.

If you can't guess which of those two jobs they're more passionate about, you need only heed Deep Throat's maxim: follow the money. Of the NCAA's $777 million budget, only 1 percent of it is earmarked for enforcement, which hardly serves as an endorsement for its priorities, or its efficacy in keeping college sports clean. It's all the more revealing to study just where the NCAA spends its relatively paltry resources for investigations.

When the *Detroit Free Press* ran a big, Sunday-front-page story six days before the 2009 season opener, alleging that the storied Michigan football program had blown past the limits for practice—sparking stories in almost every national media outlet—the NCAA spent fourteen months, and cost the university and former head coach Rich Rodriguez about a million dollars in legal fees, to determine that, yes, the Wolverines had unwittingly exceeded the NCAA rules by performing stretching exercises an average of fifteen minutes more per week than the rules allowed.

Yet when it came to the NCAA's attention that dozens of University of North Carolina football and basketball players had, from 2007 to 2011, availed themselves of either "aberrant" or "irregularly" taught courses, defined by ESPN.com as those which entailed "unauthorized grade changes, forged faculty signatures on grade rolls and limited or no class time," the NCAA did nothing. It argued that because a few of the students in those classes were not athletes, it was a university matter, not an NCAA one, and left the scandal for the university to clean up. The UNC chancellor decided it was a big enough blemish to warrant stepping down, even though he had had nothing to do with it.

If ensuring that athletes are bona fide students is not part of the central mission of the NCAA, from its very inception in 1905, you have to wonder what that mission might be. But there was little coverage or outrage over the UNC academic-fraud case, so the NCAA paid little price for ignoring it.

Likewise, the NCAA also refrained from making any judgments on the Baylor basketball case in which one player killed his teammate and the head coach lied about it and the Virginia lacrosse case in which one player killed his girlfriend, a member of the women's team. In both cases, the NCAA suffered no public outcry for its inaction.

When the NCAA does go after someone, as Branch pointed out, it typically focuses its "public censure on powerless scapegoats." Not the athletic directors or the head coaches—whose millions can buy teams of topflight lawyers—but the assistant coaches, the low-ranking administrators, the poorly paid tutors, and the players.

That's when you realize: the NCAA is no longer an enforcement agency, but a marketing company. Once you grasp that, everything the NCAA does—and doesn't do—suddenly makes sense, including its decision to all but dismantle the Penn State athletic program. As ghastly as Sandusky's crimes were, followed by the potential cover-up by university leaders who should surely have known better, these are serious criminal matters, better suited for the FBI than the NCAA. But the country was understandably apoplectic, at a time when criticism of college athletics and the NCAA was reaching a fever pitch.

The NCAA's decision to suspend its own convoluted due process—the same one that can investigate fifteen minutes of stretching for fourteen months—and rely entirely on a report Penn State itself had commissioned to come up with sweeping sanctions, in just nine days, went a long way toward quieting those critics, at least for a time.

Mike Mauti didn't have to read Taylor Branch's piece to understand the house of mirrors the NCAA had become, because he'd been living in it for almost a year.

"The people who run college football, the NCAA, they're so far removed, they have no idea what it's really like," he told me, as he sat on the couch under the window in Fitz's office, just off the weight room, before Thursday practice. "The bottom line is, you can't have that much power and that much money and look out for the best interest of the college athlete at the same time.

"If they were, they wouldn't be letting other coaches camp out on our campus to recruit our players. The sanctions had nothing to do with our program, with what we're doing here—but they're letting boosters at Miami pay for their players' abortions."

As of April 2013, the NCAA was in the middle of botching an investigation of reports that University of Miami alums provided gifts to athletes including "memorabilia, cash amounts both large and small, dinners, strip-club trips, prostitutes, and even an abortion."

"I know for a fact there are players getting paid," Mauti said. "Guys I know are getting tens of thousands of dollars a year. They give you credit cards until they run out. There's a lot of money involved. One hundred thousand dollars? Over the course of five years? Easily.

"I was offered money. They don't come out and say they're gonna give you this money. Players at other schools, they know the way things work. It's a different culture at other places. They go through the churches, and the [car] dealerships, and the good old hundred-dollar handshakes."

The NCAA's leaders seem entirely unable, unwilling, or both to pursue the stories those of us inside the industry hear constantly. They rarely act on such rumors until local reporters, working with a tiny fraction of the NCAA's resources, do the job for them and shame the NCAA enforcers into action. This familiar cycle does little to bolster our faith in the enterprise. (Mark Emmert and the NCAA declined to answer my questions.)

"They're not serious," Mauti said. "If you really wanted to discipline the teams that are doing the cheating, if they really wanted to cut out the corruption, they'd do their investigations and punish the schools that do that. It can't be that hard. Everyone knows who they are.

"But they have to *want* to go after the cheaters. It's not up to the public to determine that—it's for them. Otherwise, what is the NCAA for? What do they do?"

Joe Paterno surely had his blind spots, but how to run a clean program was not among them. He had trained the whole town—not just the team, but the *town*—so thoroughly in the oddities of the NCAA rulebook that to this day even the baristas at Starbucks know they can't give the players so much as a free latte. (I've witnessed this scene at the counter a few times—a must-see for cynics.)

The team's longtime adherence to even the silliest of NCAA rules—and there are plenty—is rightly a point of pride in Happy Valley. But for decades it was also a point of pride for the NCAA, which often held up Paterno's Penn State program as a shining example other schools should aspire to.

Again, if you view the NCAA as a marketing organization, this also makes sense. If they are occasionally forced to admit that some of their member schools' alumni pay for abortions in Coral Gables, that boosters give six-figure "gifts" to Cam Newton's father, and that USC's "friends" bought Reggie Bush's family a house, the NCAA needs at least some successful programs—Duke basketball, Notre Dame football—to wear white hats. Otherwise, we would have to conclude that nice guys can only finish last in big-time college sports. For decades, Penn State football stood as proof that the system could work.

Thus, when the Sandusky scandal broke, Penn State fell so far, and so publicly, the NCAA's leaders felt they had to do something big and dramatic to—as they say—"protect the brand." And so they did.

Yet, in spite of the kangaroo court that is the modern NCAA, I am struck by how many schools, coaches, and athletes play by the rules anyway and are quietly proud of it. Perhaps most surprising, despite everything that has happened in the past twelve months, the people in State College have continued to follow their strict orthodoxy, whether anyone cares or not.

Mauti returned to where he almost always returned: his teammates. "We've had great locker-room guys here, guys who knew what it was all about. Sean Lee. Devon Still. But this is the best locker room I've been around in my five years. Really."

He pointed to a phrase on the weight room wall, BURN THE SHIPS, coined by Spanish general Cortés, who, legend has it, told his men they could not go back the way they had come because they had ignited their boats. Retreat was not an option. They would conquer, or die trying.

"Burn the ships? Man, we already did that," Mauti said. "Sink or swim? We're not going to sink no matter what happens on Saturday, or any day.

"For our senior class, we know our days are numbered. We only have a certain number of these practices and games left."

Looking back on his decision to commit to Penn State in July of 2008, did he think he made the right decision?

"Oh, yeah," he said. "Oh, yeah."

Friday, September 14, 2012: O'Brien had two basic problems: the present, and the future.

Atop the first list was Saturday's game at home against Navy. But by Fridays, as Bo Schembechler used to say, "The hay is in the barn." The game plan had been installed, the big practices were behind them, and they were down to fine-tuning. Every coach still worked to get an edge, but by the end of the week that edge was most likely to be found in executing fundamentals, not reinventing the wheel.

This realization left them a slice of time to look ahead to the most urgent item on the second list: recruiting. O'Brien opened the session by stating the obvious: to fill next year's roster, they had serious needs "up and down the line." But with only fifteen scholarships, they did not have the luxury of simply bolstering weak positions. Like Northwestern—though for different reasons—they would have to get creative.

"It's imperative we find good football players—especially in the situation we're in—wherever they play," O'Brien said. "And we need to crank up the walk-on program. It's an *honor* to be a walk-on player here. Maybe we can find a diamond in the rough."

He mentioned one such diamond in the rough he'd talked with the previous night, who had boiled his choices down to Harvard or Penn State. *"That's* the kind of guy we're looking for."

O'Brien's plan was two-pronged: compete for the Academic All-Americans like John Urschel, the kind Harvard, Stanford, and Northwestern recruited; and get the best players in the region who grew up dreaming of playing for Penn State, guys like Pittsburgh native Mike Farrell, and then try to find talented walk-ons like Matt McGloin and develop them. O'Brien no longer regarded battling Alabama and Ohio State for Florida's five-star recruits an efficient use of their limited resources.

"I know you guys have connections in Georgia and Florida and Texas," O'Brien said to his assistants, "and that's great—but we need to focus on the kids nearby. Two thousand players have signed D-I scholarships within six or seven hours of here. A lot of top teams get good players from our area. We've got to make sure we get the bulk of our roster from our backyard.

"You look at Zordich, from Youngstown. Football is important there. They live it and they breathe it. Those are the guys we've got to get."

O'Brien's to-do list for the present and the future overlapped on Saturday, when they had scheduled recruits to see Penn State's game against Navy. A win would help their cause on both fronts.

"If we win the coin toss, we'll take the ball," O'Brien said, returning to the game plan. "We're going to take our chances. We're going to keep doing what we're doing, playing our asses off, but we are the better team. We have better football players than Navy. There is no question about it.

"We've *got* to win this one Saturday," he said, for the hundredth time that week.

• • •

The roller coaster of energy the coaches and the players must ride every Saturday bottomed out once they walked into the library-quiet locker room, having to kill the Hour of Death before they could run out the tunnel.

"We just need to get a lead," O'Brien said to Ted Roof, explaining why he wanted to take the ball first. On defense, O'Brien added, "They can run, but they can't pass. Let's make 'em pass, get 'em out of the triple option," the offense Navy used to great effect.

Then, to everyone else in the room, and to no one at all: "We just need a win. I don't care if it's six to three. Just give us a win."

"Any win," Coach Mac agreed, "is a good win."

During warm-ups, a big cheer went up, then another. What could they possibly be cheering about during warm-ups? Kicker Sam Ficken, who went 1 for 5 at Virginia, made his first warm-up kick—then his second. That's all it took.

O'Brien was all for staying calm under pressure, but he was smart enough to recognize the odds had shifted. He told his coaches and his offense they would go for it on everything but "fourth and ridiculous"—or even better, not need to kick at all.

After warm-ups, O'Brien walked into the players' room on his way to the coaches' room and told the players at least three times they needed "laserlike focus" and said "Do your job!" at least four times. "Focus on every play, all day!"

Mac McWhorter followed up with "There is a *huge* difference between just hustling, and *straining* on every play! That's what we need."

Some teams might have felt more pressure before a bowl game—but not this one.

Jordan Hill, the usually quiet defensive lineman, had a towel on his head, stewing. Then he jumped up and walked through the locker room. "Both sides of the ball. We're going to *work* today, y'all! We're going to *work*—all day, every play! You heard me! And when we come back in here, we're gonna have a party!"

Penn State won the coin toss, and as O'Brien promised, they made the unconventional decision to take the ball first.

Starting on his own 28-yard line, McGloin went to work, finding Garry

Gilliam in the flats to get out to the 40—which also got the hungry crowd going and allowed the players to take a breath.

After McGloin ran for 7 to the 49, setting up a third and one, O'Brien called for the quarterback sneak. They had gone over this simple play in great detail all week, breaking down film of Tom Brady doing it again and again. "Look it up," O'Brien had told McGloin. "In twelve years in the NFL, Tom Brady has not failed once on a quarterback sneak. Not once."

McGloin took the snap and—just like Brady—staggered his back foot, waited one beat, got his pads as low as he could, and drove forward right behind his center. He got his 2 yards, and a first down.

With a new set of downs, McGloin pumped, freezing defenders in place, then launched a 45-yard bomb to Robinson on the left side, who had blown so far past the coverage, he had to wait for McGloin's pass and was tackled at the 14. On second down, on a play-action fake, McGloin rolled to his right, stopped, then passed to true-freshman tight end Jesse James, a carpenter's son from Pittsburgh. Touchdown.

Navy then called a time-out—possibly to ice Ficken. His extra-point attempt was weak, but it made it over the crossbar—enough for a big cheer. Penn State, 7–0.

Penn State's defense—driven by the highly motivated duo of Mike Mauti and Jordan Hill—stuffed the Midshipmen in short order, giving the ball back to McGloin, who faked to the right, turned left, and then, smooth as silk, flew another long pass to Robinson at the 20, who cut right, lost his man, and glided into the end zone for the score. With 6:40 left in the first quarter, Penn State led 14–0.

No one on the sidelines or in the stands looked terribly relaxed, however. They knew their problem wasn't getting the lead, but holding it. When Navy marched down to Penn State's 5-yard line, their fears seemed justified. But on third down, Penn State blitzed, forcing Navy quarterback Trey Miller to toss one up in the air, which Gerald Hodges easily intercepted.

McGloin took advantage, leading his team on another long drive, capped by a floater over the middle for an easy touchdown. After Ficken's point-after attempt went wide right, however, O'Brien knew he would not be attempting many 40-yard field goals anytime soon.

Taking a 20–0 lead into halftime would have pleased another team, but not this one. "One thing's for sure," Roof said to his fellow coaches, "this thing ain't over!"

"We gave up only three points our first two halves, and we lost 'em both," Coach John Butler added. "We haven't won a second half yet."

When O'Brien addressed the offense, he told them, "We've been in this position the first two games, and we didn't finish the deal. *Finish the deal today! Finish the deal today!*"

After O'Brien's chalk-talk, the veteran Gerald Hodges said to rookie Jesse James, "You got yourself a nice little touchdown there, eh?" James just nodded and grinned, but Hodges already knew James would remember that moment the rest of his life. Even with all the weight on them, at times the Penn State players could still just be players.

O'Brien addressed the team before going out. "Defense: Keep running around and getting after them like I told you. They can't handle you. Offense: Keep moving the chains. Now get in here. Finish on three.

"One-two-three *finish!*"

Penn State had to pay for getting the ball first, and Navy seemed determined to make the price high. The Midshipmen started on their 34 and soon faced a fourth and 1 on their own 43. Showing admirable guts, Navy went for it, ran the triple option—and got 17. Penn State kept the pressure on Miller and came within a whisker of sack after sack, but Miller almost always got free to make the play. But on fourth and 16, from Penn State's 35, Penn State's blitz forced Miller to throw it away.

With McGloin's confidence growing before the crowd's eyes, he led his offense down to Navy's 25-yard line, then tossed a pass over the middle. Tipped! But right into the hands of Robinson, for another touchdown—the negative of the play against Ohio that had turned that game around. Luck was finally going Penn State's way.

Up 27–0 in the third quarter, even the Lions thought they had the game in hand, and the happy chants started.

"*Bill O-Bri-en!*"

The band played, "Heyyyyyyy, hey, baby! I wanna know, oh, oh—if you'll be my girl," to which the students inevitably added, "Just for the night!" For the first time in almost a year, Penn Staters could enjoy the simple, goofy fun of a college football game.

Ahead 34–7 in the fourth quarter, O'Brien sent in the backups—hoping they would be encouraged not to transfer—while the sun set between the press box and the end-zone balcony. It had been a near-perfect day.

The ticker-tape scoreboard flashed a few results from around the league. The Big Ten was running through its patsies that weekend, winning ten of twelve games. Indiana lost to Ball State, 41–39, which didn't count for much, but tenth-ranked Michigan State was upset by nineteenth-ranked Notre Dame, which did. Northwestern beat Boston College, 22–13, while Ohio State had to fight off an unranked Cal team at home, 35–28, suggesting the Buckeyes' dream of a perfect season was probably delusional.

The ticker reported Penn State's attendance at ninety-eight thousand. This would have brought heartbreak to the Michigan crowd, which had never dipped below one hundred thousand since 1975. But the Lions' six-year streak had already been broken at the opening game of the 2011 season, months *before* Sandusky was arrested, thanks to the overpricing of tickets through a misguided and ill-timed seat-license plan called the "Step Program." This had caused attendance to drop by about three thousand a game in 2010, when the program was introduced, again in 2011, and would again in 2012.

The ticker scrolled more news: "Penn State student-athlete graduation rate: 88 percent. D-I average is 80 percent," which drew one of the bigger cheers of the day.

When the game ended with a reassuring 34–7 outcome, the Lions joined the Midshipmen to sing the Navy alma mater, then ran to the other end zone to sing Penn State's song with their student section.

On the song's fourth and final verse, which eerily states, "May no act of ours bring shame," the students didn't mumble or skip it. They shouted it.

For some, it was a reminder. For others, a declaration.

In the locker room, the mood was less joy than deep relief. "Great job, men!" O'Brien said. "But that's just one! That's just one! Like I told you last night, we can get on a roll here if we stay sharp, stay hungry, and stay together!"

"*Yeah!*"

"The game ball," O'Brien said, "goes to Michael Zordich!"

In the coaches' room, Coach Mac bellowed, "Any win's a good win!" Then, almost immediately: "If it wasn't for the last drive, with Hodges going the wrong way, then I'd be happy."

Eight seconds is all it took to dispense with "any win is a good win."

They were back to normal.

CHAPTER 12

THE RICHEST RIVALRY

On the fourth Saturday of the 2012 season, September 22, the Michigan football team would take on Notre Dame for the fortieth time, in a rivalry that went back 125 years—the oldest in major college football.

Michigan and Notre Dame started going at it when they first met in 1887—by accident. The Michigan football team was traveling to Evanston to play Northwestern when they learned the "Purple" were backing out. So they got off the train at South Bend instead and literally taught those Notre Dame boys how to play football.

After the Wolverines won that first contest, 8–0, Notre Dame treated their guests to a hearty banquet. The mood was so friendly that Notre Dame president Thomas Walsh felt compelled to give a toast, assuring the Michigan players that a "cordial reception would always await them at Notre Dame."

Promises, promises.

No self-respecting Michigan or Notre Dame fan cannot repeat the history that follows. This synopsis is for the rest of you.

In 1895, representatives from seven schools—Michigan, Purdue, Illinois, Chicago, Northwestern, Wisconsin, and Minnesota—met at the Palmer House in Chicago to create what we now call the Big Ten. Because Notre Dame was still an embryonic team at a small, struggling school, no one considered inviting them to join.

Notre Dame's relationship with the Big Ten became more complicated after coach Fielding Yost arrived at Michigan, and a player named Knute Rockne enrolled at Notre Dame. In 1910, Yost accused Notre Dame of using ineligible players and cut the series off. On the various all-American teams that big-name coaches selected in 1913, only one coach left Rockne off his list—and that man was Fielding Yost.

Things got worse after Rockne became Notre Dame's coach in 1918, and then blew up beyond repair in 1923—at a track meet. Yes, a track meet. Rockne got into a shouting match with Yost over the distance between the hurdles Michigan had set up. Yost vowed then and there that Notre Dame—which had desperately been trying to get into the Big Ten—would never be admitted.

The animosity between these two giants ran at a fever pitch the rest of their lives. When a Spalding salesman tried to get Rockne to order new equipment, Rockne kept repeating that he was already overstocked with everything he needed. Finally, just before turning to go, the clever salesman sighed and said that was a shame, because Yost liked Spalding's new footballs so much he'd ordered three dozen.

"He did?" Rockne snapped. "Then I'll take three dozen and a half."

The teams ended the embargo during World War II, when they split two games, before cutting off the rivalry again. Another tradition that goes back almost as far as the rivalry is the mistrust between the teams' leaders. Like all great traditions, this one has outlived its originators. Michigan's Fritz Crisler didn't trust Notre Dame's Frank Leahy any more than Rockne trusted Yost. Pressed to explain why, Crisler cited this example: Whenever someone asked Leahy if he wanted a cigarette, he'd say yes, then just play with the thing without ever lighting it. "Why," Crisler asked, "doesn't he just say he doesn't smoke?"

This might sound like the silly stuff of family squabbles, and in the intimate realm of college football rivalries, that's exactly what they are.

What makes Notre Dame so different from other teams?

"I can't put my finger on it, but all I know is it's here," Father Theodore Hesburgh told me. He should know, having served as president of Notre Dame from 1952 to 1987, transforming Notre Dame from a middling college into a world-class university. "You've got to call it spirit. Notre Dame is both a mystery and a miracle."

But if you look at Notre Dame's history, its image, and its students, the mystery is a lot easier to understand.

Today, with more than 100,000 Catholics marrying non-Catholics each year, it's hard to appreciate how ostracized Catholics were until just a few decades ago. Before World War II, store signs reading IRISH NEED NOT APPLY were common. In areas where few blacks lived, Ku Klux Klan members frequently substituted the Irish and Italians as targets for their hatred—especially in Indiana, where the Klan flourished.

It did not matter to the Klan that Notre Dame has always made a point of welcoming anyone who cares to visit or attend the school. In 1842, when Reverend Edward Sorin founded Notre Dame, he admitted anyone who could pay even partial tuition, often in livestock, regardless of their race or religion.

This is the environment Knute Rockne entered when he took over the Notre Dame football program in 1918. To establish his team's legitimacy, Rockne badly wanted to join what is now the Big Ten. The conference schools, led by Yost, not only refused him, they banned member schools from playing Notre Dame.

The reasons were complicated. Many resented Rockne's habit of bending eligibility rules, but many of them had bent the same rules before cleaning up their programs in the 1920s, Michigan included. At least some of the coaches—most notably U-M's Fielding Yost—despised Catholics, Rockne, and losing in equal measure, and playing Notre Dame meant facing all three. Rockne's all-time winning percentage of .881 remains the best mark in college football history.

That 1923 track meet gave Yost the opportunity he needed to blackball Notre Dame for good.

Unfortunately for the Big Ten, the ban worked.

Notre Dame's leaders initially cursed their independent status, but not for long.

"Independence has meant so much to us," the late Reverend Edmund Joyce, Notre Dame's athletic director for thirty-five years under Hesburgh, told me in 1997. Without being tied to a regional conference schedule, the Irish have been free to play teams all over the country. "That made us into the single national power with a national following."

That started with Rockne himself. No sports figure in modern times did a better job of making lemonade from the lemons he'd been handed than Rockne. Once Yost made it clear Notre Dame had no chance of joining the Big Ten while he was alive, Rockne didn't waste any time licking his wounds. Instead, he scheduled the best competition in the biggest stadiums in the largest cities—where most Catholics lived.

When the Irish came to town, the hard-luck Catholics got to see an unapologetically Catholic university dominate that most red-blooded of American games, football. What Joe Louis and Jackie Robinson did for African Americans, Notre Dame did for Catholics. So many Catholics listened to Notre Dame games on the radio, you could walk down the street in the Catholic section of any big city and not miss a play.

He also scheduled games in Yankee Stadium—in front of the national media—and in Los Angeles, in front of Hollywood hotshots.

And that's why Notre Dame didn't shrink without the Big Ten, but grew into the only college team with a national following.

Well, that, and hundreds and hundreds of victories.

As the football team's fortunes rose, so did the school's reputation. Reverend Joyce was right: the team's independence allowed it to become the nation's only squad with a national following.

But it took President Hesburgh to figure out how to transfer Notre Dame's success on the field to success in the classroom. What started out as a podunk private school that would accept live cattle for tuition is now among the most respected universities in the world.

While Notre Dame's academic reputation was steadily rising, the reputation of its football team—which made it all possible—was steadily falling. The Irish earned at least one national title every decade from the twenties to the eighties—eleven total—but not another since 1988.

But there is good news for Notre Dame: in 2012, *U.S. News & World Report* ranked Notre Dame the seventeenth best university in the country—a higher ranking than the football team had enjoyed in years.

Coach Rockne must have been spinning—but Father Ted was surely thrilled.

For the next thirty-five years, arguably the sport's two most legendary programs, situated just three hours apart, did not play a single game—but once again, Notre Dame seemed to fare pretty well without the Wolverines, winning six national titles during that span.

At a banquet in the late sixties, Notre Dame athletic director Moose Krause leaned over to his Michigan counterpart, Don Canham, and said, "Don, Michigan and Notre Dame should be playing football."

They were the two winningest teams in the game's history, they both had earned reputations for doing it the right way, and they were only three hours apart. Canham couldn't argue against the logic of it.

After a few years of touchy negotiations, they relaunched the rivalry in 1978, and it was an immediate hit. The games were so good *Sports Illustrated* put the rivalry on the cover four times in a decade, plus four features—each time eclipsing the NFL's opening weekend, and tennis's U.S. Open.

The rivalry has everything college football fans love: in addition to history and tension, it boasts classic uniforms and stadiums, and unequaled parity. The night before the rivalry restarted, Moose Krause said, "When we look back twenty-five years from today, we will probably see that Michigan won half of the games and Notre Dame won half of the games."

Going into the 2012 rematch, since Krause made his prediction, Michigan had won fourteen, and Notre Dame thirteen, with one tie. Guess Mr. Krause knew something.

For most of the past thirty-four years, the game held a special place at the beginning of the season, giving Michigan a perfect symmetry of rivals: Notre Dame to start, Michigan State in the middle, and Ohio State at the end. But the Notre Dame rivalry might be the most interesting: it is Michigan's oldest; it is Michigan's only real rival outside the Big Ten; and it's the one game that's guaranteed to attract national attention every year, even when both teams are down. For years, it also kicked off college football nationwide and gave even casual fans a marker of the seasons: when Michigan played Notre Dame, fall had begun.

On his Facebook page, *Wolverine* writer Andy Reid boiled down our love of college rivalries quite efficiently.

"GO TEAM! BEAT RIVAL!

"Rival's fans are rude and ill-informed, and their coach is morally ambiguous. And don't even get me started on the relatively poor physical appearance of Rival's female students. Or our team's historical dominance of Rival. Yeesh."

Reid could have added that Rival's graduates make less money and often find themselves working for alums from your school—probably due to Rival's appallingly low admissions standards. Or, if you prefer, you can take the other side, pointing out what heartless, money-grubbing snobs Rival's fans are, fostering an insufferable arrogance that makes beating them so sweet.

But even while reveling in their differences, college football fans have far more in common than not—though they'd never admit it. They speak the same language, value the same history (though they might tell it a little differently), and follow the same rituals. They even love their opponents' customs—particularly if they can make fun of them.

Because sports columnists and pundits often follow college football on Saturdays and pro football on Sundays, they tend to lump them together as the minor league and major league of the same sport. But college football fans do not. They lump their alma mater's teams together—football, basketball, hockey, and more—and are happy when any of them beats their rival's counterparts.

In 2005, former Michigan athletic director Bill Martin commissioned a professionally conducted survey, which revealed that Michigan football season-ticket holders are doggedly loyal, with slightly more than half of them holding their seats for more than two decades. They are about 50 percent more likely to buy Michigan *basketball* season tickets than season tickets for *any professional team*. Only 9 percent of Michigan season-ticket holders also bought season tickets to any professional team, and this survey was taken when Michigan basketball was down and the Detroit Red Wings and Pistons were just a few years away from their latest titles.

This tells us a basic truth: College football fans don't just love football. They love *college* football—the history, the traditions, the rituals, and the rivalries that surpass those of the pro game. They are attracted to the belief that it's based on ideals that go beyond the field, do not fade with time, and are passed down to the next generation. And that loyalty spans the spectrum of your school's teams. No Ohio State football fan is going to cheer for Michigan's basketball team. Ever.

With few exceptions, professional rivalries are passing fads based on personalities. The Magic-Bird battles of the eighties were legendary, but when the NBA tried to market the 2010 Lakers-Celtics Finals as a rematch, no one bought it. But when Alabama and Auburn get together, you don't need Joe Namath or Bo Jackson to make the fans care.

When you talk to college football fans, it doesn't take long to hear them say the same things: their "student-athletes" are better than your "student-athletes"—in every way. Their school is superior to your school, which their football program conveniently demonstrates. In other words, they care as much about the values as the victories. Rival fans prove this when their teams start losing and they invariably cite their unusually high academic and ethical standards as the reasons—something fans of losing NFL teams can't hide behind.

But how deep does their devotion go? Are they willing to put their money where their mouths are?

The players are constantly being tried, but they are not on trial. The fans are. They pay for the seat licenses and the cable bill and the alternative jerseys—not to mention the hotel rooms and the restaurant bills and bar tabs that keep college towns humming.

The entire enterprise of big-time college football is based on the assumption that the players will continue to play, and the fans will continue to pay. But this raises a question too few have stopped to ponder—one that the NCAA, the leagues, and the universities that play big-time sports should be asking: What would it take for fans to stop opening their wallets—obscene prices, eroding traditions, ridiculous league realignments, the end of treasured rivalries? Does the fans' irrational passion for their favorite college football teams have a limit—and if so, where is it?

I've come to view the fans as frogs sitting in a shallow pot of water, with the suits turning up the heat ever so slightly over a long period, until finally it's boiling, but the frogs just sit there, until it's too late.

But, it turns out, it's a myth: Even frogs are smart enough to eventually jump out of boiling water. Are we?

To find out, I was going to hop into the pot of water myself and see how hot the moneymakers could turn it up before I jumped.

It was also a fine excuse to realize one of my long-standing dreams: traveling in a monster recreational vehicle to a football game with a bunch of buddies. (Okay, I dream small.) The idea came to me just six days before the Michigan–Notre Dame game, so I had to work fast. My first calls went to friends who owned monster RVs, but one was in Canada and the other was married, so they were out.

I then enlisted Bob "Chili" Spence and Brian "Westy" Westrate, two bar buddies from our college days at Rick's American Café in Ann Arbor, then roped in Nick Standiford, a former hockey player and student of mine turned law student. Nick naturally had the least money, so we put him in charge of finding the RV.

Nick found a local operation that was willing to rent us a thirty-two-foot highway yacht that slept six to eight, with no charge for the generator, propane, insurance, and the first three hundred miles—with no special license required (or, apparently, background check on my driving record, which may or may not reveal an endless string of speeding tickets going back to high school). All of that for just $750.

Heck, divide that by five guys, and it came to $150 each for a three-day weekend, and even a horrid hotel within thirty minutes of Notre Dame would cost twice that. Okay, so food, gas, and parking would be a few bucks more, but so what? We couldn't afford *not* to do this!

But, by Wednesday, we still hadn't recruited anyone else—and at some point, it *is* too many dollars more. So, we either had to kill the dream or come up with Plan B, which we did: put the offer on Facebook and let our friends make their case for the remaining one or two spots.

I had absolutely no idea what to expect. Would my little contest elicit a flood of responses from witty and willing friends—or crickets?

The early answer was crickets, confirming the obvious: this bizarre little dream was not shared by sane people. I'd be driving my car to South Bend on the morning of the game, then turning right back around to save the two-night minimum at the Holiday Inn Express in Elkhart, Indiana ("The City with a Heart!"), which is forty minutes from the stadium in gameday traffic.

I had just set myself up for a major public face-plant.

But within the next few hours, I received over a hundred responses.

Rent it, and they will come.

My friends responded from Florida, New York, and Chicago. I heard from a friend of a friend in Mississippi: "Awesome! Ready to fill my gas tank up and head North!!!" And the best part was, he was dead serious.

I heard from teachers of friends, daughters of friends, and people I'd never met before—often pitching for their student, dad, or husband. I heard from Rod Payne, Michigan's all-American center in 1995, who had won a Super Bowl with the Baltimore Ravens in 2000, and from the mother of Steve Kampfer, who had just won the Stanley Cup with the Boston Bruins, offering to bring a replica of the cup.

"I am confident by Saturday night," I replied, "we would not know the difference. 'Big silver thing with beer in it? Yeah, that's Lord Stanley's. Drink up!'"

You say "road trip" and people just want to go. John Steinbeck captured the impulse in *Travels with Charley*, his account of circling the United States in a pickup with his dog:

"And then I saw what I was to see so many times on the journey—a look of longing. . . .

"'Don't you like it here?'

"'Sure it's all right, but I wish I could go.'

"'You don't even know where I'm going.'

"'I don't care, I'd like to go anywhere.'"

Even better if you have a fun destination and a cause to rally around— like a college football game.

Contestants in our Facebook derby mentioned road trips they had taken in the seventies, eighties, and nineties. For the Michigan crowd, this included trips to Notre Dame in 1978, when the rivalry resumed after thirty-five years; to Ohio State just about every even year, when they play in Columbus; and to Penn State in 1997, when Michigan, on their way to a national title, blew out the second-ranked Lions. One told of the trip he'd just made to Dallas, where he fed 138 Wolverines before the game against Alabama.

The desire to hop on board ran strong in these fans.

Out of this pile of entries emerged a few aces: Jim Carty, a former *Ann Arbor News* columnist turned attorney; his boss, Alan Harris, who thought he could get us free RV parking; and Tim Payne, aka the Rhino, a college friend who was famous for his ability to drink a beer at the speed of gravity, minus friction.

"One of the best days of my life," he wrote, "was the day I was declined admission to ND and thus attended U of M."

We had our band.

Nick and I drove to HW Motorhomes in Canton, Michigan, where we gave Dan White a $1,000 security deposit in exchange for the keys. When he asked where we were going—the voice of experience, no doubt—he lit up.

"Now *that* sounds like fun," he said.

When the RV guy—who's been on, heard about, or cleaned up after every kind of trip imaginable—envies your journey, you're onto something. Turned out he was a big Michigan State fan, who named his daughter Kelly so her full name described MSU's two official colors. "I much prefer the college game," he said. "The NFL, I can barely watch it. Just mercenaries. But the college kids, they mean it. It makes all the difference."

Our gang meant it, too. Westy loaded something called the Big Trunk of Mystery on the Magic Bus. I knew better than to ask.

Rhino asked me, "You got room for the coffin?"

"What's the coffin?"

"You'll find out."

I found out: it was a gleaming white Cooler of the Gods, measuring two feet by three feet by six feet. When I asked Rhino how many beers it could hold, he didn't hesitate. "Two hundred and twelve," he said. "The two hundred and thirteenth you have to put in your pocket. Because that's just too many."

The dream had become a reality. We were on the road, looking for adventure, and whatever came our way.

Friday night, we got the Magic Bus through a Taco Bell drive-through—$40—and found a chain bar, where we dropped another $100 or so and ran into Matt Cornicelli, brother of Joe, part of our Sunday-morning team on WTKA. Matt grew up in Ann Arbor, went to Notre Dame, then returned to U-M for medical school.

"This game is always special for me," he said. "For a lot of people—that's your family. Your ties go back generations. I think Notre Dame fans are more loyal. But, for me, because of my Ann Arbor roots, the last three years have been the *worst*. The. Absolute. Worst."

And for good reason: Michigan scored three consecutive last-minute comebacks over solid Notre Dame teams. The most dramatic was the 2011 clash, the first night game in Michigan history, when the Wolverines completed an unforgettable 28-point fourth quarter to win on the game's final play, a jump ball launched from Denard Robinson to Roy Roundtree in the corner of the end zone.

"After the night game last year," Cornicelli said, "I walked out of the stadium and collapsed. I knew Joe and my friends in med school were going to give me so much shit. We had the lead, and we knew we'd find some way to screw it up. And we did.

"I said, 'I give up.' And I lay on the sidewalk.

"After five or ten minutes, my fiancée had to say, 'It's not that bad. Get up. It's not worth lying on the sidewalk.'

"I got up. I had to.

"That game! I don't care if we go six and six the rest of the year. We *have* to win that game. If it happens again . . ."

It was a sentence Cornicelli could not finish.

We returned to the Magic Bus and scrambled for the best beds. Despite the Rhino snoring like, well, a rhinoceros, I had finally gotten to sleep when the Magic Bus started rocking, thanks to two security guards who wanted us to leave their lot. Westy and Chili woke up first, and drove us to a grocery store, where they dropped $300 to fill the Magic Bus with everything we'd need. But we soon realized we had not considered a couple big-ticket items—namely, tickets.

"No, seriously, do we have tickets?" Rhino asked repeatedly.

"No, dude, we don't," I replied repeatedly. "But it'll work out."

It turned out everyone already had a ticket, and I had a press pass, which left only poor Rhino out. We promised to find him one as game time approached.

Another sizable expense we hadn't considered: $300 to park an RV anywhere near Notre Dame Stadium.

On Saturday morning, Westy and Chili set up our canopy, with mountains of food, beverages, foam fingers, and, naturally, a skull-and-spine-shaped beer bong. Westy pinned his U-M–themed baggy boxers to the corner of the tent as a flag, and the party was on.

Westy opened up the Big Trunk of Mystery to reveal a pile of bizarre wigs and costumes, which were actually just horrible fashions from the seventies, such as a three-piece denim suit, inappropriate for all occasions. These guys might have taken it to the extremes, but really, they were just doing what everyone else already was—embracing the *college* in college football, and the opportunity to step back for a few hours into your school days, wear crazy clothes, play the old music, do the old dances, and forget for a little while that time has marched on.

Whether they knew it or not, the marketers of college football were selling something similar to the fountain of youth: a ticket to the past. That it required substantial suspension of disbelief, didn't last longer than an afternoon, and often resulted in a pounding headache didn't dull the appeal.

The water might be nearing the boiling point for us frogs, but at least it was our water, and we'd been swimming in it for generations.

"The thing that makes college football different from everything else," Jim Carty said, "is this: in theory, we all took the same classes as Denard Robinson. You don't have that in pro sports, that connection."

When we finally turned our attention to finding Rhino a ticket, we were in for a shock: $300, $400, or even $500 for a single seat. According to SeatGeek.com, the average price of a ticket for that game was $371, making it the nation's most expensive ticket of the year to date. At the end of the season, it would finish fourth, behind only Alabama-LSU ($566), Texas-Oklahoma ($463), and Alabama-Auburn ($406). Poor Michigan fans would find three more of their contests in the top ten—Ohio State, Alabama, and Michigan State—ranging from $356 to $301 respectively, making Michigan the nation's leader for big-ticket games.

And this brings us to a surprising finding. For a group of guys who would not think twice about dropping $750 for an RV, a few hundred for each fill-up, $300 for groceries and beer (and then more beer), and $300 for one day of parking—not to mention a bunch of ancillary expenses that added up pretty fast—when I asked them who would pony up that kind of money for a ticket to the game, not one of my six traveling partners said yes. They told me $200 was their limit, if not lower.

That included the Rhino, who said even if he did have a ticket, he would have sold it for that price and watched the game on our twenty-four-inch color TV in the RV. Which, it turned out, he did anyway, just without the black-market profits.

We were willing to engage in plenty of irrational behavior to follow our passion, but I had just discovered that these frogs had a jumping point.

About 3:00 p.m., I headed to the stadium. This wasn't the intimate scene Northwestern offered—you could see Notre Dame Stadium for miles, with tailgaters packing the acres around it—but it wasn't the hot, smooth sea of pavement Jerry World presented, either.

I passed hundreds of RVs and thousands of revelers, including a few dozen hovering around the coolest RV I'd ever seen, painted like the famed Michigan football helmet. Its owners, Tom and Jackie Anderson, are both dentists, living in Ludington, Michigan, in the northwest corner of the Lower Peninsula.

"I was in the navy in the late eighties," he told me, wearing a classic block-M baseball hat—he kept his actual wolverine carcass hat on the bus—and a blue sweater, while swirling a beer. "I saw a bus on the side of the road, near the Great Lakes naval base in Illinois, and I thought, 'One day, I'll have a bus like that to tailgate in.'

"So, six years ago, when I saw this old Greyhound on eBay, I knew that was it. I bought it and started to convert it."

"It's always a work in progress," Jackie said, but it looked pretty finished to an outsider, with a tap protruding from its side, and a three-foot-tall bobble-head Bo standing sentry. Inside, it's set up like a rock-and-roll star's tour bus, with a bonus seat from Michigan's ninety-nine-year-old Hill Auditorium. He has three flat-screen TVs, a table from the long-defunct campus bar Pretzel Bell, and autographs on the walls from Gary Moeller, John Beilein, Red Berenson, and Brady Hoke—plus a horn that he got from Amtrak, which is technically against the law.

"The RV is okay for sleeping," he said, "but it's built for tailgating! We wanted to make a gathering place."

Judging by the happy crowd partying around his bus, he had clearly succeeded. For the honor of hosting the best party in the lot each Saturday, however, it cost them about $1,500 a week.

"We've done it for so long," he said. "We don't plan on doing anything else on football Saturdays."

"Because you're an alum," Jackie said, "it's part of who you are. A family thing. It's my mom, who's seventy-two. It's my kids. I don't think I'd sit in the freezing cold every week if it wasn't family."

With game time fast approaching, I had to keep moving—which meant passing a fan's gigantic Notre Dame helmet, big enough to stand up inside; a recording of Kid Rock singing "'Sweet Home Alabama' alllll summer long"; and mixed parties with Michigan and Notre Dame fans, even "mixed couples," if you will. In the parking lot, hundreds of flags flew high to help friends find their tailgates, but also to identify loyalties. The ND banner always flew below the Stars and Stripes, but above the national flags of Ireland, Italy, and Poland.

I passed a live band that one tailgater had hired, playing a friendly mix of reggae on acoustic instruments. I asked the lead guitarist, "Are you playing for beer, or money?"

"A little of both!" he said, and went back to his song.

It was hard to say which team had more on the line in that game. The Irish were still undefeated, though they had barely snuck by Purdue, 20–17, in the final seconds. Then they had a big win over tenth-ranked Michigan State the previous weekend, which bumped Notre Dame to eleventh. It also catapulted captain Manti Te'o onto the cover of *Sports Illustrated*, which told Te'o's Gipper-like story of losing his beloved grandmother and girlfriend in the same week, before going out to make a season-high 12 tackles against the Spartans.

For Notre Dame backers, that was enough. They were already whispering they might have their twelfth national title in their sights, and their eighth Heisman Trophy winner in Manti Te'o.

On the other side, a preseason eighth-ranked team and its own Heisman candidate, Denard Robinson, were both one game away from knocking themselves out of consideration for national titles or awards.

The previous weekend, Michigan beat up on the University of Massachusetts, 63–13. Okay, U-Mass was pretty bad. But the Wolverines had done exactly what they were supposed to do that game, and done it well.

Still, as I wrote in my previous book, Michigan fans aren't happy unless they're not happy, so it was not surprising to hear fans complain about Robinson's performance in that game. Mind you, Denard ran for over 100 yards and a touchdown and passed for almost 300 yards and 3 touchdowns.

And that, to one caller, was the problem: "I'm sick and tired of living and dying with Denard!" In other words, Robinson was too good for that fan's taste.

This only proved my theory: the two toughest jobs in the state of Michigan are goalie for the Detroit Red Wings and quarterback for the Michigan Wolverines. You can never do enough.

This was Robinson's third season as Michigan's starting quarterback, and at some point during each of those seasons he'd been listed as a strong candidate for the Heisman Trophy. Still, some fans complained that he ran too much, that he didn't pass well enough, and he didn't beat enough of the big teams.

It didn't help matters that Michigan's second-year offensive coordinator, Al Borges, seemed uncertain how best to use Robinson, which often resulted in this thoroughbred being used as a plow horse. In fairness, Robinson didn't pick these coaches, and they hadn't picked him, preferring the drop-back passer in the Tom Brady mold.

But it was not true that Robinson had a weak arm. I've seen him, goofing around after practice, drop to one knee on the goal line and launch the ball sixty-five yards. And when the coaches let him roll out of the pocket, which is what he was recruited to do, his accuracy and touch increased dramatically.

But all these points obscured a far bigger one: how lucky Michigan fans, students, and alumni were to count Denard Robinson as one of their own.

When other schools offered him money and cars and girls and even tuition for his sister, he decided instead to go to Michigan, where he was offered a scholarship, a chance to compete, cold weather, and long, expensive flights for him and his parents. He took it.

Robinson backed up Tate Forcier their freshmen year, 2009. But the following spring, Robinson outworked Forcier to become the starting quarterback.

Since then, Robinson had broken just about every Michigan record for quarterbacks, a batch of Big Ten marks, and a few national records, too—and he still had ten or eleven games to go.

Robinson probably wouldn't have gotten into Michigan without football, but he was making the most of it. He went to class every day. He studied every night. He never drank, but he bowled every week. He didn't just quote his parents—"Denard, they can take football away from you, but they can't take your education!"—he believed it. And he would graduate on time.

He had the chance that night to finish a great chapter of his legacy, with a third straight big game against Notre Dame—the kind that would test Matt Cornicelli's faith.

The program, the pregame ceremonies, and the scoreboard all made a big deal out of the 125th anniversary of Notre Dame football—and with it, the 125th year of this rivalry.

At 6:41, a military plane boomed over head—shortly after Notre Dame athletic director Jack Swarbrick approached Michigan's Dave Brandon on the sideline and handed him a letter. Brandon slipped it into his coat pocket, unopened. Few saw that, of course, and fewer probably noted it—but a few days later, everyone in that stadium would understand its significance.

When the Dropkick Murphys' signature song, "I'm Shipping Up to Boston," blasted through the speakers, everyone stood up. The fight everybody here had waited a year to see was finally about to start.

But if this was a battle between two heavyweights, it looked like their best days were behind them. Despite the calm, dry, warm weather, the teams traded turnovers as if they were being paid to give the game away.

With little over five minutes left in the first quarter, on third and 8 from his own 14-yard line, Robinson connected on a pass to former backup quarterback Devin Gardner—marking the first reception for either team.

It seemed to spark Robinson, who hit 5 of 6 passes on that drive for 59 yards, then added a 15-yard run to give the Wolverines first and goal from Notre Dame's 10-yard line. Instead of calling for another Robinson pass, or even a run—which he did better than any other quarterback in the country—offensive coordinator Al Borges called for him to hand off to five-foot-six tailback Vincent Smith, who rolled to the right, then cocked his arm to throw the second pass of his college career.

It was a strange enough plan to begin with, but the idea looked even worse after two Notre Dame defenders rushed him, forcing Smith to throw wide just to avoid them—right into the hands of Notre Dame's Nicky Baratti.

What confidence Robinson had mustered seemed to slip away. With the coaches apparently advising Robinson to pass first and run second, he ended Michigan's next four possessions with interceptions, followed by a fumble.

If there's one thing opposing teams feared, it was Robinson's fast feet. If there's one place they wanted to see those feet, it was stuck in the grass in the middle of the pocket while he looked downfield.

For this, the former sophomore Big Ten MVP was blamed. But as Einstein said, "If you judge a fish by its ability to climb a tree, it will live its whole life believing it is stupid." Robinson was born to run, not stand, so seeing him stuck in the pocket was probably as big a relief for opposing coaches as it was maddening for Michigan fans.

Notre Dame converted two of those turnovers into 10 points, and that's how the first half ended, 10–0. If national viewers suspected Michigan and Notre Dame of relying too heavily on their lofty traditions before this game, the first half would not have gone far in convincing them otherwise.

Our friend Rhino, back in the Magic Bus, fell asleep through the second quarter, while saving a cool $370.

You can't go far in Notre Dame's press box, however, without running into that tradition, starting with a long row of framed *Sports Illustrated* covers that led up to legends like 1987 Heisman Trophy winner Tim Brown, who was sitting in the press box with his young son. His NFL career with the Oakland Raiders was almost as impressive, with nine Pro Bowl selections, leaving him on the edge of induction to the NFL Hall of Fame.

But when I asked which team he liked playing for most, he didn't hesitate.

"The college experience is just hard to duplicate," he said, in his typically precise manner. "Playing at Notre Dame for me was so special. You're playing for the Blue and Gold, all the tradition—Rockne, Gipp, the Four Horsemen, the Echoes. Where else can you find that?

"I picked Notre Dame. All my teammates picked Notre Dame—and for probably all of us, that was our first choice."

He contrasted that with the NFL draft, which is just that: they pick you, and you go. Brown tried to dissuade certain teams, and while he was happy to play for the Raiders, it was not the same as Notre Dame.

"The NFL is a business, man! There, I focused on putting food on the table. Mama needs a new purse, and baby needs new shoes! The NFL is just a different mind-set. It was more about going to work and respecting the game."

When I asked him which experience he'd like to live again, he said, "Oh, college! Playing here at Notre Dame, and being a student here, meant so much to me.

"I will never forget the last day I was here, the day after my graduation. I was sitting in my apartment, by myself. And I remember thinking, 'I do not want to leave this place. I do not want to move on.'"

On his last day in the NFL? "I did not have that feeling!" he said with a laugh. "I was ready to move on. I was *eager* to move on! What's next?!

"There is nothing like playing college football—and just about everyone who played in the NFL will tell you that."

In the second half, it didn't look as if anyone on the field that day except Manti Te'o, who already had two interceptions, would ever get the chance to compare the two. It was only the fourth week of the season—a season in which I'd already seen 0-2 Penn State host 0-1 Navy—and this was by far the worst football I'd witnessed.

But despite the Wolverines' woes, they were behind only 13–3 late in the game when they got the ball back on their own 30-yard line. This was the moment Irish fans had come to dread—thanks to three straight years of dramatic, last-minute Michigan comebacks, the last two engineered by the magician who'd just got the ball: Robinson.

One of those Irish fans, Matt Cornicelli, watched with bated breath as Robinson rediscovered the same rhythm he had lost after Smith's interception, hitting four passes on four straight snaps for 51 yards to Notre Dame's 24-yard line, then running to the 7.

Michigan still had four minutes left, and all three of its time-outs— plenty of time to tear out Irish hearts once more. If you polled all the people in the stadium at that moment, a majority would probably have predicted that was exactly what was going to happen—again.

College football fans take their losses hard because they take them personally. All the tradition and history and hoopla lead up to this moment, and only this moment. There is no home-and-home rematch, no playoff game to point to, no chance for these teams to wipe the slate clean. College football makes you wait an entire year and come back with a new team to get a chance at revenge, and the wins and the losses go in columns that have been kept by six generations.

It's every bit as all-or-nothing as electoral politics, but far more brutal. If that sounds like hyperbole, ask yourself: Would Matt Cornicelli lie on the sidewalk in agony for ten minutes if his presidential candidate lost that November? Would anyone?

This was the heart-in-throat moment everyone had come for.

But when the Wolverines needed it most, their offense broke down again. Michigan had to settle for a field goal, for a 13–6 margin with 3:27 left.

Whatever hope Michigan had, it evaporated when its defense gave up three straight first downs, allowing Notre Dame to set up for every coach's favorite play: the victory formation, when the quarterback takes a knee, the benches empty, and the game is over.

At least one Cornicelli would not be lying on the sidewalk that night.

We reporters ran down the stairs from the press box to the field. Chris Balas, who writes for the *Wolverine*, said, "It's going to be unbearable," referring to his readers' predictable despair over Michigan's 2-2 record. "It's going to be, 'Everyone sucks,' all over again."

For the Irish, however, the celebration had already started—and showed no signs of stopping. Walking outside the stadium, I heard something that sounded like water rushing through Hoover Dam. When I turned back, I realized it was the fans—but how did they make that noise? It came from a spot in the concourse where fans from four directions converge: from the stadium, from the left and the right of the concourse, and from down the huge staircase, ten people across—while yelling from the balcony halfway down and from every other direction.

They yelled for the hell of it—and each time someone yelled, it inspired someone else to yell, too. Yelling begot more yelling, until you could hear them yelling from this spot halfway around the outside of the stadium.

"*Undefeated! Undefeated!*" a diminutive coed screamed.

If this didn't wake up the Echoes, nothing would.

On the drive home the next morning we tallied our expenses, divided six ways. For each man on the trip, it looked like this:

RV rental—$125
Gas—$100
Parking—$50
Food—$150
Drink—$100
Tickets—free, this time
Stories to tell our friends—priceless

We'd spent over $500 each that weekend—and none of us had purchased a ticket, which would have added another $350 or so. But we had no regrets, and before the Magic Bus had crossed the Michigan state line, we had already begun planning our next road trip for 2013.

• • •

The week before the 2012 Michigan game, Notre Dame had joined the suddenly active Atlantic Coast Conference, which was gobbling up Big East members at the same time it was trying to keep other conferences from doing the same to its schools. The move would give Notre Dame's other teams, especially basketball, a promotion from their membership in the Big East, which was rapidly falling apart.

The ACC was so eager to lure Notre Dame, it let the Irish remain independent in football, while the Irish agreed to play five ACC football teams a year. Both parties would earn bigger paychecks. But some observers immediately recognized that Notre Dame's decision could threaten its rivalry with Michigan, though probably no one expected it to happen so fast.

While we were driving home that Sunday afternoon, Dave Brandon pulled the letter out of his coat pocket that Swarbrick, a former law partner and Internet CEO who had never worked in an athletic department before Notre Dame hired him in 2008, had handed him right before Saturday's kickoff. That's when he learned that, as their agreement allowed, Notre Dame was ending one of the greatest rivalries in sports, canceling their games from 2015 through 2017, with no future dates scheduled. By informing Michigan minutes before the kickoff, Notre Dame could count the 2012 game as one of the three the agreement required they play after either side informed the other it planned to break the rivalry off, giving the Irish two remaining home games to Michigan's one. All of it was all legal—and none of it was well handled.

In fairness to Swarbrick, if Brandon—who had a similarly strong business background, with no prior experience working in athletics or education—determined that it was in Michigan's financial self-interest to cut the rivalry off, he almost certainly would have done the same thing, and in the same manner. Neither party seemed overly concerned with goodwill.

For decades, Notre Dame's leaders had wisely traded on their football success to become a national academic power. Mission accomplished, they discovered they were now free to sell that same tradition for money.

So much for Father Walsh's promise to the Wolverines that a "cordial reception would always await them at Notre Dame." The tradition of distrust between the schools' leaders, at least, was alive and well.

Notre Dame would replace Michigan with teams like Wake Forest and Clemson, while Michigan would replace Notre Dame with—well, probably teams like Wake Forest and Clemson, if not Central Michigan, Western Michigan, and Eastern Michigan.

But within that equation, Notre Dame was making a couple of bets: first, that the athletes, who had come to Notre Dame partly to play teams like Michigan, wouldn't raise a peep, and Swarbrick was surely right about that; and second, that all those RVs that Michigan fans drove to South Bend could readily be replaced by RVs driven by fans from Virginia or North Carolina or Georgia Tech.

The players don't have any real choices. But the fans do, and whether they're willing to keep shelling out a thousand bucks for a football weekend—or will start spending their Saturdays going to soccer games or mowing their lawns—remains to be seen.

The NFL was created as a business to make money, but the college game was supposed to have higher ideals. That was getting harder to argue. With each year, each season, and each decision, it was becoming increasingly apparent that the people who love college football have less and less in common with the people who are running it.

CHAPTER 13

A TOAST TO OPEN HEARTS

Friday afternoon, September 28, 2012: Hang around the Midwest long enough and you'll hear just about every Big Ten fan say, "I love fall!" It makes a lot of sense when you experience our famously frigid, gray winters, and our surprisingly steamy summers—and even more sense when you see how Big Ten football provides three months of relief from it all.

In Big Ten towns, life begins anew not in spring, but in fall—the blooming flowers be damned. Come May, the school year has just ended and everyone's leaving.

But in the fall, the students and professors return right on schedule, concerts and shows pack the calendar again, and the whole cycle starts over. If you're lucky enough to follow the football season campus by campus, you'll also notice the founders of Big Ten schools had a knack for planting their campuses on the hilliest, most beautiful land around, usually with a river running through them.

You often hear people in Big Ten country say, on a cool, crisp fall day, with the colors just starting to turn, "Perfect football weather." For us, it's a recognized climatological condition.

Yes, we know football started between Rutgers and Princeton, and was advanced by Yale. But we think it was born here, on these sprawling campuses among the cornfields, the perfect setting for the perfect game.

It was on just such a perfect fall Friday I approached the world's most verdant campus. You know you've arrived when Grand River Avenue crosses M.A.C. Avenue—which you would pronounce "MAC" Avenue, because you're not from here. Locals spell it out as "M-A-C," a nod to its origins: Michigan Agricultural College.

That was the school's given name in 1855, the same year taxpayers gave birth to Pennsylvania Farmers High School, now known as Penn State. The two schools were the "First of the Land Grant Colleges," commemorated by a three-cent stamp on their centennial. Both received their land from their states, predating the Morrill Act, which President Lincoln signed into law in 1862. The idea was simple, and utterly American: after most states had established their flagship universities—almost always called the University of Blank, à la the universities of Oklahoma, Iowa, and Michigan—to provide a liberal arts education to future professors, doctors, and lawyers, the government created over a hundred landgrant schools to give more practical training in agriculture, science, and engineering. Some of these schools started life as their state's Agricultural College, or A&M (for agricultural and mechanical), but today are usually called Blank State University, as in Oklahoma State, Iowa State, and, yes, Michigan State.

Every state that is home to this familiar pair of schools—U of Blank, and Blank State U—including Washington and Oregon, Utah and Colorado, Kansas and Oklahoma, and Mississippi and Florida, just to name a few—breeds uncannily similar stereotypes: the U of Blank students are the rich, elitist bookworms, more likely to come from out of state and more likely to leave when they graduate, while the Blank State students are the local, friendlier, fun-loving partyers going to a "cow college" and more likely to stay in-state when they finish.

These stereotypes don't have that much to do with contemporary state universities. Just about any class you want to take at University of Blank, you can take at Blank State University, taught by similarly skilled professors (or more likely lecturers or grad students these days), surrounded by similarly motivated classmates. The number of students at University of Blank who don't drink on Thursday nights is probably equal to the number of students at Blank State University who milk cows. But the very fact that these once disparate schools are becoming increasingly similar makes fans of both schools work that much harder to keep the old distinctions alive.

This is what Sigmund Freud called the "narcissism of minor differences," which he described as "the phenomenon that it is precisely communities with adjoining territories, and related to each other in other ways as well, who are engaged in constant feuds and ridiculing each other" and exhibit extreme "sensitiveness . . . to just these details of differentiation."

The good doctor Freud probably wasn't analyzing American college football, but no one has ever explained the nature of these rivalries better. It matters that contemporary students can still hurl the same insults their fathers and grandfathers did. And it matters that college football teams, from Maine to Hawaii, still draw most of their players from their region. Those players grew up on those stereotypes, and picked their schools accordingly.

These labels have lasted less because they're still valid than because they're persistently perpetuated by both sides, and have been for generations. If you dropped a Michigan State student in Ann Arbor, or vice versa, no one would know he's from the Other School—until he expressed his opinions on his current location. The arguments and insults that would surely follow are ultimately all that matters. The differences may be small, but if both sides care about them that much, they're big enough to keep the school's identities separate.

The schism between Michigan and Michigan State runs a little deeper than most, with the first drops of bad blood between them falling before Michigan State even existed.

On the heels of Ireland's potato famine, America's education leaders realized they needed to treat agriculture as a science, one that could determine the most productive practices, and teach them to farmers. This created the rush of land-grant colleges—but where to put the state of Michigan's?

In Kim Clarke's great research on the subject, she unearthed a revelation that will prick the pride of the Wolverines: the university's first president fought fiercely to host the "cow college," arguing that the state's premier agricultural school should be under the auspices of the state's flagship university.

"O say, farmers of Michigan, that our great desire is to make the University useful to you and we are determined to do it," wrote President Henry Philip Tappan. "It is better to have one great institution than half a dozen abortions," he added, marking the first recorded insult from a Michigan man to the school that did not yet exist.

Michigan professor Alexander Winchell followed Tappan's plea by trying to overcome the objection that starting an agricultural school in Ann

Arbor would take longer than starting a new one in East Lansing. "Let us remember," he wrote, "the evils of delay are only of two years continuance, while the evils of an unfortunate location will be enduring."

And there is your second recorded insult.

When Michigan lost that battle, Winchell concluded the new school "cannot be more than a fifth-rate affair. . . . I cannot believe the best thing has been done."

And there's your third.

The Wolverines could wail all they liked. The folks at the new school quickly realized they were onto something good.

In 1925, Michigan Agricultural College changed its name to Michigan State College of Agricultural and Applied Science (MSC), and again in 1955 to Michigan State University of Agricultural and Applied Science. Finally, in 1964, it became simply Michigan State University— reflecting the expansion of its curriculum and the growth of its research.

I didn't know it then, but the next day I would meet the man whose vision made Michigan State what it is today.

As you wind along Grand River Avenue, Michigan State's campus emerges on your right. By the time you hit M.A.C. Avenue, you can already see this is no "unfortunate location," but quite simply one of the world's prettiest campuses. Built on some ten thousand acres, with the Red Cedar River cutting through the middle, it's a picture of rich green grass and thick, sturdy trees surrounding redbrick buildings, with enough space among them to enjoy all three.

The other side of Grand River is lined with the shoe stores and sandwich shops, the bookstores and the bars typical of every Big Ten town— and that's where I was headed.

I walked over to Harper's and took a seat on their wraparound patio, surrounded by grad students, alums, and parents in for the weekend, many already wearing their kelly green and white, or scarlet and gray. Life was good.

It was a perfect fall Friday in the Big Ten. Football weather.

I was soon joined by Nick—yes, the U-M alum and MSU law student who hopped on the Magic Bus to South Bend. After finishing our pints of Bell's Two Hearted Ale—a Michigan thing—we headed off to a famed burger joint with the decidedly noncorporate name of Crunchy's, which is just about the last thing you want your burger to be. But according to Complex.com's City Guide, it's the sixth-best college bar in the country—and, worth noting, one of six Big Ten bars in the top thirteen. This is what we do.

Just to get in the place on a home football weekend you have to wait in a narrow alley with a single overhead light—and people do it, happily. When someone comes out, people waiting cheer and clap, because one of them gets to go in.

Inside, the darkness does not suggest a nightclub but a cozy cabin "Up North," with a fire going. The booth benches are surrounded by photos of famous sports scenes: Michigan State point guard Mateen Cleaves cutting down the nets after the 2000 NCAA basketball title game, and Steve Yzerman hoisting the Stanley Cup. Above the door to the kitchen, they've posted signs that say WE SERVE WOLVERINES—WELL DONE! and DIRECTIONS TO ANN ARBOR: SOUTH UNTIL YOU SMELL IT. EAST UNTIL YOU STEP IN IT. The dark-stained pine tables and walls have been carved and drawn on so many times, the layers look like Jackson Pollock artworks from his little-known "Wood Period."

We happened to run into an old high school friend of Nick's, Chris Pozza, who invited us to join his gang of grad students—a lucky break. In a packed house, we got to sit at the end of the long picnic bench in the middle, leading right up to the ten-foot stage at the front window. Beer arrived in two-and-a-half-gallon mop buckets. We scooped the beer out with pitchers, then passed them around while they dripped over everybody.

Crunchy's is the kind of classic campus joint that would never make it past a focus group—or its first year, if they opened it today. But it works because it's been working for so long. Generations of students, locals, and alums have come to love it and pass on its traditions. It feels good to know you're doing the same things thousands before you have done.

Only in a college burger joint do local customs like two-and-a-half-gallon mop buckets full of beer, pictures of Bubba Smith and Magic Johnson, and discussions of how a Michigan State professor invented hybrid corn to feed the world come together at the same table, and it all makes sense. I didn't even blink when they started with the karaoke, which was less *American Idol* than campfire sing-along, a sort of Cornfield Kabuki Theater: everyone knew who would get up, sing what and when, and we all joined in.

"Michigan State is so unpretentious," Nick said. "I love this place!"

"You don't find anything like this anywhere near Ann Arbor," Pozza added.

The real differences between the schools, their students, and their fans might be minuscule, but in their minds, they are many, and major. Both sides cling to that belief because their identities depend on it. They all might cheer for the Detroit Lions—and given their usual failure, let's underscore *might*—but even when it's in their rational self-interest for their in-state rival to beat someone else, they just can't cheer for the Other Guys to win.

This is not a small point. The entire multibillion-dollar industry of college athletics is built on the assumption that these identities are so powerful that those who embrace them will spend irrationally on everything from licensed jerseys to seat licenses to toilet seats claiming that *they*, in fact, are "Number One!" These two schools offer the state's residents traditions that cannot be manufactured, but the people making the most money from them aren't the ones who built them.

Whether the marketers understand this or not, the future of college football depends partly on how well those traditions are protected by the businesspeople who have bought them.

Saturday morning, walking across the beautiful school grounds, you see something else that makes the Spartans' tailgate experience unique: it is the only school I've visited where the fans tailgate on the main campus itself, in the shadows of the classroom buildings students filled the day before.

Granted, some schools make it easier than others. At Oxford University in England, wrought-iron gates keep visitors out of its quads. You are not welcome. At Michigan, they recently put a half-million-dollar fence with turnstile revolving doors around Elbel Field, which used to be open to everyone, earning it the nickname "the Practice Beach." But most of the campus—outside of athletics, notably—is still open to all, and that's the rule in the Big Ten, and the nation: almost all American universities encourage visitors to wander about their campus and imagine—or remember—what it's like to be a student there.

This casual fun, I believe, has been one of the secrets of the tremendous growth of the greatest public universities the world has ever seen, and for a simple reason: people rarely support institutions they haven't seen. They are far more likely to support what they know. Picnicking on the grounds makes kids more likely to go to the university, and it makes their parents more willing to pay for it.

But no one does it better than Michigan State.

As I approached the Red Cedar River, which the TV networks have used for years for their cutaway shot, I came across the John A. Hannah Administration Building, and in front, a bronze statue of the man, his coat over his arm, forever walking across the campus. While I scribbled down the quotes inscribed on Hannah's statue, a small group of fans walked by.

"Who's that guy?" one of them asked.

"I think he used to be the president," another said.

Well, yeah—but that's like saying Albert Einstein used to be a college professor. It doesn't quite do the man justice.

Every school has its giants, of course, but those schools born around the Civil War needed bigger men than most to carve these campuses out of forests, then build them to rival the world's greatest institutions—and do it all in mere decades.

The list of icons includes the University of Chicago's President William Rainey Harper and Amos Alonzo Stagg, who put their new school on the map; Michigan's James B. Angell and Fielding Yost, who made Michigan what it is today; Notre Dame's Knute Rockne, who made Notre Dame famous, and Father Ted Hesburgh, who made it great.

At Michigan State, that man is John A. Hannah.

Born in Grand Rapids in 1902, he was a proud graduate of Michigan Agricultural College in 1923, earning a degree in poultry science. He rose to become the school's vice president, whose job description included serving as the state's secretary of agriculture. He married the president's daughter, then succeeded him as president in 1941.

Hannah's timing was unusually good, with the G.I. Bill opening the doors for 2.2 million returning veterans nationwide, and the state's auto industry entering its golden era, generating unprecedented wealth for the state's citizens, who dreamed bigger dreams for their children. Seemingly unrelatedly, the University of Chicago's football team dropped out of the Big Ten in 1939.

Hannah cleverly exploited all three opportunities. Back when state schools were funded by the state, Hannah knew he needed more help from Lansing, which had long favored the flagship university in Ann Arbor. So, while U-M's President Harlan Hatcher rolled up to the capital in a chauffeured Lincoln Town Car, the unassuming Hannah hopped in his pickup truck for the trip up Michigan Avenue to the statehouse — and got more money each time from his old friends in the legislature.

When Hannah gathered enough funds for a new dorm, he built a beautiful brick building with green trim, filled it with former GIs, then took their tuition and built the next dorm — and kept doing it, for decades. At the same time, he lobbied hard to take Chicago's place in the Big Ten, over the strenuous objections of Michigan's coach and athletic director Fritz Crisler, a proud Chicago alumnus who had played for Stagg.

In 1947, President Hannah fought back by hiring Clarence "Biggie" Munn, who had been Crisler's former captain at Minnesota, and his former assistant at Michigan. To gain stature, the next year Michigan State started an annual rivalry with Notre Dame, which was only too happy to help the upstart Spartans stick it to their mutual enemy.

When the Spartans finished both 1951 and 1952 as undefeated national champions, even the powerful Crisler could no longer justify keeping them out of the Big Ten. The Spartans enjoyed their greatest success during Hannah's last two decades, claiming four more national titles and a 14-4-2 record against the "Arrogant Asses" in Ann Arbor.

Hannah attended every Spartan football game, home and away, for "a ridiculous number of years," his daughter told me. *Ripley's Believe It or Not* even published a piece on his streak. He recognized the central role the Spartans' success played in raising the profile of the former cow college, which in turn helped attract more state funding, more skilled students, and more first-rate professors to East Lansing — following a familiar formula.

Hannah's strategy transformed the humble Michigan Agricultural College of just six thousand students into the forty-thousand-student Michigan State University, a major research center good enough to be admitted to the prestigious Association of American Universities — and he did it all in about two decades, arguably the fastest growth in the history of higher education.

Perhaps most impressive, what President Hannah built has endured, surviving Michigan's turbulent economy, the Big Three's troubles, and the Spartans' sporadic performance. In the forty-two years since Hannah retired, they have won only four Big Ten titles and no national crowns.

One side of the statue's base quotes President Hannah's speech to the National Conference on General Education, on November 3, 1961: "If educators are agreed on anything, it's that the fundamental purpose of education is to prepare young people to be good citizens."

The other side takes a line from his penultimate State of the University address, on February 12, 1968: "The university is an integral part of a social system that has given more opportunity, more freedom and more hope to more people than any other system."

President Hannah greatly increased all three through improved state funding, the G.I. Bill—and football.

Michigan State University would not be half of what it is without him.

Of course, football Saturdays also bring your foes to your campus, and I saw plenty of Buckeye backers among the Spartans. One group, all dressed in scarlet and gray, set up their chairs and tables in a clearing and were nice enough to invite this Wolverine to join them.

"Urban Meyer's been the best fit with his school since [Nick] Saban went to Alabama," said Brandon McCurry, twenty-eight, who now lives in Jacksonville. "He's a Buckeye through and through, born and bred. Cooper couldn't beat Michigan because he didn't understand the culture."

"Urban's whole mentality is speed, and national championships," added Rob Young, twenty-seven, from Findlay, Ohio ("Flag City, USA"), between beanbag tosses.

"And national recruiting," McCurry said.

"Tressel was more conservative," said Eric Corle, twenty-eight, from Grand Haven, Michigan. "Urban's more aggressive. We like that."

"Eleven and one is not good enough!" said Dana Chalupa, twenty-five, who's getting her PhD in sociology at Bowling Green. "It's not!"

When a sweet sociology graduate student tells you 11-1 is not good enough for Ohio State, you have just seen what pressure looks like. Year in and year out, no coach in the Big Ten has more pressure to win than Ohio State's—something Tressel, Cooper, and Earle Bruce could have told Meyer, and probably have. The tenures of Ohio State's last five coaches all ended in firings.

How did these fans explain the uncommon intensity Buckeye fans brought to their team? "The whole state is Buckeyes," Corle answered. "No split loyalties. And no pro teams in town." The NHL's Columbus Blue Jackets, obviously, didn't count.

"The last time the [Cleveland] Browns won the title [in 1964], Jim Brown was the star," McCurry said. "And the Bengals have never won it."

What did they make of the Big Ten's apparent demise, relative to the SEC?

"The Big Ten's the oldest conference in the country," McCurry said, "but the population in the Sun Belt is changing everything."

"Like recruiting," Young said. "Down there, you've already got the cream of the crop. Then you take the cream of the cream. And because they oversign recruits [an unethical but legal practice, analogous to over-booking flights], they get to keep it all."

"Academics in the SEC are not as important as they are in the Big Ten," McCurry said, then chuckled. "Except at Vandy. But what does that get them?"

I turned the conversation to the Michigan–Ohio State rivalry.

"Best rivalry in college football," Young said.

"In sports," Corle added.

"If you're not hated, you're doing something wrong," McCurry said.

"I'm looking forward to that," Young said. To what, exactly? "To being hated again. Like we were. But maybe even more, this time. If we keep winning this year, we're gonna be hated everywhere—and that's gonna be nice!"

Of the programs I researched, Ohio State makes the boldest bid for winning. Not at all costs: they graduated 74 percent of their players that spring—up from 63 percent just two years earlier—ahead of Michigan and every other Big Ten school but Northwestern and Penn State. But Meyer pledged to do better. Since his six Florida teams all finished in the top three in the SEC in both Academic Progress Rate (APR) and graduation rates, often trailing only Vanderbilt, and every senior on his

2008 national title team graduated, there was no reason to doubt he was serious about academics.

But the Buckeyes' recent past, and the comments from their president to their fans, suggest their priorities are not the same as Northwestern's — or Michigan's. Putting aside president Gordon Gee's unfortunate comment — "I'm just hopeful [Tressel] doesn't dismiss me!" — and Maurice Clarett's steady stream of damaging quotes, the hits still kept coming. Just a few days after my visit to East Lansing, Ohio State's third-string quarterback Cardale Jones tweeted a PR man's nightmare: "Why should we have to go to class when we came here to play FOOTBALL, we ain't come to play SCHOOL, classes are POINTLESS." You could argue that anyone whose grammar and punctuation were that bad and was not even a starter is exactly the kind of person who should take most advantage of the educational opportunities being offered, but that's a side point.

To be fair, when even twenty-five-year-old grad students declare that 11-1 is not good enough, everyone feels the pressure to win — from the president to the third-string quarterback. When the standard is an undefeated national championship season — not this year, even these fans conceded, but soon — it is obviously impossible for Meyer to surpass their expectations on the field.

But he could off the field, with higher graduation rates, and fewer negative stories. If he could do all that, he could strike a blow for college football itself. The best answer to "Everyone cheats" is "We don't — and we still beat you."

That, of course, would only earn the Buckeyes still more resentment around the league — which would please these fans immensely.

While we were out singing "500 Miles" with a hundred of our best friends at Crunchy's, Ohio State head coach Urban Meyer was sitting in his hotel room half an hour away, racking his brain for something to motivate his team. He wasn't searching for the usual pregame fodder about sticking together and playing their best. He needed something better, because he felt their challenge was bigger than just playing a tough Big Ten team.

"We were 4 and 0," he told me, "but we still weren't very good. And Michigan State had whacked us pretty bad the year before. We couldn't move the ball against them."

But Meyer's biggest problem wasn't a football problem, but a fundamental one: trust.

"The kids wouldn't let us coach them," he said. "Whenever you take over a new program, there's going to be pushback—but it had gone on long enough. They were still in the evaluation stage with us—and going into your fifth game, that's not good."

Zach Boren, the senior captain, "was actually one of the biggest offenders. It was always, 'Why are we doing this? We didn't do it this way before! We won games and went to the Rose Bowl!' You put in all the time and effort, and you start to get a little angry that they're not coming along."

So, the night before the Michigan State game, Meyer stewed in his hotel room, trying to come up with something to create a breakthrough and end the war of wills between the coaches and the players so they could join forces against their foe.

"I started thinking of the pageantry and the tradition of Ohio State football," he said, something he knew well from growing up in Ashtabula. "And that's when I came up with it. So I decided, at breakfast, I'd give a real impassioned speech."

The next morning, while tens of thousands of fans enjoyed their burgers and brats at their campus tailgates, Meyer tapped his glass, then stood up in the hotel banquet hall to address his team. "Ohio State's got a lot of great traditions," he told them. "The Victory Bell, the Buckeye Grove, the Senior Tackle. We've got all these great traditions—so why can't *we* start one?

"We need to come together. We need to be one. We could cut our fingers and sign our names in blood, but I don't think we can do that with the Internet," he said, getting a chuckle. "Might make some news.

"So let's make a toast to each other," he said, and lifted his glass of water, inviting them to do the same. "Let's start today. Open your hearts, and let us coach you. All in!"

They clinked their raised glasses and drank their baptismal water.

"This will go down in Ohio State tradition as one of the great moments."

It *could*, anyway.

"Whenever coaches do things like that," he told me, "it's risky. If it doesn't work, you're all of a sudden in a storm that you can't manage. You put it out there, and they don't take it, then you panic and start getting gimmicky. Secret handshakes, slogans on T-shirts, all that. And then you're fishing. You're lost.

"It only works if you win. When they asked Francis Schmidt in 1934 how he planned to beat Michigan, and he said, 'Michigan puts their pants on the same way we do—one leg at a time,' that's awesome. But if Francis Schmidt said that, and his players went out there and got their asses kicked, would they start giving out little gold pants?

"It only works if you win."

ESPN set up its *College GameDay* crew in East Lansing that day to showcase a classic Big Ten battle between fourteenth-ranked Ohio State, at 4-0, and twentieth-ranked Michigan State, at 3-1. The Spartans had lost to Notre Dame, but beaten a ranked Boise State team. Both teams had visions of a division title.

The stands were packed early—never a sure thing with the modern student population—and in full bloom with a student whiteout. But enough Buckeye fans were in the northeast corner and in the balcony to make some noise when the players gave them something to cheer about.

The Buckeyes brought their band, too, which they call "The Best Damn Band in the Land," or TBDBITL for short, and the moniker is more than bluster. They are damn good.

With a three-thirty kickoff, the view from the press box was worth taking in. When you look out through the back windows, away from the field, you see Munn Ice Arena, the Breslin Center for basketball and concerts, and in the distance the capitol dome five miles up Michigan Avenue—the trip Hannah made often in his pickup truck—all surrounded by green, green, and more green.

But the view out the other side, past the field, is even better. MSU can't boast a golden dome, a mountain range, or a Great Lake, but looking out on the brick buildings and the thoughtful landscaping, with mature trees, open fields, and pathways cut artfully through all of it, it makes you appreciate what President Hannah had envisioned.

On the game's first possession, Buckeye quarterback Braxton Miller needed only eight plays, one third-down conversion, and less than three minutes to cover 75 yards for the game's first touchdown. It looked as if it could be a long day for the Spartans, but they stopped two Buckeye drives with an interception and a fumble recovery.

But it could have been a much better half for the Spartans, too. Their star tailback, Le'Veon Bell, had disappeared; first-year quarterback Andrew Maxwell's passes were off, and when they weren't, his receivers dropped them; and their kicker missed a 42-yard chance before halftime, so the Spartans went to the locker room down 7-3. For anyone but a Big Ten fan, that was probably reason enough to change the channel.

After the teams started the second half by swapping field goals, Maxwell and his receivers finally got in sync, connecting for a 29-yard touchdown that featured crafty moves and poor tackling. The scoreboard didn't ask questions: 13–10 Michigan State, with 4:49 left in the third quarter.

The Buckeyes had already survived a close battle against Cal at home, and the next week they couldn't shake University of Alabama–Birmingham until the five-minute mark. This was hardly a dominant Ohio State team, but the 2012 squad was nothing if not resilient.

But Urban Meyer carried a burden the rest of the Big Ten did not: if the league's only national-title-winning coach could not succeed at the league's only consistent national contender from the previous decade, the Big Ten was doomed. And if the team didn't vindicate Meyer's morning toast, he might be, too.

On just the fourth play of the Buckeyes' next possession, Braxton Miller fired a bomb down the right sideline, slipping it just past the defender's fingers into the hands of Devin Smith, who ran straight to the end zone for a 17–13 Ohio State lead.

But just as quickly as Miller had flashed his promise, he showed his inexperience. At the start of the fourth quarter, he got hit hard and apparently assumed he was down, so he spun the ball on the field—but the whistle hadn't blown, it was ruled a fumble, and the Spartans got the ball. Could they take advantage?

The Spartans' drive stalled at the Ohio State 31-yard line, forcing them to settle for a field goal to move within one point, 17–16, with 7:07 left.

It seemed like the right decision at the time, but a few minutes later Meyer's speech seemed to kick in. The Buckeyes started with the ball on their own 18 with 4:10 to kill. Meyer was in no mood to take chances passing the ball against a good defense, but he wasn't too eager to give the ball back to Le'Veon Bell, either.

"We had to move it, the hard way," Meyer told me. "It was our O-line against Michigan State's very good D-line, on national TV. We didn't do a lot of option. We just ran it straight up the gut. On a third-down play, we ran right over Reid Fragel—pure strength on strength. That's when you go 'Wow.'"

Quarterback Braxton Miller made a gesture many interpreted as the "Superman," when he pulled his fists apart on his chest, as though busting out the S on his shirt. He was actually communicating a very different message: "Open your heart," the point of Meyer's breakfast toast, "which is the opposite," Meyer said. "And that's what they did: they opened their hearts.

"It was not just *what* they did on the field, but *how*. They grew up, right then. Boys became men that day."

At the center of it was senior captain Zach Boren, whose blocking at fullback was crucial to that drive.

"We hadn't really played very well in any of our nonconference games," Boren told me. "It was time to get better, time to become a team. When Coach said, 'It's time to buy in,' we took that to heart. And that's what happened out there. The last four minutes of that game, that was something. We held the ball the entire time. Carlos Hyde was just chewing up yards, like there was nothing they could do."

"After the toast," linebacker Etienne Sabino told me, "we were going to do it for each other. It wasn't cocky, but it was confident. And from that point, our play just elevated from there. No doubt we were going to find a way to win."

After Ohio State's offense fought for three straight first downs, Meyer called for the victory formation, with the shade sliding over the field.

No one would have confused the game that day for the Patriots versus the Colts—or Alabama versus LSU, for that matter—but no one sitting in the stands or watching it on TV had any such expectations. They had come to see a big game between two Big Ten teams. While the Spartan fans were surely disappointed, everyone had gotten what they'd paid for: an all-out battle between two longtime foes who left everything on the field.

The postgame handshakes complete, Meyer ran with his players to the northeast corner, where the Buckeye fans gathered. Standing in the middle of the mob, surrounded by his players, he was beaming.

The drums and sousaphones belted out a few rock anthems, to which the fans, players, and coaches responded with rhythmic fist-pumping. The postgame routines are truly tribal, the modern equivalent of dancing around the fire after the kill. Then they put their arms around each other to sing "Carmen Ohio," the alma mater, with emphasis on "O-hi-o!" Running up the tunnel, Meyer leaped up to high-five a fan.

No one who has ever met Urban Meyer would ever call the man soft, or stupid. He knew his team needed a lot of work to compete at the national level. But he also knew that in college football, unlike every other sport, you almost never face any opponent twice, and just one loss can knock you out of the running for the national title or even the conference crown. Because one loss can be too many, one victory matters most in college football.

This game might have been a sloppy, simple, one-point victory over an average opponent—but the Buckeyes had won. The Spartans got nothing. So the Buckeyes, and only the Buckeyes, got to go home happy.

And their coach went home convinced, for the first time, that this was his team, and they were finally in it together.

At Michigan State, they host the visiting team's postgame press conference in a portable classroom parked near a loading ramp. To get there, you have to walk up the tunnel and past Ohio State's equipment truck, painted gray with white and black stripes at the top, with eleven gigantic, green BUCKEYE award stickers, and, in big, bold letters, THE PEOPLE. THE TRADITION. THE EXCELLENCE.

Waiting for Meyer to show up, all you could hear was the loud loading of the truck by the student managers: bang-bang-bang.

Meyer showed up with his son, wearing a Braxton Miller number 5 jersey, while his dad wore a relaxed, satisfied expression—the rarest of sights for a college football coach in season.

"This was my Big Ten baptism," Meyer said, after praising the Spartans. "It was a war—two sledgehammers going after each other. I know the Big Ten's taken some heat, but that was a great game.

"That ranks as one of [my] top wins," which was saying something. "This was fantastic. We're happy to be 5 and 0, with a chance to go 6 and 0."

After he finished, he stood against the fifteen-foot concrete wall that borders the loading area, with his right arm around his wife and his left arm around his son, to savor five minutes of peace.

Ohio State's Sports Information Director Jerry Emig brought a series of players down the ramp for the reporters, like chum to sharks. While they devoured their subjects, Meyer was able to walk out unnoticed with his son. He passed a table stacked with Styrofoam boxes of chicken tenders, an apple, and a banana, grabbed one for himself and one for his son, then walked up the ramp, where he was cheered by the Ohio State fans behind the ropes.

Behind him, his players—all dressed in shiny black sweats—grabbed boxes for themselves, then gave their parents hugs at the rope line. They could look forward to a satisfying four-hour ride home of cheerful talk and text messages.

"That was a big win for our program," he told me. "Big win."

"On Saturday, September twenty-ninth, 2012, at eleven twenty-two a.m., we became a team. And they proved it seven hours later.

"By the time we got on the buses, something had changed."

After the game, I walked back across the campus toward Grand River Avenue. Most of the tailgaters had packed and gone, but I saw a few hearty souls drinking beer, jawing, watching their generator-powered TVs, and even playing a friendly game of cornhole. A loss does not ruin the day for Spartans the way it does for Wolverines and Buckeyes, but their energy had taken a hit. They were no longer standing, but sitting in chairs in circles in the growing dusk.

The Red Cedar glowed. Walking over it, I could still hear loud talking and laughter and music thumping, but I couldn't see the people, gathering in hidden pockets scattered throughout the green paradise.

The gorgeous campus didn't seem to know its team had lost.

The Wolverines had the week off. They had finished the nonconference schedule at 2-2, which put them at the bottom of the Big Ten, but with plenty of company. Four other conference teams started league play at 2-2, four at 3-1, and three were a perfect 4-0: Ohio State, Northwestern, and Minnesota.

In the first week of Big Ten play, Nebraska won a thriller over Wisconsin, 30–27, to move to 4-1 and a No. 21 national ranking. That set up a showdown with the No. 12 ranked Buckeyes in Columbus the next weekend.

Northwestern took care of Indiana, 44–29, to remain undefeated at 5-0. The Wildcats were just one win off their total from 2011. They would sneak into the Top 25 at No. 24—another indication of the lack of respect the Wildcats typically receive. They would get their chance to make their point in Happy Valley, where the Wildcats hadn't won since 2004.

Just to make that game worthwhile, however, the Lions had some work to do. After their ignominious 0-2 start, most of the pundits had written them off, but the players didn't bail.

Their first Big Ten opponent, Illinois, entered the game with the same 2-2 record as the Lions, with bad losses against Arizona State and Louisiana Tech. The Illini were led by first-year head coach Tim Beckman—the man who flew eight coaches out to State College in late July to scoop up as many transfers as he could get. Despite the effort, he got exactly one: freshman Ryan Nowicki, a scout team offensive lineman. Beckman did, however, manage to become the focal point of the Penn State players' rage, which they intended to release in full when they visited Memorial Stadium on September 29.

"They were basically trying to break up our team," said Jordan Hill, who actually drove around Penn State's campus like a cowboy herding cattle when he heard Illinois's coaches were afoot. "And really, not only our team, but our brotherhood."

"I've never seen a locker room so intense, so on a mission," Spider Caldwell said, grinning. "I almost felt sorry for Illinois. I knew what was coming. And our guys did not disappoint!"

Mauti led the charge, getting a sack, forcing a fumble, and making two interceptions. One of them he returned 99 yards before getting tackled by their wide receiver on the 1-yard line.

Mauti—still overflowing with anger—stayed out for Penn State's punt team and launched himself downfield on a 60-yard sprint. The Illini sent a receiver to block Mauti, who launched the poor guy into next week, then blew up the returner. "There's no better feeling than that."

Well, maybe one.

Before the game, Mauti promised himself he would find Coach Beckman and personally tell him to fuck off. When Mauti finally caught eyes with him, however, he opted for a bit more discretion, spitting on the ground in front of him. That, and Mauti's sack, forced fumble, and two interceptions, he reasoned, "are the best fuck-yous available."

The players might not have realized it at the time, but the bigger statement made that day was for themselves: they were unified, they were not going to go quietly, they were going to fight back. Every day.

The plane ride home was happy and relaxed, but with No. 24 ranked, undefeated Northwestern coming to Penn State the next week, there wasn't much time to celebrate.

CHAPTER 14

INFERNO AT THE HORSESHOE

Friday Night, October 5, 2012: The night before No. 20 ranked Nebraska's nationally televised night game against undefeated Ohio State, the Buckeyes' biggest game to date, there was only one place to go: Plank's Café & Pizzeria, deep in Columbus's historic German Village, just south of downtown.

Open the old wooden door that reads PLANK'S 1939 and you enter a Buckeye fan's paradise: dark and warm, with low ceilings, wooden walls and pillars. You have to look hard to see the wood, though, because just about every flat surface is covered with framed, autographed photos of Woody Hayes, Jim Tressel, or Archie Griffin; the most extensive collection of college pennants I have ever seen; and dozens of personalized license plates nailed to the wall with stamps like USBUILT and IMABUKI.

I came for the beer, the pizza, and the ambience, but this being Plank's on a Friday night before a big game, it wasn't too surprising to run into some fellow ink-stained wretches: Kyle Rowland, who writes for the popular Buckeye blog Elevenwarriors.com, Jeff Svoboda, who writes for *Buckeye Sports Bulletin*, and a friend of theirs, Aaron Stollar, a former sports editor of *The Lantern*, Ohio State's student newspaper.

Stollar compared the previous week's Ohio State–Michigan State 17–16 slugfest to West Virginia's wide-open 70–63 win over Baylor, the highest-scoring game in Big 12 history, and concluded, "It looks like two different sports out there."

His snippet of stats pointed to a bigger issue: the Big Ten against the World, with the first round—Michigan-Alabama—going to the World in a landslide. Stollar further predicted college football would go the way of college baseball: that is to say, South, literally, a shift that was about to accelerate since Southern high schools had started exploiting seven-on-seven leagues and other loopholes to play year-round. This was not merely the boast of a Southerner, but a cold, hard look at the future from an Ohio State alum, speaking from the short side of the equation.

The bigger picture wasn't much brighter, with the gathering class-action lawsuits against the NCAA to compensate players for brain injuries, an issue that was causing many parents to prohibit their kids from playing the game in the first place.

"Will football soon be rugby, or bullfighting," Stollar asked, "just a niche sport that's too dangerous for 'civilized' Americans?" On his list of niche sports, he could have added horse racing, boxing, and IndyCar racing, whose popularity had diminished greatly over the decades—with all three downfalls triggered by greed.

It might seem like a strange question to ask while drinking beer in a shrine to the sport, but Stollar was actually going easy on college sports by leaving out Ed O'Bannon's lawsuit against the NCAA for selling the athletes' likenesses to EA Sports video games, among other things—just another death star whizzing toward Planet NCAA.

While we chatted away over jukebox standards, an older man kept scurrying from the bar to the tables. He was such a sight it was hard to focus on the conversation. He had white coconut hair, chomping on an unlit cigar at the end of his amusingly sinister smile—similar to the Joker's—and wore a white shirt, a green bow tie, green floral-print suspenders, green pants rolled up like plus fours, and white-and-green, horizontally striped socks. Predictably, a few patrons called him "the Leprechaun."

"I don't give a damn what I look like!" he barked, then cackled.

The man was no hired hand but Tommy Plank, grandson of Walter Sr., the bar's founder, and son of Walt Jr., who had passed it on to the next generation. The family has since opened two more bars in town.

Tommy often crashed on a couch in the upstairs office, and not just because he was so dedicated. He used to "pound a fifth of Jack Daniel's and a case of beer every day," according to Tom Montell, a regular patron and friend, who'd joined us. Having stopped cold turkey years ago, Plank rechanneled his energy to gardening, and he was so good at it, *Better Homes and Gardens* gave his backyard, "Enchanted Forest," a five-page photo spread.

Another surprise: Tommy used to play shortstop for Ohio State. "Good fielder," he said. "Couldn't hit a watermelon."

Plank initially came off as impatient and irascible, but if he liked you — and ultimately, he seemed to like most people — he became incredibly generous. After a friend and I talked to him for a while, he said, while dashing off to get something, "George! Make sure they get another beer. I know a hobo when I see one. And you two aren't hobos!"

"Walter Sr. had been the head of the Buckeye Boosters for years," George said, recounting the bar's history while pulling two complimentary mugs of Yuengling, "America's oldest brewery." "A lot of our regulars grew up in this neighborhood. This is where we came when we were in college, and where a lot of us met our wives.

"Then folks moved to the suburbs — Dublin, Upper Arlington, Bexley — but for all our big events, they come back here. Games, sure, but also birthdays, christenings, rehearsal dinners, weddings, graduations. And deaths. Hey, the family needs to have dinner between viewings. And we do a good wake.

"But never, *ever*, schedule your wedding for a fall Saturday. You're going to have a hundred pissed-off people packing the living room or the banquet hall's kitchen watching the game. You just don't *do* that!"

Buckeye fans also appreciate it if you don't have the poor taste to die on a game day, too.

At the bar, the talk returned to football, a subject Plank complains he hears too much about each fall, but we couldn't help ourselves.

"When Terrelle Pryor sold his gold pants, are you kidding me?" Montell asked indignantly. "The guys from the seventies said, 'He did *what*?!'"

After Pryor's blasphemy became public, Archie Griffin himself brought the players to his home to explain to them the value of Ohio State football tradition. You could argue, however, that if Pryor could sell a pair of tiny gold pants for $3,000, he didn't need the lesson. He knew better than anyone else exactly what Ohio State football tradition was worth. In that sense, he was doing exactly what the athletic directors, the league commissioners, and the NCAA were already doing — selling the fans' favorite traditions back to them. Of course, when Pryor did it, it wasn't considered smart business, but scandalous.

"Money can't buy you love," Montell's friend Lenny Smith added.

True, but it can help pay your mother's rent, which is why, Pryor told the media, he needed the money. It was a clever move for someone I hadn't heard a good word about in Franklin County, because who could go after a guy paying for his mom's rent?

There, in a nutshell, you have both the foundation of college football—the fan's unconditional love for tradition—and one of the battalions attacking it: players who resent businessmen exploiting their performance and the fans' devotion. (After all, someone was willing to pay $3,000 for that trinket.)

Money can also buy you facilities, and Ohio State's are "top-notch!" Montell said, and he was surely right about that. "And, hey, it's cold here in the winter!" he said, explaining the $19.5 million Ohio State had spent in 2007 to renovate the twenty-year-old Woody Hayes Athletic Center. "This is not USC. We *need* facilities! And if you need facilities, you should get the best. We are Ohio State!" he said, banging his mug on the counter for punctuation.

"Everyone hates us," Smith said. "But you gotta understand—we're not that bad!"

And they're not. They're not even that different—if you take out the 5 percent who seem to have been raised by wolves.

But, in a weird way, the Buckeyes were flattering themselves. Yes, the rest of the Big Ten hated them. And for the most part, the Buckeyes liked it that way. But given the Big Ten's two national titles since 1968, it's unlikely that the people at USC, Texas, or Alabama spend much time hating the Buckeyes, let alone Michigan or Penn State—or even thinking about them.

In fairness, however, the Buckeyes don't give those teams in the South and West much thought, either. They're too obsessed thinking about their beloved Buckeyes.

"At Ohio State hockey games," Michelle King told me over breakfast with her husband, both Michigan graduates now living in Columbus, "no matter who's playing, when they say, 'There is one minute remaining in the period,' the crowd yells, 'Michigan still sucks!'"

"Last spring," Kevin King said, "we went to a Division III basketball game in Bexley [just outside Columbus] to see a friend's kid play for Capital University. This was an important game for them, it was close, and they still stopped to yell, 'And Michigan still sucks!' And I swear—I *swear*—I saw the point guard mouth the words."

"That's when it hit me," Michelle said. "The point guard for a D-III basketball team loves his school less than *he hates Michigan*."

Across from us at our shared table, a smart-looking, thirty-one-year-old grad student named Andy Pfeiffer, wearing a long-sleeved, white T-shirt with OHIO STATE in small letters on the left, was reading the paper. He told us he was from Dublin, a posh suburb of Columbus, and had gone to Duke for undergrad. He was now getting his MBA at night at Ohio State.

"Duke and UNC, that's a good rivalry," he said. "But UNC's a good school, a nice place. There's respect between them. But Michigan . . . ?" He chuckled. "Let's just say there's less respect."

I had to follow up on Michelle's observation. "Would you say you love Ohio State more than you hate Michigan, or vice versa?"

"I love Ohio State more," he decided, but only after taking a few beats to think about it. "But you have to understand that, during the Cooper Era, we really built up a lot of anger." And less toward Cooper, apparently, than Michigan.

This, to me, was the beauty of a great rivalry: yes, the inevitable bad patch does generate bitterness, but it can actually be absolved by the next generation, by dragging your rival through an equally bad patch. Players who might have been four or five during the losing streak can erase the stains on the souls of those who came before.

Glory is transferable.

Because Pfeiffer seemed like an intelligent, reasonable person, I had to ask, "Why do you hate Michigan so much?"

He smiled, he chuckled, then he wiped the grin off his face, looked me dead in the eye, and said, "Because my dad raised me right."

I do believe he meant it.

Because the Nebraska–Ohio State game wouldn't start until 8:00 p.m., after our late breakfast we watched some football at the Kings' home. Michigan put away Purdue in the first quarter, 21–0, en route to a 44–13 stomping, to push the Wolverines to 3-2 overall. Most important to the staff and players, however, Michigan stood at 1-0 in the Big Ten, with a weak 2-4 Illinois team coming next. Their quest for a Big Ten title had just begun.

The Northwestern–Penn State game was far more compelling—even before they kicked off. The Wildcats' goal was to stop their four-year slide and prove, yet again, that they could play with the Big Boys. At 5-0, with three victories over BCS conference teams, they were making a strong case, but they still didn't get the kind of respect they deserved.

When I asked Northwestern's head coach, Pat Fitzgerald, "You're no longer everyone's favorite homecoming opponent, are you?" he said, "Oh, we still are. But now we'll ruin your homecoming."

Sure enough, Penn State had scheduled Northwestern for homecoming weekend. Could the Wildcats come through on Fitzgerald's promise and ruin the Lions' day?

Tough call. Penn State had won three straight to return to a respectable 3-2.

Only then were they willing to admit that "after those two losses, we were terrified that everything people said would happen to us—that our program would all fall apart—might come true," Zordich told me. "It was a possibility—and that's what kept us going."

"Short and sweet," Mauti said, "we knew we'd *better* win, or we'd look like the world's biggest blowhards. After saying all that stuff on ESPN, we had established ourselves as the spokesmen. If we're going to be up front when it's good, we'd have to get up there and represent when it's bad. That's a big double-edged sword."

Yes, they were riding a three-game winning streak, but they knew "those teams weren't the best teams," Zordich said. "We couldn't stop there and still make our point."

The Lions' oft-stated belief that if they could just win a few, they'd get on a roll, would be tested on the season's sixth Saturday. A loss to Northwestern, however, with Ohio State, Nebraska, and Wisconsin still on the docket, would almost certainly doom Penn State to an indifferent 6-6 season, or worse.

The fans of both teams would be watching intently—in person and on TV—but this was a players' game.

Former walk-on quarterback Matt McGloin entered the game leading the Big Ten in passing, and he looked good from the start, giving his team an early 10–0 lead. But Penn State dropped another punt—echoes of the opener against Ohio University. Kain Colter, who set Northwestern's school record of 704 total yards against Indiana the week before, quickly converted Penn State's mistake into a touchdown, 10–7.

Near the end of the first half, Penn State moved the ball to Northwestern's 34-yard line, but not close enough to dare a field goal attempt with their shaky kicker, backup-turned-starter Sam Ficken, who had gone 1 for 5 against Virginia four weeks earlier. So, on fourth and four, O'Brien went for it, but on a broken play, McGloin chucked an ill-advised pitch-pass to Zordich, who couldn't gather the low toss.

The cameras showed O'Brien throw his head back in disbelief, Jordan Hill drop his face in his hands, and Zordich, his palms up, look back at McGloin: *Really?*

Northwestern—a program built on calculated risks—went to the air, gaining a dubious pass-interference call. An injury brought O'Brien onto the field, ranting at the refs. Pat Fitzgerald walked out, too, put his arm around the ref, and said with a grin, "I know he coached Tommy Brady and the Pats, but you don't have to listen to his NFL bullshit."

That got O'Brien—who had great respect for Fitzgerald, and vice versa—even hotter. "Screw you, Fitz!" Or words to that effect.

The TV cameras showed the shouting match, and it blew up accordingly. But to the guys on the field, it was just some good, old-fashioned trash-talking between former linebackers, whom they knew had great mutual admiration. The coaches themselves described it as a couple Irish Catholic guys from Chicago and Boston engaged in a little jawing, like pigs in mud.

"I loved it!" said Mauti, who heard it all. "That's football. That's a couple linebackers. You know they loved it, too."

Immediately after, Fitzgerald was walking on his team's sideline, through his players. He knew his team and proved it when he said with a grin, to no one in particular, "I shoulda just kicked his ass," leaving a wave of players laughing in his wake.

"Those guys were getting into it," quarterback Kain Colter recalled, laughing. "We know the respect they have, but it got us all fired up, and we loved it."

With thirty seconds left in the half, the Wildcats got their touchdown, their 14–10 lead, and their opponent—who had never trailed at halftime all season—on the verge of collapse. Pull this off, and Northwestern would be 6-0—a record even the national press couldn't ignore. Talk of their magical 1995 season would surface again.

I headed to the Horseshoe on another beautiful fall day. The weather each weekend had been almost perfect. But we Midwesterners know it can't last.

I stopped at the Horseshoe's north side to see the rotunda, which was modeled after the Pantheon's—with a twist. Look closely and you'll see each coffer was painted blue, with a maize flower in the center—about the only scraps of those colors you can find anywhere in Franklin County.

The answer to this mystery goes back to Ohio Stadium's creation. The Ohioans' pride in their university and its most famous structure was so great, the university received donations from every one of the state's eighty-eight counties for its completion.

Although the Buckeyes had already beaten neighbors Ohio Wesleyan and Oberlin in their new home, they saved their dedication game for October 21, 1922—and invited Michigan to be their guests. The gesture reflected the growing rivalry between the schools, soon to surpass Michigan's rivalries with Chicago and Minnesota.

The Buckeyes went all out on the festivities, which included a twenty-one-gun salute, a "parade of distinguished guests," and a full house of seventy-two thousand fans. If you want to understand the role college football played in solidifying the relationship between the state university and the students, faculty, alums, and citizens, October 21, 1922, in Columbus, Ohio, is not a bad place to start.

"All walks of life were represented," Ohio State's student newspaper, *The Lantern*, reported, "when leaders came from far and near to pay their respects to the Ohio State University's new athletic plant." They were less likely to visit campus to dedicate the new chemistry building.

But what of those yellow flowers and blue squares? Buckeye fan Mike Burkhard, forty-two, waiting outside the landmark for friends, knew the story: The Buckeyes made a friendly wager with the Wolverines. If Michigan beat their hosts—well, you can guess.

The only blight for the Buckeyes on that seemingly perfect day was the outcome: Michigan 19, Ohio State 0. (As Michigan's Fielding Yost liked to boast, "We put the *dead* in dedication!") The temptation to paint over

226

those maize flowers must be great, but in the Horseshoe's ninety years, to the Buckeyes' lasting credit, they have never welshed on the wager.

"It's kinda neat," Burkhard said. "It shows the respect for the best rivalry in the game. But it sticks in the craw a bit, a constant reminder. But that's part of the beauty of a great rivalry, too."

But none of it counts for much if fans stop looking up at the rotunda and forget their history. Institutional memory runs strong at schools like Ohio State, but fans will continue to learn Buckeye history and pass it down only if the team continues to be successful, and fun to watch.

"Tressel was a great coach," Burkhard said, "but that was boring football. We want to win national titles, and to do that, we have to compete with the SEC. You just can't do that with smashmouth football anymore—not against a team like Alabama. The Big Ten's been smacked in the teeth a few times lately. That's getting old—and needs to stop!"

As we talked, a band of Nebraska fans walked by, one wearing the trademark "Cornhead" hat.

"Bringing in Nebraska was a great move," Burkhard said. "They're everything the Big Ten's about: tradition, respect, good football, great program, and they're *into it*.

"That's the Big Ten. That's us."

And that is Ohio State's challenge: to preserve its rich history and stay connected with its Big Ten brothers, while beating the best of the best down South.

Fully five hours before kickoff, Buckeye tailgates covered the parking lot, the surrounding fields, and most of Columbus, it seemed. It wasn't hard to find a tailgate with a big-screen TV to watch the second half of the Northwestern–Penn State game—and, just for standing there, a free bratwurst.

"Every year they get better and better," Zordich said of Northwestern. With Penn State going into the second half down 14–10, "we knew we had to give them everything we've got."

To open the second half, McGloin handed off to Zach Zwinak six times and passed to him once on a drive that regained the lead, 17–14. But the Wildcats countered with a smooth 11-play drive—requiring only one third-down conversion—then returned a Penn State punt 75 yards for a touchdown, to take a 28–17 lead right before the fourth quarter.

"I honestly felt that was the best game we played all season," Colter said. "We had great focus, great fundamentals. Very solid."

"We really thought we were going to beat them," defensive end Quentin Williams said. "We really did."

The guys on the other side recognized the threat for what it was. "You could easily see how our team could have said, 'That's it. We're done,'" Mauti said.

"When you're in those situations," McGloin told me, "if you're nervous and don't believe that you're gonna come back and win the game, how do you expect everyone else to respond? I never thought we were going to lose that game. It didn't feel like we were down by eleven. That's what this team's all about: keep scratching and clawing to the end."

When McGloin walked into the huddle, with the ball on Penn State's 18, and his team down 28–17, he looked at his teammates and said, "I love moments like this. This is what makes teams great. We wouldn't have it any other way."

Then he proved it, leading his troops on one of their biggest drives of the season, an 18-play masterpiece featuring 7 runs and 2 catches by Zach Zwinak, and 8 for 9 passing by McGloin. They converted four third downs, and when they finally failed on third and goal from the 4, O'Brien went for it.

McGloin responded by hitting Allen Robinson for the touchdown.

O'Brien then decided to go for two. Zordich converted to close Northwestern's lead to 28–25.

"Then our D just ate 'em up," Zordich said.

It helped that in that fourth quarter, Penn State's defense faced their student section, often at close range.

"It got *loud*," Mauti said.

"Then it got *LOUD* loud!" Zordich said.

"You get up after a big play," Mauti said, "and you point to the crowd, and the response is so immediate, it's like being a conductor. It's so loud, your whole body goes numb. It's like a drug. So intoxicating."

"That is *the* best drug you could ever find," Zordich said. "When you're on offense, it's the opposite. You need to get the play in, and they know that, so they're quiet. But as soon as you run the play, they go, 'Whoooo!' And you can hear them."

And that's what happened next. After Northwestern bombed the punt down to Penn State's 14-yard line, the Lions went on a 15-play drive that took 5:38 off the clock.

"You could feel the tension building on every play," Mauti said.

On fourth and two from Northwestern's 19-yard line, down 28-25, O'Brien didn't hesitate to go for it. This thrilled the crowd, which was accustomed to watching the previous staff run quarterback sneaks on third and five.

McGloin didn't see what he wanted, however, and started scrambling. Wide receiver Brandon Moseby-Felder recognized the situation, slipped behind his man, and got open for the first down and then some, getting down to the 6-yard line.

"Great instinct play," Zordich said.

On third and goal from the five, McGloin faked the toss, rolled to the right, then ran full speed to the right corner of the end zone, culminating in a leap that was as ungraceful as it was unnecessary, just inside the right end-zone pylon. "Hey, it got the job done," he told me with a grin.

Touchdown. With 2:37 left, Penn State had finally taken a 32–28 lead.

"Our defense comes back out, and it's crazy as hell again!" Mauti said.

With Kain Colter at the controls, however, you could not count the Cardiac 'Cats out. But on fourth down, his pass fell incomplete. Penn State's ball.

O'Brien knew if they didn't get another first down, they would give the Wildcats one more shot. On third down, the call went to Zordich, who got around the defensive end on the left side. Then Moseby-Felder made "a great block on the safety and sprung me open," said Zordich, who bolted down the left sideline. "When you're running with the ball, you can hear the crowd get louder, yard by yard, and that just gets you going faster."

The Wildcats collided with him near the end zone, and the refs signaled a touchdown. But upon review, they moved the ball back to the 3. O'Brien ran the same play again, and Zordich bounced his way into the end zone. Northwestern's 11-point lead had been reversed: 39–28, Penn State.

"*That* got loud!" Zordich said. "I was excited and screaming and stuff, and it felt like the whole damn team was on top of me. I tried to make my way to the sideline—you're excited about it, but then you think, 'I can't breathe! I'm gonna pass out!'"

When the game ended, the players ran straight to the student section to sing the alma mater—which Mauti calls, without irony, "one of the best traditions we've started this year."

If the NCAA can erase thirteen years of victories with the stroke of a pen, why can't a college team create a tradition in weeks?

Mauti's father, Rich, stood with the lettermen right behind the team, singing the alma mater. He put his arm around Coach Butler and said, "Hey John, it doesn't get any better than this." But Butler didn't respond. When Rich turned to look at him, he found out why: tears were rolling down his face.

"And that's why I love this place," Zordich said. "Coach Butler, he's only been here for a few months—and I think it just smacked him. The coaches, they care about this place, they love it. They care about us."

The players rang the victory bell endlessly—a few coaches did, too—then ran into the locker room.

"Man, we just ran a hundred plays on offense against a damn good team," Mike Farrell told me. "When we needed the ball back in the last quarter, the defense absolutely *killed* it. The whole team just laid it on the line, and that's what it took.

"Man, *everybody* was running in and just jumping around—coaches, too! It wasn't like you're a player and you're a coach and you're a manager. It was just *everybody* jumping around. It was just about the guys in the room—like O-B had been preaching throughout the year through all the tough stuff: just us.

"This is the most fun I've ever had playing football, and a lot of guys in that room would tell you that."

Instead of limping to the locker room at 3-3 with more questions than answers, the resurgent Penn Staters were 4-2, on a four-game winning streak, and undefeated in the Big Ten.

If a college football program can be measured by its press box, then Ohio State is clearly shooting to be the best. The box is part of a $194 million renovation, which they completed in 2001, but they didn't scrimp on the scribes—which is rare. The food is the best in the Big Ten, featuring first-rate bratwurst, stick-to-your-ribs ribs from City Barbeque, and a McCafé stand where the staff sets out an endless supply of smoothies, frappes, and McFlurrys, all with a smile—and all for free.

When you sit down, the view is—once again—something to savor. But unlike the vistas at Penn State, Northwestern, Notre Dame, or Michigan State—which feature a mix of natural scenery and beautiful buildings—in the Horseshoe all you can see is the Horseshoe. But it's enough.

You look out at a wall of fans right across from you in the upper deck, wearing scarlet, then to the student end zone, a thick bloodred that glows in the night lights, and it feels like all of them are right on top of you. And when you're on that field—and I've been down there during games—it's downright intimidating.

The Horseshoe is framed by two sentry towers at the north end zone, and two at the end of the horseshoe. (They don't make stadiums like this anymore.) Ringing the 'Shoe are the names and numbers of seven of the Buckeyes' greatest players, five of them Heisman Trophy winners. Then they list their six national titles, five from 1942 to 1970, plus 2002. Last but not least, they reserved a spot to honor Woody Hayes, who won thirteen Big Ten titles, and all but two of those national crowns.

The place makes its point: great things are expected here.

When a game is hyped this much, it's not surprising when both teams get off to a skittish start—all defense and punting and fumbles.

Suitably, it was not either team's offense but Ohio State's defense that opened the scoring, midway through the first quarter, when Bradley Roby intercepted Taylor Martinez's pass at midfield and ran it back 41 yards for a 7–0 OSU lead.

But Nebraska responded by finishing the quarter with six first downs to Ohio State's zero, and two touchdowns. By the end of the half, Martinez had showed the crowd what the preseason buzz was about by generating 24 points.

Buckeye fans might have wondered if their defense was much better than the one that went 6-7 the year before.

"It was a big night game," Ohio State linebacker Etienne Sabino told me. "Everyone was a little bit too excited and playing outside of ourselves. You do that, and you forget the basics of tackling, and making the plays that come to you."

Meyer took a longer view. "When we get to the Nebraska game," he told me, "we're still not a great team. We'd found ways to win, but we hadn't put one solid game together yet."

But if the Buckeyes' defense couldn't stop the Huskers in the first half, in the second quarter the Buckeyes' offense came alive. Led by sophomore Braxton Miller, whose reads, judgment, and accuracy had improved greatly from just a week earlier at Michigan State, Ohio State scored four touchdowns in the second quarter alone, for a 28–24 halftime lead.

It wasn't great football. It might not have even been very good football. On the two teams' eight trips to the red zone, they both scored every time. But it was undeniably *exciting* football, and the crowd was eating it up.

At halftime, the Best Damn Band in the Land put on a dazzling show celebrating, of all things, video games. Hey, they knew their audience. They played their canon, then jumped into an impressive depiction of classic video games, with the band members forming the moving pieces. After running through Pac-Man, Frogger, and Tetris, they finished with Super Mario Bros., topping the castle with an OSU flag, which naturally dropped down and crushed a hapless Michigan banner.

This is the kind of show fans stick around to see—and should.

In the second half, Ohio State's offense picked up where it left off, and the defense caught up. Martinez could manage only one touchdown—against two more interceptions—while the young Miller showed better poise, skill, and simple ability, racking up four more touchdowns to give his team a comfortable 56–31 lead with 10:27 left.

"For the last three quarters of that game," Meyer told me, "we played like we were one of the best teams in college football—almost flawless. We ran for four hundred yards, and our quarterback was on fire.

"We kind of got our identity as an offense that second half. We were flopping around before that—but then Carlos [Hyde], Braxton, and the O-line starting taking over games."

Even Zach Boren, the stubborn senior captain, was a convert. "The Nebraska game, that's when we turned it up," Boren told me. "That's when we realized there is something to play for that year."

Down 56–31 late in the game, the Huskers were done—evidenced by Bo Pelini's decision to call for screen passes, which is not how you dent a 25-point gap.

But Urban Meyer wasn't.

With two minutes left in the game—which set a stadium attendance record of 106,102, breaking the mark set by the USC game in 2009—and

Ohio State comfortably ahead, Meyer's offense did not set up in the victory formation to take a knee and kill the clock, but let Carlos Hyde run up the middle a few times to get the first down, then around the end for a 16-yard touchdown to bury the Huskers, 63–38.

Meyer had his scalp.

The reporters, collected near the end zone to run to the postgame press conferences, couldn't help but chuckle. Meyer had just given Nebraska a little taste of SEC football for the Huskers to enjoy on their long flight home.

Ohio State holds its postgame press conference in a big, white room under the stands, with bright fluorescent lighting. On this night it was packed with fifty to sixty reporters, maybe more, facing a wooden podium with a plaque on the front:

OHIO STATE
FOOTBALL
Est. 1890

Coach Meyer opened by thanking the crowd. "I never want to let that go without telling the fans, 'That's tremendous,'" he said, leaving his script. "It's cool to watch the fans buy in. From the bottom of my heart, I appreciate it."

In these settings, Meyer stood in contrast to Tressel, who was careful, nice, and polite, but had the knack for saying nothing for twenty minutes. Meyer is unfailingly direct and honest—whether you like it or not.

When a reporter asked, "When you first got here, you said you wanted this place to be 'an inferno.' Is that what you saw?"

Meyer replied, "I didn't like the first couple weeks. I saw fans too far away, and players with their headsets on. That's not what we want. We want people to enjoy *their* Ohio State players."

With the victory, plus Minnesota's defeat the previous week and Northwestern's loss earlier that day to Penn State, Ohio State was already the last undefeated team in the Big Ten, and would be the only conference team in the Top 10.

On that night, you could see Meyer's challenge clearly: He had to respect Ohio State's past, and the rabid fans who revered it, while leading the program into the future to battle the new kings of the sport. And he intended to do it for a program that would never have to apologize for anything.

The Buckeyes were 6-0.

"Don't tell anyone this," one Ohio State employee told me, "but I hope we lose just one game. If we go undefeated this year, the pressure next year will be insane."

CHAPTER 15

SING TO THE COLORS

Long before I knew the difference between a post pattern and a flea-flicker, I was captivated by the sight of Michigan's marching band gathering inside the stadium tunnel, flags high. The announcer's baritone boomed over the speakers, with a trademark phrase any Michigan fan can mimic: "Laaaaaadies and gentlemen! Innnnn-troducing the two-hundred-and-thirty-member Meeeeeshigan Marching Band! Baaaaaaaand—take the field!"

You'd hear the drum major's sharp, staccato whistles, then the urgent thumping of the drums as the band high-stepped out of the tunnel, expanding magically to create a perfect block *M*. It got me going every time and was the first reason I fell in love with football Saturdays.

In junior high, the game became the thing. I knew the players, the plays, and even who the bad guys were. But I still loved the band.

One Saturday every fall, the band's size doubled. The newcomers, wearing all manner of ragtag Michigan regalia, were older folks, but they marched almost as fast, twirled their batons just as well, and sounded just as good as the young, snappy college students. I learned that these reinforcements were the alumni band, back to relive their college days. I looked forward to their return every fall, and they never disappointed.

So, before the Michigan Marching Band went the way of the Michigan–Notre Dame rivalry, I wanted to find out what made it so special.

Friday, October 12: On a sunny, fifty-five-degree Friday, I walked down to Elbel Field, home to two softball diamonds, two sand volleyball courts, and enough room in the middle for impromptu football, soccer, lacrosse, rugby, and ultimate-Frisbee games. It wasn't named for a wealthy donor but for a music student named Louis Elbel, who wrote Michigan's famous fight song, "The Victors."

The marching band has practiced here for over a century. This is where families bring their kids for a free concert every fall weekday, and where the alumni band gathers to begin its reunion on the Friday before homecoming. The mood this year, as always, was fun and light, fueled by cold beer and warm stories, but even this merry band of some 350 alums could not ignore the changing climate of Michigan football.

Garland Campbell, a tall African-American man with a tidy mustache, played tenor sax from 1979 to 1983, literally following in his father's footsteps. He had flown in from California, as he did every year, to see his coterie of old band buddies.

"Who was first chair in high school?" he asked his friends.

"All of us!" replied Jack Miner, a euphonium player whose son now plays trumpet in the band.

It's the shock most freshmen face. Athlete or engineer, you learn that a lot of people in college can do what you can do.

For these folks, that first hit home at band camp—though it's no camp. Potential band members move into the dorms two weeks early and spend just about every waking hour at Revelli Hall. The tryout is brutal. The musicians in your section form a circle, with each person facing outward, eyes closed, head down. The candidate stands in the center, and plays the piece. Then the next person plays, and the listeners vote on who sounds better.

The winner slides up the row, the loser slides down, and so it goes until the last candidate has played. Slide too far down and you won't make the band—a merciless process.

Of the 380 who qualify, only 270 play at halftime (the rest stay in their seats), and just 230 play the pregame concert. So if you rank between 271 and 380, you practice just as hard, but you play only after the game, when all but a few hundred fans have left.

You're judged on marching, too. The test sounds simple enough: play "The Victors" while marching twenty yards. But you have to march *exactly* eight steps for every five yards: "8 to 5" is the slogan, each step measured at exactly 22.5 inches.

236

"Let me tell you," Campbell said, "after your eighth step, the ball of your foot damn well *better* land on that yard line!"

Players used to complain about two-a-day hitting practices (something almost no one does anymore, thanks to NCAA limits on scholarships and practice times), but when you're at band camp, you get:

"Three-a-days!" Campbell said.

"Try six-a-days!" said Andy Pervis.

"No one's wearing makeup," said Stephanie Pervis. "Nobody's even showered."

"We smelled!" Campbell said. "But who cared? We *all* smelled!"

It creates a bond.

Despite the load, the band's collective GPA hovers around 3.4, even though typically half the members are engineering students who take their classes on the North Campus, a twenty-minute bus ride away.

Then there are the tangible benefits: two credits and $100 a year to dry-clean your all-wool uniform—which is too thick for Notre Dame in early September, and too thin for Ohio State in late November. The band members often pocket the Benjamin as a bonus—the kind of sophomoric sleight of hand for which the NCAA would suspend a player and put a program on probation.

Likewise, if the band were an NCAA sport, the twenty-five hours per week of scheduled practice would be cut to twenty, while the extra practices any section leader can call after practice would be considered "voluntary."

"Yeah, 'voluntary'!" Campbell coughed, getting laughs.

In the band, at least, common sense still ruled.

Saturday morning, October 13: On a cold, rainy Saturday morning I got to Revelli Hall by 8:00 a.m., but it was already packed with 350 alumni, ready to rehearse. John Wilkins, a dapper man wearing a navy-blue suit, a maize-and-blue tie, a full head of salt-and-pepper hair, and the demeanor of, well, a band conductor, took the podium. He started leading the pack twenty-one years ago when the athletic department asked the alums to fill in at hockey and basketball games when the student band members went on vacations.

Wilkins had a message for his fellow alumni: "We are on a mission to fully endow the program, so the [student] marching band will be fully independent and *not* at the mercy of . . . *other departments"*—his pause got a laugh. They all knew he was talking about the athletic department—"which may or may not have the funding for us going forward."

The need to protect the marching band is nothing new—but the urgency was, thanks to the near miss in Dallas.

"The endowment," Wilkins continued, "will fund the entire program, including staff, instruments, composers—arrangers cost more these days!—facilities, and, yes, travel!" They all got the joke.

The mission, he said, was not just to pay for plane tickets or tubas. "It's to make sure that *what we are,* and *what we do,* will not be compromised, for as far as we can see." He let that sink in before delivering the punch line. "To do all this, to endow the entire program, we need to raise forty million dollars."

A few heads tilted back—but then Wilkins went in for the kill. "We are already *halfway to our goal.*" He paused to let the alums' surprise rise to the rafters. "Our goal is *one hundred percent participation.* Track that?"

They cheered. They tracked that.

Wilkins turned his attention to the day's music.

"We're gonna run out there onto the field," he said, "make the crowd drop their Cokes and hot dogs, and we're gonna play 'The Victors Trio.'"

They leaped into the medley, but Wilkins soon put his hands up, tapped on his stand, and gave them a pained expression. He told the percussionists to play their part again.

"Good!" he said with warm sarcasm. "I hear a rhythm similar to what *we're* doing!" Wilkins got a laugh, and the percussion section got the point.

Next came "Let's Go Blue!" then a lighthearted campus classic, "I Want to Go Back to Michigan." Someone in the glee club—no one knows who—wrote it well more than a century ago, and the bars mentioned are long gone, but every current student (and their parents) would understand the lyrics:

> *I want to go back to Michigan,*
> *To dear Ann Arbor town,*

Back to Joe's and the Orient,
And back to some of the money I spent.

Oh! Father and Mother pay all the bills,
And we have all the fun,
In the friendly rivalry of college life, Hooray!

The band members' heads bobbed in unison. Some had been away for decades, but no one needed to tell them when to swing their trombones or lift their shiny sousaphones to the sky. Somehow, this had been grafted on to their collective DNA, and it looked like it was there to stay.

"Give our percussion a hand!" Wilkins commanded. "They were wonderful!" He had forgiven their sins.

Then he called up the director of bands from 1970 to 1995, Professor H. Robert Reynolds, a kindly man in his eighties, bald on top with white hair running down the sides.

"Okay!" Reynolds called. "'The Yellow and Blue'!"

This is the alma mater, a sentimental ballad, the emotional grace note of the Michigan canon.

Reynolds waved his wand for the first note, but he was soon so displeased that his hands fell away in disgust, and the band stumbled to a stop. (One mystery solved: they really *do* watch the conductor.)

"Noooooo!" he said. "Play it with *enthusiasm!*"

A drummer yelled from the back, "Play it for the band!"

This time, even a tin-eared writer could tell the difference. They were no longer playing the notes. They were playing the *song*, with the spirit behind it.

The best moment wasn't on the field, before the largest crowd in college football that day, nor inside the stately Hill Auditorium, whose acoustically perfect design was copied by Radio City Music Hall, where the band plays at least once a year to a packed house. It was in the dark silence of the stadium tunnel, where no one could see or hear them. This was the time they treasured most, alone in the dark, and they sang—not played, but sang—the alma mater, to themselves, and for themselves. They had not, after all, been picked for their voices.

"Singing the alma mater in the tunnel beforehand means as much to us as playing 'The Victors' in the stadium," Thomas Rhea told me.

"My last time in the tunnel, as a senior," said Paul Sutherland, '08, "the emotion . . . I'm not embarrassed to admit it, I cried. A lot of us do, and that's when the younger people in the band see that and realize what this means. A junior came up and hugged me. There's no judging. There are not many situations where you see people that visibly moved."

They walked into the tunnel and lined up, in order, along the cold, dank wall; 350 of them, in five rows, from the top of the tunnel near the parking lot all the way down to the field, the crowd, and the M GO BLUE banner outside.

Their ages spanned the spectrum. There could be a dozen or so from your year, but the band is so big, you might not even know those who showed up from your class. There is no alumni band uniform, but almost everyone wore something from their Michigan days. Their arms were bent at ninety degrees, instruments in front, pointing down. A few had dug up a pair of the white gloves they'd been issued years before.

The song started with a single note—an A-flat concert pitch played by a trombone—then a measured pause, followed by 350 voices softly singing words written only twenty years after the Civil War;

> Sing to the colors that float in the light;
> Hurrah for the Yellow and Blue!
> Yellow the stars as they ride through the night
> And reel in a rollicking crew;
> Yellow the field where ripens the grain
> And yellow the moon on the harvest wain;
>
> Hail!
>
> Hail to the colors that float in the light
> Hurrah for the Yellow and Blue!

"When you get to heaven," Marianne Swenson said, with red eyes, "that's what they'll be playing."

The trip will be paid for.

CHAPTER 16

IT MATTERS TO US

After beating Northwestern in thrilling fashion, Penn State got the next Saturday off. Northwestern recovered nicely against a decent Minnesota team, 21–13. Ohio State expected a cakewalk against Indiana, but had to fight off a late Hoosier charge to win 52–49. That gave the Buckeyes a record of 7-0, and 3-0 in the Big Ten. Their dreams of a division title and a perfect season were very much alive.

Despite the bone-chilling rain on homecoming weekend, the Wolverines did just about everything right in their 45–0 beatdown of Illinois. But the students had the following Monday and Tuesday off for fall break, so many of them had skipped the game to take a four-day weekend at home. That made Michigan's next game against Michigan State a better chance for a reunion.

Almost everything we love about college football is economically irrational: marching bands, alumni bands, tailgating, the hundreds of volunteers working around the stadium, even amateur athletics itself.

Almost everything that threatens its future is profit-driven. TV networks insist schools play almost every day but Sunday—out of respect for the NFL, not the Sabbath—and at 9:00 p.m. on Saturdays. The NCAA added a twelfth game, so powerful teams can pound punching bags in contests no one wants to see. It's allowed another game for conference championships, and even more for the playoffs to come. Schools use the windfall from the games to pay increasingly outrageous salaries for coaches, athletic directors, and the guys in silly coats who run bowl games.

All of these pose a threat to the health of the game—and the young men who play it—but for now, let's focus on the bowls. Those who run them need us to believe their games are rewards for teams that had a great season, that the games offer players and fans a much-wanted vacation, and that these events are nonprofits, while the schools make a killing.

These claims are nice—and would be even nicer if any of them were actually true.

Forty years ago, college football got by with just eleven bowl games. Back then, when your team got into a bowl game, you knew they'd done something special. Those twenty-two invited teams were truly elite, and so were the bowls—like the Orange Bowl, the Sugar Bowl, the Cotton Bowl, and the Granddaddy of Them All, the Rose Bowl.

But in the past four decades, the number of bowls has more than tripled, to a staggering thirty-five, so the bowls need seventy willing teams. But there are just 124 Division I teams to choose from, and by definition, only 62 are above average. So some bowls settle for teams that didn't even finish in the top half of the *sport*—let alone their conferences. This year, thirteen bowl teams don't have winning records. When your team gets into a bowl game today, you know they must not be on probation.

So we now have such timeless classics as the the Meineke Car Care Bowl, the AdvoCare V100 Independence Bowl, and the legendary TaxSlayer.com Bowl. How many TaxSlayer.coms fit into a bowl? It's a question for theologians.

What used to be a special trip is now a chore. If players are not going to one of the elite bowls, most would rather skip the fifteen mandatory practices, and a trip to Shreveport, Boise, or Detroit, and stay home for the holidays.

Fans feel the same way. Few bowls sell out, and a third of them draw fewer than forty thousand fans. You could fire a cannon in those stadiums, then find the cannonball and fire it again, and still not hit anybody.

This is all silly excess, but it crosses the line into corruption when you look at the finances. The bowls are nonprofit and want you to believe schools make out like bandits. But the only ones *not* profiting are the schools and their players. It's the bowls themselves that make the money—and the coaches and the athletic directors, who receive bonuses for dragging their teams to these backwaters.

Here's how the scam works: The schools have to pay for their flights, hotels, and meals—which adds up fast for 150 players, coaches, staffers, and university VIPs. Then the bowls force them to buy thousands of tickets they can't give away—and that sets up the final outrage: the bowls make the schools accept far less than the advertised payout, right down to nothing, which, according to *Death to the BCS*, is exactly what the Motor City Bowl actually paid Florida Atlantic in 2009.

Only half the teams lose bowl games—but almost all of them lose their shirts going to them.

That's bad enough, but get this: the men in the ugly blazers who run these "nonprofit" bowls walk off with hundreds of thousands of dollars in salary—all for setting up one game a year that no one wants to play or watch.

How to fix this mess? Simple: Prohibit forcing schools to buy tickets they don't want. Make the bowls actually pay the schools what they proudly announce they're paying them. And while we're at it, make them pay for the schools' travel expenses, too.

If the bowls think it's still worth it—and the better ones will—great. Everybody wins, just like the old days.

But if the bowls don't, they can close shop and end the charade.

They would not be missed.

Given all this—and more—it's tempting to ask which side will win in college football: passion or profits?

Without the passion of the players and the fans, there would be nothing to profit from. The more passion we feel, the more profit others make. But this can create a vicious cycle. If our passion becomes an insatiable appetite, will it merely tempt the suits to take advantage for more profit, and will that in turn start to strangle the very passion that made those profits possible?

If so, where is the tipping point—and how long before we get there?

So far, few tailgaters behave like demanding superdonors. They may grumble about this coach or that play, this season or that rival, and they will always find fault with the offense and the officiating. But they don't expect anyone in power to listen because they don't presume to own any of it. Yet if you added up the financial contributions of the hundred thousand Michigan fans tailgating within a mile of the stadium, the total would make them a powerful donor, indeed.

Almost without exception, the fans have grudgingly accepted the changes engulfing college football. But as Bill Martin's survey suggests, they care less about the overall quality of play—let alone the professionals who perform at a higher level—than they do about their team's traditions, and their connection to them.

You have to wonder if anyone operating the turnstiles has ever asked, will the fans always pay? Or will they get so fed up with the shifting kick-off times, the subpar opponents, and the skyrocketing cost of sitting in a cold seat, waiting for the endless TV time-outs to end, that they finally pack up their grills and go home—for good?

The night before the Michigan–Michigan State game, I joined a group of about twenty friends who had flown from every time zone in the country for their annual Michigan football weekend. The conversations ran the gamut, but they never strayed too far from Michigan football—the magnet that draws them together every fall.

But all was not well in Arborville. Instead of the usual armchair quarterbacking, this time the natives were getting restless with bigger concerns.

"They are ruining college football," Jason Conti said, a view echoed by many that night. Why? "Because the essence of college football is not a national title. That's as cheesy as a unicorn. It's tomorrow's game against Michigan State. It's regional rivalries that go back generations.

"Honestly, I don't give a damn if Alabama wins the national title by a hundred points," he added. "If we beat State tomorrow by three, I'll be thrilled."

The next morning, I walked down to the massive high school parking lot kitty-corner from Michigan Stadium, where, every football Saturday, hundreds of RVs and countless cars disgorge coolers, grills, generators, footballs, cornhole boards and beanbags, and a sea of tailgating fans.

I ran into an old friend of mine, former Michigan cross-country coach Ron Warhurst. He won two NCAA titles as a runner and two Purple Hearts in Vietnam. As a coach, his runners won eight Big Ten titles, and twelve Top 10 finishes in the NCAA.

Warhurst looked around at the thousands of people happily spending about $500 on that day's game—and many of them much more. Two golf courses across Main Street were just as full. So was the stadium parking lot and dozens of residential blocks within a mile of the Big House.

"You look at all this, you look at how much money people spend, and how much those guys make," he said, pointing a thumb at the Big House, "and you have to think, one of these times the players are going to run out of that tunnel, sit down on the benches, and refuse to play until they get paid.

"One of these days."

William Friday, the former president of the University of North Carolina, told the writer Taylor Branch that if a certain team—not his own school's—reached the NCAA basketball championship game a few years ago, "they were going to dress and go out on the floor, but refuse to play."

Because the team didn't make it to the finals, we'll never know if they would have followed through. But any team in the tournament could do it, jeopardizing the $1 billion March Madness generates in TV ads alone, the highest ad revenue of any sporting event.

Just as Warhurst postulated, any football team could do the same—which demonstrates just how fragile the game's foundation really is.

As the salaries of coaches and athletic directors escalate, while the players' income remains stuck at zero, it's not hard to imagine a point when the players finally say, "Enough."

With Michigan riding a two-game Big Ten winning streak and a 4-2 overall record, ESPN had planned to cover the game. Then Michigan State lost to a weak Iowa team in overtime, giving the Spartans a record of 4-3 overall and 1-2 in the Big Ten. ESPN went elsewhere, leaving the game for the Big Ten Network.

The fans weren't going anywhere. The stakes for Michigan–Michigan State, always high, were higher than usual in Ann Arbor this year, since the Spartans had won the Paul Bunyan Trophy—four feet of carved kitsch—four years straight.

Thanks more to sputtering offenses than great defenses, the first quarter ended 0–0. In the second quarter, Michigan faced third and goal on State's 7-yard line, but Denard Robinson's toss to Roy Roundtree in the end zone wasn't close, so Hoke took the field goal. The Spartans failed to convert on a third and one from Michigan's 21-yard line, then their kicker missed the 38-yard field goal attempt. The half ended with Michigan ahead, 6–0.

ESPN was looking pretty smart.

Sportswriter Steve Grinczel, who's covered more than twenty of these matchups, said, "I can't recall a Michigan–Michigan State game with so little sizzle."

But the crowd's energy never waned. They hadn't planned their tailgates for weeks or spent hundreds or thousands of dollars to watch twenty-two professionals in the cold pursuit of perfection. They'd paid to see college kids they cared about play with unbridled enthusiasm. Both teams were providing that in spades.

In the second half, State's first-year quarterback, Andrew Maxwell, finished a 10-play drive by finding Paul Lang wide open in the end zone, making the easy toss for a 7–6 lead. The Wolverines countered with their third field goal to go ahead 9–7.

In the fourth quarter, MSU coach Mark Dantonio—never afraid to roll the dice—faced a fourth and 9 deep in his own territory and called for a fake punt. The Spartans executed it perfectly, got to midfield, and kept driving to Michigan's 2-yard line. It looked as if State had made the play of the game. Then Dantonio's nerve let him down, and he settled for the field goal and a 10–9 lead with 5:48 left.

After State got the ball back, with just 3:07 left, Dantonio did Michigan a favor by passing twice instead of running the ball to kill the clock. Michigan got the ball back on its own 38-yard line, with exactly two minutes left.

Against Notre Dame, Michigan had failed to score a touchdown, and in nearly four quarters against the Spartans, the Wolverines still hadn't crossed the goal line—but incredibly, they were still very much in the hunt. On second and 11, from Michigan State's 41-yard line, Robinson completed a crucial pass to Drew Dileo to set up a last-second field goal attempt from 38 yards—exactly the distance from which the Spartans' kicker had missed in the second quarter.

By any objective standard, the game had been horrible. Neither team could crack 200 yards, rushing or passing, a mark Robinson routinely reached by himself as a sophomore—in the first half. But the crowd didn't seem to care. It was a close, hard-fought game between two ancient rivals—exactly what the fans hoped to see—and it was all going to come down to the last play.

After the 2009 Michigan–Michigan State game—which the 1-4 Spartans pulled out in overtime against the 4-0 Wolverines—all-American punter Zoltan Mesko told me the outcome hammered home a basic truth: "Fans have so much invested in these games that a ball tipped by six inches can change the chemical composition of a million brains."

Sound crazy? It's actually more than that, 2 or 3 million brains on each side of the equation. Now, once again, a few million brains teetered on the edge of agony and ecstasy.

When kicker Brendan Gibbons ran out to the field, punter Will Hagerup stood on the bench, helmet off, rubbing his face, muttering, "Oh my God. Oh my God."

One hundred and thirteen thousand people were on their feet. One hundred and twenty Michigan players were standing on benches.

Brendan Gibbons stepped into the kick, drove his foot straight through the ball, then watched it go up, up, up—and straight through the uprights.

Good!

It's unusual for fans to swarm the field at the end of a Michigan–Michigan State game. This time, a Spartan beat writer told me, "I almost got trampled."

Against the night sky, the scoreboard flashed the dates of Michigan's "century" wins: the 100th in 1901 against Case College, the 200th in 1915 against Mt. Union, the 300th in 1932 against Michigan State College, leading up to . . .

900: October 20, 2012.

MOST WINS IN COLLEGE FOOTBALL!

Another jolt for maize-and-blue brains.

Michigan had invited dozens of top recruits for the game. They might have seen a better game, but they couldn't have seen a better show. Winning begets winning, and Hoke's recruiting skills were attracting historic quantities of blue-chip players.

If the teams had worn different uniforms or played in a stadium built with taxpayers' dollars for millionaire professionals, the game would have been seen for what it was: a dog of a dog, with thirteen penalties and exactly one touchdown. Michigan had won simply because the Spartans missed their 38-yard field goal, while the Wolverines had made their 38-yard field goal.

But the identity of these schools and their fans, their fraught relationship, and the long history between them had powered the contest—and the Big House contained more of those commodities than any NFL concrete doughnut could ever hold. That's why, if the Spartans had made their kick, or the Wolverines had missed theirs, millions of brains would have fired the opposite direction in an instant.

Another year, style might have mattered. Michigan fans would have complained about their "lucky win," the lack of a single touchdown, and the 2-point victory over an increasingly mediocre foe.

But not this year. Having endured their longest losing streak in the series since 1962, Wolverine fans were euphoric.

"The world is back to normal," one Michigan fan said on Facebook.

"Order restored," wrote another.

"Ugly Trophy—but OUR ugly trophy."

"Thank fucking god."

At the press conference, a reporter asked walk-on-turned-senior-cocaptain Jordan Kovacs if the 12–10 game was "dull."

"Against anyone else, yes," he said. "We won it for the guys who came before us."

I walked back through revelers partying in the dark—who were in no hurry to pack up and leave—then past houses and yards and all the places I'd seen on the way down, then long lines stretching out of the bars on campus and downtown. The previous week's blowout against lowly Illinois was not the real homecoming. This was.

That's when I realized Jason Conti had been right the night before when he'd told me, "The essence of college football is not a national title. That's as cheesy as a unicorn. It's tomorrow's game against Michigan State. It's regional rivalries that go back generations. . . .

"If we beat State tomorrow by three, I'll be thrilled."

Michigan beat Michigan State only by two—but Mr. Conti was no less thrilled.

CHAPTER 17

"ALL THE THINGS WE ADMIRE"

On October 20, fans around the league saw scoreboards that said: PUR-DUE 22, OHIO STATE 29 FINAL (OT).

Fans surely concluded that Ohio State had dodged another bullet. It was actually a cannonball. A loss to either 2-3 Indiana, which Ohio State had beaten in a squeaker, 52–49, or a 3-3 Purdue team, at home, would have turned the Buckeyes' hopes of a miracle season to confetti.

But the scores didn't tell the whole story.

It had started two weeks earlier, when senior linebacker Etienne Sabino broke his leg early in the Buckeyes' impressive win over Nebraska. Urban Meyer scanned his depth chart at linebacker and saw gaping holes. Starters Storm Klein and Ryan Shazier were also hurt, as was Shazier's backup, Cam Williams. It wasn't clear how they could run practice, let alone field a defense against Indiana and Purdue.

During a break in Meyer's weekly show with Jim Lachey—a former Ohio State tight end and Pro Bowler turned radio host—the coach bemoaned the state of his surviving defensive backfield.

"Hey," said Lachey, "last year when we had three or four guys out, [fullback] Zach Boren wanted to switch to linebacker. He's a natural."

Meyer looked pained and growled, "I hope we're never that desperate."

But at the Tuesday practice after Nebraska, Meyer was realizing they were exactly that desperate. His gaze settled on none other than Zach Boren.

"Go to defense," Meyer said.

Boren didn't have a clue what the defense was doing, but he traded a red jersey for a gray one without complaint and jumped in.

A couple plays later, Meyer had second thoughts. He went to Boren with an expression that said, "I must have been crazy," and told him, "Go back to offense."

Then, with Boren out, the coach watched the defense's intensity deflate like a leaky balloon. He walked over to Tom Herman, the offensive coordinator, and said, "You don't have Boren anymore."

Herman was none too pleased, but there was no alternative.

"Within ten minutes of the switch," Meyer recalled later, "Zach Boren is a starting linebacker at Ohio State—and this is Ohio State. Even with injuries, we have linebackers here. Very few people could have done that. The more I think about it, the more I think no one else could have done that.

"In my entire coaching career, this will go down as one of the top five moments of truth, one of the biggest decisions I've made."

Or, if it didn't work, one of the dumbest. But that's the nature of big decisions.

Against Indiana, with two minutes left, the Buckeyes had held a comfortable 52–34 lead, but Indiana put up 15 points in thirty-five seconds. With just 1:05 left, the Hoosiers' onside kick rolled around Ohio State territory before the Buckeyes smothered it for the win.

Afterward, Meyer had some direct words with his defensive coaches.

"We were guilty of poor tackling and loss of leverage—fundamentals," Meyer told me. "Indiana was cutting back on us, getting outside of us, and that's bad coaching. So from that point, we put in five to ten minutes every practice focusing on tackling and leverage.

"You don't like something, you don't just go into the coaches' room or the team room and complain about it. You fix it. You put in an action plan and you execute that plan. We built practices around that action plan."

The next weekend, it was the offense's turn to be tested. In the Horseshoe, with the clock ticking down, the 3-3 Boilermakers led the Buckeyes, 22–14. Things got worse when quarterback Braxton Miller took a bone-rattling hit. With Miller en route to the hospital, Urban Meyer turned to his backup quarterback, Kenny Guiton.

In the off-season, the coach had almost sent Guiton home to Houston. But Guiton stayed, and turned his fate around.

"We have a mantra: 'Competitive excellence,'" Meyer told me. "And that means when your number's called, you're ready. There are only two ways to get ready: mental reps, and game reps, and backups don't get enough game reps. So we tell all our backups to be right behind the starters on the practice field and watch your man. It might be you next."

So whenever Braxton Miller was running plays during practice, Kenny Guiton was standing ten yards behind him, throwing an air ball when Miller threw the actual ball. When Meyer looked over near the end of the Purdue game, he saw Guiton already snapping his helmet. He was ready.

The Buckeyes were down by 8 with forty seconds left and 76 yards to go. Their starting quarterback and their best wide receiver were out. But Kenny Guiton marched the offense down to the end zone, and then got the conversion to tie the game. In overtime, the Buckeyes won.

"That's it, right there," Meyer said later. "Competitive excellence."

Northwestern didn't fare so well. After righting the ship post–Penn State against Minnesota to get to 6-1, and all but guarantee another bowl invitation—and another chance to do that stuffed monkey bodily harm—the Wildcats returned to Evanston to face the 4-2 Huskers. Northwestern held a lead at the end of the first, second, and third quarters—then lost, 29–28. If the defeat at Penn State had been tough, this one was brutal.

After the thriller over Northwestern, Penn State's record stood at a respectable 4-2. It gave the coaches and the players something fans don't often consider: the ability to enjoy their bye week in peace, savoring what they'd just accomplished, instead of replaying a painful loss in their minds—and on the screens—for two solid weeks.

But trouble loomed. The Iowa Hawkeyes had beaten Penn State eight of their last ten meetings, half of those by 3 points or less. Penn State's losing streak in Iowa City included a classic contest in 2008, when the second-ranked Nittany Lions arrived with a 9-0 record and left with a 24–23 loss, their hopes for a national title shattered. Every fifth-year senior remembered that game bitterly.

Adding a little pregame spice, one Iowa player bragged to the press that the Hawkeyes were known as the bullies of the Big Ten.

"O-B got it right," Zordich recalled, "when he said, 'What happens to the bully when he gets punched in the mouth? He can't take it! He's not the bully anymore!' So that was our plan."

The jacked-up Lions scored on their second drive, and their third, their fifth, their sixth, and their eighth, to go up 31–0 just twenty-seven seconds into the second half. When the game ended, 38–14, the Big Ten playground was looking for a new bully.

After the game, O'Brien gathered his team in Iowa's famed pink visitors' locker room and said, "It's one thing to be a bully. It's another thing to be a badass."

The players erupted. The flight home was a party fueled by five straight wins.

The celebration ended when the plane landed. The week preparing for the 8-0 Ohio State Buckeyes would be all business.

"It's the biggest game of our careers," Mauti told me.

"It's *the* statement," Zordich said.

The Navy game had stopped the bleeding. Victories over Illinois, Northwestern, and Iowa provided revenge and redemption, while solidifying the team like cement. Now, a victory over undefeated Ohio State before a rabid home crowd would provide more joy than State College had felt in years. It would establish, unequivocally, that Penn State was alive and well and not going anywhere. It could be the booster shot that ensured a healthy program through the remaining three years of sanctions.

"Hey, it's fun now," Jordan Hill told me at the team dinner Wednesday night. "We're just going out playing, and playing for each other. We don't want to screw this up for our teammates. Once we make a play, *everyone* is gonna be jumping around and going nuts."

It didn't hurt that the Buckeyes are Penn State's biggest rival—and biggest enemy. "Not a big fan of them—not at all," the stoic Hill stated. "Just something about 'em. I'm a Penn State guy, and you're an Ohio State guy, and we just don't get along."

Once again, Penn State's opponent made comments that got in the media, with Ryan Shazier tweeting, "We're going to try to show them who is Linebacker U."

"It's more than football," Hill told me. "It means so much more to this team. It shows fight—and the type of people we are. I'm not talking just football players. I'm talking Penn State as a whole—the alumni, and the students here now. You gotta be a Penn State guy to know what it means.

"Man, I'm ready to go right now!

"This is our moment. This is our turn."

• • •

On Friday morning, October 26, before the biggest game of O'Brien's college coaching career, he met with three members of the academic staff. The breadth and detail of their discussion was striking. They covered more than a hundred players, focusing on the forty with one issue or another, right down to how each player was doing in every class.

Most of these discussions came down to one thing: Was the young man making a sincere effort to improve, or was he trying to take advantage of his professors, advisers, and coaches? In most cases, the news was good—there's a reason Penn State's football program consistently ranks among the nation's highest in academic success—but in a few, warnings went out to keep an eye on so-and-so and let him know his margin for error had evaporated.

For those who scoff at the term *student-athlete*, this meeting—and many others—made it clear that if the schools didn't require varsity athletes to learn, many wouldn't go to college at all, let alone graduate. This part of the equation, at least, works a lot better than advertised.

What was easily Penn State's most maddening hurdle, however, was a consequence of the NCAA's sanctions, which not only allowed the players to transfer without penalty—and invited opposing coaches to recruit them—but permitted the players to quit the team, stay at Penn State, and keep their scholarships.

Those scholarships could not be replaced—but the NCAA still held the football program responsible for the academic fate of those students, without allowing the program to enforce class attendance. If a player who'd quit the team but stayed in school flunked out, the program's Academic Progress Rating (APR) would take a hit. And that could cost Penn State still more scholarships.

Plenty of players were still in the balance, but the team seemed to be on track for another stellar semester—the kind that NCAA president Mark Emmert's former athletic department at LSU could only envy.

"It's amazing," O'Brien said. "Amazing. This guy Emmert comes out and says, 'There is a culture of football here at Penn State,' then these numbers come out and say ninety-one percent of our players graduated, and ninety-four percent of the African-American players. What was LSU's average?"

But even if they tarred and feathered Emmert in State College's town square, it wouldn't help Penn State one iota.

That brought O'Brien to his next meeting, with recruiting coordinator Bill Kavanaugh. If academics had been made tougher by the NCAA sanctions, recruiting had become Herculean.

The public focused on the bowl ban—which insiders believed was probably the least punitive of the sanctions—while O'Brien and company worried far more about the effect of reducing Penn State's scholarships from twenty-five to fifteen for each of the next four years, while prohibiting the school from replacing the scholarships of any players who quit or transferred. Since the attrition rate at peer programs like Michigan and Ohio State usually resulted in perhaps sixteen or seventeen of the original twenty-five scholarship freshmen finishing their senior year, at similar rates Penn State could have four straight senior classes of fewer than ten. That could be a death sentence, by slow poisoning.

This only increased the pressure on recruiting. In other programs, after being given a draconian punishment that was more akin to the disastrous Treaty of Versailles than the wise Marshall Plan, that might also increase the temptation to cut corners. To O'Brien's credit, he was taking the opposite approach: trying to discover the hidden gems who would appreciate what Penn State had to offer—without the bowl games and baubles other programs could promise.

To those ends, they went over their list, sifting through piles of dirt for the shiny nuggets others might miss—the two- and three-star players with good work ethics, good grades, and a strong desire to play for Penn State. In a football-rich state such as Pennsylvania, that usually meant staying close to home.

Despite all their handicaps, the class of 2013 was shaping up to be— well, better than expected. They actually had twenty scholarships to offer, thanks to five carryovers from 2012 that went unused during the transition. Twelve players had already promised to come—including one of the best tight ends in the country, Adam Breneman from Camp Hill, Pennsylvania, near Harrisburg, and Christian Hackenberg, a five-star quarterback from Fork Union Military Academy in Virginia—leaving scholarships for eight more players. If Penn State could hang on to this group and add a few more, they could play competitive football for at least one more year—which would give them the chance to climb the same hill all over again the next year.

He'd already had a full day of meetings and media, but O'Brien still had to squeeze in a personal task before running the team meeting, practice, practice review, the team meal, more meetings, and finally lights out.

On a cold, gray Friday afternoon, I saw two men in the farthest corner of the third practice field, with Mt. Nittany in the background. I had to walk a hundred yards or so, on the crisp grass and hard clay, to recognize that it was strength coach Craig Fitzgerald and head coach Bill O'Brien, doing a workout I'd never before seen conducted anywhere.

They ran to the 30-yard line and back, then pushed a sled with lead plates on it back out to the 30, then ran over to a huge tractor tire, grabbed a sledgehammer, and beat the hell out of the tire with ten full swings—then they did it all again, again and again, a series of tasks that looked like a Caveman Triathlon.

Fitz looked stylish in his blue shorts and loose-fitting, gray, nylon T-shirt, but O'Brien looked like a fraternity couch waiting to be picked up from the curb: gray T-shirt over a blue long-sleeve shirt and blue sweatpants, all loose and rumpled. His T-shirt was turning dark with sweat. You would not pick this guy for your magazine cover, but you might for your farm.

He was not doing all this to appease his doctor, his wife—a graduate of the Georgia State University School of Law—or his vanity. He was one of the few contemporary coaches who'd rather do without the attention that came with the job. He was not doing this for his seven-year-old son, Michael, already a jock's jock, who frequently came to practice to play catch with anyone who would throw the ball back.

Bill O'Brien was doing all this for his ten-year-old son, Jack, who was born severely handicapped and would live his entire life in a wheelchair. Because Bill and Colleen could never seem to settle on a caretaker to look after Jack while they went about their busy days, it was their job to get their eighty-five-pound son in and out of his wheelchair several times a day, every day. O'Brien wanted to be sure he was strong enough to do the job and give their oldest son, as they so often said, "the best possible life."

• • •

Ohio State and Penn State had earned the right to play a meaningful, nationally televised game by playing surprisingly good football when both were expected to stumble.

Because both schools were on probation, however, and neither was eligible for the Big Ten title game or any bowl games, T-shirts inevitably popped up with lines like INELIGI-BOWL, BATTLE OF THE BANNED, and the particularly tasteful SCREWED V. TATTOOED. Their status in purgatory only increased the stakes. Both teams could still win the Leaders Division, even if they couldn't go on to the title game.

If they couldn't play for all the marbles, the ones that remained were that much more valuable.

The morning of the season-opening game against Ohio University, McGloin had eaten his breakfast quickly, then put himself in a trance, listening to his music with his eyes wide-open while bobbing his head back and forth. *Wired* would be a fair description.

Exactly eight weeks later, McGloin looked like a different man: calm, relaxed, poised. Ready.

After the breakfast plates had been cleared, O'Brien pored over the last details with his quarterbacks, focusing on McGloin.

"Right from the start," O'Brien said, "be ready for the speed of the game. Both teams are going to be jacked up. Get adapted, get adjusted. In warm-ups, work on the urgency of your throws. You're going to have to deliver it fast today.

"Once you're in your rhythm, everyone else will follow you. They *feed* off you. Your tempo is their tempo. Once in a while, we'll put you under center to give them a running look, but not that often."

They reviewed their signals one last time:

O'Brien hiked his pants up. McGloin said, "Zero-Flood."

O'Brien made a magician's move. "Rabbit."

O'Brien made "glasses" with his fingers. "Joe-Pa."

O'Brien sped up his signals, but McGloin never missed. He answered with confidence, pausing only occasionally, never having to check the play chart.

Finally O'Brien asked, "Can you believe how far you've come in the last nine months?"

"Yeah, I can," McGloin said, and they both laughed.

"Your Scranton is showing," O'Brien said, their code for McGloin's cocky, steel-town attitude. "Yeah—well, good. It's true. You've got this—and this is the same stuff we did with the Patriots.

"Now, you've got to know: I'm going to do anything I can to jack this crowd up. If I'm yelling at a ref, you stay calm. This is the most fun you'll ever have. You'll remember this the rest of your life. So, you just keep your poise."

In just a few hours, the hands of the young man to my left would have 100 teammates, 1,100 lettermen, 108,000 spectators, 600,000 alums, and millions of fans depending on them.

Reading the situation, O'Brien said, "Hey, remember what Peyton Manning said pressure is?"

"'Pressure's what you feel when you don't know what the hell you're doing,'" McGloin recited. "'Study your tip sheet.'" With a glint in his eye, McGloin couldn't resist adding, "Peyton Manning. Good quarterback. Maybe the best."

"Shiiiiit," O'Brien said with a stubborn grin, knowing exactly the comparison McGloin was making—to O'Brien's guy, Tom Brady.

"Eli's pretty good, too," McGloin added. "Two rings!"

"Fuck you," O'Brien said, since Eli's second ring was at O'Brien's expense. They both laughed again. "Meeting dismissed. Now let's go kick some Buckeye ass."

Earlier in the week, I'd talked with athletic trainer Tim Bream, a quietly intense, wiry guy who wears the kind of reading glasses that can break apart in the middle, hanging from a rubber strap around his neck. Craig Fitzgerald described him as "sharp, smart, quick. Comes in at five, leaves at eight every night. Guys trust him, trust his ability, and they know he cares about them."

From what I'd seen over several months, that all sounded about right.

Bream, a native of Gettysburg, was a student trainer at Penn State from 1979 to 1983, which included the 1982 championship team. He worked his way up to the NFL, where he served nineteen years for the Chicago Bears. He and his family were happy in Chicago, but when the Penn State job opened up after Paterno's firing, Bream didn't think too long before taking it.

"Some of my peers looked at me, like, why are you leaving this?" he said in his glass-enclosed office looking out on the training room. "My university was getting beat down so bad, I wanted to give back a little bit, not just send money or write letters to the editor. How many people get an opportunity like this?"

The position also provided a chance to work with college kids again.

"In the NFL, the players still have the gleam in their eyes for the first two, three, maybe four years, where they'd play for free. But after they get through that first contract, they're married, they have kids, they have business interests, and they *have* to be there. They do their work, but it's a job. It gets mercenary to a certain degree. You'll see very few Brian Urlachers, who go to one team and stay there.

"These guys," he said, motioning through his window to the players getting taped, "are tired and all that, but they genuinely enjoy playing football, and the experience that goes with it."

And that's what sold Bream on the decision: working with the students, from the football players to the student trainers, in the largest undergraduate training program in the country. "The whole thing was getting back to teaching young people. And when I thought about it, that's what I missed in the NFL, the academic component."

A couple hours before the blue buses left for the stadium, O'Brien was sitting back on his hotel bed, going over his play sheets, with ESPN's *College GameDay* on the TV.

"I just can't give more credit for the job's he's done," Kirk Herbstreit said, talking on TV about the man who was going over his play sheets a few feet from me. "And Mike Mauti reminds me of Ryan Fitzpatrick in Buffalo."

"Mauti will *hit* you!" Desmond Howard added.

"This is *not* your father's Penn State offense!" Lee Corso added. "They ran ninety-one plays in their last two wins."

For these reasons, Corso and Howard picked Penn State to pull the upset, while Ohio State alum Herbstreit stuck with the Bucks.

Whatever reassurance this might have provided was lost on O'Brien, who barely looked up from his work. But when I mentioned why Bream left the Chicago Bears for Penn State, O'Brien became engaged. He'd faced a similar decision: stay in the best league with the best coach and the best quarterback, or take over a college program that looked to be going to hell in a handbasket?

"*This* is college football," he said, referring to the unprecedented season they'd been going through. "You take it all away, and that's what's left. These guys are playing for a lot more than bowl games. They're playing for all the guys who came before, the guys on their team, their classmates in the stands—and Joe! They're playing for Joe!"

O'Brien was undeniably surprised by the severity of the NCAA sanctions. He'd turned down the Jacksonville Jaguars' offer to become their next head coach to accept Penn State's offer, partly because he was told there was little chance that Penn State would receive more than a slap on the wrist. Yet, for all the headaches it created in the present, and the worries for the future—for O'Brien more than anyone else—he was not so consumed by his daily tasks that he was missing what was unfolding before his eyes.

"When you coach at this level, you really do have an effect on kids later in life," he said, a list which would surely include Matt McGloin. "After this year, he will have learned how to work, study, and prepare like an NFL quarterback. When you win, good things happen to you—and if we continue to win, a large part of it will be due to his play. And I tell you what: if he continues to play well, he could get into an NFL camp. I would love for this kid to be the All–Big Ten quarterback. How great would that be? He's got a shot."

On that day, McGloin was leading the league's quarterbacks in just about every category. But could the former walk-on really be the league's best?

McGloin would face the main obstacle to that goal, Ohio State's Braxton Miller, later that day. In just a few hours, the winner of that duel would take a big step toward being named the Big Ten's best quarterback.

The players go stir-crazy trying to kill the hours before night games. Five meals help, as does serial napping, but when they were finally packing up to board the buses, a little after two, it was still a relief.

The strength staff stood at their stations by the three blue buses, handing out Gatorades and taking attendance. On the school buses, the players put their heads down, their caps on, and their earpieces in, bobbing gently to their music. It is not a ride for chitchatting.

It was fifty-nine degrees and gray, with rain expected by game time. On the tree-lined route to the stadium, most of the leaves had fallen, with only the bloodred ones still hanging on. The corn from the university's fields had been harvested, but the Mushroom Research Farm seemed to be running at full speed.

"Been on one of these buses?" Kirk Diehl asked me, as we sat together in the last row.

Yes, I said, for the Ohio and Navy games.

He grinned. "You ain't seen nothing yet."

After the buses groaned up the hill, bouncing all the way, they hit a T-stop, then turned right. This is still on the far outskirts of university property—farmland—but you could already hear the crowds ahead. Whatever I'd seen the first two games had been doubled for this one. The nationally televised night game helped, but five straight wins helped more. These tailgaters had their mojo back. They were even a little blood-thirsty.

When the buses pulled up outside the stadium, the crowd was even thicker, holding up sticks with the stars' faces on them: McGloin, Mauti, Zordich, Stankiewitch, Hodges, Hill. They still flashed the signs from the first game: YOU STAYED WITH US and WE STAND WITH YOU.

When the players walked into their locker room, there was no gazing at the names on the backs of their jerseys. This was not opening night. The players were focused.

Before the team prayer in the dark showers, Larry Johnson Sr., in his lyrical manner, repeated, "This is your finest hour. We were meant to be here. We're here for a reason. Let it flow through you." He reinforced those themes in the team prayer, leading up to lineman Nate Cadogan's unscripted sermon.

Cadogan's sermon built slowly, then grew louder, and faster. When Cadogan was finished, Zordich stayed behind to kneel by himself in the corner for a solid five minutes.

Back in the coaches' room, their self-imposed silence had only grown heavier, broken by big shouts coming from the locker room. The players had formed a circle in the middle, with Fitz in the bull's-eye, smashing a Buckeye helmet with a sledgehammer. Spider has traded helmets with each opponent they've faced over the years, giving him an excellent collection he keeps on shelves in the equipment room—now minus one.

When Fitz walked back to Spider's window, shards of the Buckeye helmet in hand, he channeled his inner John Belushi from *Animal House*: "Sorry about your helmet." Spider grinned and nodded. He'd get another one.

Inspired by Fitz's gesture, Jordan Hill stood up and announced, "Fuck quiet! We're getting *loud* today!" He bounced a circular path in the center of the locker room and said, "When we get a big play, we *all* celebrate! We score a touchdown, we *all* celebrate! The whole fucking team—every play, all day! The Buckeyes are gonna learn, this is Penn State! This is Penn State!

"This is Penn State!"

O'Brien didn't have to add much to that.

Before their first game, they walked out to the tunnel. Before Navy, they trotted.

Before Ohio State, they ran.

Penn State won the toss, deferred as planned, and watched Sam Ficken, whom they feared had strained his leg, boot the ball deep into the end zone—answering at least one question.

Ted Roof's defense answered a few more when it forced Ohio State to punt on its first six possessions. But it could actually have been better—and perhaps should have been.

On Ohio State's second possession, with the ball on Penn State's 44-yard line, Braxton Miller looked to the right flats for Corey Brown, but threw almost directly to Penn State's defensive back Stephon Morris. Seeing nothing but green in front of him, the crowd stood up—only to watch Morris drop the ball.

Not long after that, Miller threw an easy interception chance right at Stephen Obeng-Agyapong, who might also have run it back for a touchdown—if he hadn't dropped it.

Throw in McGloin's long ball to Allen Robinson, who dropped it, and Penn State had blown three great chances for touchdowns in the first quarter alone. These were not turnovers or missed assignments or points allowed. But winning big games like that usually takes someone to step up and make big plays.

The first quarter ended 0–0, and it looked as if the first half would, too, with ten straight scoreless possessions. On the last of those, Penn State drove from its 21-yard line to Ohio State's 20, but even on fourth and 7, O'Brien refused to attempt a field goal, and not without reason.

Ohio State took over from its own 17 and went backward. On fourth down, Penn State's Mike Hull broke through the Buckeye line to block Ben Buchanan's punt, which Mike Yancich recovered in the end zone.

Touchdown. Penn State, 7–0. The tinderbox ignited.

On Ohio State's next possession, on third and 5, the Lions sacked Miller, forcing the Buckeyes to punt from their own 27. With about five minutes left in the half, Penn State had a good chance to score another touchdown and head into halftime with a 14–0 lead. But the refs threw a questionable flag for holding on Penn State, which gave the Buckeyes a first down, and a new start.

Braxton Miller finally looked like the Big Ten's best quarterback on a 33-yard dash down to Penn State's 6-yard line, but Penn State's defense held again. On third and goal from the 1-yard line, with less than a minute left, Mauti had running back Carlos Hyde lined up, but the right tackle blatantly held him—but not blatantly enough for Big Ten refs, who made no call as Hyde ran into the end zone.

When the half ended a couple plays later, the scoreboard said 7–7.

During halftime, they brought out Penn State's deans and other officials to recognize the university's academic achievements. They all received warm applause. But they also introduced President Rod Erickson and acting Athletic Director Dave Joyner, who were enthusiastically booed.

Why the organizers had invited the two wasn't a mystery. There is no college football without a college, and universities need presidents and athletic departments need directors. Why the two men didn't anticipate being booed, however, was a mystery.

The game had been reduced to a thirty-minute sprint, but all the advantages seemed to be Penn State's: they had left far more plays on the table than Ohio State had, including three dropped chances for interceptions; the defense had sacked Miller an incredible five times;

McGloin looked comfortable, hitting 8 of 14 passes for 116 yards, and no turnovers, to Miller's anemic 4 of 12 for 25 yards; and Penn State would get the ball back to start the second half.

O'Brien marched toward the coaches' room, thought of something, stopped, turned around, and marched to the middle of the locker room. "Hey, shut the hell up! Offense"—he pointed their way—"quit making mistakes! Defense"—he pointed again—"keep doing what you're doing. Keep your stinger!" He punched his hand. "Let's fuck 'em up!"

"*Yeah!*"

Quarterback coach Charlie Fisher, a kindly man who could play Andy Griffith in Mayberry, tapped McGloin on his elbow and quietly said, "You're doing a good job."

O'Brien met with the offensive staff in the coaches' shower room. "We gotta relax! We can't have these penalties and bad plays in the middle of drives. We start out every series second and ten, first and twenty, that gets old. Cut that crap out. We do, and we're scoring! We're moving the ball! We're averaging five yards a carry. We've got these guys!

"Let's use more comeback and go routes."

To the team, O'Brien said, "Our D's playing their asses off. Their D is playing like they're tired. They're not hitting shit. Twenty-eight isn't tackling shit. Let's get after 'em *now*!"

"They didn't work like we worked!" Mauti added, almost hyperventilating while strapping his helmet on for the second half. "They sure as hell aren't leaving here with a perfect record!"

"We've worked too hard!" O'Brien shouted to the team. "We've come too far to stop now. So leave it all on the field for thirty minutes. Let's go!"

The crowd—fresh from booing its president and AD—came back to life when their team returned, cheering them heartily. The stars seemed aligned for a Penn State surge—but that's not how it went.

Ohio State's kick went only to the 4-yard line. But after Bill Belton dropped it, then scooped it up in a panic, he could only get to the 11.

Zach Zwinak rushed for 6 yards to the 17, before McGloin got sacked back to the 8-yard line. On third and 13, exactly the sort of situation O'Brien had hoped to avoid, McGloin dropped back, looked around, and fired over the middle—right into the stomach of Ohio State linebacker Ryan Shazier, who ran the ball straight to the end zone: 14–7.

And just like that, every advantage Penn State had going into the half had been wiped clean.

The Lions gamely took their next possession down to Ohio State's 4-yard line, but a holding call and Zwinak runs of 1 and 0 yards forced O'Brien to settle for a Sam Ficken field goal: 14–10.

Adrian Amos finally made Miller pay for his errant passing with an interception, but a sack forced Penn State to punt. Or so it looked, until punter Alex Butterworth rolled out to the right and saw Derek Day wide-open on the right sideline. But the Buckeyes exploited Butterworth's hesitation, and the ref's apparent inability to recognize pass interference, resulting in Day's bobbling the ball before it hit the ground.

The scoreboard said 14–10, but the game was over. Penn State had had every chance to jump out to a crowd-rousing lead, but dropped balls and bad penalties prevented them from taking advantage.

Ohio State took over the ball and then the game, finishing their next three possessions in the end zone. Penn State's two late touchdowns showed resolve and made the final score look better, at 35–23, but they weren't enough to make the visitors sweat.

The Lions and their fans were deeply disappointed, but Urban Meyer could afford to take a broader view. Three months later, back in his spacious office in the Woody Hayes Athletic Center, filled with books, motivational messages, and a couple tables and couches for recruiting, he remembered the moment clearly:

"Here's what I don't hear talked about enough: the students, the players, and the former players. They are the heart and soul of college football.

"In the fourth quarter of that Penn State game [when Ohio State had a 35–16 lead], I took a couple moments to look around and soak it in.

"I saw 110,000 people in that stadium, all wearing white. They were into it—big-time—one of the greatest environments I have ever coached in.

"And then I looked out onto the field. You look at these players. Those guys did nothing wrong. Nothing wrong. Not one player on that field did anything wrong.

"But they weren't playing for a Big Ten title, or a BCS bowl game, or a Top Ten ranking. All that had been taken off the table. All of that was gone. Both teams, all those players, had already had their hearts ripped out, and for nothing they did—and they were playing like it's the Super Bowl. Man, both teams, *every player I saw*, they were putting everything on the line, everything they had, every play.

"Why do they do it? It's for the love of each other, and their school, and the great game of college football. Everything else was stripped way. There was no other reason they did that.

"This is why the game was invented one hundred and fifty years ago. On that day, there were no BCS conversations, no ESPN deals, no NFL draft. Just a bunch of eighteen- and nineteen-year-old kids giving themselves up for each other, their school, and the game. They were not playing for anything else.

"*That* is pure college football. You have two teams playing their hearts out like that—how can you not love it?

"I was actually thinking about all that in the fourth quarter. Those guys on the field, they were playing for all the things we admire. And the crowd could see that. You could feel that.

"When you're standing on the sidelines of the Penn State game that night, you see it, the heart of college football. It wasn't about the media, or the TV contracts, or the commissioners, or the schools jumping conferences every day.

"It was a bunch of eighteen- and nineteen-year-old kids training hard for each other and competing their hearts out every day in practice and games.

"Period.

"That's it.

"There is no more after that."

CHAPTER 18

THE BATTLE FOR THE BROWN JUG

According to the *New York Times'* Nate Silver—yes, *that* Nate Silver, who correctly predicted every state in the 2012 presidential election— the nation's three biggest college football fan bases are Ohio State's (3.2 million), Michigan's (2.9 million), and Penn State's (2.6 million), for a total of about 8.7 million fans, which is more than the entire Pac-12 combined. These three schools usually lead the nation in home attendance, too.

Of the nation's twenty biggest college football fan bases, seven are Big Ten teams', and only Northwestern is not in the top fifty. The nation's oldest league has 17.5 million fans, by far the most, followed by the SEC, the ACC, the Big 12, and the Pac-12, in that order. That statistic—not national titles—determines the value of TV contracts, the lifeblood of college football today.

The real "product" college football is selling is not professional perfection—the SEC currently comes closest—but passion, which constitutes another argument for preserving the charm of the game, instead of "going pro."

These stats teach a few less obvious but equally important lessons, too. If these teams depended solely on their students and alumni for support, they would have only about a fifth of their current following, since the "subway alums" constitute roughly 80 percent of their fan base.

Turning our attention back to the Big Ten's "Big Three" programs, and the 8.7 millions fans who follow them: their gigantic stadiums hold more than three hundred thousand fans, but that still leaves 8.4 million of their followers on the outside looking in, which those fans eagerly do through TV and the Internet. If you want to know why the Big Ten Network was the first conference network, and is by far the most successful, that's where you start: 17.5 million fans, dwarfing the next-biggest fan base, the SEC's, at 13.6 million.

And that's why the Big Ten Network now reaches an estimated 53 million households: because it can.

The Big Ten's 17.5 million fans undoubtedly include just about every demographic you can name in substantial numbers, but it's what they have in common that's most important here: a shared love of their favorite Big Ten schools and the conference itself, its history and traditions, right down to their memories of the same games.

I haven't met all 17.5 million Big Ten fans, or even the 2.9 million who follow Michigan. But I've met a lot of them, and some I've known my entire life, including the gang I grew up with in Ann Arbor—the same guys who went door-to-door with their cornets in grade school, playing "The Victors" for their neighbors, and played tailback for Jim Harbaugh in junior high.

The early habit we all acquired now drives our Saturday get-togethers. In much the same way that our grandparents used quilting circles and our parents used potlucks and dinner parties, watching Michigan football games over the years has been our principal means of staying in touch.

It helps that we know the schedule, and the games are always on Saturdays (at least in the Big Ten—for now), even if the kickoff times these days can run the gamut, and sometimes aren't announced until a week or two before the game. As we've gotten busier, we're lucky to catch a few games together each season, but Big Ten football remains one of the soundest institutions left in the Midwest to anchor your social life.

We settled on the Michigan–Minnesota game—an easy pick, since that weekend Ohio State was scheduled to crush lowly Illinois (and did, 52–22, to go 10-0), Penn State was traveling to pedestrian Purdue (and rebounded nicely, 34–9, to improve to 6-3), and Northwestern had a bye week, standing pat at 7-2.

One of the joys of the watch party is setting up the watch party. While your ritual may vary, I suspect the pattern is about the same for the rest of the 17.5 million Big Ten fans that get together across the country to watch their favorite teams take the field. Second only to inside jokes, the most common comments in both our e-mails and game-time banter are the endless complaints about our favorite team's offense. Doesn't matter the coach, the coordinator, or the quarterback, this stream of criticism transcends all eras and offensive systems.

The reason is simple: When you've been living and dying with your team since you were too young to know you were doing so, you've had a lifetime to think about the subject, and your views are heartfelt. You have skin in the game. And the offense is usually the easiest target.

But the 2012 season contained more than the usual carping about Bo Schembechler's "three yards and a cloud of dust," which might have been dull, but it did the job for decades. James Carville, the political guru who backs his home-state Louisiana State Tigers, has made a side job of criticizing Michigan's boring offense. In 2004, he said, "Michigan plays gutless football. Always has and always will. You could put the New England Patriots in Michigan uniforms and they would still lose to OSU two out of three times and lose the Rose Bowl two out of three times."

The phrase that would probably make most Michigan fans wince stands out: "always has and always will." Intentionally or not, the political guru put his finger on the triple bind of tradition, passion, and results. Michigan fans care about winning, but they also care *how* their team wins. Results alone aren't enough. Remember, passion trumps perfection, or we would have quit watching college football a long time ago—or the Little League World Series, for that matter. Like its Big Ten brothers, Michigan needed to win, but in a way that honored its fans' beloved traditions.

But underneath their endless griping about the offense was a deeper, though rarely stated, concern: that Michigan's reliance on its proud tradition and conservative ways prevented it from keeping up with the faster, innovative offenses—the kind that Appalachian State and Oregon used in back-to-back games to give Michigan football the wake-up call of all wake-up calls. If these fears were founded, the team the fans loved so much would soon be relegated to also-ran. While they don't require perfection to love their team, losing doesn't foster love.

The breadth of this fear—and the hope of a renaissance—became manifest after Michigan hired Rich Rodriguez, the father of the spread-option offense, in December of 2007.

Throughout the 2012 season, I had been surprised to learn how many

Big Ten fans—particularly Buckeye fans, I'd noticed—viewed Michigan's bold move as a clarion call for the rest of the league, hoping it would force their teams to embrace the future, too. If Rodriguez succeeded at Michigan, they believed, more Big Ten schools would start hiring coaches from outside the conference with faster, more innovative offenses, and soon the Big Ten would again start beating the best from the South and the West.

But at the end of Rodriguez's third season, a 7-6 campaign capped by losses to Wisconsin, Ohio State, and Mississippi State in the Gator Bowl by a combined score of 137–49, Dave Brandon let Rodriguez go. The renaissance never materialized. As Rodriguez himself said to his staff, minutes after being fired, "It was a bad fit from the start."

A week later, Brandon hired Brady Hoke, who was less celebrated but more familiar. He led Michigan to an 11-2 record his first year out, including a long-awaited win over Ohio State, and a BCS bowl victory.

But 2012 had not been as kind, with the Wolverines getting gutted by Alabama, falling over themselves against Notre Dame, and worse, losing a laugher to Nebraska the previous week after Robinson went down with an injured elbow. The coaches seemed utterly unprepared for this emergency. Instead of giving the ball to heir apparent Devin Gardner, whom Rivals had ranked the nation's top high school quarterback in 2009, the coaches kept him at receiver to shore up the weakened ranks there and put redshirt freshman Russell Bellomy under center. He promptly went 3 for 16, with 3 interceptions. Nebraska caught as many of his passes as his own receivers did.

This resulted in a 23–9 embarrassment—with the Big Ten title on the line, no less—which marked Michigan's third game without a touchdown, along with the Notre Dame and Michigan State contests. It also ignited a predictable flame out on the blogs, with fans wondering why Michigan's coaches didn't have a Denard Emergency Plan in place, why Devin Gardner hadn't been put into duty, if Robinson would return that weekend against Minnesota, and if he couldn't, would the coaches put Gardner in or Bellomy?

Under that was a bigger question: Was Michigan moving forward, or backward? And what did it all mean for the "Michigan brand"—which is what Brandon was selling?

"Greetings," former Harbaugh tailback Brian Weisman wrote to the gang, to set up our little party. "I question the quality of the game we intend to watch, but not the idea itself. I can make at least half the game, which is probably more than how long the game will be in doubt (in favor of U-M if Denard plays, in favor of the Golden Gophers if Bellomy plays). I have to give a shout-out to Michigan's offensive coordinator for having no 'plan B' for Denard getting hurt.

"So, our special teams are actually quite good this year for the first time in a long while, our D is getting stronger and stronger, yet our offense is very spotty, and just a big hole when Denard is on the sidelines.

"The Big 10 blows—and RichRod [now at Arizona] beat USC in his first try. It's all a jumble!!"

And that's why we watch.

Throughout the long NFL season—with four exhibition games, sixteen regular-season contests, and up to four playoff games—thirty-two teams compete for just one trophy, the Vince Lombardi Trophy. Never mind that Lombardi himself hated the Super Bowl, resented having to play in it, and wasn't that fond of the eponymous trophy, either.

But in college football, 124 teams will play not one exhibition game— it is the only sport without them—jumping right into a twelve-game season. A few will play a single conference title game, and half of them will finish with a bowl game. Fourteen games, max. Still too many, in my opinion, but a far cry from the NFL's maximum of 24.

Those college teams will compete not merely for one trophy, but 102 trophies—not even counting the manufactured trophies the conferences, bowls, and the BCS now pile on. The best college trophies don't go to league or national champions, but to the winners of rivalry games, games that stir deeper passions than the Super Bowl ever will. Honestly, do the Baltimore Ravens even hate the San Francisco 49ers? Hardly. They don't even know them—and some of them could be playing for the other team next year. You can't say that about the annual game between Georgia and Georgia Tech, officially titled Clean, Old-Fashioned Hate.

Those 102 rivalry trophies are the result of organic tradition, not corporate marketing. College rivals have played for seven bells, four buckets, and two spittoons, not to mention beer barrels, bourbon buckets, peace pipes, and even a shot glass—which leaves little room for the winner to engrave its name.

The game between Montana and Montana State is officially titled the Brawl of the Wild—surely one of the most testosteroni contests around—with the winner getting . . . a painting. That's right, a painting. Okay, it's a painting of their two mascots, a bobcat and a grizzly—but still.

The victor of the epic clash between LSU and Tulane gets—yes—a rag.

But the best of the batch—considered the oldest in all of football—is the Little Brown Jug, which has been awarded to the winner of the Michigan–Minnesota game since 1909.

The story goes like this:

In 1903 the Michigan football team was riding a 28-game winning streak. Coach Fielding Yost so distrusted Minnesota he directed the team manager to buy a container to store their own water during the game. Thomas B. Roberts walked into a dry-goods store and bought a putty-colored jug for thirty cents.

It didn't seem to help much. In the waning minutes of the game, Minnesota tied Michigan, 6–6, setting off a near riot when Gopher fans charged the field before the final gun, forcing the refs to call the game a tie. The Wolverines scrambled off the field to avoid the mob, leaving their clay water jug behind. Back in Ann Arbor, the penurious Yost decided he wanted the thirty-cent jug back. Minnesota athletic director L. J. Cooke replied, "We have your little brown jug; if you want it, you'll have to win it."

Historian Greg Dooley has learned that story has been beefed up over the years—but that's part of a real rivalry, too.

The Wolverines returned to Minneapolis in 1909 and beat the Gophers 15–6. They walked across the field and reclaimed their water jug, initiating a ritual generations of players have repeated for over a century.

A rivalry was born—all centered around a thirty-cent water vessel.

Thanks to that jug, Minnesota and Michigan played every fall from 1919 through 1998—eighty seasons in a row, making Minnesota Michigan's longest unbroken rivalry. According to the *Minneapolis Star Tribune*'s Patrick Reusse, "For the first fifty of those seasons, Michigan was the number one rival on Minnesota's schedule. Not Iowa, not Wisconsin, but Michigan."

When the Big Ten added Penn State, the league teams naturally could not play each other quite as often, which included interrupting the Michigan-Minnesota series in 1999 and 2000, and again in 2009 and 2010. But when the addition of Nebraska forced the league to create two divisions, they wisely put Michigan and Minnesota in the same division, securing the annual ritual for the foreseeable future.

Or so we thought.

Soon after the usual suspects arrived at my place to watch the game, they were disappointed to see Denard Robinson still on the sideline.

But the gang was excited and relieved to see Devin Gardner in at quarterback, instead of Bellomy. The Wolverines had a chance. On Michigan's first possession, however, Gardner got sacked on third and 2, and on the second, he threw an interception. Maybe he wasn't quite ready for prime time, after all.

The Gophers, who entered the game with the same 5-3 record Michigan had, weren't doing much either, until the second quarter, when they went ahead, 7–0.

"Here we go."

"This sucks."

"I can't believe we're going to see another season go down the drain."

The Wolverines were in danger of getting buried early. Even when Denard was healthy, their offense had shown little stomach for comebacks. In the four games they had trailed, they had only come back against Michigan State—with four field goals.

Things looked even bleaker on third and 17 from Minnesota's 45-yard line, when Gardner appeared to be caught deep in the backfield for yet another sack. Instead of throwing the ball away, however, Gardner trusted his instincts, cut a deep loop back to his left, 15 yards behind the line of scrimmage, then found Drew Dileo camped out by himself in the end zone and launched the ball across his body. It had just enough juice to get to Dileo before the defenders caught up. Touchdown.

The play capped a 91-yard drive, and seemed to mark a change in Michigan's fortunes. The Wolverines followed it up with a 90-yard drive to take a 14–7 lead into halftime.

It was time to move the chips and salsa aside to make room for the Hawaiian Heartstoppers, two large ham, bacon, and pineapple pizzas, and pick up our complaining where we'd left off.

"Hell, we spend most of our time bitching," Paul "Barney" Barnett said. "We even had the nerve to bitch during the Tom Brady era."

Undaunted, we started bitching anew, this time about the wild uniforms that Notre Dame had worn for certain games, which added a blue stripe down their trademark gold pants, with a leprechaun logo on the side. They even messed with the very helmets NBC featured in a special segment seemingly every week—always mentioning that the equipment managers repainted them before every game, with real gold—replacing them with a bizarre gold-and-navy-blue version, again with the leprechaun on one side. Bleacherreport.com gave them an F—which sounded to us like grade inflation.

"If I was a Notre Dame fan," Barney offered, "I wouldn't be one anymore."

"My *God*, are those ugly," Weisman added. "Why do *they* need to change their uniforms? They're *Notre Dame*, fer crissakes!"

"Why do *we*?" Barney said, referring to the five different uniforms Michigan had already donned during the Brandon era, midway through its third season. These included "throwback" jerseys for the September 10, 2011, night game against Notre Dame, with a series of blue and yellow stripes on the shoulders suggesting bumblebees, whose design went all the way back to September 10, 2011. Michigan's jerseys have never had stripes—and when you saw what they looked like, you gained a new appreciation for just how wise Michigan football's founders had been.

We didn't have to ask why. The answer was easy: the $79.99 price tag on the Michigan Adidas "Throwback Premier Jersey."

When fans complained about the "special" uniforms, Brandon often replied by saying how much the players like them. But no player in his right mind would ever speak out against the athletic director's pet project.

Until they graduate, that is, and even then, cautiously. When I raised the matter with David Molk, the nation's best center in 2011, he said, "I remember when the players were the main attraction." I quoted Molk back to the crew, who pointed out that Michigan football had attracted crowds of one hundred thousand or more for thirty-five consecutive years—a total of 242 straight games, to that point—before Brandon introduced the "wow experience."

But our far-bigger complaint was the soaring price of actually going to the games, which had become prohibitive for young families, like the ones in my living room.

"How can they claim to have a waiting list for season tickets when they try to sell you 'ticket packages' for one Big Ten game and two los-ers?" Barney asked. "And even for those, they're asking you to pay for a 'Personal Seat Donation.'"

My friends have discovered that paying the premium, however steep, is not nearly enough to satiate the beast. After you get to the game, the marketing begins anew. Because every game is televised, fans have come to expect about twenty commercial breaks per game, most lasting one to two minutes. To loyal fans, who sit in a stadium that is too hot in Septem-ber and too cold in November—and often too rainy in October—this feels as galling as taking the time, money, and effort to drive downtown to a local store, only to have to wait there while the clerk talks on the phone with someone who didn't bother to do any of those things. The most important man in the stadium is not the quarterback or the coach or even the athletic director, but the anonymous person on the sideline wearing the red gloves. He signals the refs when to stop the game for TV ads, and when they can start the game back up.

Michigan and Notre Dame have long been the only two stadiums to forbid advertising in their buildings—a point of pride for both fan bases—but at U-M, it's creeping in on the concourse pillars, which fea-ture ads for two banks, an oil company, a car company, and StubHub; and on the big screens, where endless promotions try to get you to buy tickets to other sporting events, or to host your corporate event or wed-ding in the stadium, all while those season-ticket holders wait for the man with the red gloves to restart the game.

If fans want to escape the rock music—in lieu of the marching band— or loud solicitations for soccer tickets, they can go to the concession stand, where a bottle of water costs four bucks, a container of popcorn five, and a hot dog six. One friend calculated that taking her husband and two kids to the games—without dinners or hotel rooms—costs about $500 per Saturday, more than a day at Disney World. And Mickey never loses or snows on you.

For all these reasons, my friends—who developed what they thought were lifelong habits of attendance as kids—have found themselves in the last few years rarely going to the stadium anymore.

The straw man of the hour was Michigan athletic director Dave Bran-don. Brandon talks a lot about "brand loyalty," but that combines two words that, to a college football fan, aren't related. College football fans are fiercely loyal, but their loyalty is to something they most definitely do not see as a brand, rather something much deeper. If Michigan football ever lost loyal fans like my friends in the living room, who were raised on Michigan football, could it win them back?

Clearly, Brandon was betting that the endless branding would keep them in the fold. And perhaps if not, other fans could replace them.

But Jim Duderstadt was not so sure — and he's given this more thought than most. Michigan's former nuclear engineering professor, dean, and president, who authored the book *Intercollegiate Athletics and the American University: A University President's Perspective* in 2003, had worked at the forefront for reform in the 1990s, and still weighs in on the subject in national publications.

"A lot of schools and colleges are hiring a lot of staff in the branding area," he told me, "which I think is both expensive and dangerous. They're building their marketing departments, their Internet presence, and hiring outside marketing companies for their bicentennials. When you do that, who owns your history? Who tells it?

"You'll see that the budget for the athletic department has skyrocketed in the four years Dave Brandon has been here."

And, in fact, from the $100 million budget Brandon started with in the 2010–11 fiscal year, it has quickly expanded to $137.5 million for 2013–14. (This does not include the estimated $340 million in capital expenses for the athletic campus's new master plan).

In June 2013, Brandon presented his budget to the Regents, adding, "I tell our coaches we have an unlimited budget for achieving championships and receiving incentive-based pay."

Brandon will more than cover the $37.5 million increase in operating expenses with a projected $146.4 million in revenues, for an $8.9 million surplus. Three million of that will come from the one-time NHL "Winter Classic" to be played at the Big House on January 1, 2014.

But far more will come through a 30 percent increase in football season ticket prices, from $50 per game for the 2009 season, before he took office, to $65 per game for the 2012 season. While ticket prices remained stable in 2013, seat license fees jumped that year from 20 percent for the best seats — from $500 to $600 — to 60 percent near the corners, an increase from $125 to $200.

When you include both the ticket prices and the seat license fees, season ticket holders saw a per-game price increase anywhere from 34 percent (to $150 per seat per game on the 50-yard line) to 51 percent (to $75 per seat per game in the end zone).

The few analysts I've talked with who've compared the numbers have been alarmed by the increases, but Duderstadt is more concerned about "how little of these revenues are actually spent on student-athletes—for financial aid, academic support, and health care—and instead are spent on the expansion of facilities and the staff, in areas such as marketing, fund-raising, communications, other auxiliary activities, and coaching salaries. In the revenue sports, these are approaching levels that are truly extreme and quite unwarranted when compared with other university activities."

Once again, the budget numbers back up Duderstadt's concerns.

The budget spent on scholarships, for example, over which the athletic department exercises little control, grew steadily by about 5 or 6 percent a year, from $16.2 million in 2010–11 to $19.7 million in the 2013–14 budget, while staff salaries have grown from $34 million to $49 million, or about a 45 percent increase. This expansion included a 62 percent increase in administrator compensation, from $7.4 million to $11.5 million.

Although far from the department's biggest item, "Operating and Administrative Expenses" have nearly doubled over those same four years, from $8.6 million to $16.5 million.

What does the additional $7.9 million go for? In the 2010–11 fiscal year, the department spent $473,000 on "Marketing, Promotions and Ticketing," but in 2013–14 it will spend $1.54 million on those things, an increase of 225 percent. (This does not include the marketing personnel hired.)

During the 2010–11 fiscal year, the department spent $444,000 on "Professional Travel and Conference Dues." In the 2013–14 budget, it tripled, to $1.324 million.

An item titled "Hosting, Food and Special Events" increased in the same four years from $436,000 to $2.6 million—an increase of almost 500 percent.

"It's a different operation now," Duderstadt concluded. "And most of the expenditures are *not* associated with what's going on on the field, but it's the branding business—and I think it's a house of cards.

"There are a lot of good, smart, young coaches in the Big Ten. Urban Meyer is one. They're going to be a dominant force at Ohio State for years to come—and Dave's going back to the Domino's days, as Stephen Colbert said, of putting ketchup on cardboard and selling it as pizza. Branding will not fool the fans forever. No matter how much you build the brand, if you don't have the product, sooner or later it gets you."

Even if it does, the expense of it all has stunned Brandon's predecessor, too.

While Bill Martin has steadfastly kept his silence after leaving office in 2010, Brandon has spoken critically, publicly, and frequently of the previous administration.

Soon after Brandon was hired, he often boasted to audiences that he planned to let a third of the 275 employees he inherited go, and within a year and a half he had accomplished his goal. Because almost all of them had signed "nondisparagement" clauses in their buyouts, Brandon knew if he stopped short of mentioning names, he could speak freely without being challenged from those he was disparaging.

Of the eighty-five employees who were no longer with the department, "some of them have been natural retirements," Brandon said to an audience in June of 2012. "Some of them have self-selected to other places because maybe they resist change. That's not good. We had other people that couldn't perform at the level we needed. The skill level was not there to be able to carry out the change and the aspirations and expectations of our department."

He replaced the eighty-five employees he let go, then hired an additional thirty-three, expanding his marketing department from three people to more than a dozen, and his development team from nine to twenty-eight full-time staffers, to create a total workforce of 308 employees.

"We've gone through a period of change that certainly results in a completely different organizational structure," he told his audience. "We are much stronger."

Why was the previous administration so weak, in his opinion? Because their attitude, he said, was simply that "We're Michigan. We didn't want to change. We were stuck in 'This is the way we do things at Michigan.' If we didn't like the way things were going, we would just sing the fight song."

This got a laugh, so Brandon repeated it often, but it also got back to those employees who had left, for various reasons. I have talked with more than a dozen of them, and several people still in the department, who predictably feel unappreciated each time Brandon's public comments about the previous administration show up in the press.

(Both those who have already left and those who are still working in the department insisted on anonymity. Brandon himself declined my request for an interview, and did not allow anyone else in the department to speak to me, including staffers, coaches, and players.)

The former staffers often prefaced their comments by stressing that they were not targeting Brandon, but defending the record of the Martin administration, and their main concern was the future of the department.

To those ends, they almost uniformly pointed out that their team left Brandon some $400 million in capital improvements—in the form of fourteen state-of-the-art buildings, both new and renovated, including the Big House—plus about $10 million in annual operating surpluses and over $50 million in the reserve fund. Further, they generated the plans and the funds for the renovations to the basketball and hockey venues, which were completed after they left.

"From my perspective," said one, who is not given to bold statements, "it's hard to appreciate how positive the situation was that Dave inherited. In the history of intercollegiate athletics, has there ever been an AD who received the keys to a department that had all that?"

Another said, "Dave confuses disagreeing with being unwilling to change. If you're not a yes-man, you better get your résumé ready. He has gotten rid of anyone who disagreed, and since he leads by fear and intimidation, there is no one there who is challenging any of his ideas. That can be very dangerous for the future of any organization."

"For the record," another added sardonically, "I cannot recall one person ever singing 'The Victors' as an administrative exercise."

Thus, by the time I met with Bill Martin in early 2013, three years after he had stepped down, he was willing to make at least a few observations he had previously kept to himself.

"Look into how much is spent on marketing, then look at how effective it is," he said. "Look at the increase in men's basketball attendance this year," he added. Michigan's top-10 men's team played twenty games at home, attracting capacity crowds of 12,693 for fifteen of those games, with only two under 10,000. "That would happen if you didn't spend one penny on marketing. You don't have to do marketing at Michigan. We have the fans. We have the support. We have a great reputation. All you have to do is win. If you win, they will come. You just need to make it as affordable as possible for your fans."

And that means keeping unnecessary expenses down—like marketing, and just about everything else that isn't directly connected to the field.

"For all the talk of 'return on investment,' it isn't that complicated," said Martin, who has made many millions himself as one of Washtenaw County's biggest real estate developers. "When you invest in the student-athletes, the facilities, in coaching, you see a return. The rest is for show."

So why do it? Duderstadt has a theory:

"Brandon comes out of a CEO world—and even a million-dollar salary is chump change for those guys. So it has to be a personal payoff to be out in front of a crowd of one hundred thousand, cheering for you. You don't get that as a CEO."

You also don't get to stand on the sidelines, chest-bump the players when they come off the field, and sign autographs standing next to Denard Robinson after the games.

"Brandon always says he's 'building the brand,'" Duderstadt says. "But of what? Dave Brandon. That's the brand he's building."

In the third quarter, the Gophers threatened to tie it up before Gardner hit Jeremy Gallon in the end zone to take a 21–7 lead. The Wolverines never looked back, finishing the job 35–13, to retain the Brown Jug.

The cameras focused on longtime equipment manager Jon Falk hauling an old-timey-looking trunk onto a table, and unlatching two locks to let the linemen pull out the 109-year-old trophy.

Brown Jugologist Greg Dooley provided a "very conservative" estimate that the Little Brown Jug would fetch anywhere between $15,000 to $25,000 on eBay—or roughly eighty thousand times the thirty cents Yost's manager Thomas B. Roberts plunked down at the Minnesota dry-goods store in 1903. The value has multiplied so many times for one simple reason, and it's not the Jug's age, or its quality. It's because a lot of people have cared a lot about the Little Brown Jug, for a very long time.

Judging by the smiles on the players passing the Jug around and hoisting it over their heads, however, they were not looking to sell it at any price.

CHAPTER 19

THE MUDBOWL
AND THE BIG HOUSE

Friday, November 9, 2012: The Wolverines returned to Ann Arbor with the Little Brown Jug on board, a bowl-eligible 6-3 record, a 4-1 mark in the Big Ten, and a decent shot at winning the Legends Division. They had lost to Nebraska, but Nebraska had already lost to Ohio State. One more loss for the Huskers—who had to come from behind to beat Michigan State, 28–24, the previous week and were hosting an improving Penn State squad that weekend—and Michigan would take the division lead with only two games left.

But Michigan's next game was against a resurgent Northwestern squad, one that came to the game with a 7-2 record, its only blemishes being late losses to Penn State and Nebraska. If the Wildcats could beat the Wolverines this weekend, they'd also have a crack at the division crown. The loser of this game would, however, effectively be out of the running.

In the old days, this wasn't a contest. In Schembechler's twenty-one years as Michigan's head coach, he lost to every Big Ten team at least once, except one: Northwestern. But the Wildcats had beaten Michigan four times in their last thirteen games, almost a third. With Pat Fitzgerald in his seventh year, the Wildcats had the kind of stability that Michigan, Ohio State, and Penn State could only envy.

That Friday I walked down State Street to see my two favorite barbers, Jerry Erickson at Coach & Four, and Red Stolberg at State Street Barber Shop. Both shops always do good business before a home game, but they seemed unusually busy.

Erickson clued me in: "Mom and dad are coming!" he said. "Parents Weekend! Gotta get cleaned up, especially if they want to get taken out to the big steak house and get wined and dined!" The students filling his seats nodded and grinned.

And how did Erickson's customers feel after their team had kept the Jug? "Everybody's happy!" Jerry said. "Northwestern's not bad, but we've got the home-field advantage. Not gonna let the home crowd down. Not on Parents Weekend!"

"They got a little confidence now, and a little momentum—and they'll do it. Go Blue!"

I walked a few doors down the street to see his cousin Red Stolberg, whose outlook tends to be more circumspect. But like everyone else, he was happy to have the Jug in town, along with the parents.

"Opening Day, Homecoming, Parents Weekend, a good rivalry game—it all makes a difference," he said, pointing to the young men waiting for their haircuts. "I see business go up because mom's coming up for the game! Got to get a trim. Got a lot of guys coming up the past few days for that."

Ann Arbor's Convention and Visitors Bureau estimates that a good football weekend pumps $10 million into the local ecomony—and that doesn't include Michigan's take, which approaches that figure from stadium revenue alone.

The buzz Stolberg was hearing, however, was not about the football team, but the men's basketball team, which had just been ranked fifth in the preseason polls.

"Fans are kind of excited about the team," he said, "but they've also got more people complaining about the basketball seats—tickets cost more, you get moved if you don't donate enough, all that. A lot of the old guard, folks who've been going to the games for years, rain or shine, they're getting moved by the big-money folks, the corporations. I know a lot of guys turned in their tickets. They ain't happy!"

If the situation for season-ticket holders at the Big House was getting tighter—with higher ticket prices, seat licenses, and the like—it was nothing compared to what the basketball regulars were dealing with.

One of them is my accountant, Gary Rogow, who earned his bachelor's degree from Michigan and had purchased basketball season tickets for three decades—including a lot of lean years, when attendance was down because of poor coaching, NCAA sanctions, and the economy, when only the hard-core fans kept coming. Rogow is a pretty calm, studied individual—an accountant, in other words—and I'd never seen him worked up about anything until I asked him about his basketball tickets.

In football, he pointed out, so long as you're willing to pay more for your tickets, you can keep them. "Your money was as good as the next guy's money," he said. "Just because someone was a bigger donor didn't mean he could take your seats. You had the right of first refusal. Loyalty was rewarded."

In basketball, the opposite was suddenly true. Your choice of seats was entirely dependent on Michigan's new "priority points" system, which gives 20 points for a U-M degree, 40 points for a varsity letter, and 1 point for every year you've bought season tickets. That sounds pretty good, until you learn they also give 1 point for every $100 you "donate." Thus, if you graduated from Michigan, earned a varsity letter, and bought your season tickets for twenty years, you could still be surpassed in the priority-point pecking order by someone who never went to U-M or earned a letter or attended a game, once they donate more than $8,000. Many were willing to spend that much—and much, much more.

"Donors are far more important than you," Rogow said. "It doesn't matter if you've been buying season tickets for twenty years, even when the team was horrible and Crisler was empty, and they have never been to a U of M basketball game in their entire lives. A two-thousand-dollar donation to the athletic department gets you as many priority points as twenty consecutive years of buying season basketball tickets. They can buy eight seats—including yours. Who says you can't put a price on loyalty?"

At the Michigan athletic department, they've calculated the exchange down to the dollar.

"The athletic department's attitude is 'We don't care how many years you sat there. But thanks for sticking with us until now. Good-bye!'

"I could go on," Rogow concluded, "but what's the point?"

There are a few points, actually. The first: Rogow is far from alone, but many other loyal fans cannot afford to keep their tickets or have chosen not to.

"Just because you *can* charge them more," Bill Martin told me, "doesn't mean you *should*.

"What you want to do—and we said this from my first day—is graduate your student-athletes, make sure everyone is representing the university in a highly ethical manner, run winning programs—because that's part of our DNA—and pay our own way.

"How you do that," he added, paraphrasing the philosophy that Michigan's athletic department had followed for over a century, "is pay all your bills, invest in first-class facilities and coaches, endow scholarships, have a little reserve to protect the future, and never be a burden on the institution, so the cash can flow uphill" (to the university's central administration for need-based scholarships).

"You're not there to ring up the cash to the nth degree. It's a nonprofit model!"

That's why, during the 2008 recession, Martin's administration actually lowered ticket prices and gave free full-page ads in every football program to the Big Three automakers, who have generously supported the department for decades. It's also why Martin insisted on being paid a dollar for each of his first two years as athletic director, then agreed to the going rate of about $300,000 per year thereafter. Already a multimillionaire, Martin turned down the president's offer to double his salary, and all bonuses. When he traveled to New York on university business, he and his staffers flew coach on Northwest Airlines, then took a cab in the city, or the subway, or, most often, simply walked.

Dave Brandon is estimated to be worth tens of millions, but he is now paid three times what Bill Martin received. For the first time in Michigan's history, the athletic director makes more than the president. When university business calls Brandon to New York, he often flies out on a donor's private jet, then pays a limousine service to drive him to meetings around the city.

Back in Ann Arbor, for his first two years Denard Robinson borrowed his teammates' beat-up cars—Thomas Rawls's pickup truck was particularly popular among the players—before he bought a rusty clunker of his own, a Pontiac Grand Am, possibly a '98, though he wasn't sure. His protégé, Devin Gardner, picked up a little blue coupe, which had "wires hanging out from the engine over the front bumper, and half the back bumper missing," teammate Elliott Mealer told me. "Devin couldn't have resold that thing to a blind man. So, no. No one's giving us cars."

After a point, the contrasts start to matter.

• • •

If you're running a Fortune 500 company, virtually every expense and every decision can be justified by your company's profitability.

Brandon requires reporters who cover Michigan athletics to get approval from his office before contacting players' parents and their high school coaches, who have no affiliation with the university, or the reporters will get their press passes pulled. Under Brandon, the staff frequently calls reporters to chastise them for printing what they perceive to be negative stories, or simply unflattering statistics. And the staff delays Freedom of Information Act (FOIA) requests as long as possible, charge far more than their peer institutions for each request, and then provide as little information as possible — including basic data like coaches' contracts. (In fairness to the athletic department, *The Michigan Daily*'s Stephanie Steinberg's in-depth investigation revealed that Michigan's central administration ranked last of the five Big Ten institutions she studied on all those counts.)

"Every interview and press conference the [athletic] department sets up is presented as a huge favor, not just them doing their jobs," one beat writer told me, echoing the sentiments of his peers. "They show amazing contempt for the media — and really free speech itself."

When Brandon's staff makes Indiana basketball fans wearing red shirts leave the Michigan student section; when he charges tens of thousands of dollars for archived footage available in U-M's libraries for virtually nothing; and when he regularly attends Executive Officer meetings to which he is not invited, he is merely making sound marketing decisions — for a corporation.

Controlling the message, protecting the brand, and accessing power are pillars of the successful American executive. It's less clear that those practices reflect the values of a public university.

But when he seems to go out of his way to alienate the football lettermen by eliminating the fifty to one hundred tickets the department always kept on hand for former players to purchase at full price for individual games; or when he takes over their annual Chili and Cornbread pregame tailgate and moves it from the Big House plaza to the indoor football building; or when he tries to usurp "Victors Night" from the lettermen, which they quietly underwrite without asking for anything in return — it's not clear why even a corporate executive would do those things.

But it does establish that he, and he alone, is in charge—and there's surely managerial merit in that.

Of course, the fans can rightly say those are the problems of the press and the former players. None of those things directly affect the fans' experience. But ticket prices do.

"You've got to be careful that you don't price your fans out of the experience," Martin told me. "Don't put your fans in the position where they think, 'Why go to the games? What else can I do with my time and my money?'

"You need to make certain a thirty-five-year-old guy with a couple little kids can afford to come to your event."

That brought Martin to a larger point. "My thesis about sports in America," he said, raising an index finger. "We've reached the saturation point. You see this in the NFL, and the NBA. The quality of TV has improved so much, you can stay home, see a great game, and not shell out twenty bucks for parking, ten for a beer, five for a bottle of water, and sit in your Barcalounger and scream your head off and know no one's going to get mad at you."

Even the ones who can afford to keep their tickets are increasingly discontent with what they find at Crisler Center, for which Bill Martin raised funds and developed plans to renovate with an attached basketball practice facility, new weight rooms and offices, new lower-bowl seating, and a gorgeous concourse, to which Brandon added a fancy waterfall near the front. Everybody loves the renovations, but it's the "wow" factor that Brandon persistently promotes that has left some of them, well, less than wowed.

"He talks about the 'wow factor,'" Duderstadt told me, "which I saw up close at the Michigan State and Indiana basketball games. The 'wow factor' was a lot of loud, piped-in music, flashing scoreboards, and endless ads."

After Martin took years to remove all the advertising from Crisler, Brandon has brought the advertising back with a vengeance. If you complain about the noise to the people at Guest Services, one fan told me, they will give you earplugs. Granted, the students are surely more amenable to the piped-in music than the older patrons, and the coaches and players like the energy it provides, but everyone agrees the atmosphere is becoming less like the collegiate kookiness of Duke's Cameron Crazies and more like the smooth, shiny productions of the Detroit Pistons.

"The fact that they put the Michigan pep band so far away," Duder-stadt said, "I mean, way, way up there, while they're blasting rap music—it just doesn't seem like college sports to me.

"I'll be generous and say, I don't think Dave Brandon 'gets it'—but he's not stopping to ask me or anyone else. I'm not sure where he gets his feedback, or if he gets any at all. It's full speed ahead."

Searching for the silver lining, Duderstadt added, "The one good thing they have is a bigger student section, where they're right down there, all together. But very few university people are in that crowd anymore." (And, in fact, the new student section was created under Martin.)

As one friend of mine—a U-M graduate and employee—told me after he took his sons to Crisler for a game, "Michigan athletics used to feel like something we shared. Now it's something they hoard. Anything of value they put a price tag on. Anything that appeals to anyone is kept locked away—literally in some cases—and only brought out if you pay for it. And what's been permanently banished is any sense of generosity."

The suits will find your fun, buy it up, and charge you for it.

Back in his barbershop, Red Stolberg had his own theory.

"Ten or fifteen years ago," he recalled, waving his razor in the air, "they had six or seven thousand folks on the wait list for football season tickets. The last five years, you want a ticket, you got it. I don't know what the actual numbers are—or if they'd tell ya!—but the demand is a lot softer than it used to be, I can tell ya that."

Since his cousin up the street, fellow barber Jerry Erickson, taped tickets for sale in his big picture window, Stolberg had a decent sense of the shifting market.

Here's the bigger point. College football fandom depends on the same force that buoys our nation's currency: faith. Since the United States left the gold standard, the US dollar has value only because billions of people around the world think it does. When a critical mass of people stop thinking that, our dollars will be worth no more than Confederate scrip—without the eBay memorabilia value.

College football isn't nearly as important, of course, nor as serious. But the ecosystem works the same way. Going to a football game at Michigan, Ohio State, or Penn State is great largely because over one hundred thousand people at each stadium think it is. If the sellouts stop and the empty seats increase, the fans start questioning why they're paying such incredible fees for a "wow experience" that cannot attract a sellout.

Former Michigan athletic director Don Canham once explained to me his simple strategy: everyone wants to eat at the restaurant with the line out the door. His first goal was to create the illusion of a sellout with Band Day, when thousands of high school musicians filled the seats for the weaker games; Scout Day (ditto); and $2 student tickets for all the games. Soon, the illusion became real, the place sold out, the wait list grew, and the price went up. But even he never thought anyone would pay more than twenty bucks—*twenty bucks!*—for a football ticket. And he was telling me that the year he passed away, in 2005.

But few predicted the creation and incredible growth of the Big Ten Network, which inspired other conferences to follow suit and dramatically increased revenue for college sports across the board.

At no time is this more obvious than during March Madness, which generated a record $1 billion—with a *b*—dollars in ad revenue in 2013, including an increase in Internet revenue from $32 million to $60 million in a single year, a trend that will surely continue.

But all this was occurring against the backdrop of something new and surprising: "swaths of empty seats" at the arenas hosting the NCAA tournament games, "and declining TV ratings," according to PennLive.com. "This is how the NCAA has decided to run its single most lucrative event. Given the return the NCAA and networks have seen on the digital platforms, it's not going away."

In other words, if you like off-track betting parlors and the empty stands they create, you're going to love the future of big-time college sports.

Saturday, November 10, 2012: Instead of thinking about the business of football or basketball, or handicapping the final quarter of the race for the Big Ten title, after I woke up on a cold, rainy Saturday morning, I headed across the Diag and up South University to walk back in time toward something called the Mudbowl.

In 1933, Alabama won the Southeastern Conference's first title, Columbia University won the Rose Bowl, and Michigan once again took home the Knute Rockne Memorial Trophy as the national champion, with a man named Jerry Ford playing both center and defensive line. That's the year the Mudbowl was born.

For seventy-nine years, every fall the Michigan SAE fraternity—whose house looks like a medieval castle, complete with a turret overlooking the grounds—has made its pledges dig up their front yard, flood it with water, and voilà! Their lawn becomes a mud bowl, ready for the annual football game.

Nineteen thirty-three was a different world. Seventy-nine years ago, the leap from the Mudbowl to the Rose Bowl—played that year in a "small lake," making it almost as muddy as the SAE's front yard—was a lot smaller than it is today. Oh, and a new venture called the National Football League was little over a decade old, but few cared very much, and even fewer still in State College, Columbus, Ann Arbor, or Evanston.

Fast-forward eight decades, and college football is a lot closer to the NFL than it is to the Mudbowl—which still doesn't charge its hearty spectators a dime to watch.

By 10:00 a.m., a full crowd estimated at a couple thousand (they don't have turnstiles or seat licenses at the Mudbowl) had already lined the bowl-shaped outer rim of SAE's front lawn, which runs from the South University sidewalk down to the patch of watery mud.

The "field," which doesn't have a blade of grass on it by game day, is not quite twenty-five yards by fifty yards. But that's okay, because it's not quite rectangular, either, or even flat. It runs uphill from west to east about four feet. The SAEs naturally gave the deeper end to their opponents, the Fijis, who'd won a playoff for this honor.

The play wasn't pretty, but it was fierce, with almost every down resulting in at least one player getting jammed face-first into the swamp, followed by a five-man shoving match, which usually ended with at least one more player eating mud. If you could claim anything was "beautiful" about a game that was literally the ugliest ever played, it's that they were playing this hard for nothing more than bragging rights. No money, no fame, just pride—which might explain why neither side backed down an inch.

On one play, the Fijis had the SAE quarterback on the run. He escaped his attackers, only to tackle himself by tripping in the mud and wiping out. Although he was clearly down—his mud-covered T-shirt told you that—a Fiji slogging by still felt the need to dunk the quarterback's face into the mud, which started yet another fight.

That's when it hit me: All of us watching this primal contest had gone further back in time than just seventy-nine years. We'd flown all the way back to November 6, 1869, and we were watching the first American football game between Rutgers and Princeton. It was glorified rugby—an excellent outlet for excess testosterone, and an effective catalyst for school spirit.

The forward passes the SAEs and Fijis threw were new, but everything else had been done before, countless times—and these players were showing all of us why football had caught on in the first place. It was cold, it was chaotic, it was crazy, but the pure energy pulled the crowd in, just as it surely did four years after the Civil War. The banks were packed with people the entire game, and I didn't see a single soul leave. (Of course, not having any TV time-outs helped.)

Every Michigan football player I've ever talked to about the Mudbowl was dying to play in it. I know of at least a few who—at the risk of Schembechler killing them with his bare hands—snuck out of the Campus Inn hotel early on Saturday morning to see the spectacle for themselves, before dashing back to catch the team buses to the Big House. It's not hard to understand why, given the forty-hour-plus workweeks they go through just to play big-time college football, they might envy the Mudbowlers, and their primal fun.

If you added it all up, the frat brothers might have had the better deal. After SAE dispensed with the Fijis 30–21, they naturally celebrated by diving into the mud—all the brothers, not just the players.

Satisfied, I walked down South U, past the Diag and the President's House on the right, the first in town to have indoor plumbing, and the picturesque law quad on the left, toward the Student Union, where John F. Kennedy introduced the idea of the Peace Corps from the front steps during his presidential campaign.

As I turned left down State Street, the crowd grew thicker with each block, while the lines separating homes and tailgate parties got blurrier. With each step, I was walking away from college football's distant past and toward its present. But the people I was looking for might, I hoped, give me a glimpse into the game's future.

They were not football legends, just a couple twenty-three-year-olds. I was in search of Michigan family—literally. And the history I was after wasn't that old—just a few weeks, when Adam Offerman proposed to Ally Stencel in the first half of the Air Force game.

I tracked them down outside a students' house right across Division Street from Elbel Field, and right across Hoover from Revelli Hall—ground zero for tailgaters.

Offerman had paid for a scoreboard announcement between the first and second quarter of the first home game that fall, then started scheming with Ally's parents and her best friend to pull it off.

"I had no idea," Ally said. "It was just a typical tailgate. My dad kept saying, 'Beautiful day for a tailgate!' About ten times!"

"That man can *not* keep a secret!" said her mom, Linda.

As the first quarter came to an end, "my mom makes me start reading the scoreboard, every announcement. Someone put up MOM, HAPPY FIFTIETH BIRTHDAY! And she asks, 'Why didn't you do that for me?' Then they showed the band on the screen. 'Look at that! How cool is the drum line?'

"'I've *seen* it! Yes, it's cool! What *is it* with you people?!' But it worked. The next one, I was actually looking. I saw it: ALLY STENCEL, WILL YOU MARRY ME? And I froze!" A couple months later, recounting the story, she got a bit glassy-eyed all over again. "I was shaking!"

Shaking, yes—but not answering. So Offerman had to ask, "Is that a yes?"

"Yes!" she said. *"Yes! Yes! Yes! Yes!"*

"Our whole section stood up and cheered," Ally recalled. "It was a very quiet event—shared with 112,000 of my closest friends."

You can pop the question anywhere in the world, so why do it at the Big House, in the middle of a game? Offerman picked this place and that time because Michigan football is how they met, and he knew how important it was to his girlfriend.

"We've been sitting in the same section for ten years," Ally's mom, Linda, said. "It's all walks of life, but after a while you know everyone, and your section feels like family." Many of those 112,000 people really *were* among their closest friends.

This happy little scene could not have happened, at least not in the same way, at a Michigan basketball game. Here was a glimpse into one possible future: if Michigan applies its basketball-ticket policies to football and starts selling Section 38's seats to the highest bidders, how many fans will want to get engaged surrounded by high rollers they've never seen before?

Decades from now, will the Offermans' kids be so attached to Michigan football that they'll want to copy their parents?

By noon, the gray skies had still refused to give way, dumping a cold drizzle on the ticketholders waiting for kickoff.

Northwestern's players didn't care. They couldn't have been more excited to be there. Thanks to the expanded Big Ten, the Wildcats hadn't played in the Big House since 2008, when no one on the current roster had made the trip.

"You hear about it, and you see it on TV," Northwestern quarterback Kain Colter told me. "When you drive up to it, you think you're going to see this huge thing—but it's not that big on the outside. But the one thing I'll always remember [was] the first time I was jogging into the stadium: it goes down, and it's huge. During warm-ups, I was just trying to get a feel for how big the stadium is.

"It's definitely one of my favorite stadiums to play in. It was awesome. People are so passionate about Michigan football. It really gets my juices going."

If Northwestern's blood brothers are scattered across the country—Duke, Rice, Vanderbilt, and Stanford—Michigan might serve as its closest cousin in the Big Ten. The two universities usually sit atop the league in academic standing and have developed a decent football rivalry, to boot. In ways neither party could have imagined twenty years ago, this game mattered greatly to both sides.

"I have such respect for the people at Michigan," Northwestern president Morton Schapiro told me, "and how they have achieved so much. I've given some lectures up there and know that it is a first-rate school. I've always been a Michigan fan—and I love Denard Robinson! I like to see him going to the basketball games, and how he always has a smile. I root for him—when he's not playing us!"

The crowd got an answer to one pressing question when Michigan's offense took the field: Devin Gardner was starting at quarterback. Then they got another: Northwestern no longer feared the winged helmets, the Big House, or the Wolverines' forty-two Big Ten titles, either.

The Wildcats sent Michigan's offense to the bench after three downs, then mounted an 80-yard drive, led by the elusive Colter, who mixed up his passes and runs all the way to Michigan's end zone for a 7–0 lead.

Amazingly, that marked the first touchdown Michigan's defense had given up in the first quarter of any game since the opener against Alabama, and the first points of any kind since Michigan's second game, against Air Force. When the man with the red gloves allowed play to resume, the Wolverines responded with a 10-play, 78-yard drive to tie the score 7–7, then converted a Colter fumble into another touchdown for a 14–7 lead.

After Northwestern tied the game at 14–14 before the half, the Wildcats had made one thing clear: they were done playing Michigan's patsy.

In the second half, the Wildcats converted a couple third downs to go ahead, 21–14, then tacked on a field goal for a 24–14 lead.

"Michigan wasn't as loud as I thought it was going to be," senior Northwestern defensive lineman Quentin Williams told me. "It was nice to hear so many fans quiet like that for three and a half quarters. We were on top of the world for a little while."

Michigan could have collapsed and conceded the better bowl game and the shot at the Big Ten title to the upstart 'Cats, but Gardner proved just as tough as his mentor, Denard Robinson. On third and 17, deep in Michigan territory, Gardner sent a bomb to tiny Jeremy Gallon, who beat double coverage to get down to Northwestern's 28. Gardner followed with an easy pass to the equally small and speedy Fitzgerald Toussaint, who ran it into the end zone to close the gap to 24–21, before the third quarter ended.

With ten minutes left, and tension rising in this do-or-die game for both teams, the stubborn sun finally pushed away the gray to give the fans a great show on a great day. No one would be asking for a refund after this game.

Gardner gave the fans what they wanted with an impressive 91-yard touchdown drive to go ahead, 28–24, only to see the 'Cats fight back with a touchdown of their own to retake the lead, 31–28.

With 4:46 left, the Wolverines' hopes seemed to fly out the window when Gardner's pass was intercepted and returned to the 50. When

Pat Fitzgerald showed some guts by going for it on fourth and one at Michigan's 41, with Colter barely getting the first down, it looked as if Northwestern might have just sealed the deal. But the 'Cats couldn't get another first down, which "would have won the game right there," Fitzgerald said.

The Wolverines got the ball back on their own 38-yard line with just 18 seconds left, and no time-outs. If you were a betting man, you'd still take the Wildcats—and you'd have a hard time finding anyone to take the Wolverines.

Gardner dropped back and launched a high-arcing, wobbly duck, which looked more punt than pass. It was ripe to be intercepted, and that's just what Daniel Jones planned to do—although just knocking the ball down would have left Michigan at its own 38-yard line with six seconds left, and would probably have done the job.

Jones went for the pick—but he jumped too soon, giving the more patient Roy Roundtree a path to the ball. Roundtree could not catch it cleanly, but he managed to tip it back up into the air like a volleyball player, as he fell to the turf at the 9-yard line. The ball, amazingly, fell right back down to him, and he secured it against his helmet. But it was a catch, fair and square, and didn't even require a review—rare, in this era.

"I remember the pass like it was yesterday," Quentin Williams said two months later. "I saw the ball go up—and I'm like, 'Awesome, we got 'em.' Then I saw him catch it, and I'm like, 'Wow, we're really screwed here.'"

Roundtree bounced back to his feet, displaying his boyish enthusiasm, and pointed the ball at the fans, looking as happy as a frat boy in mud. Just seconds earlier, those same fans had feared a demoralizing fallback to another 6-4 record, and another trip to the TaxSlayer.com Gator Bowl, but now they responded as if Roundree was their leader, unleashing all the noise 112,510 people can make.

"They were going crazy then!" Colter said. "Kind of hard to believe, but just a few seconds before, we had the game won."

Roundtree's teammates, standing on the sidelines and on top of the benches, started jumping and hugging each other, as you'd expect. But it was a little more surprising to see the middle-aged men in the garish sport coats from the Rose Bowl and the Capital One Bowl start hugging each other, too. Although they were paid six figures to "scout" potential invitees to their bowls and perform an objective analysis, they weren't even bothering to fake it. They didn't want Northwestern, its relatively paltry two hundred thousand alums, and weak TV ratings. They wanted the Wolverines—and the money they would bring.

Gardner had no time for celebrations. He ran up to the line of scrimmage, took the snap, and spiked the ball to stop the clock. Brandon Gibbons trotted out to attempt a game-tying, 26-yard field goal.

One fan, hanging over the rail, holding her head, let out an involuntary, "Oh my God!"

Two years earlier, Michigan's kickers could convert only 4 of 14 attempts. But last year, the same kickers made 15 of 19. This year, to that point, Gibbons had made 13 of 15.

So, what would it be—the 2010 Gibbons, or the 2011–2012 versions?

Gibbons stepped toward the ball and blasted a perfect strike: 31–31. Everyone but the Wildcats hugged again: the fans, the players, even the bowl reps.

The crowd knew all momentum had suddenly shifted Michigan's way—and some important Northwestern backers did, too. "To be honest," President Schapiro told me, "after watching Michigan pull off a minor miracle to tie the game, I wasn't that optimistic in overtime."

On Michigan's overtime possession, Gardner rolled out to the right and ran straight through the right corner of the end zone for the go-ahead touchdown.

On Northwestern's turn, facing third and one on the 16, Colter's draw play got stuffed by Kenny Demens, inspiring the band to break into "Temptation" and the fans to yell, in unison, "You suck!"

On fourth and two, Pat Fitzgerald sent Tyris Jones up the middle. But once again, Demens read the play perfectly, eluded his man, and sent Jones hard to the turf.

The Wolverines had held up, won the game, and kept their dream of a Big Ten title alive. Vincent Smith and Denard Robinson hugged, then found Roundtree to hug some more.

The crowd got the moment they had waited for, while the Wildcats got a swift kick in the gut.

"That was probably the worst loss I ever had in my football career," Colter told me. "It was a really hard-fought game, but it was a game we feel like we should have won. Once you lose that kind of momentum, it's really hard to get it back."

When you walk up the famed Big House tunnel, you can keep going straight out to the parking lot and join the tailgaters, or you can turn to your right and join the raucous celebration in the Michigan locker room, or you can turn to the left for the postgame press conferences. Take that left-hand turn and the first stop on your right is Michigan's pressroom, which is usually crammed with four or five dozen reporters and cameramen, and half as many photographers working behind them.

But if you keep going through the catacombs of the old stadium and hit the far wall and turn right, and right again, you'll reach the infinitely smaller—and usually far unhappier—visitors' postgame pressroom.

Here the Northwestern beat writers—most of them working for the *Daily Northwestern*, plus a couple from Chicago—waited for head coach Pat Fitzgerald.

While killing time, one student reporter asked another, "Is this the worst ever?"

The second one thought about it, then said, "No, the Outback Bowl," where the Wildcats had their chance, on January 1, 2010, to taste their first bowl victory since January 1, 1949. They twice spotted Auburn, which would win the national title the next year, a 14-point lead, but came back both times, tying the game with 1:15 left.

In overtime, they held Auburn to a field goal, then attempted a 37-yarder themselves. The ball hit the upright—and bounced back. No good. But the officials called Auburn for roughing the kicker—who had actually been injured on the play—giving Northwestern a first down and the ball on the 9-yard line.

On fourth and goal from the five, Fitzgerald sent in his backup kicker, a freshman. With the Auburn players still not set, Northwestern ran a version of the fumblerooski—but got knocked out of bounds at the two. Auburn had the victory, in what had to be one of the hardest losses any Wildcat had ever suffered.

"No," a third student said, "this was worse. They *had* it!"

"Yeah, but the stakes in the Outback were so much higher," the second one said. "The bowl streak!"

They ended their debate of despair when Fitzgerald walked in. After snatching defeat from the jaws of victory in arguably the most painful manner possible, Fitzgerald was not gruff, short, or snarky. Although hardly happy—the man is as competitive as anyone else in the league, which his hoarse voice revealed—he opened by saying, "First, thanks to everyone for being here, especially those of you who came all the way from Chicago."

There are good reasons why Pat Fitzgerald is among the most respected coaches in the Big Ten.

Down the hall, I stopped in to catch the end of Michigan's press conference. Brady Hoke had already been through, getting a good laugh with his opening line, "Who started writing the article before the game was over?"

But the highlight was Devin Gardner and Roy Roundtree, both intelligent, engaging, funny young men. They wore Adidas sweats and glasses. Not sunglasses, but glasses. The dozens of reporters gathered there were asking about The Catch. Why did it work?

"I think it's 'cause we practice that very play," Gardner said with a grin, "just like that! Obviously, he doesn't usually tip it to himself."

"Basically," Roundtree said, "I saw Devin roll out and he chucked it. It hit my helmet, I held it—and then I pulled it in. [Then] I just jumped up. There was no review, so I'm good!" More laughter.

When someone asked Devin, who had just won his first two starts, about his new role, he cut that idea off quickly. "This is Denard's team," he said of his roommate and mentor. "And it will always be Denard's team until he leaves. He's done way too much."

Nonetheless, Gardner's growing confidence was evident when another reporter asked him, "What made you think, with eighteen seconds left, you were going to win?"

He grinned and said, "We had the ball."

Around the league, the other games unfolded as expected.

While both Michigan State and Ohio State had bye weeks, Wisconsin crushed Indiana, 62–14, Minnesota beat Illinois, 17–3, and Purdue beat a struggling Iowa team, 27–24.

Only one of those teams, Wisconsin, had been ranked at any point that season, yet only Indiana did not fill its stadium, while still attracting a respectable 85 percent of capacity.

That left the Penn State–Nebraska game, played in Nebraska's 81,091-

seat Memorial Stadium. The game drew 85,527—including one Warren Buffett, a loyal alum and fan, who sits with the regular folks—marking Lincoln's 324th consecutive sellout, an NCAA record that stretched back to 1962.

For the Penn State coaches and players, the Ohio State game two weeks earlier had been painful, but no one claimed they had outplayed the Buckeyes or lost for any reason other than Ohio State was the better team that day.

They salved their wounds by mopping up on a Purdue team that had started the season 3-1, then lost its first four Big Ten games. Penn State made it five, with a 34–9 shellacking, all but sealing the coffin of Purdue's fourth-year head coach Danny Hope.

That gave the Nittany Lions a 6-3 record overall, and a 4-1 mark in the Big Ten, where they still had a chance for at least a share of the divisional title if Ohio State stumbled against Wisconsin or Michigan, which was a real possibility.

But the Lions would have to go through Nebraska, the only Big Ten team ranked in the Associated Press's Top 25 that week, at No. 18. The Cornhuskers had suffered their only losses on the road at UCLA and Ohio State, while surviving close calls against Wisconsin, Northwestern, and Michigan State. They had not lost in over a year at their cherished eighty-nine-year-old Memorial Stadium.

Of all the teams in the Big Ten, Penn State players respected their counterparts at Nebraska the most. At least a half dozen told me how similar Penn State was to Nebraska: hardworking, nothing fancy—right down to the uniforms—no trash talk, just good, solid football.

That's why the Penn State players wanted to beat Nebraska so badly. "We were going to show the Big Ten that we're better than their Rose Bowl team," Mauti said. "We were gonna knock 'em off."

The clash of inspired amateurs produced predictably unpredictable results, with the lead jumping back and forth, as often due to a great play as a rookie mistake.

After Nebraska finished another long drive to take a 27–23 lead, Penn State marched right back down the field all the way to Nebraska's 3-yard line. Facing second and goal, with at least two chances to punch it in,

McGloin rolled out to his right and made a quick toss to tight end Matt Lehman, the walk-on from Newport, Pennslyvania.

The play was designed for Lehman to follow his blockers to the outside, and it seemed set up perfectly for Lehman to rumble home. But Lehman saw a gap and, being a rookie, he could not resist. He made a hard left cut, dipping his left shoulder toward the end zone. The Huskers crashed into him at the goal line.

And this is where Lehman made another rookie mistake: He took the ball in both hands and extended it toward the goal line, trying to break the plane for the touchdown. On fourth down, this would make sense— you'd have nothing to lose—but not on second down. The Huskers' David Santos slapped the ball out of Lehman's hands, and after a scramble, Nebraska recovered the ball in the end zone.

Kirk Diehl missed the play because he was busy escorting James Terry to the locker room to have Dr. Sebastianelli look at his high ankle sprain. On their way, they passed the referees' small locker room, where a credentialed Nebraska stadium official in a red jacket had his feet up on a folding chair, watching the game on a portable TV. Diehl had heard the cheers and asked the man what had happened.

"There was a fumble at the goal line," he said, "but it'll be overturned because the ball crossed the plane. You guys just scored."

The replay showed Lehman had, in fact, extended the tip of the ball well past the front edge of the goal line, good for a touchdown. But after several minutes, the replay official confirmed the call on the field.

"It went on forever," Mauti recalled, "and the longer it goes, the more likely they are to screw it up."

When Diehl felt the second cheer reverberate through the stadium, he knew what had happened.

And that was it. The Cornhuskers sent the Lions home with a 32–23 defeat.

"That game hurt the most," Mauti said. "We had 'em. We emptied the tank out there, and that one just hurt."

The plane ride home was the worst of the season—worse even than after the Virginia game.

"Nebraska took something away," Spider said. "It hurt a lot more than Ohio State. We really felt we should've won that game. We wanted to have that storybook ending—and we thought Nebraska was it."

After they returned to State College at 4:00 a.m.—thank you, night game—the Omaha paper and a Nebraska website posted graphically enhanced photos of Lehman's reach for the end zone, showing three-quarters of the ball clearly crossed the goal line. (Give the Nebraskans credit for such honesty.)

It was small consolation, but the Penn State players followed the same protocol they had after every setback over the past year.

"Parents were sending photos of Lehman's touchdown," Craig Fitzgerald said. "'Was he in or was he out?' O-B said, 'Who cares? Let's move on!' No bitching allowed."

That left the Lions with a ho-hum mark of 6-4, and 4-2 in the Big Ten.

They still had to play Indiana, which was 4-6 but had lost to Oregon State, Michigan State, Ohio State, and Navy by a total of 10 points and put up 49 on the Buckeyes. After that, the Lions had Wisconsin, which had lost three games, each by 3 points, but had already clinched a berth in the Big Ten title game.

Nonetheless, Penn State's seniors determined, on the flight home from Nebraska, they would not lose another game that season.

This declaration was not based on their opponents' records or Penn State's, but on nothing more than their force of will.

CHAPTER 20

"YOU CAN'T MANUFACTURE TRADITION"

November 17, 2012: In the Spartan Stadium press box, Northwestern PR man Paul Kennedy still had the Wildcats' previous week's game against Michigan on his mind. "You know, Nebraska beat us at the end of the game, and Penn State beat us at the end of the game, but we couldn't say we outplayed them. But Michigan! We *outplayed* them—and still lost. That one hurt."

It also raised the stakes for that day's game.

"I'm in the locker room after every game," President Schapiro told me. "And after that Michigan game, it was just stunned silence—something you don't see very often. Pure shock. We felt we were out of there with a 'W'—but an amazing turn of events took the game away.

"Fitz got up there and said, 'We're done with this. We're going up to East Lansing in a week, and we've *gotta* win that one.'

"I have to tell ya, that was a tough plane ride back."

Northwestern entered the Michigan State game at 7-3, and 3-3 in the league, having lost three of their last five games. They were all but eliminated from the division race—it was Nebraska's to lose, and Michigan's to pick up if the Cornhuskers dropped it—but they were still playing for their own records, and an improved bowl bid. If they beat the Spartans, they would be heavily favored to defeat struggling Illinois the next week and secure nine wins for only the sixth time in their 131 seasons. Win the bowl game, and the 2012 Wildcats' ten wins would tie them for the school's best record, sharing the podium with their 1995 and 1903 squads.

Since all three of their losses were close calls, they obviously could have won more, but if they fell apart now, they would reduce a season that had started with such promise to something that would soon be forgotten.

Across the field, the 5-5 Spartans were fighting to salvage their season. If they lost to Northwestern, they would have to win up at Minnesota's new stadium, against the reviving Gophers, to qualify for a bowl—or stay home for the first time since 2006, the year before head coach Mark Dantonio's reign began.

This was another appeal of college football: on almost any given Saturday, even late in the season, both teams were still fighting for something. By the next-to-last regular-season game in the NFL, most teams are either out of it or are resting their starters for the playoffs. Most teams end their season not with a bang against an archrival, but a whimper against another team that doesn't care, either.

The Wildcats would get no sympathy from the Spartans for their three close losses. The Spartans lost by one point to Ohio State, three to Iowa (in overtime), two to Michigan, and four to Nebraska—a total of ten points keeping them from a 9-1 record and a Top 5 ranking. Instead, they were far off the national radar, and 2-4 in the league.

The Spartans, however, were still interesting—certainly to their loyal students, alums, and fans. The Spartans' faithful sold out four of their seven home games and averaged more than their 75,005 capacity for the season—something the stumbling Detroit Lions, playing in the smaller 65,000-seat Ford Field, have never come close to accomplishing.

This gets to another difference: College football fans don't stop caring about their teams when they're losing. The bond is too strong. They may rip into the athletic director, the coach, and all the assistants they know, and go online to bomb every strategic decision made by anyone attached to the program, but they do not stop caring. If you want the acid test, it's Michigan's 2008 season, whose 3-9 record broke a 33-year string of bowl games, a 41-year streak of winning regular seasons, and the school record for most losses in the program's then-129-year history. Yet every one of their seven home games exceeded the stadium's 106,201 capacity.

Records be damned; the Northwestern–Michigan State game still mattered. And 75,101 fans showed up to prove it.

True to form, the Wildcats came out swinging, driving the ball on the game's first possession inside Michigan State's 10-yard line. But the 'Cats stalled and kicked a field goal, a microcosm of their three losses that season: start strong, fade at the finish.

The Spartans then embarked on their own impressive drive, but on third and one at the 3-yard line, they fumbled, which served as a pretty good microcosm of their season, too: play tough for a long stretch, then blow up at the end.

After the Spartans notched a safety against Colter, the first quarter score read: Michigan State 5, Northwestern 3. You had to remind yourself you were watching a football game.

When Fitzgerald was asked in the postgame press conference about the first-quarter score, he quipped, "I thought the White Sox were playing the Tigers."

Even though the second quarter was no better, the fans got louder. Northwestern's kicker, Jeff Budzien, the best in the league, hit a 43-yard field goal to give Northwestern a weird-looking 6–5 halftime lead.

The Spartans started the second half by throwing an interception to David Nwabuisi, who slithered back 43 yards for the charity touchdown, and a 13–5 lead. But the Spartans fought back with a touchdown and a 2-point conversion to retie the game, then the teams swapped touchdowns to tie the game yet again, 20–20, early in the fourth quarter. Halfway into the final quarter, Northwestern couldn't get past State's 9-yard line, so Fitzgerald called on the surefire Budzien to kick another field goal for a 23–20 lead.

With 1:29 left, the Spartans started from their own 20-yard line. This was their moment of truth.

Maxwell threw a pass over the middle to Tony Lippett, who got hit, and dropped it. Maxwell then passed to Le'Veon Bell—who wasn't hit, but dropped it anyway. Then Maxwell tried Aaron Burbridge, who got hit—possibly early—and dropped it, but the fans' call for an interference penalty didn't persuade the refs. Finally, on fourth and 10, Maxwell went to a wide-open Dion Sims—who just flat out dropped it.

Even the steadfast Spartan fans had their limit, and the last play reached it. They headed to the aisles, grumbling things like "an embarrassment" and "pathetic."

A few "victory formations" later, and it was done: a hard-fought if sloppy 23–20 game, but enough to give Northwestern an 8-3 record and put State on the verge of spending the holidays at home.

The Spartans' postgame postures expressed pure defeat. A season that had started so well for the Spartans, who had been ranked tenth before the Notre Dame game and were picked by some pundits to win the division, had become a lost year.

Standing on the field next to longtime Spartan beat writer Jack Ebling, I said, "This is not a five-and-six team."

"But they are," he said, and in the unforgiving world of college football he was right. It was that simple. They were.

The shadows had started crawling across the lush green grass. After the compulsory handshakes, the Northwestern players ran to the corner. They didn't care if they didn't make ESPN's Top 10 that night, and neither did the stripe of purple fans who descended to the rails, making their numbers seem to expand. They yelled a chant, then sang the fight song, and finally launched into a dozen rounds of "Go—U! N—U!"

I followed the teams up the tunnel, where I ran into Michigan State athletic director Mark Hollis, one of the best in the business. He had now suffered through his fifth loss by less than a touchdown, and his expression gave it away. "I've seen this one before," he said, then struggled to produce something close to a wry grin.

When I heard the Northwestern players chanting in the visitors' locker room, I asked a middle-aged woman standing in front of the steps, wearing purple, what they were saying.

"To be honest," she said, "I have no idea." But after she turned to the locker room doorway, still open, and saw them whooping and hollering and gallivanting around, she changed her mind. She did know. "Happiness!"

When Fitzgerald got to the press trailer, he started with his customary opening: "Thanks to everyone for being here," in his customarily hoarse postgame voice, then followed with his customary comments, such as "I want to wish Mark [Dantonio] and his young team good luck."

If Northwestern never quite develops the kind of wait-all-year rivalries other Big Ten schools have, you can blame Fitzgerald. You just can't hate the guy.

When one reporter said, "Fans complained about you running out the clock [last game], and today you passed the ball more," Fitzgerald replied, "Yeah, I had our FBI guys compile all those e-mails, and because of the fans, I changed. I hope that's crystal clear." But his charm made the line come off less snarky than lighthearted.

"Midseason, as a coach," he said, "you sound like Charlie Brown's teacher: 'Wa-wah, wa-wah, wa-wah.' They don't hear you. They're sick of you." But, he added, with their season heading to their biggest goal—a bowl victory—ears open and focus sharpens.

He, and the players who followed, were candid about how much the Michigan loss had taken out of them. "We had a big pit in our stomachs after the last one," said freshman Dan Vitale, who would be named the league's Rookie of the Week for his 110 yards gained on 9 catches. "This erased a lot of the demons from that."

"Singing the fight song," David Nwabuisi said, "is one of the best feelings you get all season."

Back in the Spartan Stadium press box, before packing my laptop, I took one last look at scores around the league.

Michigan took care of struggling Iowa, 42–17, to go 8-3, and 5-1 in the league. The Wolverines could still win the division title if Nebraska lost its last game, against Iowa, and Michigan beat Ohio State. Not likely— the Hawkeyes were on a five-game losing skid—but not impossible.

The Buckeyes found themselves in a dogfight in Madison, one of the nation's toughest places to play, especially a night game. Down 14–7, with the ball on Ohio State's 5-yard line and just eight seconds left, Wisconsin quarterback Curt Phillips hit Jacob Pedersen for the touchdown. But in overtime, the Buckeyes outscored the Badgers 7–0 to remain undefeated at 11-0 and clinch the Leaders Division with one game left on their schedule.

Life was pretty good for Urban Meyer—and not just on the field.

To fulfill his preseason promise to keep his family life as normal as possible, Meyer had to perform a trickier balancing act than even the average football coach because his two daughters both played college volleyball—Gigi at Florida Gulf Coast and Nicki at Georgia Tech— while his thirteen-year-old son, Nathan, was still playing Pop Warner football.

"At Georgia Tech," Meyer told me, "the AD there was nice enough to schedule their senior day on my bye week [the previous weekend]. So I got to see my middle daughter, Nicki, play volleyball. And Florida Gulf Coast scheduled a game in Toledo, so I could see Gigi play. That's a first."

Meyer didn't stop there. During the 2012 season, on Sundays, he came in an hour early to get his special teams work done, until he got a text about 10:45, telling him it was time to go see his son play football.

"That's a great thing," he said. "I go there every Sunday, and you can see him there, on the sidelines, looking over his shoulder when I show up. He notices."

As he had hoped to do before the season started, Meyer had won every game on the field while maintaining his sanity off it.

So far.

Meyer didn't need to be told that 11-0 didn't count for much in Columbus if the Buckeyes didn't get a little pair of gold pants.

The final score from State College read Penn State 45, Indiana 22. No great surprise there. The win gave the Lions a 7-4 overall record, and a 5-2 mark in the league. The Lions could still finish strong with a victory the next weekend over Wisconsin, which had already sealed an invitation to the conference title game thanks to the bans on both OSU and Penn State.

But the brief recap contained some more news: "Senior linebacker Mike Mauti left the game with an injury."

Rich Mauti had made it to every Penn State home game that fall, and the last two would be no exception. He and his wife, Nancy, had spent the week before the Indiana game at their home in Louisiana gathering all the ingredients to make jambalaya, crawfish étouffée, and alligator for the coaches' regular family dinner Sunday night, to thank them for all they'd done for their son, their family, and their school. The Mautis arrived in State College on Friday with a car full of food and planned to stay the whole week with an old friend and classmate, Penn State women's field hockey coach Charlene Morett. They would celebrate Thanksgiving at her home with their entire family, and the Zordiches, then stay for the seniors' swan song against Wisconsin.

Rich and Nancy knew it would be a bit sad to see their youngest son leave the field for the last time, but they would not miss these two games for the world.

The Penn State seniors had the schedule on their minds, too, but they were experiencing it from a decidedly different vantage point. Preparing to play their eleventh game of the season, they knew something few outside of those in Columbus knew: no matter how well they played in their last two games, no matter how many wins they posted, they would not be going to a conference title game, or a bowl game.

This was it.

"I've had tears in my eyes before every game," Mauti told me that week. "I think about it before every game. To be grateful to be healthy, to be put in a position to be able to do what I love with people I love doing it with."

Paradoxically, because Mauti had felt that way all fall, he'd failed to register that their careers would end in less than two weeks. Their five-year odyssey had been reduced to days.

It hit his fellow seniors at odd moments: sitting in team meetings with the lights off and the overhead on, eating at the training table, lying in bed late at night. When it hit them, it hit them hard.

The night before the Indiana game, a bunch of the seniors were sitting at the same table. "Guys were talking about it," Mauti recalled. "'It's getting close. Time's running out.' Until I heard that, it hadn't hit me: *this is it!*

"Then Farrell says, 'Man, last night I couldn't sleep. We only have a week left!'

"When he said that—man, it smacked me in the face like a ton of bricks. It's not just my final *year.* It's my final *week.*"

Mauti, sitting at the end of the table that night, started staring off into space. The longer he thought about it, the more his eyes welled up. After about five minutes, he got up and said, "I'm sorry, guys," and left without another word. He walked down the stairs, by himself, and "just lost it. It was the first time I full out let it all go."

"I was at the table," Zordich said. "I saw it. And I knew. I just laughed, because I was doing the same damn thing an hour before.

"And that's the beauty of it all: Everybody cares. Everybody cares."

Unlike the others at the table, however, Mauti and Jordan Hill knew their football careers would not end in November. Barring serious injury in their final two games, both would be drafted, probably in the first three rounds. For Hill, that was expected. He had been one of the few true stars returning that season, and so long as he could stay healthy—not a guarantee for a man whose knees kept him out of pads during practice—he would get a good contract and be in a position to take care of his mom and ailing father.

For Mauti, however, it was a bit surprising. After having had both knees operated on—an MCL and an ACL—he'd started his senior year as damaged goods, unlikely to be taken seriously by NFL teams, who were literally running a meat market. But with two games to go, O'Brien's NFL scouting friends had told him Mauti had proved he could still play linebacker at the highest level and would likely be a second-round pick. That portended a big payday, and a good run in the league.

All Hill and Mauti had to do was get through eight more days in good health.

But that's not what they were thinking about when they took the field that Saturday at noon, a sunny day in the low fifties—not bad for November 17. Perfect football weather.

Quite a few dreams seemed in jeopardy when Indiana took an early 10–7 lead. If Penn State lost to the Hoosiers, beating the Badgers the following week would only be that much harder, and an uninspiring 6-6 record their likely punishment.

Still in the first quarter, Indiana moved the ball into Penn State territory, heading toward the student section—the end where the Lions' defense had made its most memorable stands. When the Indiana runner headed toward Mauti's side, he stepped up to engage the lineman. He was about to disengage to pursue the runner when a smaller player from Indiana's backfield, not accustomed to blocking, threw his body into Mauti's right leg, which had been planted in the grass.

"I'll attribute it to bad football," Mauti told me, dismissing intent. "Terrible technique."

Mauti crumpled to the grass and lay on his back, twisting and turning and holding his helmet. Thanks to his history with both knees, he had no illusions about what had just happened.

His best friend figured it out almost as quickly. When Penn State's defense was on the field, Zordich always sat on one of the Gatorade jugs by the phones. That's where he was when the announcer said, "A Nittany Lion is down on the field." Like everyone else, Zordich knew that happened all the time, and the player usually walked off under his own power.

"But for some reason," he said, "this time, I popped up. 'Who is it?'"

"Mauti," someone said.

"What's he holding?"

"His head."

"Right then, I knew what it was."

By this time, the entire team—offense and defense—had drifted out to the field.

"Then we see the cart come out for him," Urschel told me, "and then we know." With that, Urschel turned quiet and dropped his head, red-eyed.

The coaches knew, too, but they also knew they had to play a football game. They swept everyone back to the sidelines—but not Zordich, who went out to meet the green Gator, which hauled players off to the locker room. Mauti's head was down, with his helmet still on, but he looked up when Zordich approached him.

"Don't worry, man," Zordich told him, and clasped hands. "We got this."

Which, between these friends, didn't mean the game, but Mauti's grueling rehab. Zordich was promising him they would go through it together, and Mauti understood immediately.

Kirk Diehl knew the drill too well. He made it to the locker-room door in time to meet the Gator. "I was thinking, 'God, we just did this a year ago.' Mike looked at me and said, 'Well, are you ready to do this again?'

"That's when it dawned on me that he remembered me helping him into the shower last year. When I handed him the towel this time, he said, 'You've always been there for me.'

"And I said, 'No, you've always been there for me.'" Recalling this, Diehl started crying again.

Mauti remembered, too. "He's got tears going down his face. He said, 'ou don't understand the kind of effect you had on me. You got me ough this year, you're the reason I'm still here, the reason I'm able to up in the morning and go to work.'"

ayone who had lived in Happy Valley that year—from professors to s—knew exactly what Diehl was talking about.

In the locker room, Diehl and Mauti were soon joined by Mauti's dad, Mauti's girlfriend—and Zordich's cousin—Julianna Marie Toscani, and longtime coach Fran Ganter, who still worked for the department. It didn't take long for all of them to lose it.

"But I knew," Mauti said, "this day was not close to over."

Back on the field, after O'Brien had watched Mauti loaded onto the Gator and carted off, he realized he had a considerable challenge on his hands. "I felt terrible for the kid," he said, and would talk to him at halftime. "But at that point we weren't playing very well. I looked back at the team and they were in a funk. They weren't there."

"You could see the entire bench deflate," Spider Caldwell said. "Zordich was in a total fog. He was gone. I was so worried, our team seemed to go flat. Another loss wouldn't have helped anything."

O'Brien agreed. He told me later, "Coming off a loss like that, the whole next week would have been that much tougher."

Before Mauti even made it to the locker room, O'Brien wisely gathered the squad. "That guy on the field, I know what he means to you, but we can't do anything for him right now but play hard. So whatever your motivation is—play well for Mauti or just play for your team—we need to pick this shit up."

They listened and, as usual, followed their coach's lead.

In less than nine minutes, McGloin hit Allen Robinson for a 53-yard touchdown, then hit him again for a 10-yard touchdown, then hit Zach Zwinak for a 16-yard touchdown. The Lions played possessed, turning a 10–7 second-quarter deficit into a 28–13 halftime lead.

But that's not what the coaches and players remember about that day.

"The rest of the game, I was just in a daze," Zordich said. "I just wanted it to end. A lot of guys felt that way. I didn't want to be on the field. We wanted to follow the cart, to be in the locker room."

They had their chance at halftime, when the players lined up to see Mauti in the training room.

"I was standing outside the door the whole time when all those guys were going in," Zordich said. "Coaches, players—everybody was crying. Everybody was crying. As much as I wanted to, I just couldn't go in there. I would have lost it. If I'd've lost it, I probably wouldn't have been able to go out for the second half."

Led by Jordan Hill, Penn State's defense held Indiana to 9 more points, while Zwinak, Zordich, and Ficken added 17, for a safe 45–22 victory, and a 7-4 record.

When the team returned to the locker room, everyone made a beeline for the training room, where they could talk as long as they liked.

"Sitting there, you're in a state of just complete—I don't want to say vulnerability—but you're just completely broken," Mauti remembered. "Defenseless. All your walls, emotionally, physically, spiritually—they're gone.

"I knew inevitably I was going to have to look Coach O'Brien in the eye. I knew that was going to be hard to do."

When O'Brien walked in, then stuck his hand out, Mauti saw his coach's hand was shaking. O'Brien opened his mouth to say something, but nothing came out, and tears started coming down.

"I was relatively composed until that point," Mauti said. "I don't remember the exact way he put it—but his voice was shaking, and he said, 'I've been around some special players, and you're one of the best I've ever coached.' We hugged. He was about to say something else, but he couldn't take any more, and he walked out.

"He left and I'm thinking, 'That's my head coach—and *he's* crying.'

"I was thinking about the last eight months, and how far we've come, from talking to him on the phone in January [after O'Brien had been named Paterno's successor], to this. If you told me we'd be crying in each other's arms in November, I'd have said . . ."

Mauti looked away, shaking his head, unable to finish the sentence.

While I was driving back down I-96 and toward US 23 from East Lansing as dusk approached, I turned on the radio to catch some scores around the country. But instead of scores, I heard this: sources indicated that on Monday the Big Ten would announce the addition of both Maryland and Rutgers to the league.

No matter what line of work you're in, you probably hear plenty of rumors every week, usually false. Sports writing seems to generate more than most, so any experienced reporter has to develop a healthy skepticism. Most of what you hear on sports-talk radio and TV shows barely raises an eyebrow. We become hard to surprise, and harder still to shock.

But hearing this, I actually shook my head. I turned up the volume, leaned forward, and locked my focus onto the announcer. *I could not have heard that correctly.*

Once I realized I had, I concluded, *No way that's true.*

My brain ticked off all the reasons why. The Big Ten is defined by the Great Lakes states—even Pennsylvania touches Lake Erie, and State College *feels* Midwestern—and to an extent, the Great Lakes states are defined by the Big Ten. The conference is the oldest and most stable by far, and conservative in almost every respect.

When it's added schools—Michigan State, Penn State, Nebraska—it has looked for a good fit, first and foremost. A league that could go almost two decades before adding a twelfth team was not a league that rushed itself into desperate decisions.

Just three months earlier, Jim Delany himself had told me, "We're not going to add teams to add teams. We like what we have. That doesn't mean we couldn't expand, or we won't. But it's like I said about Nebraska, it has to be a good fit. When you sit down and talk with their people, you know it when you see it."

If the league was going to add more teams, which didn't seem out of the question, Missouri and Notre Dame were most often mentioned. But Maryland—a charter member of the ACC in 1953, the 2002 NCAA basketball champion, and longtime rival of Virginia, Duke, and North Carolina? The Terrapins' football team was occasionally decent—but only occasionally. They were an ACC school, to the core.

As for Rutgers, a Big East member since 1991, that made even less sense, on every level—except one: the New York TV market.

It was even stranger that none of us in the press box had heard a thing—which was exceedingly rare for big news like that.

But because it came from a major outlet, I couldn't simply dismiss it. By Sunday, of course, everyone knew it was true.

The next day, Monday, November 19, 2012, Big Ten commissioner Jim Delany held a press conference in College Park, Maryland, to announce that the Big Ten Council of Presidents and Chancellors had unanimously voted to admit Maryland into the Big Ten, effective July 1, 2014. The following day, Delany would make the same announcement at Rutgers.

University of Maryland president Wallace Loh opened with a statement that was refreshingly frank for a contemporary college leader:

"Membership in the Big Ten enables us to truly guarantee the financial stability of Maryland athletics for a long, long time. It's never just about the money, but somebody has to pay the bills. And the issue at hand is the long-term viability of Maryland athletics."

Although Loh knew the decision would likely be unpopular with Maryland's faculty, alumni, and students—which is one reason why the school's leaders ignored the Open Meetings Act and met privately when discussing their decision, for which they were later sued—from his position, it was not hard to see the move as rational, even necessary.

"I came to this university two years ago and discovered there were deficits going on for several years, and nobody told me about it, and I was left with the job of having to cut teams because we're required to balance our budget, and I swore this would never happen again," Loh told the student newspaper. "Not to me, not to my successor. It was the most painful experience and I still get nightmares. . . . It put at risk the entire enterprise of Maryland athletics.

"I did it to guarantee the long-term future of Maryland athletics."

What was less clear was why the Big Ten wanted Maryland, whose athletic department was running a deficit that stood at $7.8 million a year and was growing fast, and whose average football attendance had fallen from fifty-two thousand to thirty-six thousand in 2012. (According to the *Newark Star-Ledger*, Rutgers athletics was in even worse shape, running a $26.8 million deficit in 2010–11 alone.)

The Big Ten, Loh said, was expanding to protect itself against a national phenomenon. "Attendance [at games] among college-aged students is dropping. The reason is because this generation is completely wired, and they are getting their education and entertainment on tablets and mobile devices. Everyone thinks you make your money in seats. You make it on eyeballs on a screen."

In other words, if ticket sales went down, TV ratings would make up for it. This equation had a lot of assumptions baked into it—from why attendance among college-aged students was dropping, to how the colleges could make up for it—but President Loh was surely correct in assessing why the Big Ten wanted to add Maryland and Rutgers: TV money.

Celebrated columnist Dave Kindred, writing in the *Washington Post*, sized it up this way: "Some universities had played for most of a century in leagues dictated by geography and shared values. They abandoned those alliances for bloated groupings designed to produce football revenue in multiples of anything basketball can do."

If there was another motive, no one mentioned it.

If the Big Ten truly was just a business, and its fans mere shareholders, the fans would have been content with that explanation and possibly thrilled. Business was booming.

But they're not shareholders, they're fans—and they proved it with their swift, severe, and virtually unanimous reaction.

Jonathan Chait, a Michigan alum who still writes occasionally on Big Ten sports from his perch as a political writer for *New York* magazine, didn't mince words:

"College football expansion is all about money. On this everybody agrees, and so the Big Ten's additions of Maryland and Rutgers are being met mainly with angry denunciations of their greed, along with a sprinkling of cynical congratulations for their financial savvy."

Chait didn't bother addressing the greed—it spoke for itself—and quickly set aside the not-insignificant fact that college athletic departments are legally nonprofit organizations, which don't pay taxes or shareholders, to disassemble the surprisingly weak business rationale:

"Money is obviously vital to college athletics as a threshold question. If you're running an athletic department, you need to bring in enough revenue to fund your operations. But beyond that threshold, you don't need more money. Universities are nonprofit institutions. There are no stockholders. At some point, more revenue simply means that athletic directors need to find more things to spend their windfall on."

They will tell you it's the cost of doing business—but what's the business, exactly? When *60 Minutes* interviewed Dave Brandon that fall, he said the "business model is broken." What he failed to grasp was that it is not supposed to be a business in the first place. After all, what business doesn't have to pay shareholders, partners, owners, taxes, or the star attractions, the players and the band?

This mind-set seems particularly true of the contemporary CEOs-as-athletic directors, for whom no amount is enough.

"As one digs deeper into the national character of the Americans," Alexis de Tocqueville wrote, almost two hundred years ago, "one sees that they have sought the value of everything in this world only in the answer to this single question: how much money will it bring in?"

More recently, Homer Simpson told his boss, Monty Burns, "You're the richest man I know."

"Yes," Burns replied. "But you know, I'd trade it all for just a little more."

And that's the problem. Like Asian carp invading your freshwater paradise, once the money-grubbers take over, their appetites are insatiable, and they are impossible to remove. The corporate approach has proven to be quite appropriate for running corporations, but less so for running our schools, our museums, and our national parks. If our only counter is "You can't stop progress," then we should sell our museums to mall developers, open up our national parks to the highest bidders—be they billionaires looking to build vacation homes or oil companies looking to drill—and turn Gettysburg over to Disney, so they can "maximize the brand" and give all visitors a "wow" experience.

Chait's more damning argument was that even the promised profits for which these acrobatics were being performed, might not be realized at all. The motive behind the expansion was strictly financial, with the rewards to come almost entirely from cable television. Maryland's and Rutgers's media markets—DC and New York—would greatly increase the number of households that could be forced to pay their cable companies a little extra to carry the Big Ten Network. Not fans, mind you, or even viewers, but involuntary subscribers who don't give a damn about the BTN or the league it covers—most of whom will not even be aware they're paying for it.

Cynical, sure. But, more surprisingly, potentially stupid.

"Bundled cable television pricing is not going to last forever," Chait wrote, "and possibly not very long at all. There is already a revolution in video content under way that is going to render the cable television bundle model obsolete. When that revolution has finished, the Big Ten will realize it pulled apart its entire identity to grab a profit stream that has disappeared."

Chait then addressed the fans on their terms: "You can't manufacture tradition, and tradition is the only thing college football has to offer. Without tradition, college football is just an NFL minor league. Big Ten football mainly consists on a week-to-week basis of games like Michigan versus Minnesota and Illinois versus Wisconsin.

"Those games have meaning to the fans in ways outsiders can't grasp. The series have gone on for a century. They often have funny old trophies. Every game is lodged into a long historical narrative of cherished (or cursed) memory. Replacing those games with some other equally good (or, as the case may be, not good) program is like snuffing out your family dog and replacing it with some slightly better-trained breed. It is *not the same thing.*"

If Chait was critical, he looked like Mr. Congeniality compared to MGoBlog founder Brian Cook, whose interview with Spencer Hall on the popular national website Every Day Should Be Saturday was titled "The Big Ten Expands: A Q&A with Angerbrian Ragecook."

"I guess it's a play for television sets, as everyone who thinks more money automatically justifies any activity keeps telling me," Cook said. "As if I should care about television sets in Maryland funding even more unnecessary spending. . . . At some point the money went from nice to destructive, and this is the point at which money bursts through your chest."

Hall replied, "There is literally nothing in my heart but despair when I imagine Maryland/Iowa playing a football game."

"The inevitable sixteen-team end game isn't even a conference anymore," Cook added. "You get one game against the other division. One!"

"I just don't understand the choices," Hall piled on. The DC and New York markets, he wrote, "literally WILL NEVER CARE ABOUT COLLEGE FOOTBALL."

"They don't have to care," Cook pointed out. "They just have to not watch the BTN they're paying for. For some reason. I would love to see New Jersey cable operators flat out refuse to carry the BTN."

"That's what I don't get," Hall agreed. "You're paying to ship food that will just rot in the warehouses."

CHAPTER 21

"TWENTY YEARS FROM NOW, THIS IS WHAT WE'LL BE TALKING ABOUT"

Coach O'Brien called the Mautis on Sunday after the Indiana game to let them know that no one expected them to bring the food Sunday night for the staff's weekly family dinner—or even show up. But the Mautis wouldn't hear it.

After the Cajun cuisine was served to great acclaim, "Rich thanked *us* for making it a great season," strength coach Craig Fitzgerald recalled. "Bill said, 'No no no. We thank *you* for your son. Without him, we never would have gotten here.'"

Throughout the weekend, hours after the Indiana game, Mike Mauti's phone blew up with calls and texts from teammates, former players— including Penn State legends like Paul Posluszny and Franco Harris for a half-hour talk—and even Peyton Manning, whose father, Archie, had played with Rich Mauti in New Orleans and remains a family friend.

After the senior Manning called Mike Mauti on Sunday, he texted him Monday morning: "Life's a big shit sandwich. You either take a bite, or you starve. You've had some bad breaks, but life will be good. Keep the faith."

"Couldn't have said it any better," Mauti said.

Zordich nodded. "That's what we've all been doing, all year."

But Mauti knew he had probably just played his last football game.

At four thirty on a cold Tuesday morning, three hours before sunrise, the two Mauti men—father and son—headed out for the four-hour drive to Pittsburgh to find out. Because Mike had been surrounded by people non-stop since he tore his ACL, "I was looking forward to that drive so much," he told me. "I so badly needed to be alone with my dad. One-on-one time with him is very precious. The older I get, the more I appreciate it."

Despite playing lacrosse and football at Penn State and special teams for the Saints, Rich Mauti never blew a knee. Yet, Mike knew, no one would understand what he was going through better than his dad.

"By the time I got in the car that morning," Mike said, "I'd already come to grips with the fact that I may not play again, ever. That's when I started to look at what the future would look like without football. Football is all I've known. That was sobering.

"My dad was as spent as I was. And I think what killed him is the idea that this was the way it was going to end. At four thirty in the morning, driving in pitch dark, there wasn't a dull moment in that car, and not a dry eye for two and a half hours. And that's really when I just let out all my thoughts."

Mike told his father, "I'm okay with not playing again. I've done everything that I could." Mike was not thinking just about football, but everything his team had done for the program and Penn State itself. They had given everything they had.

"Since last November," he told his dad, "I made up my mind, this is what I wanted, this is what I was committing to, all year. I was so proud to be a part of it, and the people I did it with. The friendships that I've made—the seniors, the coaches—that's what made it worth it."

"Your relationship with Z," Rich said, "makes the last five years worth it."

"That really kinda hit me," Mike told me. "That *is* what it's all about. That's what lasts a lot longer than a title: the relationships."

When the Penn State players had the bells and whistles of big-time college football stripped away by the NCAA sanctions, they discovered something better: they believed deeply in the ideals of the student-athlete experience that the NCAA had always espoused—and by the end of the season, they had proven that they believed in them more than the NCAA itself.

When Mike Mauti, a likely second-round NFL draft pick, blew out a knee for the third time and faced a future without football, that's when he fully realized the student-athlete experience was enough by itself. He did not need an NFL contract to justify his effort and experience.

"That's when I got peace, is what I'd call it, when I finally got one-on-one time with my dad. I'll never forget that car ride for the rest of my life."

By the time they arrived in Pittsburgh, Mike said, "Basically, I had hung my helmet up before I even walked into Dr. Bradley's office. I think both of us did. But my hand was still hanging on to the mask, just in case."

317

While they waited for Dr. Bradley to come back with the MRI, the Mautis had already accepted that Mike's football career might be over. But then Dr. Bradley came back and told them, "The MCL does not need to be operated on. It will heal itself, and the ACL is a standard reconstruction, with a cadaver's ligament."

Mike and his dad just looked at each other, stunned.

"I said, 'Whoa!'" Mike recalled. "With that news, I took my helmet off the hook and brought it back with me. I wasn't done.

"That's all I really needed to hear. ACL rehab is a *bitch*—and I know exactly what it is. It's just tedious. It takes time. Your whole quad shuts down and atrophies immediately. Your leg is literally like Jell-O. But, hey, the third time's the charm. In a sick way, I've mastered this."

On the drive back to Penn State, Mike told his dad, "I can do this. I could be back in camp next year, by July. That's doable. That's salvageable."

They drove back in daylight, with their first good news in four days.

When Mauti returned to the football building, he saw Jordan Hill working out, which inspired Mike to start working out himself.

"I just started cranking out sets of pull-ups. Then I go to another machine and start doing curls. And I'm feeling good, and the next thing you know I'm on the trampoline strengthening my quad, to help me get ready for the surgery. It felt so good doing it."

As was so often the case when Mauti talked, his next sentence could have applied to him, as intended, or the Penn State program, which was never far from his thoughts:

"Whoever's trying to kill me isn't getting the job done. But one day, I'm going to punch that fucker in the face."

A few hours after Mauti returned from Pittsburgh, knowing his teammates were far more upset about his injury than they were pleased by the victory over Indiana, he gave them the good news at the team meeting. He told them not to worry about him, and to focus on Wisconsin.

But he did not know that while he was riding to Pittsburgh, Zordich had made an unscheduled visit to O'Brien's office, followed by Jordan Hill. Both had the same idea: they wanted to put Mauti's number 42 on the left side of every player's helmet. As usual, O'Brien was open to their idea and told Hill to get together with Zordich, then go see if Spider could do it.

Spider called Penn State's sign department to see if they could provide 120 number 42s by Friday, the latest they could put them all on the helmets. They called him Wednesday and said yes—but they only had a few extras, so if the equipment staff botched very many, it wouldn't work.

At about the same time, Gerald Hodges asked O'Brien if he could wear Mauti's number 42 jersey that week. Knowing how close Mauti and Zordich were, O'Brien told Hodges to first ask Zordich if he wanted to wear it.

"I couldn't," he told Hodges. "All yours."

When Hodges asked Mauti, "I just broke down," Mauti recalled. "Hodges and I couldn't be more different, but one thing we have in common is passion for what we're doing: our mission, and our bond. That's why he's so special to me. He's come such a long way."

Something else was in the works that week: the athletic department planned to surprise the seniors with a special honor, but would only tell O'Brien and Spider about it. The players—and the fans—would not find out until game time.

For college football's first 130 years or so, almost every school's season ended before Thanksgiving. This allowed players and students to go home to their families and gave a comforting rhythm to the season. When they returned, finals were in swing and basketball was starting up.

But that started changing in 1992, when the NCAA permitted conferences to tack on a championship game, then approved an additional twelfth game for all schools in 2007.

After top-ranked Ohio State got blown out by Florida in the 2006 BCS title game, 41–14, some believed it was because Ohio State had fifty-one days between the Michigan game and the bowl, compared to Florida's thirty-seven—or two weeks less. The Big Ten decided to shrink the gap between the regular season and the bowl games by starting the season later and adding bye weeks.

Put it all together, and now just about every FBS school finishes its regular season the Saturday after Thanksgiving—keeping players on campus while most of their classmates go home, and creating more empty seats for the biggest rivalry games of the season.

That wasn't the Nittany Lions' concern on Thanksgiving, however—and O'Brien was working to make sure they stayed focus on their final mission.

"Think about that locker room after a win," he told them. "For some of you guys, I hate to burst your bubble, but this might be your last game.

"I don't think Wisconsin knows the type of beehive they're walking into. They have no idea. I don't know what they're thinking, being the division champs in third place. It doesn't make any sense to me.

"What *does* make sense to me is you guys are a bunch of tough sons of bitches, some of the best guys I've ever met, who are going to get after them. You are going to finish the job and come into the locker room and celebrate like never before."

They got the message, loud and clear, and—as was usually the case—soon started sounding a lot like their head coach.

"After the Nebraska loss," offensive tackle Mike Farrell told me, "it felt so shitty. And we would hate to end the season with that feeling."

"This year, it all just can't end with a loss," Zordich said. "It just can't."

At Toftrees Resort Saturday morning, the team had to kill an hour or so before hopping on the blue buses. Because Penn State had a three-thirty kickoff, most of the players watched the noon football games in their rooms.

After the University of Chicago dropped out of the Big Ten, Northwestern picked up a new rival in Illinois. In 1945, they started playing for the Sweet Sioux Tomahawk, a cigar-store Indian that was stolen and replaced by an actual tomahawk. In 2008, when the NCAA ordered members to eradicate all Native American names, logos, and the like—and received only partial compliance, witness the Illini—the two teams buried the hatchet and started playing for the Land of Lincoln Trophy, a bronze replica of Abe Lincoln's stovepipe hat, designed by *Dick Tracy* cartoonist Dick Locher.

Even during Northwestern's Dark Ages, the rivalry with Illinois has been surprisingly close, with the Illini holding a 54-46-5 lead, going back to 1892. Since 1995, Northwestern had the upper hand, 10 to 7, going into the 2012 rematch. But they had lost Lincoln's hat the last two years, so it was a relief for the Wildcats to put the 2-9 Illini away early, breezing to a 50–14 victory.

The 'Cats finished the regular season 9-3, and 5-3 in the Big Ten. They weren't sure which bowl they'd be going to, but they knew they'd be going somewhere warm. The bowl losing-streak monkey, on their backs since 1949, was on full alert.

Michigan and Ohio State do not play for a tomahawk or a stovepipe hat or a turtle or a jug, for a simple reason: every year they expect to play for the Big Ten title.

But as it was in so many other ways, the 2012 season was an exception. The Wolverines could have shared the division title with Nebraska if the Cornhuskers had lost that weekend, but they had already squeaked by Iowa, 13–7, the day after Thanksgiving. Likewise, Ohio State had already clinched its division, but couldn't go any further, so this game was, truly, for bragging rights and little else.

For both teams and their millions of followers, however, that's always been more than enough, and they played like it.

The Wolverines were out to prove that their 40–34 victory the year before, their first in eight years, was no fluke, and the rivalry was back. The Buckeyes, who entered the 2011 game with a freshman quarterback, an interim coach, and a 6-5 record, were out to prove that that loss really *was* a fluke, and that they were back. Further, they were just one win away from a perfect season—only the sixth in school history, a greater rarity than the Buckeyes' seven national titles.

Ohio State rode Braxton Miller's 52-yard pass to Devin Smith to set up their first touchdown just 2:19 into the game. But Michigan came back with a 75-yard bomb to the irrepressible Roy Roundtree to tie the game, and the battle was on, with the old enemies trading the lead seven times before it was done.

Thanks to his injured elbow, Robinson couldn't pass, but he could run. With Michigan down 17–14 with 1:30 left in the half, the coaches put Robinson in at quarterback, on their own 25-yard line. He ran for 8, then broke another tackle when two Buckeyes hit him at the same time and left him standing, free to run 67 yards for the touchdown.

The Buckeyes countered with a 52-yard field goal to end the half behind, 21–20. No matter who won, all indications were that the rivalry had returned, in full force.

Despite the score, Urban Meyer wasn't worried. "Up to that point, we had been one of the top-two teams for red-zone production," he told me. "But Braxton was not playing particularly well, and you have to give credit to Michigan's defense.

"The score was real close—you can't get any closer than twenty-one to twenty—so the plan was simple: take care of the ball, and let's finish."

After the first quarter, Ohio State honored its 2002 national-champion team on its tenth anniversary. Their coach, Jim Tressel, had cost the current undefeated team not just an invitation to the Big Ten championship and to a BCS bowl game, but a shot at a national title. None of that stopped the 2002 players from hoisting Tressel onto their shoulders and marching him around the Horseshoe, to the cheers of the 105,899.

The Buckeyes do not run a renegade program, but they once again demonstrated they don't seem to care if their actions make others think they do.

If Meyer was impressed with the Wolverines' defenders after the first half, he hadn't seen anything yet: they kept Miller and company out of the end zone the entire second half.

But Michigan's offense seemed to forget everything it had done so well in the first half. The Wolverines gained 219 yards in the first half, and just 60 in the second, never crossing the 50-yard line the entire half. Michigan's defense allowed the Buckeyes just two field goals, but it was enough for the Buckeyes to seal a 26–21 victory, Ohio State's sixth undefeated season, and Meyer's first pair of little gold pants as Ohio State's head coach.

"That was a great win," he told me, breaking into a rare, full-blown smile. "One of my top five."

But the best part, for the new Urban Meyer, was yet to come. As soon as the game ended, with the students rushing the field all around him and his son, he started asking, "Where's my wife?" He asked someone to find her, and his daughters, who'd come back for Thanksgiving, and get them to the locker room.

"I've never done that before, either," Meyer said, "but I knew this was the only time I might have the chance.

"So I had my wife, my two daughters, and my son in the locker room together, all arm in arm, singing that great fight song.

"I don't think I'll ever forget that."

In Big East action, Pitt led Rutgers 21–0 at halftime, in front of a half-empty Heinz Field, home of the Pittsburgh Steelers, while Maryland had fallen behind North Carolina, en route to the Terrapins' sixth straight loss, to close out a 4-8 season. The Big Ten fans who noticed were not impressed.

● ● ●

Back in State College, Penn State's seniors boarded the blue buses for the last time.

Although it was not a sellout—a crowd of 93,505 showed up (thank you, Thanksgiving)—the folks who stayed in town or traveled an average of four hours to get there made sure they were heard.

The fans lined the buses' route, while the seniors gazed out the school-bus windows, filing away the final images to pull up decades later. The usual suspects were there, flashing their signs—WE ARE ONE, PRIDE, and the fourteen people spelling out W-E A-R-E P-E-N-N S-T-A-T-E—but the first of the day's surprises met the players at the tunnel. When they got off the buses, they saw the fans covering the grass embankments, waving blue signs that said LEGENDS, and white signs that said EVERY ONE OF YOU, and others holding up the individual faces of the seniors—*all* the seniors. The seniors noticed.

Zordich made it a point to get off the bus with Mauti and walk into the locker room together. Zordich put his arm around his best friend and lifted his left hand to point to the players' stalls.

"Check this out."

There, Mauti saw the famed white helmets hanging from their hooks—every one of them featuring a dark-blue 42 on the side.

Mauti shook his head, pushed Zordich away, bent over for a moment, then walked straight to the showers to lose it by himself. After he had composed himself, he returned to thank Zordich, Hill, and Spider, who'd worked with his staff sticking them on the night before.

"You better like it, you sonovabitch," Spider said, smiling. "I spent five hours on them!"

After the routine warm-up on the field, the seniors returned to the field, one by one, when the announcer called out each name. They ran back out between two rows of lettermen, band members, and cheerleaders to meet their parents at midfield. The last four, in order, were Hill, Mauti, Zordich, and McGloin.

The families had already gone through plenty of tissues when the announcer turned the crowd's attention to the seats on the east side, under the press box. There, the crowd flipped up their cards, which tried to spell out ONE TEAM and THANK YOU SENIORS in the student section, but because the top layer was empty, due to Thanksgiving vacation, you could only make out TEAM and SENIORS.

The announcer then asked the crowd to look toward the east skyboxes, where the years of the school's undefeated, national, or Big Ten championship seasons lined the silver fascia. The list was long: 1894, 1909, 1911, 1912, 1920, 1921, 1947, 1948, 1968, 1969, 1973, 1982, 1986, 1994, 2005, and 2008.

After the announcer finished, a gray plastic tarp hanging to the right of the last year, 2008, dropped, revealing the big blue numbers: 2012.

Whatever tissues remained were quickly put into service.

After your players go through what amounted to a senior banquet attended by their families and 93,505 adoring fans, how do you get their heads screwed on straight to play the game?

O'Brien did his best by keeping his final pregame speech short and intense, and conspicuously routine.

"We're going to go out there and give them sixty minutes of Penn State football! Now let's go!"

But it quickly became clear that O'Brien's best efforts could not be enough.

Wisconsin's Montee Ball, the Big Ten's best runner in both 2011 and 2012, started the day by cutting through Penn State's heralded defensive line for 7 and 9 yards. One play later, from Wisconsin's 43, quarterback Curt Phillips hit Gordon Melvin for a first down, but Melvin didn't stop there, running all the way to the end zone.

Four plays, 74 yards, 1:53 into the game: 7–0, Wisconsin.

Penn State responded with a now-trademark, 15-play drive. Nine of them were runs by Zach Zwinak, including the last 4 straight, to cover 41 yards, every one of them hard. The contrast between the slippery, fleet-footed Ball, who was happy to sneak out of bounds instead of being hit, and the blood-and-guts Zwinak, who plowed relentlessly forward like a linebacker-seeking missile, reflected the teams they led. But Zwinak's method worked just as well, and tied the game at 7–7.

The Badgers didn't seem to mind too much, returning the following kickoff back to their own 47-yard line. From there, Jar Abbrederis ran through the Lions for 24 yards, then let Ball finish the job with three straight runs to get to the end zone, for a 14–7 lead.

As General Patton would say, the Badgers were going through the Lions like crap through a goose.

"First two drives?" Coach Johnson said afterward. "Scary. Scary. It happened so fast. I told them, 'We're fine. Just keep fighting.' It was no time to panic. And I tell you, we went to work—and Jordan [Hill] had a defining moment. He was hurt, and he played.

"I knew he knew he was about to pounce."

"I was still remembering what they did to us last year," Hill told me, referring to the 45–7 beating the Lions suffered in Madison, to give them a disappointing 9-3 record. "This time we knew it was our last game—there would be no bowl game—and after everything that happened to Mauti, there was *no* way we were going to lose that game. No. Way. It just wasn't how the storybook was supposed to end."

Hill told his fellow defenders, "The bullshit's gotta stop. We're not doing that. We came too far for us to be playing like that right now."

He said later, "All we needed was one stop to get things rolling. And that's what happened."

The rest of the half, Penn State's offense managed to cross midfield just once, to Wisconsin's 40, but it never gave Wisconsin a short field, while Penn State's defense clamped down. The result: eight straight punts between the two teams.

In the coaches' room before the game, O'Brien had said, "What Wisconsin does on offense plays right into our hand. Right to Jordan Hill." Hill seemed determined to prove his coach right.

What started out looking like a disaster for the Lions had settled down to a straightforward, no-nonsense Big Ten battle—already one of the best of the season.

After the coaches met in their room at the half—"Thank God our D held us in," O'Brien said—they fanned out to talk strategy with their position groups.

O'Brien told the offense the coaches had a new strategy to attack Wisconsin more effectively in the second half.

"We're going to run more Z-formations, more wheel and sub routes," he said. "Matt [McGloin], I'm not going to freeze you as much. Just run the plays. Let's get into a rhythm and get going.

"Let's *run* and work those formations—and we *got this*."

"No more penalties. Stay on track. We had a good drive there, and a penalty took us out.

"Lot of football left. Lot of football left."

It was not hard to see that, in just twelve games, O'Brien's command of his team had become even greater, and his sense of where they were and what they needed even more precise, his energy more finely focused.

O'Brien turned the offense over to Mac McWhorter and the position coaches, but charged back a few minutes later to say, "Hey, offense! When I do this"—he punched his left palm—"that's 'whoop speed.' That means you run, you *sprint* to the line, you spot the ball, and you *go*! Got it?!" They got it.

Defensive coordinator Ted Roof closed his session with the defense—which, after Wisconsin's first two drives, had been superb—by telling them, "Thirty more minutes. Don't bring anything back."

O'Brien addressed the entire team one last time. "Thirty minutes of your best fucking football! We've figured out a few things on offense. Defense, keep holding 'em. *And we got this!* Thirty of your best fucking football. *Right now!*"

This was a conductor who had his orchestra in the palm of his hand. There was no translation needed between them. They had always been in this together, but by their last half as a team, you could barely feel a line between them.

They knew their entire twelve-month odyssey was going to end in half an hour, one way or the other.

The Lions started the second half on their own 17-yard line—about the same spot they started the second half against Ohio State, when they promptly gave up a pick-6, and the game.

This time, McGloin calmly hit passes of 14, 6, and 37 yards, in between six runs by the workhorse Zwinak for a hard-fought 20 yards, leaving the Lions with third and goal from Wisconsin's 6-yard line. McGloin's pass to Moseby-Felder fell incomplete, setting up a fourth and goal from the 6.

A couple months earlier, after Sam Ficken had gone 1 for 5 on field goals and 1 for 2 on extra points against Virginia, O'Brien would have been sorely tempted to go for it. But since the Lions' fifth game against Illinois, Ficken had quietly hit nine of his next ten field goals, including his last seven straight.

He had improved so much, Ted Roof had been sufficiently impressed to tell Jim Bernhardt before the game, "Hey, wouldn't it be fitting if Sam Ficken got a chance and won the game for us, today?" It says enough about Ficken's turnaround that no one thought Roof was joking.

O'Brien sent Ficken out, without fear, and Ficken nailed it: 14–10. After Hill's defense delivered two more three-and-outs, Ficken kicked another field goal, this one from 32 yards, with confidence: 14–13. It extended his streak to nine straight field goals.

After Penn State's defense sent Wisconsin's offense back with yet another three-and-out, McGloin went for the kill, passing to Allen Robinson—who was having a breakout season—for 19 yards, then 15, before hitting true freshman Jesse James, who was wide-open on the left side. McGloin was rewarded with the pleasure of watching James run all the way down to the 3-yard line. From there, probably everyone in the building knew Zwinak was getting the ball, including the Badgers, but no one could stop him.

Penn State 19, Wisconsin 14, with 13-plus minutes left.

What to do? Kick the extra point, or go for the 2-point conversion and the 7-point lead?

"Bill made the decision to send out the offense for the two-point conversion," Jim Bernhardt recalled. "And he made it decisively. But then he seemed to play devil's advocate, just to see if he'd made the right call. He said, 'It's just the beginning of the fourth quarter.'

"I said, through the headset, 'Hey, this isn't a basketball game. You might not get another chance at this.'"

O'Brien stuck to his guns. Once again, there probably wasn't a great deal of mystery about who would get the ball—and once again, it didn't matter. Zach Zwinak pounded up the middle for the 2-point conversion.

Penn State, 21–14, with 13:19 remaining.

After Wisconsin's two quick touchdowns, everyone could see Penn State's defense had settled down and kept them out of the end zone. But probably few realized they had forced Wisconsin to punt the ball eight straight times, five of them after three-and-outs. And the key, by all accounts, was Jordan Hill.

Like just about everyone else on the Lions, Hill had a few motives for giving everything he had in those final minutes. In his case, that included his father, Larry, who had grilled him after every high school game so intensely, Jordan admitted with a laugh, that sometimes he stayed at his cousins' house Friday nights just to avoid it. During the Blue-White game weekend, right when they were getting out of the car in the Lasch Football Building parking lot, Larry collapsed in Jordan's arms, suffering a stroke. He'd spent the last three years in a wheelchair, which is where he was sitting in the front row of seats right behind Penn State's bench. After everything these players had been through, good and bad, it was hard to imagine anyone needing additional motivation not to "bring anything back," in Coach Roof's words, but Hill had it.

If the Illinois game was Mauti's, the Wisconsin game was Hill's.

"That was his Michael Jordan 'flu game,'" Zordich told me. "He played, man. He played."

That he did, notching 12 tackles and 3 tackles for a loss, including 2 sacks.

"For a D-lineman, those are good numbers for a *season*," Mike Farrell said. "Jordan did that in a *game*. He was *possessed*."

"I just didn't want to lose," Hill told me a few days later. "I just didn't want to lose. That's all it came down to. The whole time, I had last year's Wisconsin game in my head. And I'm just not going out like that. We came too far."

On the Badgers' ninth possession after its two touchdowns, they whittled their way down to Penn State's 20-yard line, poised, it seemed, to tie the game. But when Phillips fired the ball near the end zone, Jacob Fagnano, a walk-on from State College, stepped up to intercept the ball and return it to the 19.

With exactly five minutes left, Wisconsin still had all three time-outs, but Penn State could probably kill the clock—and secure the win—with a couple first downs. Three downs later, however, the Lions had to punt, leaving Wisconsin with an ample 3:51 to cover 66 yards.

Despite another Jordan Hill sack, the Badgers conducted their best drive of the day, chipping away with simple passes by Phillips and solid runs by Ball, to get down to Penn State's 2-yard line, on third down, with less than a minute left.

With all the surprise of a Zach Zwinak run up the middle, Phillips gave the ball to Montee Ball. Hill knew the Badgers would double-team him, but he had a plan.

"I watched a ton of film on them, and you don't have to watch too much to know what they're going to do on the goal line," he explained. "All the times they played teams who used four-three defenses, like ours, only *one* time they didn't run to the left. I thought, 'All right, they're not gonna change because it's Penn State. That's what they're gonna do.'

"I was supposed to split the guard and center—but I knew they'd come after me, so instead of doing that, I faked to that gap and cut to the left of the center, and I got him." Ball, that is—for a loss of 2 yards, forcing the Badgers to use their third and final time-out, with 23 seconds left, to set up their fourth-and-goal play from the 4-yard line.

In a do-or-die situation, Phillips dropped back and fired quickly to Jeff Duckworth, right on the goal line—as far from Hill as they could get. It was enough for the touchdown. Wisconsin didn't feel like testing their luck twice, opting for the extra point to tie the game 21–21, with 18 seconds left.

Just a few days earlier, McGloin had told quarterback coach Charlie Fisher that he had never played in an overtime game. Well, this was his chance.

Penn State went first. In three plays, they could only gain 6 yards on a Zwinak run. O'Brien did not hesitate to send out Ficken for the 37-yard attempt. Ficken's kick curved left, but slipped just inside the upright for 3 points and his tenth straight field goal.

Penn State, 24–21.

Now, which Penn State defense would show up—the one that had let the Badgers slice through on their first two possessions, or the one that stymied Wisconsin for nine straight scoreless possessions?

On first down, Montee Ball could only gain one yard before Hill stuffed him.

On second down, Penn State's Sean Stanley got into the backfield, sacked Phillips, and forced a fumble. The ball spun around on the grass for a few seconds, with a couple Lions missing chances to grab it, before Wisconsin recovered it.

On third down and 9, Phillips dropped back, intending to throw the ball to Jordan Fredrick on the left side—but whipped it right into the belly of Penn State's Glenn Carson.

"I thought it was over!" Hill said. "I started running off the field!" But Carson was so surprised by the misdirected pass, he failed to drop his arms down fast enough to secure the ball, which bounced off his gut to the ground. A stadium full of fans held their heads.

Wisconsin head coach Bret Bielema had little choice but to attempt a 44-yard field goal, while Carson stewed on the sidelines, beside himself.

"Glenn was a mess," Mauti said, recalling seeing the conscientious Carson on the sideline, distraught. Mauti yelled to the coaches, "Get Jesse James in there!" Craig Fitzgerald and John Butler did a 40-yard sprint, grabbed James, and threw him into Carson's spot on the field-goal defense unit.

"If we had to go into double overtime," Mauti said, "Glenn was done."

The snap was good, the hold was perfect. Kyle French stepped in to kick it.

Days later, Urschel recalled the moment in slow motion.

He was next to Mike Farrell on the sideline, "sitting with the O-line group, hand in hand, eyes closed. We couldn't even watch the kick. I don't know if I was praying," the mathematician said, "but I was doing something of the sort."

The Lions' defenders charged and jumped. DaQuan Jones's hand, and Jesse James's elbow, looked to be in perfect position to make the block. If the kick were straight, they probably would have knocked it down. But it twisted left, left, left—and sailed wide of the pipe.

"Then we heard the crowd," Urschel said, "and we knew."

"They all came hard, and Jesse just barely missed it!" Coach Johnson recalled. "Then they all looked at the goalposts—and they all had eleven separate reactions. Scattered! Amazing."

While his teammates jumped up and down, spun in circles, and hugged, Jordan Hill knew exactly where he was going.

"I took my helmet off and threw it. I was out there like a running back dodging people, to run up on the stands to see my father. I jumped on our little speaker box and jumped over the rail."

He found his father, in his wheelchair. Jordan hugged him and thanked him for being there for him. "That was really it, man. My best moment at Penn State."

"Yeah," Jordan said, nodding with the deepest of smiles. "Yeah."

• • •

After minutes of mayhem, the team finally gathered in front of the student section, arms on shoulders, to sing the alma mater.

"The alma mater's been there for a long time," Zordich told me later.

"But it sounds like it's written for us," Hill said, referring to the now famous line "May no act of ours bring shame."

"It gives me goose bumps when we get to that part," Mauti said. "At the end of the day it wasn't *us* who did the shaming, but we're there to say, 'We're doing the good things. We're keeping our word.'"

But the Lions had won more than a football game, gained more than an 8-4 overall record, and accomplished more than a 6-2 conference mark, which was good enough for second place in their division, right behind Ohio State and one game ahead of Wisconsin, which would go on to the Big Ten title game.

The players had achieved their primary goal, stated in front of the ESPN cameras on the practice field in July, of simply sticking together and not giving up, no matter what happened.

In the process, they accomplished far more. They had saved the program and helped restore their university.

The victory bell rang out for minutes, with each player giving it a pull before running up the tunnel to the locker room. The scene inside was as wild as a party can get without music, women, or alcohol. The players and coaches and managers jumped around, hugging, high-fiving, hooting and hollering.

If you wanted to see what twelve months of pent-up frustration, anger, effort, determination, and desire look like when fulfillment of a distant dream finally pops the cork, this would be it.

After a few minutes of mayhem, John Butler and Craig Fitzgerald got the players to form a mosh pit in the center of the room and coaxed Bill O'Brien to run into the middle of it.

"Every time he looks at you, he's intense," Zordich said of O'Brien.

"Even after a touchdown," Hill added, "he throws his arms up, but he's already looking at the clock, thinking about the next play."

Not this time—for once.

He ran into the middle of the mosh pit, twisting on his fall to face the ceiling.

"He had both of his arms up," Mauti recalled, "and his eyes were closed, and he was smiling. That was the first time I ever saw him relaxed! A completely euphoric smile, nothing else on his mind. Almost like he went weak in the knees, letting everyone just hold him up.

"That's easily my best memory."

"That game was basically our whole story," Hill said. "If we had to pick one game to represent everything we've been through? Easy. Wisconsin. They punched us in the face, they did what they wanted—and then we fought back."

"When we come back twenty years from now," McGloin said, "this is the game we'll be talking about."

The late November night was pitch dark and getting cold, but the happy tailgaters showed no signs of leaving.

The coaches and their families went to O'Brien's house for a celebration that was more relief than revelry, while the seniors had rented out the Gingerbread Man in town for an invitation-only party. Players and parents, brothers and sisters, friends and girlfriends—just about everyone they cared about was in that room.

Coach Larry Johnson was not there, which didn't surprise anyone. He is not a big drinker, and it's not how he wanted to end the night. But he might have stayed up longer than any of them.

He got to bed early. But, he said, "I couldn't sleep all night. Tossing and turning. Thinking of this play and that. Thinking about the last field goal.

"I tried to envision every kid's face after the game—their reaction, their smiles. I wanted to see them all before I went to sleep. I thought of Jordan climbing up to his father in his wheelchair in the stands.

"When I was leaving the locker room, Zordich grabbed me. 'Coach Johnson, I just want you to know, you were always there. You mean so much to me.'

"And I walked out with tears in my eyes.

"For me, the 2012 season was the best season I've ever had as a coach, at any level. Maybe the highlight of my life, outside the birth of my kids.

"I've had a few sleepless nights this year. I carry things with me. I take everything personal. I take the weight of the world on my shoulders.

"But that was the best sleepless night I ever had."

EPILOGUE:
"HOW MUCH MONEY DO THEY NEED?"

By the end of the 2012 season, Ohio State fans got exactly what they wanted: the enmity of everyone else in the Big Ten. And they savored it.

Urban Meyer knew his undefeated inaugural season would only crank up expectations for his second year as head coach. Buckeye fans would want not just another perfect record—including a victory over That Team Up North—but their thirty-fifth Big Ten title, and a national crown to go with it.

When Meyer had returned home to Ohio, that was exactly the problem he had wanted.

When he stood up to give his "team toast" the morning of their game against Michigan State, he promised his players they would not be forgotten.

They'd kept their end of the deal by letting the coaches coach them, and going undefeated. He kept his by hoisting a huge scarlet banner in their field house—*2012 12-0*—right alongside the banners commemorating Ohio State's national titles. He also ordered championship rings, with Ohio State's trademark big block *O* at the center replaced with *12-0*. On one side, the engraving said LEADERS [DIVISION] CHAMPIONS; on the other, O.S.U. 26, T.U.N. 21—with *TUN* standing for "Team Up North."

Naturally, their website, programs, and other official publications were all singing the same song, too—one Michigan fans hoped not to hear again.

Two weeks after Michigan's loss to Ohio State, the Michigan athletic department sent letters to season-ticket holders, announcing that their

333

"Personal Seat Donation" levels were being "adjusted"—upward, of course.

Michigan's record of 8-4 had not been as good as Northwestern's 9-3. But it was close enough to allow the sponsors of Tampa's Outback Bowl to pick the Wolverines—and their 2.9 million followers—over Northwestern's much smaller fan base.

Michigan's reward was facing an SEC powerhouse, the tenth-ranked South Carolina Gamecocks. But even that appealing matchup couldn't sell out Tampa's 65,857-seat Raymond James Stadium. The official attendance of 54,527 seemed substantially higher than the actual attendance, which left balconies and end zones barren.

As the designated home team, the Wolverines were expected to wear their classic dark-blue home uniforms. Instead, they wore their eighth different look in the past two seasons: snow-white jerseys with yellow numbers, which were impossible to read, in person or on TV. Michigan fought hard, but lost to South Carolina in the final seconds.

Michigan's junior left tackle, Taylor Lewan, was named the Big Ten's offensive lineman of the year and a first-team all-American. He was a likely first-round NFL draft pick, which would be worth many millions of dollars to the young man.

When Lewan called a press conference in January, everyone expected him to announce he would forgo his senior year for an NFL contract. Instead, he said he had decided to stick with his teammates and graduate on time. For this, the experts said he was stupid or crazy, or both. He did not seem to care.

Over the winter, Brady Hoke appeared at a clinic for high school coaches in Kalamazoo. He spoke with admirable candor:

"We had a shitty season, to be honest with you. Proud of the kids, how they kept moving forward, but it wasn't the year Michigan deserves."

Hoke took a big step toward better years with his second top-ten recruiting class, and was shooting for the nation's number-one class for 2014.

In April, Dave Brandon announced that season tickets for Michigan students would now be general admission, to encourage students to arrive on time. He simultaneously increased the price of their season tickets 23 percent, with the extra revenue earmarked for recreational sports. So, he said, "No one can make a claim, even though they want to try, that we're doing anything here that's financially motivated."

All this had my gang in Ann Arbor complaining about issues bigger than flying the marching band to Dallas, or wearing white jerseys with yellow numbers in Tampa. Were the students leaving Michigan football, or was Michigan football leaving the students? And if it was the latter, what would the future look like when the surplus of goodwill that previous leaders had built up over a century was squandered in just a few years?

"College football is getting to be like a bad high school relationship," said Tim Petersen, one-half of Jim Harbaugh's junior high backfield. "You keep getting abused, you know you should swear it off, but you can't get yourself to let it go."

Paul Barnett, a.k.a. Barney, was the guy whose parents had played in the Michigan band, the one who had gone door-to-door with his grade-school friends and their shiny cornets and trombones, playing "The Victors" for their neighbors.

He still went to a few games a year, mainly because his kids wanted to go. "And there's still some small sliver of the magic of college football left," he said, "and I like to think—perhaps naively—that it could come back.

"But I'm just about through with Michigan football."

Forty-seven seconds into Northwestern's game against Mississippi State in the TaxSlayer.com Gator Bowl, Bulldogs quarterback Tyler Russell dropped back to pass downfield, then turned his torso to toss a screen pass.

Senior Quentin Williams, Northwestern's 255-pound defensive end, hadn't caught an interception all year. But he read the play perfectly and intercepted Russell's throw at the Bulldogs' 29-yard line, then ran for the end zone as fast as his ponderous frame would allow. He made it, barely.

With less than two minutes left to play, Northwestern led Mississippi State, 34–20. The same Quentin Williams chased down the same Tyler Russell and sacked him for a 4-yard loss. It was the last play of Williams's football career. It allowed the Wildcats to run three straight victory formations to end the game, and they savored every second.

After the final seconds ticked off, Northwestern's players, parents, coaches, and even President Schapiro stayed on the field for a full half hour. It was Northwestern's second bowl victory in the school's 131-year history, their first since 1949, and the first after four straight bowl losses for the fifth-year seniors. It was the goal they had talked about privately when they met in January 2012, and it was the goal they had talked about publicly at the Big Ten meeting in July. It was the one thing they had wanted most.

Back in the locker room, they gathered in the center. They had gone 10-3—Northwestern's first 10-win season since 1995 and only its second since 1903. They were the only Big Ten team to win two games against SEC teams—and not pikers, either, but squads that finished 9-4 and 8-5. And they had won more games—forty, for the fifth-year players—than any other senior class in Northwestern's history.

They knew what to do: sing the fight song, one last time. But this time, there was something new—the monkey.

"Man, when they were done with it," Pat Fitzgerald told me, "there were just remnants, no signs of a corpse." He pulled out his iPhone to show pictures of the locker-room carpet, which looked as if it had been covered in snow.

"That damn monkey," Kain Colter said, grinning. "I feel bad for whoever had to clean that up."

Every Penn State player, coach, and staffer had played, coached, or worked for teams with better records, most of them the previous season. Some had won conference titles, national titles, even Super Bowls. But they all said the same thing: this season had been their favorite. And they agreed that a bowl game would have added nothing to their experience.

"You go to a bowl," Mauti said, "you're spending time away from your family, in a hotel room Christmas Eve, New Year's Eve. Unless you're playing for something—unless you're in a BCS bowl—man, it's hard.

"I don't want to crap on the bowl system, but we knew about all that. We'd already done it. But this year, we played our last game at home in front of our families and our friends. We wouldn't have it any other way."

But the players were concerned about their coach's future at Penn State.

Two days after the season ended on that glowing field of grass, I sat at the O'Briens' breakfast table. Bill and Colleen made it clear they wanted to stay in State College.

"We like it here," Bill said. "She likes it here, and the kids do, too. We love this team, the families. I love the values here, and I believe in them."

But as he was talking, his cell phone buzzed so often it almost danced off the edge of the table. It wasn't friends or well-wishers calling. It was the athletic directors at Boston College, Tennessee, and Arkansas, and the NFL's Philadelphia Eagles, Cleveland Browns, and San Diego Chargers. They all wanted to know one thing: What would it take to get O'Brien to jump?

The Monday after the football season ends, college and pro alike, is traditionally the day when the athletic director, the general manager, or the owner calls in the head coach to assess the season just past and to plan for the seasons ahead.

But not at Penn State. At least, not in 2012.

While O'Brien's phone was blowing up, his boss, acting Athletic Director Dave Joyner, was on a hunting trip. It was the opening day of Pennsylvania's deer season.

O'Brien shrugged it off, but not Mike Mauti.

"That *enrages* me," Mauti told me. "Let's lay it out there: *he's* the reason we did all this. They hire anyone else, this season doesn't happen—and who knows where the program is? *He's it.* If O-B leaves in the next three, four, five years, it's *their* fault, not his fault. It's not because of him. It would never be. It's because they didn't do their jobs and do what's right."

O'Brien decided to stay anyway.

"You could wrap my whole thing up with this," Spider Caldwell said. "Looking back when Bill was hired, at first I was a little disappointed we didn't hire a Penn State person.

"But you know what? We ended up hiring a Penn Stater. He just went to Brown first."

In December, I drove back to State College to sit down with the coaches and players one more time.

When I sat down with Matt McGloin and the three Mikes—Mauti, Zordich, and Farrell—I promised myself I'd ask about a couple things I'd been curious about.

In the locker-room celebration after the Wisconsin triumph, I had noticed that Dave Joyner had never showed. I assumed he was trying to avoid the appearance of basking in reflected glory. Penn State's president, Rodney Erickson, did come down to the locker room, but because no players greeted him, I assumed they didn't know who he was. But when I asked the seniors about it, they told me the real story.

Ever since Dave Joyner and Gerald Hodges had come close to blows in the team room a year earlier, the seniors had made it clear they wanted Joyner nowhere near the team, even during pregame warm-ups. Joyner had complied, never so much as ducking his head into a team meeting.

As for President Erickson, all the players actually had recognized him, but they chose not to acknowledge him.

When the NCAA sanctions had come down and the Penn State program was being bashed on the cable news shows and in the national newspapers and even in the players' own e-mail inboxes, no one in the university's administration building had said a word in support of the players—despite the fact that, of all the parties involved in the Sandusky scandal and its aftermath, they had clearly done no wrong.

"In the past year," the normally calm Mike Farrell said, "the only visible thing the trustees did successfully was cover their asses with the Freeh Report."

"Who was stepping up and taking it?" Zordich asked. "We were. They never stood up for us. Not the president, not the AD. They were silent. Silent. Thanks. Who was standing up for us? O-B—and that's it."

I asked Zordich about my memory of President Erickson standing alone in the locker room, smiling stiffly, clenching his hands and releasing them, uncertain what to do. I thought I had seen him make eye contact with Zordich from about ten feet away, and Erickson looked as if he was about to say something. But Zordich just continued staring at him, until Erickson turned away and walked out.

Zordich confirmed my memory, then explained what had happened. "He was so out of place, and you knew that he felt out of place. You could feel how uncomfortable he felt.

"You could say, yeah, he's the president of the university. But he had absolutely no business there, as far as I'm concerned."

His teammates nodded in agreement.

Of course, the seniors had played their last game. They would be leaving campus and starting their new lives in just a few weeks. They had nothing to lose by excluding the AD and snubbing the president.

Bill O'Brien did not have that luxury. The athletic director was his boss, and the president was his boss's boss. The sanctions would run for three more years. If O'Brien intended to protect Penn State football into the future, he would need the help of every official he knew.

When O'Brien saw President Erickson in the locker room, he gave him a hug.

But that didn't change the central truth of the previous twelve months. As Jim Bernhardt had put it, "Our kids knew how to handle the situation better than most of the adults. That's what I'll always remember."

I also felt compelled to ask the seniors about the Big Ten's bringing in Maryland and Rutgers.

It was quickly clear they agreed with 83 percent of the almost 1,000 respondents on MGoBlog, who concluded the decision had nothing to do with the quality of the two universities' academics or even athletics, but money. Worse, Maryland had twenty-eight players leave that season, *without* sanctions, and Rutgers was taking a beating for not reporting their abusive basketball coach and then hiring an athletic director with a checkered past of her own. The two schools were not exactly enhancing the Big Ten's reputation.

"As soon as we first heard that the Big Ten might be adding two new teams," Mike Farrell said, "it seemed like a done deal overnight. One of my first thoughts was that it didn't seem to be in the best interest of the student-athletes. How much sense does it make to have kids traveling from Nebraska to New Jersey and vice versa to compete, especially in sports that play on weekdays, when classes are in session?

"No matter what anyone thought about the new universities that were being added, the glaring catalyst was money."

"The *fans* see everything, sooner or later," Mauti said. "They're catching on."

"Men have played this game throughout history, for their own reasons," Zordich concluded. "Now it's just currency for someone else to sell.

"I worry about the future of the game, because what they're going to be playing in twenty years will have nothing to do with what we had.

"The suits are ruining the whole thing, for money.

"It makes enough fucking money.

"How much do they need?"